SCREENPLAY

SCREENPLAY

WRITING THE PICTURE

2ND EDITION REVISED AND UPDATED

BY ROBIN U. RUSSIN
AND WILLIAM MISSOURI DOWNS

SILMAN-JAMES PRESS   LOS ANGELES

Library of Congress Cataloging-in-Publication Data

Russin, Robin U.
Screenplay : writing the picture /
by Robin U. Russin and William Missouri Downs. -- 2nd ed. rev. & updated.
p. cm.
ISBN 978-1-935247-06-7 (alk. paper)
1. Motion picture authorship. I. Downs, William Missouri. II. Title.
PN1996.R84 2012
808.2'3--dc23

ISBN: 978-1-935247-06-7

Cover design by
Wade Lageose

Printed in the United States of America
Silman-James Press
www.silmanjamespress.com

Contents

FADE OUT

Acknowledgments

Lew Hunter, Howard Suber, Richard Walter, Hal Ackerman, Bill Froug, Stirling Silliphant, Jerzy Antczak and all the others at UCLA film school, for showing us the way; Steve Peterman, for putting up with our asking him how to be funny; Derek Burrill, Jeff Kunzler and Patrick Seitz for helping us navigate the mysteries of video gaming; Val Stulman, John Shannon and Rob Rinow for being great students and now teaching us a bit about writing for the web; Lou Anne Wright for her long months of editing and advice; Todd McCullough for letting us use his webisode script; Sandra J. Payne, Ken Jones, Cathlynn Richard Dodson and Rich Burlingham for their careful reading of the manuscript and thoughtful suggestions, which helped make this a better book. Barbara Rosenberg, David Hall and Matt Ball for getting us into this mess in the first place; Michelle Vardeman for making sure we cleaned it up; and lastly to Gwen Feldman and Jim Fox at Silman-James Press, for seeing the merit in this book and, more importantly, publishing it.

R. U. Russin
W. M. Downs

Robert and Adele Russin, for raising me with the belief that I could live the life of an artist, because they lived it themselves; Sarah Russin and my kids Olivia and Ben, for putting up with me no matter what; James and Cookie Goldstone, for being my first and dearest film-world mentors; my colleagues at the University of California, Riverside; and Milah Wermer, patron saint of all that is dramatic, ecstatic and "marvelous!"

Robin

Lou Anne Wright—the love of my life.

Bill

FADE IN...

Preface

"What's all this business of being a writer?
It's just putting one word after another."

—Irving Thalberg

Welcome to the second edition of *Screenplay: Writing the Picture*. What's new? Well, a lot is the same; the principles of great screenwriting remain the same. We've also kept references to classic films that we consider worth your checking out if you don't know them already. But we've trimmed references to things that no longer apply (or exist, for that matter), and included dozens of revised and updated examples. Newly included are chapters on writing webisodes and video games, but we no longer include a playwriting chapter because we've now written a complete guide, *Naked Playwriting* (also published by Silman-James), which we modestly believe is the best book on the subject out there, and which should answer all your playwriting questions.

As we said before, this book is not written by screenwriting gurus. We are not trying to sell you special formulas, secret methods, tapes, computer programs or gung-ho three-day seminars. We are not going to show you how to write a screenplay in twenty-one days or twenty-one steps. Nor are we going to tell you there is only one true path to success; we offer no easy how-to formulas. Rather, this is a down-to-earth guide written by two writers who came from the heartland of America, moved to Hollywood, were lucky enough to get into UCLA film school, struggled for years, made many mistakes, wrote every day and in the end, against all odds, succeeded. Both of us are "produced" writers (something akin to being "made men" in the Cosa Nostra), meaning we've actually sold screenplays and had movies or television shows produced from them, and we've both made our livings as writers. And we preach only what we've learned and practiced ourselves—every day. There are no shortcuts in screenwriting, no magical recipes besides talent, an understanding of the basics and then some very, very hard work. We wrote this book to help you find your talent and understand the basics. The hard work is up to you.

We will not cheerlead or sugar-coat how difficult it will be for you—for anyone—to succeed in writing for "Hollywood." In fact, we have some good advice for anyone who isn't absolutely driven to write movies or television: think long and hard before you commit yourself to it. To paraphrase a line from *Scent of a Woman*, it's just too damn hard. Writing itself is too hard; or as Gene Fowler (journalist, screenwriter and author of the John Barrymore biography *Good Night, Sweet Prince*) put it, "Writing is easy. All you do is sit staring at a blank sheet of paper until the drops of blood form on your forehead." And writing for Hollywood is worse. Movies and television are the Big Game for writers these days, and everyone wants to play. Not that there aren't enormous satisfactions and rewards, both artistic and financial, if you do succeed. There are. But only a tiny fraction of you will make it. That's just a fact, and anyone who says different couldn't give you directions to Warner Brothers Studios if he were standing on Warner Boulevard. Of course anything really worth doing is hard, success in any truly challenging endeavor is a long shot, and the fact of the matter is that you'll never know whether or not you have what it takes if you don't try.

Do you have the talent to succeed? Only time and hard work will tell. Talent is something neither you nor we have any control over, anyway, so forget about it. Focus instead on the various techniques that screenwriters must master in order to write exciting, entertaining, well-structured screenplays, so that if you do have talent, you can make the most of it.

That's what this book is all about. We've included detailed chapters on techniques and fundamentals that many screenwriting books and gurus gloss over or skip completely. We've divided it into five easy-to-use sections so that you can treat it as a textbook, a reference guide, or something to read from cover to cover. The first section covers the basics: who is going to read your script and how to impress them. If you can't get by the readers in Hollywood all your effort is for nothing. You impress readers by giving your script a proper, professional format, choosing interesting themes, finding the world and developing effective characters. We'll show you how.

The second section tackles structure. Rather than trying to sell you on one theory or approach, we examine storytelling methods from Aristotle to modern computer programs. We take you through the principles of power and conflict and how they grow from scenes to sequences to a well-structured screenplay. We include chapters on how to design your screenplay using scene cards and how to structure the beginning of your screenplay so that it grabs everyone's attention. We finish the structure section with an advanced chapter on genres. Each genre arises from certain emotional sources and expectations, and each has its own unique demands. Identify these and you'll solve many of your structural challenges before you begin.

The third section reveals the nuts and bolts of writing the script. We detail techniques to help you write strong, visual narrative and powerful dialogue. After you have pounded through the first draft, what follows naturally is rewriting. How do you know what needs to be fixed, saved or thrown away? How many drafts are needed? How can you test what you've written? When is your script ready for the market? We give real-world methods and advice to answer all these questions.

Marketing is the fourth section of the book. It's a sad fact, but most screenplays that are submitted—after the months of brain-wracking effort that went into writing them—get rejected. Once your screenplay is done, you must plunge into the market and self-promote. We show you how to approach agents and producers, take meetings, do pitches—in short, how to start the process of becoming a professional. Is any of it easy? No, it's all really, really hard. But we'll give you the tools you need to attempt it.

The last section of this book covers related fields, including writing for television, webisodes and video games.

In short, this book is intended to help you choose, develop, and perfect your stories, avoid common mistakes, and get you up to speed as a professional screenwriter so that you'll look like you've already got a dozen screenplays under your belt rather than only one or two. What's more, you'll have some idea of what to do next. It is said that people make their own luck by searching out opportunity and being prepared when opportunity appears. We've written this to help you make your own luck; you're going to need it.

One other thing. We each have our MFA in screenwriting from the UCLA School of Theater, Film and Television, and we're mighty proud of it. Under the stewardship of Lew Hunter, Richard Walter, Hal Ackerman, Bill Froug, Howard Suber, Cynthia Whitcomb and the rest of the fine faculty, past and present, UCLA has achieved recognition as the premier screenwriting school in the world, and counts hundreds of successful (that is, working) screen and television writers among its alumni. At a recent awards ceremony for UCLA screenwriting graduates, honoree James Cameron noted (with typical reserve) that now that he'd received the approval of UCLA's film school, the critics could all go to hell. Although this book of course reflects our own views and experiences, we owe a huge debt to what we learned at UCLA, and to these wise mentors. They taught us well.

PART ONE

THE BASICS

How to Impress a Reader

Format

Theme, Meaning and Emotion

The World of the Story

Character

1

How to Impress a Reader

Why Am I Reading This Joker's Work?

Today's screenwriters are among the most intelligent, imaginative and skilled storytellers of our time. But one thing must be clearly stated from the start: they are writing (and you, hopefully, will be writing) movies. Screenwriting is a very particular kind of storytelling. It's a craft as well as an art. Perhaps the first, and in some ways hardest, truth for new screenwriters to accept is that, while some rise to the level of classics and even get published, screenplays are not intended as literature. They are blueprints for films. And just as blueprints show only the essential plan, elements and structure of a building, the screenplay must show only the essential plan, elements and structure of a film. If you want to write something intended to be read for its own literary merit, write a novel, short story or poem—even a stage play—not a screenplay. It's true that some screenplays are now being published, but these are usually put out in the wake of having been made into successful films and are often not the original script anyway, but transcriptions of the produced movies.

You'll be writing a spec script. "Spec" is short for speculation script. A spec script is a screenplay that the writer has created from an original idea or from some underlying material (book, life story) to which he or she's acquired the rights. It is not a work for hire, and it hasn't been sold yet. This is the opposite of a "shooting script," which is a screenplay that has been sold and prepared for production. A spec screenplay is never going to be read, nor should it be written, for its own sake. It exists to persuade a very limited group of people (agents, producers, professional readers, directors and/or actors) that it can be the basis for something else entirely: a must-see motion picture.

This isn't to say that it doesn't matter how well or how badly a script is written: it does. Your spec script, in addition to being a blueprint, is a selling tool (which is why it's sometimes called a "show script" or "selling script"). You are hoping to sell the reader on your idea for a movie, which means the more skillfully you tell your story, through well-written narrative and powerful dialogue, the better it will be received. An illegible, poorly worded screenplay is as sure to turn off a reader as a poorly drawn blueprint is to turn off a home-builder. Good writing convinces a producer that even if this isn't the script for him, you're a strong, talented, imaginative writer to be remembered. For the same reason, a well-written spec is essential as a writing sample if you're hoping to land an assignment.

It may seem strange, at the beginning, to worry so much about who is going to read your screenplay. What has the reader got to do with how you write? You haven't even gotten started yet. But it's critical for exactly that reason; you must think of the reader before you begin because, in a larger sense, your reader is the first member of the audience to see your film—your film, not your script.

WHO *ARE* THOSE GUYS?

If you're very lucky, your script will be read by an important agent, producer, director or actor. But that's rare; it's more likely that your script's first "audience member" (outside your friends and family) will be someone known as a script reader (sometimes called a story analyst) whom the above-mentioned agent, producer, director or actor has hired to read for them. This isn't because they don't want to read the script themselves; they simply can't. They may have thirty-plus screenplays a week submitted to them by agents, studios, managers, friends, as well as the guy they met in line at Starbucks, who wouldn't give up until they agreed to look at his script. Agents, producers, directors and actors do read; it's just that they will personally try to get to the screenplays that seem likeliest to get made, meaning scripts that have been sent along by someone who already has a production deal or who is high enough in the showbiz hierarchy to be considered a strong bet to get a deal. Scripts with strong "elements attached"—great actors, directors or tens of millions of dollars already committed to them—are the first to get read, and read most carefully.

The rest of the scripts—including yours—will go to one of their hired, tired readers, usually a bright young person who has or is working on an English or film degree, who also has written a screenplay or two (unproduced, or he wouldn't be reading) and who is therefore primed to be judgmental about yours. Which is, after all, why he's there, although he probably, secretly, resents it a little ("Why am I reading this joker's work when my script is the one people should be looking at?"). This reader is the lowest rung on the development ladder, the plankton in the choppy ocean of Hollywood production. And yet, in a strange way, the reader is the most influential person in the business. He is the gatekeeper, the first line of defense. Nothing he dislikes goes any further at his production company; when he "passes," the company has passed. When he says "consider," then those higher up might read the script; readers only have the power of condemning to death, not of bringing to life. The reader's synopsis and opinion goes into the computer—"the system"—for future reference and, if that opinion is negative, nothing short of a death threat or the producer's favorite actor pleading on bended knee will get your script considered at that company again.

Now this lowly yet awesomely powerful reader is wearily contemplating the ten or so screenplays—meaning 1,200 pages—he must plow through by Monday, on top of trying to finish the next draft of his own screenplay. And all for maybe forty or fifty bucks a script. And so that precious story, which has occupied your every waking thought for the past six months, which is so compellingly worthy of being filmed that you can practically taste the celluloid, is now lodged somewhere in his foot-thick stack of other hopefuls. You're just praying it isn't near the bottom. You're just begging that he will not turn his thumb down, for any reason you can prevent. The screenplay's fate is in the reader's hands, and so is yours.

Coverage: "Pass or Fail"

The reader's report is called coverage, and it will include such items as your name, the title, length and genre of the script, the date read, who submitted it and who the reader is. It will also provide a one- or two-sentence summary, as well as a one- or two-page synopsis and a paragraph or so of comments as to the script's merits, or lack thereof. There are boxes in which the reader rates various aspects of the script—story, writing, character, sometimes dialogue—on a scale of excellent/good/average/poor. If the coverage is good or excellent, then the producer may read it. If the coverage is average or poor, the script is rejected. Coverage differs from one company or agency to another, but they all have one thing in common: the screenwriter is not allowed to see it, even if he asks to. Coverage is an internal report and for the producers' eyes only. On the following pages are examples of what coverage looks like.

Unfair as it seems, this simple abstract, written by possibly the least experienced person in the company, will determine the fate (at least, in the negative) of your script there.

So there's a bit of luck involved, and more than a bit of personal bias. In spite of these vagaries—or because of them—your script has to be as powerful and entertaining as possible.

WHAT ARE THEY LOOKING FOR?

When you cut through all the personal opinions, tastes and prejudices, the question remains: What are these readers looking for, and what will make them pass your script on to that important agent, producer, director or actor for further consideration? Simple. They're looking for a script that can become a must-see movie, a sure hit. It must convey a strong "film sense" and be written in a straightforward, economical, easy-to-read manner by someone who has a marvelous style and terrific understanding of story and character. They're not asking for much.

CREATIVE ARTISTE FILMS

TITLE: "THREE THOUSAND"

AUTHOR: J. F. LAWTON

SUBMITTED BY: G. G.

FORM: SCREENPLAY

ANALYST: R. R.

CIRCA: PRESENT

SUBMITTED TO: M. S.

DATE RECEIVED: 7/12

PAGES: 120

LOCATION: LA

GENRE: DRAMA

LOG LINE: A streetwalker is paid 3000 dollars to be a week's companion for a multimillionaire.

"THREE THOUSAND"— SYNOPSIS

VIVIAN, 22, is a tough, pretty Hollywood streetwalker, hooking since she was sixteen. She cares for another street girl, KIT, a childlike coke addict. One evening Vivian is picked up by EDWARD, the middle-aged driver of a rented Mercedes, who made a wrong turn onto the Boulevard. Edward is a multimillionaire takeover artist who built his family's old wealth into an enormous fortune. He is in LA to take and wreck an ailing defense contractor. Irritated with his bimbo/model girlfriend back in New York, he takes Vivian back to his penthouse at the Beverly Wilshire on a whim.

Stripped of her street clothes and makeup, Vivian is a lovely girl, and Edward is fascinated by her toughness and brass; after one night, he offers to hire her for the week he is in town, for 3000 dollars plus the clothing and jewelry she will need to fit in as his companion. She is wary and a little frightened by the prospect, but goes along for the money. Edward is a man who loves power games, and he forces MR. THOMAS, the manager, to accept the fact that he is keeping a hooker in his room.

The main power game that concerns him is with KROSS, the man who built the defense company Edward is there to wreck. He instructs Vivian to buy clothes for their upcoming dinner together with Kross. Vivian goes into Beverly Hills in her own street outfit, and is terrified and humiliated by the shop owners. She turns to Mr. Thomas of all people to help her, and he turns out to be a nice guy. He sets her up with some friends and she comes back transformed, looking—if not feeling—like a sophisticated beauty. The dinner is troubling to Vivian—she doesn't understand the business terms, but she does understand the power play. Kross is a once-proud, dynamic man who built half the WWII fleet, but Edward strips him of any dignity in his hardball presentation of terms. Kross vows to fight Edward at first, but Edward knows he is bluffing.

Vivian is further upset when Edward invites WILLIAM, one of his lawyers—who owns a high-priced escort service—over for a drink. They make crude jokes at her expense, and Edward even offers William a go at her. When William leaves, Vivian is furious—how dare he treat her like a piece of meat? She makes her own terms and decides who she will and will not do business with. Edward is shocked and touched by her self-respect, and apologizes. She is absolutely right—he thought she had no feelings about that, that he had been treating her royally, but he made a mistake.

He decides to treat Vivian to a ride on his Lear jet and a night in San Francisco at the opera. He tells her that opera is in the blood, either you love it or you don't; breeding makes no difference. He rents her a gorgeous fur for the occasion, which she adores. The performance is Aida, and Vivian weeps for hours at the story of the slave girl hopelessly in love with the Pharaoh's son. Edward is both intrigued and irritated by her emotionalism. When he is asleep, she says words she has never said before: "I love you." But she has no illusions.

Vivian takes a free afternoon and a limo to visit Kit, whom she finds hungry and coked up. Kit sees how well she's doing and tells her that Edward will probably marry her. Vivian, upset, tells her to shut up, and that they'll go to Disneyland together when the week is over.

She is also disturbed by her second dinner with Edward and Kross, who comes in a broken man. Things reach a crisis when William comes on to her, offering to take her into his escort service. She angrily refuses, and he tries to assault her. Edward arrives and punches William, but not before he's bruised Vivian.

The week is up, and Edward decides to drive Vivian back to the Boulevard. He lets her keep all her clothes except for the rented fur. She is distant and unhappy the whole way, and he gets irritated, thinking she is mad about the fur. But as she reenters her old, seedy world, Vivian loses control and starts hitting Edward and pounding at his car. Alarmed, he chides her for ingratitude and tosses her out, along with her 3000 dollars.

Drained and listless, she takes Kit to Disneyland.

____XXX ____RECOMMEND _____CONSIDER _____PASS

	Excellent	Good	Fair	Poor
Story Line	X			
Characters	X			
Writing	X			
Structure		X		
Dialogue		X		
Originality		X		

COMMENTS:
This is a terrific script. The characters are fully believable, with no false notes. Vivian is tough and capable in her own environment, but understandably childlike when put into the penthouse. Edward is a perfect power-master, trying to control the lives of those around him for his own pleasure, even when he himself isn't fully aware of it. The business talk feels accurate, but never boring—it is the hard, cutthroat talk which makes or ruins people's lives. This is not an upbeat story—it is a story of haves and have-nots, and of the vast chasm that separates them. But it is an intelligent and moving moral tale, well worth a look.

OVERALL RATING: Good to Excellent

MAGELLAN FILMS, INC.

TITLE: "Photoplay"

AUTHOR: Gil Smith

FORM: SCREENPLAY

PAGES: 139

ANALYST: B. S.

GENRE: FILM NOIR

SUBMITTED BY: Gil Smith

DATE RECEIVED: JAN. 27

CIRCA: 1945

LOCATION: NEW YORK

LOG LINE: A street photographer gets involved with the wife of a hoodlum and finds himself in a murder mystery.

SYNOPSIS: FLOOGEE, a street photographer who finds his photos anywhere—sometimes chasing fire engines, sometimes prowling the alleys—is a hit, with a show in the Museum of Modern Art. There he meets society wife SHERRY, and flirts with her; she is intrigued by him, and wants to spend a weekend away from her brute/rich husband JAMES following Floogee around. But someone has slashed some of Floogee's prize photos, and a goon named BRUISER is threatening him about them—especially now that a book of Floogee's photos is about to be published. Floogee, out with Sherry, finds a corpse on the sidewalk, murdered, and photographs him. The police, all crooks and apparently in consort with James—who has underworld ties—seem to have a conspiracy to tie Floogee to the murder. It turns out that Bruiser is Sherry's lover, pretending to be her brother so that James will hire him to run his nightclub, unsuspecting that he is having an affair with Sherry. The disputed photos—unknown to Floogee—show Sherry a few years earlier as a hooker being felt up by Bruiser, which explains his alarm over their publication. The stiff is someone Bruiser killed to protect some of James' business interests. At the end, Bruiser is about to kill Floogee, but Sherry, now in love with Floogee, kills Bruiser first. James is exposed, as are the corrupt police in cahoots with him.

COMMENTS:

An almost incomprehensible jumble of half-realized plot twists. The characters are interesting, but have little chemistry with each other; nor are any of them particularly pleasant. Floogee is not well defined, a cocky asshole who both knows the streets and doesn't, knows a lot and doesn't, has photos of everything and doesn't know what they mean, remembers things photographically and yet doesn't recognize one of the women in his prize photo as the woman he is now after. Once we learn what the fuss was all about, it is a big letdown, hardly worth the wait. Not much to care about, and an excruciatingly overcomplicated version of an essentially simple, boring story. The only real interest here is the angle of the street photographer, and I've read other scripts that use this character to far greater effect. The 1940's setting is almost irrelevant to the story.

	Excellent	Good	Average	Poor
Story			X	
Characters			X	
Premise				X
Commercial Appeal				X

RECOMMEND

CONSIDER

X PASS

Would You Go See It?

Now that you know your audience, what does it take, what does it mean, to write a good movie? Strong characters? A terrific story? Absolutely. But there is more. Put yourself in the reader's place: is this film (script) going to be an exciting, moving experience? Is it going to be not just an interesting film, something you might like to see sometime, but the very first film you'd choose on any given weekend? Is this the movie you'd decide to take the time to go see at a theater, or at least to choose from the thousands of titles available on your internet movie service? This is what your reader is asking as he goes through your script.

Reality Check

Also, you have to be somewhat realistic. If you're writing a tragedy or a huge period epic, for example, you're cutting down your chances of making a sale no matter how good the script turns out to be. In spite of many great successes that would seem to prove the contrary, studios don't consider such stories "commercial" unless they are brought in with some heavyweight talent attached. And sometimes not even then. The Oscar-winning films *The English Patient* and *Braveheart* nearly didn't get made, and never would have been made if they had started as spec scripts by unrepresented writers. *The English Patient* was based on an award-winning novel that was the passion of a veteran producer and an award-winning director; even so, one month before it was about to begin production at Fox, the studio got cold feet and insisted that the filmmakers cast the inappropriate (but high-profile) Demi Moore instead of Kristin Scott Thomas in the lead female role, or the deal was off. The producers wisely refused and luckily found another home for the film at Miramax. But it could have gone either way. In the case of *Braveheart*, the writer happened to be a personal friend of Mel Gibson and got him to read it. Even then, it took Gibson several years to decide to bring it in to Warner Brothers, where his company is based. And even with his attachment, the studio balked; it wasn't until another studio agreed to split the cost—and the risk—that the movie got made. We're not saying, "Don't write a period epic," or some other difficult material. We are saying that if you do, you're going to face an uphill battle getting a reader to consider it. By the way, in the above coverage examples, the first script, *Three Thousand*, did get made—as *Pretty Woman*. Although the screenplay was so good that it was purchased, the studio ultimately couldn't live with the down ending. And so, instead of the tragic, anti-Cinderella story the writer had intended, it became the opposite: a Cinderella comedy with an upbeat ending.

Film Sense and Nonsense

There are things film can and cannot do. It can show us things and make us hear things: the environment, characters acting or reacting to it or to each other. Film can show us planets colliding or the nervous tick of an eyelid. It can roar with the big guns of war or whisper with a lover's voice. But it cannot give us a character's internal state, past history or future dreams, unless those things are externalized in a visual or aural manner. Internal moods, smells, tastes, attitudes must be described in such a way that a director can direct them, an actor can act them, a cinematographer can photograph them or a sound person can record them. If you can't see it or hear it, or an actor can't play it, don't write it. Writers with film sense take the reader on a journey not primarily of words, but of images. Readers are looking for scripts that allow them to see the movie.

Short and Sweet

Shakespeare observed, "Brevity is the soul of wit." To wit: being long-winded is boring, and being boring is a cardinal sin in all storytelling, but especially in writing for the movies. The phrase "cut to the chase" originated as an editing term; when things were dragging in a film, the editors cut to something exciting, like a chase. More importantly, they cut out whatever was written, or even committed to film, that impeded the forward motion of the story. So don't give them that chance. Make every moment of your story essential. Keep your writing as tight and sharp as possible: Don't use three words if two will suffice. This applies to dialogue, too; even if you have a character who is meant to be long-winded, you still must try to make every word meaningful. The film industry is awash in a tidal wave of screenplays, most of them bad. So whoever ends up finally reading yours will be in a hurry to find out if the darn thing is any good. Writing actively and economically makes for a cleaner, faster read.

Motion is the nature of film. You are trying to convey not a painting, but an actively changing picture. Each page is regarded as roughly a minute of screen time. You want the reader to forget she is reading words on a page and begin to see the film, minute by minute, its characters acting and talking, moving fluidly through time and space. While in a novel there is the luxury of describing people and locations for pages on end, this kind of writing stops the action (motion) of a film dead in its tracks.

This means there cannot be long, unbroken paragraphs of description. There's nothing a reader reacts to with greater fear and loathing than a page of dense, uninterrupted, overwritten prose. There are always exceptions, such as the memorable opening of Eric Roth's script for *Forrest Gump*. But this was a work-for-hire assignment, not a spec screenplay, that allowed Roth certain liberties. (Even so, his long, poetic descriptions of Forrest and the floating feather last only a page, and then the rest of his script is far less dense.) Dialogue should be equally economical. Again, there are exceptions, such as the long, entertaining dialogue passages in *Pulp Fiction*. But this film works because Tarantino has a unique knack for making such dialogue essential to the theme, subtext and world of the story. Right after *Pulp Fiction* was released, Hollywood was inundated with scripts superficially attempting to copy his style, almost none of which were made.

You will always find and may create exceptions, but it is a general rule to try to keep your writing as brief as the character and situation will allow.

WAR STORIES

Robin

I worked as a reader myself for several years before I sold my first screenplay, during which time I covered almost two thousand scripts. I tried to be fair, and I know most readers do, but the fact is that I was, and they are, overworked, paid too little money, hoping for something better to come along in their careers, and sometimes less than objective. After reading a hundred high-school romance scripts, or futuristic actioners, it's easy to become jaded and sarcastic, and any hint of cliché or ineptness, any false note, may be reason enough to condemn a screenplay (unless the reader is working for an exploitation company, in which case cliché is required). On the other hand, readers are your allies, because they are always looking for that great script they can bring in to the producer as proof that they deserve to be promoted. And they are the only ones who are guaranteed to read your script all the way through (or at least scan it), because they have to in order to do their synopsis. So don't give them any excuses to mark your script down. I speak from experience.

WAR STORIES

Bill

Years ago, while putting myself through UCLA film school, I worked as a secretary for Interscope, a Hollywood production company. I was in charge of sending scripts out for coverage. The banality of my job gave me time to concoct a wicked scheme. I took one of my screenplays and sent it to a reader under a pen name, so my boss wouldn't discover what I was up to. If the coverage came back good, I was going to show him the script, but the coverage came back, "This is the worst screenplay ever written." So I sent it to another reader, a female reader, and gave my title page a female author. It came back, "Not bad. We ought to have her in and see if she has anything else." Finally, I placed the script in a William Morris cover and wrote on the title page, "A new screenplay by William Goldman, Jr." I was passing myself off as the son of the author of *Butch Cassidy and the Sundance Kid*, *Marathon Man*, and *The Princess Bride*, certainly one of the most popular, talented, and richest screenwriters in Hollywood. This time the coverage came back, "Some problems, but wonderful." Not one word of the screenplay was different. Coverage isn't fair. It is a necessary evil. All you can do is reduce the margin of error.

The more white space there is on the page, the easier it is to contemplate reading, and the more likely it is that the script will convey the motion of a potential film.

WRITING IN STYLE

Assuming the common strictures of brevity, clarity and "film sense," every screenwriter has his or her own style. This both affects and is affected by what is being written. A writer's natural style can to some degree provide a clue as to the kind of movies he or she is best suited to write. This is because each genre has its own feel and demands. An action script, for instance, is usually written in a terse, aggressive, spare style with limited dialogue, which moves the reader at maximum pace through its story. If that's the way you like to write, action might be your field. A character drama or romantic comedy takes more time to develop character relationships and is far more reliant on mood and dialogue. If this kind of writing matches your interests and strengths, you might be well-suited to write the next *Juno* or *The Descendants*, not the next *Inception* or *Fast & Furious*. In other words, you should write in a style that feels natural to you, and your style should be consistent with the kind of films you are trying to write. If it isn't, you may need to change it, or change genres (for more on genres, see Chapter 11).

Some think it's good for students to try out a number of different genres and styles until they figure out what's right for them, and within the context of a college program this may be true. However, once you do determine a preference, stick to it for a while. You need to create a consistent identity for yourself in a very crowded field that is becoming more crowded every day. Producers have only so much time and attention, and that is usually limited to projects coming in from known sources. When you flicker across their radar screen, you want them to sit up, take notice and remember your particular signature.

Be careful to choose a genre or style that truly reflects what you want to be working on for the foreseeable future. The unfortunate fact is that Hollywood pigeonholes writers. The same harried producer or reader mentioned above, once familiar with a writer's first work, will tend to identify the writer with that particular work and will be confused if something radically different appears on her desk.

It's not that you shouldn't write different kinds of scripts, but you should identify your strengths and primary areas of interest and focus your efforts there. You'll get where you want to go faster. Once you're well enough established in one area (and financially comfortable enough that you can take a chance), go for it and break the mold.

FINAL THOUGHTS

The moral of all this is that, just as in quantum physics, the observer has a fundamental effect on the observed; in this case, your screenplay. Over time, the process of how screenplays are read and judged has helped to define what makes for good screenwriting, which in turn anticipates the reader's concerns. Remember, the reader is your audience. He's tired, bored and bombarded with horrible scripts. But he's also looking for strong blueprints for wonderful, exciting movies. With these first lessons in mind, let's start learning how to write a screenplay that a reader can't resist.

EXERCISES

1. Write a list of your top ten favorite movies. Now identify what it is about each that appeals to you.

2. Read any screenplay and then create your own coverage for the script. Use the examples of coverage in this chapter as a template.

2

Format

Looking Good

The first thing a reader looks for is proper format. You may think that formatting the script is a pointless (if required) chore, but one that has little to do with the larger concerns of your screenplay. In fact, proper format, having evolved out of years of production and reading demands, is as essential to the craft and conception of screen stories as meter is to poetry. You don't start writing a sonnet or a lyric until you have an understanding of the form. Screenplays are not formless; they are demandingly structured, and their format both reflects and helps to create that structure.

Improper format is the surest way to get your script tossed in the rejection pile. You may think that "technical" errors having "nothing to do with story" will be forgiven, but they won't. When an experienced reader comes across a script that doesn't look professional, her assumption is that the writing isn't professional either, because that's usually the case. Typos, punctuation errors and poor grammar will also annoy readers and get scripts tossed. If a writer doesn't know the correct format, can't spell or construct a sentence intelligently, why should readers assume he can construct a proper story? The old saying "You can't judge a book by its cover" doesn't apply to screenwriting. Producers, directors and readers always judge a script by its appearance.

What follows are the basics of how to format a spec screenplay (as stated in Chapter 1, "spec" is short for speculation script). This format also applies to spec MOW (Movie of the Week) and spec hour-length television (one-camera) shows like *House, Breaking Bad* and *Homeland*. Sitcoms (three-camera shows) have a unique format that is covered in Chapter 17.

A caution: Most of the scripts you can buy are either bound books and re-formatted for that form, which is different than your script format should be; or if you can actually find actual drafts of screenplays at rare specialty stores like Book City Script Shop or Script City, they'll likely be shooting scripts, and again will have a slightly different format from a spec (speculation or show) script. Nowadays with a little effort you can also locate thousands of downloadable scripts from various websites as well, but it's a crapshoot as to which draft may have been uploaded and whether the format has been preserved properly in transmission. More often than not it hasn't.

FORMATTING AND FORMATTING SOFTWARE

Achieving the proper format no longer requires tabbing and spacing to get your character names, dialogue and narrative all lined up. There are software programs designed to help screenwriters (and television writers). The industry-standard screenwriting programs are Final Draft, Movie Magic Screenwriter and SceneWriter Pro, which are all pricey, and offer features you may not yet need. All of them can be ordered online or found at a specialty store, if you're in a city large enough to have one. There are also two pretty good free programs as of now that you can download from celtx.com and scripped.com. Any of these will automatically provide the correct format templates for you, but even so these can be confusing to use—most of our students still get things wrong at first, even using a specialized program. So pay attention here: stick to the spec format we've laid out for you, and you'll look professional.

If you don't have the money for one of these programs, you can usually achieve similar results with your own word processor, if you don't mind spending a little time. On PCs, the format-creating feature is usually called "templates," and on Macintosh it's often listed under "styles" or "style sheets." Crack open that word-processing manual and learn how to program your computer so that with a push of a button you can format narrative, dialogue, character titles, slug lines and all the rest of it. If you use the "Macros" feature you can also program your computer to enter an entire scene header or character name with the push of a single button.

SETTING UP YOUR SCRIPT

Title Page

The title page is a simple white sheet of paper that usually doubles as the front cover. Just as with covers, the title page should not have any fancy graphics, pictures, wacky typefaces or other distractions. Some beginning screenwriters think that an eye-catching title page will help separate their script from the pack, and it does: it practically shouts at the reader that this is a script by a rank amateur. We know you can find counterexamples, mostly horror scripts with "bleeding letter" typefaces and/or graphics, but keep in mind that most unusual title pages you see on shooting scripts were probably put on by the production company after the film was produced or when it was going into production as a shooting script.

All that's needed on the title page is the following:

1. An exciting title, all caps and centered, about a third of the way down the page. The title can be plain, or it can be underlined or in quotation marks, but not both.
2. Your name, centered and double-spaced below the title, but not in caps. It's acceptable to write "by" or "An Original Screenplay By" (if the story is wholly original) beneath the title and above your name.
3. Your contact information (agent, manager, your own phone, address and e-mail address), not in caps, placed in the lower right-hand corner.

4. If the script is based on secondary material (adapted from a book, true story, short story or play you have permission to adapt, or someone else's story in some other form) describe such collaboration or material below your name, centered and not in caps.

Your title page should look something like the example on page 20.

Title Page No-No's

Avoid the following common mistakes. Just because you've seen them doesn't make them correct.

1. Don't use fancy typeface. Courier 12 point is preferred, although New York, Bookman and Times will do—on the title page <u>only</u>.

2. Don't announce a copyright or WGA registration number on your title page. This is a waste of ink. Your work is legally considered copyrighted as soon as it's written, and if someone's really going to steal your idea a WGA registration number isn't going to stop them. (Complete WGA registration and copyright information is covered in Chapter 15.)

3. Don't try to make your script appear more legitimate by adding statements like "Property of Harry Johnson and Associates," "Owned by Johnson Films" or "A Harry Johnson Production." This fools no one. The film business is a pretty tight community, and anyone actively working in it is probably familiar with most of the real companies in the business. Even if you have incorporated yourself as a "production" loan-out company for tax purposes, putting such information on the title page still does nothing for you as far as selling your script. In fact, it may create the assumption that the script is already burdened with attached producers, and most companies prefer a script with no producers attached, unless they're very experienced and well connected, because they have their own production team and don't want to pay extra salaries or percentages of profit. So trying to appear "professional" in this manner may actually hurt your chances at a sale.

4. Don't indicate on your title page whether this is the "First Draft," "Second Draft" or "Final Draft." These listings are for your own personal use and shouldn't appear on a spec script. No one cares which draft it is; all they know is that it's the draft they're being asked to read. Any other information is unnecessary. In fact, if you place "First Draft" on the title page you may raise the concern that you haven't taken the time to send a well-developed script, and if you put "Second" or "Third Draft" on it, it may look like it's been shopped around and had something wrong with it. It's like selling sausages. You don't want or need your buyer to see the process of how they're made—or if the sausages look like they might be old...

Binding

Screenplay binding is simple. Scripts are three-hole-punched and bound with brass brads or lesser-used Chicago screws. Plastic ring-binders, fancy clamps, metal strip couplers, embossed leatherette spring-notebooks or any other form of binding you can think of are unacceptable. The industry standard is brass brads or Chicago screws only. The best brass brads are made by ACCO. Use their No. 5 or No. 6 industrial, heavy-duty style fasteners. They come in boxes of a hundred and are typically available (or can be ordered) at stationery or office supply stores. The cheap, brass-colored brads you get at discount stores are too flimsy. Most professional screenwriters use only two brads per script, one in the top hole and one in the bottom, the middle hole left empty. It's just cooler that way, more Zen.

Covers

Covers are optional. Some writers use them, most professionals don't. If there is a cover or jacket on a screenplay, it's usually added by an agency or manager. Each agency has its own special cover that proudly identifies it as the submitter of the screenplay. If you do want to use covers, they should be simple, three-hole-punched card stock, in a single color. Never write, print or glue anything on the cover; no designs, drawings, quotes, decorations, family photos, not even the title or your name. Simplicity is the rule.

No Character Page, Quotations or Dedications

A cast of characters page, where each character is described, is a standard feature on a play script but is never done on a screenplay. After the title page the script begins. Although there have been notable exceptions to this, there also usually should not be any "meaningful quotations" to set the reader in the right mood nor any dedications. These are clutter.

The Basic Page

Use plain, white, 8½-by-11-inch, three-hole-punched paper. No colors, no borders, no onion skin, just regular old 20 lb. bond paper. Only one side of each sheet is used. (Some agencies or production companies will make their own double-sided copies to save paper. You may come across a double-sided script from time to time, but it is never correct for a spec script.)

Fonts, Printers and PDFs

In spite of all the fancy typefaces your computer can do, the text of your screenplay should look typewritten, meaning simple Courier 12-point pica font. Period. No boldface, italics or bigger or smaller fonts for emphasis. Real writers don't get fancy with their typeface. They let their story, not their font, carry the drama. The font should also be extremely readable, so use a

Title Page Guide

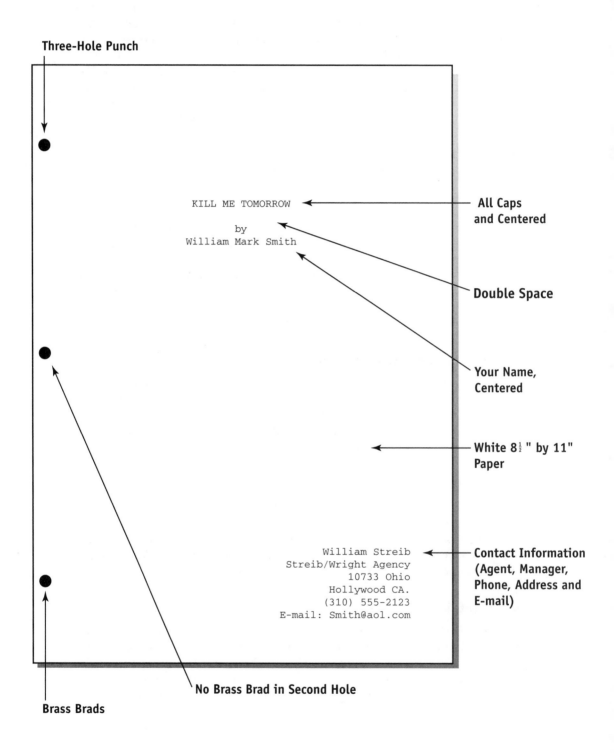

good quality printer if you're sending a hard copy. Most places like screenplay competitions and those rare agencies that are willing to look at new writers usually accept PDF copies via email or online upload, which can save on printing costs. Your screenwriting program will either offer an option to Save, or Export, or Print to PDF.

Margins

One inch on the top, bottom and right-hand sides of the page is the norm. The left margin is larger (1½ inch) to allow for the three-hole punch and brads. You can get away with cheating the right margin down to ¾ inch if you need to, but not more.

White Space

The first impression is important. A properly formatted script tends to have a lot of white space. This means the white of the paper, not the ink, seems to dominate the page. When directors, producers and readers open a screenplay and see lots of tight paragraphs, poor spacing and hard-to-read fonts, they are immediately turned off. A well-formatted script gives the reader breathing room.

Page Numbers

Page numbers appear in the upper-right corner. The title page is not numbered.

Page One / Fade In

You do not put the title on the first page, only on the title page. Page one begins with the words FADE IN: or FADE UP: or the less common OPEN ON:. These words, followed by a colon, are capitalized and placed flush with the far-left margin:

```
FADE IN:
```

Scene Headers

Scene headers (also known as slug lines or the more formal master scene headings) are captions that identify where and when a scene takes place. The scene header begins with either INT. meaning "Interior" or EXT. for "Exterior." Then it states the location, followed by a dash (—) and the time of day (almost always DAY or NIGHT, very occasionally DAWN, DUSK, MAGIC HOUR, or CONTINUOUS in the event that the scene follows a continuous action from the previous scene). Scene headers are placed flush with the far left margin (1½ inches from the left edge of the page). They are always in caps and followed by a double space (hard return). Here are examples of various scene headers:

```
EXT. GENE'S SWIMMING POOL — NIGHT

INT. DOG HOUSE — DAY

EXT. AN OLD GAS STATION — DUSK

INT. HOLIDAY INN CONFERENCE ROOM — NIGHT
```

In a spec screenplay, the scene headers are not numbered. Scene numbers are a production concern, and are added only when the script is sold and being readied for production; in other words, when it's being turned into a shooting script. However, it is important that, when you return to certain locations in your screenplay more than once, your scene headers for each recurring location should appear identical, other than time of day, if that variable has changed. This too is a production concern because it alerts the production crew in a clear, economical fashion as to the number of locations, days and nights required to schedule the production. But it is also a reading concern because scene headers help the reader easily recognize a new or recurring location and see the transition from scene to scene without having to work at it. Recently it's become fashionable to boldface your scene headers, and some programs are auto-set to do that. But it's neither a requirement nor that commonplace, so do it if you like, or don't. We prefer the cleaner, non-boldface look.

Narrative

The scene header is followed by a double space, then what is known as the narrative, narration or business. Screenplay narrative describes the physical action as well as the location and mood. The purpose of narrative is to make your reader see the movie. Narrative is single-spaced and aligned to the widest paragraph margin, 1½ inches from the left edge of the page and 1 inch from the right. Do not justify the right margin.

Here is a scene heading followed by narrative:

```
EXT. ROW HOUSE UNITS — NIGHT


A chain of old Chicago row houses, shackled together
with common walls and porches. A solid sequence of Sears
siding and shutterless windows stretches to the horizon,
a dank cutout of the city's nightline.
```

Narrative is kept brief, written in present tense and broken into short, readable paragraphs. (Chapter 12 is devoted to writing good narrative.) Within the narrative there are two elements that are usually capitalized. Character names are written in caps the first time the character appears in the screenplay, but not in subsequent scenes, unless the character is actually going to be played by another actor. For instance, if we meet SAM as a child, and later

Screenplay Spacing Guide

```
FADE IN:                                           1.

EXT. MIDDLE CLASS NEIGHBORHOOD - DAY

Late autumn. A small Midwestern town. The year is 1969.

Not that autumn was any different than now. It's just
that then, you were allowed to burn your leaves in the
gutter.

MR. STRAYER is doing that now. And from the crackling
fire smoke fills the bare branches overhead, making
everything almost roar to life with the sights and
smells that say, "grab it now before winter comes".


The POSTMAN, a fat but healthy man, passes Mr.
Strayer's colorful ice cream truck and hands him a
pile of junk mail.

                    MR. STRAYER
          More of the same, Joe?

                    POSTMAN
          More of the same.

With a vengeance, Mr. Strayer tosses the junk mail
into the burning leaves.

                    NARRATOR (V.O.)
          I grew up in a Norman Rockwell
          painting. Well, almost. Our
          postman was a homosexual. But
          you couldn't tell from the
          outside, so no one really cared.

                    MR. STRAYER
          Ice cream? On the house.

                    POSTMAN
          Gotta watch my weight.
```

Double Space after "FADE IN"

Double Space after Slug Line

Break Narrative Up into Short, Readable Paragraphs. Narrative LowerCase, Single-Spaced

Caps First Time a Character Appears

No Space Between Character Name and Dialogue

Double Space after Dialogue

Double Space after Narrative

Dialogue LowerCase Single-Spaced

Screenplay Margin and Tab Guide

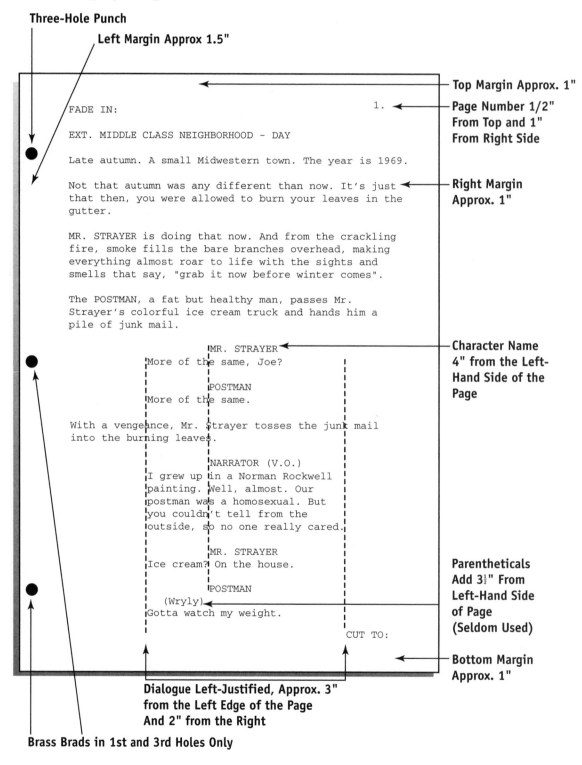

Three-Hole Punch

Left Margin Approx 1.5"

Top Margin Approx. 1"

Page Number 1/2" From Top and 1" From Right Side

```
FADE IN:                                          1.

EXT. MIDDLE CLASS NEIGHBORHOOD - DAY

Late autumn. A small Midwestern town. The year is 1969.

Not that autumn was any different than now. It's just
that then, you were allowed to burn your leaves in the
gutter.

MR. STRAYER is doing that now. And from the crackling
fire, smoke fills the bare branches overhead, making
everything almost roar to life with the sights and
smells that say, "grab it now before winter comes".

The POSTMAN, a fat but healthy man, passes Mr.
Strayer's colorful ice cream truck and hands him a
pile of junk mail.

                    MR. STRAYER
          More of the same, Joe?

                    POSTMAN
          More of the same.

With a vengeance, Mr. Strayer tosses the junk mail
into the burning leaves.

                    NARRATOR (V.O.)
          I grew up in a Norman Rockwell
          painting. Well, almost. Our
          postman was a homosexual. But
          you couldn't tell from the
          outside, so no one really cared.

                    MR. STRAYER
          Ice cream? On the house.

                    POSTMAN
              (Wryly)
          Gotta watch my weight.

                                       CUT TO:
```

Right Margin Approx. 1"

Character Name 4" from the Left-Hand Side of the Page

Parentheticals Add 3½" From Left-Hand Side of Page (Seldom Used)

Bottom Margin Approx. 1"

Dialogue Left-Justified, Approx. 3" from the Left Edge of the Page And 2" from the Right

Brass Brads in 1st and 3rd Holes Only

we come back to him as an adult (second actor), we would again write SAM in caps. Secondly, sounds (music or sound effects) may also be capitalized in the narrative:

```
KONIGSBERG closes his eyes and with a flinch squeezes the
trigger. CLICK! A dud.
```

Capping sounds can serve to give them emphasis, but in fact the practice survives from the old studio days, when contract writers sent their scripts straight into production. Capping quickly alerted the production and post-production sound crews to music and sound effects in the script, and it remains a standard feature on all shooting scripts. While it is not necessary in a spec, many older writers still capitalize sounds out of habit. Many younger writers do not. This one's your choice.

Character Headings

Character names are placed on the line immediately preceding the dialogue, and are capped and indented 4 inches from the left-hand side of the page. They are never centered. Character names are followed by a single space, after which comes either the dialogue or a parenthetical.

Dialogue

Dialogue is indented and left-justified 3 inches from the left edge of the page and approximately 2 inches from the right. It's single-spaced below the character heading and is not right-justified. Here is an example of character heading and dialogue:

```
                WALTER CRONKITE
        Today the U.S. Court of Appeals set aside
        the conviction of Dr. Benjamin Spock,
        author of 'The Common Sense Book of Baby
        and Child Care.' Dr. Spock was arrested
        and convicted of conspiracy to counsel
        draft evasion...
```

Dialogue must never be "orphaned" by letting a page break or intervening narrative separate it from its character heading. The following is wrong:

```
BILL, the football team's center, emerges from the tunnel
twenty yards away.


                BILL
        Hey, Mark. Come on, buddy. It's over.

Sweat drips down Mark's nose. He doesn't answer or move.
```

```
                    Mark, they're closing up. Let's go.
```

Instead, the second line of dialogue must include a new character heading. Some writers add a (CONT'D), short for "continued," to the character heading when a character's dialogue is interrupted by a bit of narrative:

```
        BILL, the football team's center, emerges from the tunnel
        twenty yards away.


                            BILL
                Hey, Mark. Come on, buddy. It's over.


        Sweat drips down Mark's nose. He doesn't answer or move.


                        BILL (CONT'D)
                Mark, they're closing up. Let's go.
```

However, this can be extremely cumbersome if you're shifting dialogue around and forget to remove the (CONT'D)'s from dialogue that is no longer interrupted. Again, it's just more clutter that doesn't need to be there. A new character heading is all you need. The only time a "continued" is required is if a page break interrupts the dialogue. When this occurs, the word "CONTINUED" or "MORE" should appear in parentheses at the bottom of the page and the speech finished on the next page. Example:

```
                        WALTER CRONKITE
                Today the U.S. Court of Appeals set aside
                the conviction of Dr. Benjamin Spock,
                author of 'The Common Sense Book of Baby
                and Child Care.'

                                            (MORE)


        _____Page Break


                        WALTER CRONKITE (CONT'D)
                Dr. Spock had been arrested and convicted
                of conspiracy to counsel draft evasion.
```

You do not want a page break to interrupt a sentence; the break should occur at the end of a sentence. If you have a very long sentence and have no choice but to interrupt it, add an ellipsis to the end of the last line on the bottom of the outgoing page and to the beginning of the dialogue at the top of the next page:

```
                        WALTER CRONKITE
                Today the U.S. Court of Appeals set aside
                the conviction of Dr. Benjamin Spock,
                author of 'The Common Sense Book of Baby
                and Child Care'...

                                            (MORE)
```

```
_____Page Break
                    WALTER CRONKITE (CONT'D)
... and long regarded by new parents
or the post-war generation as the top
authority in the care and upbringing
of young children. Dr. Spock had been
arrested and convicted of conspiracy to
counsel draft evasion.
```

Widow Control

A "widow" is a character heading or scene header that is left by itself at the bottom of a page, while the dialogue or narrative continues on the next. This is a widowed scene header:

```
EXT. JOLIET STATE PRISON GATE — DAY


_____Page Break
Guards inspect Frederick Shapiro's briefcase. His
starched collar and gold tie-pin set him apart from the
usual public defenders who use this gate.
```

Widows make a script look unprofessional, and can easily be avoided, if you're writing on a computer, by creating a format style in which the scene header or character heading is always kept with the following narrative or dialogue. (In Microsoft Word, for instance, there is a "Keep With Next" command.) In any event, always check your script's pagination. If a scene header or character heading falls at the bottom of a page and is separated from the narrative or dialogue on the following page, move the character heading or scene header to the next page.

Parentheticals

A parenthetical, also known in slang as a "wryly," is a small stage or acting direction placed in parentheses between the character heading and the dialogue. Parentheticals are usually indented 3½ inches from the left edge of the paper. They are single-spaced and set one line below the character heading:

```
Jim hugs Sam in an overly affectionate embrace. Betty
watches, annoyed.

                    JIM
          (wryly)
I love you, man.
          (to Betty, in French)
And of course, you too, my sweet.
```

Most beginning writers use far too many parentheticals. Professionals try to avoid using them at all. Your narrative and dialogue should be written well enough that parentheticals are not needed. As a rule, actors and directors actively detest parentheticals as a screenwriter's intrusive attempt to interfere with their jobs, and they cross these directions out if they bother to read the script at all. Parentheticals are acceptable if you're indicating that someone is speaking in another language (which you are writing in English so the reader can understand it) or if there are several characters in a scene and your speaker is addressing first one, then the other. In the above example, the second parenthetical is acceptable, the first is not.

Other acceptable parentheticals are (V.O.) or (VO), which means "Voice Over," and (O.S.) or (OS), which means "Off Screen." (VO) is used to indicate dialogue that the audience can hear but characters in the scene cannot. For example, if one character is "silently" telling us her internal thoughts, or if a narrator describes a scene, this would be indicated with (VO). (OS) means that the dialogue or sound can be heard by the characters, but the source of the sound is not visible on the screen, such as someone shouting from another room or a car honking outside. (Some screenwriters use (O.C.), for "Off Camera," which means the same thing. (OS) is more popular.) (V.O.) and (O.S.) parentheticals are placed beside the character heading, like this:

```
                    MARTY (O.S.)
          You'd better get your butts down here
          right now!
```

Some writers prefer the abbreviations; others attempt to avoid parentheticals at all costs and substitute the word "VOICE" for (O.S.) or (V.O):

```
                    MARTY'S VOICE
          Are you coming, or not!
```

Another occasionally used parenthetical is (beat), which indicates a brief hesitation or pause, and is not the same thing as a story beat (see Chapter 8). If this parenthetical is used sparingly at dramatic moments or for comic effect, then it is acceptable. (See Chapter 13 for more information on parentheticals.)

Cuts, Dissolves and Continueds

At the end of a scene, screenwriters sometimes place the words CUT TO followed by a colon flush with the right-hand margin:

```
                                            CUT TO:
```

This simply means that the movie is now changing to a new location or time. But it is not necessary to place CUT TO: after every scene. There's an obvious cut every time there's a new scene header or slug line (meaning a new scene), so why be redundant? Sometimes the words FADE TO: or DISSOLVE TO: are used to indicate that the end of a scene melts into the beginning of the next. This should be used sparingly and for specific effect, for instance, when going into a dream sequence or a flashback, or when the time change between scenes is great. CUT TO: should also be reserved for times when you want to draw attention to the scene change for specific effect, such as when bouncing between a pursuer and his pursued in a chase, or when going from a very quiet scene into a loud one.

Shooting scripts will have a (CONTINUED) at the top and bottom of every page. This is done to let the production crew know that whatever scene is happening at the bottom of this page continues on the next page (as if they couldn't figure this out for themselves). (CONTINUED)'s are an old tradition in shooting scripts, but are not necessary or desirable in a spec script. Leave them off; they clutter the page and add nothing to the read. Most computer screenwriting programs allow you the option of using or turning off the (CONTINUED) and CUT TO: functions. We advise turning them off. You'll save page space and script length.

Fade Out

The last line of a screenplay is usually FADE OUT. This is capitalized and is right-margin-justified.

Capitalization

Here are what should be capitalized:

1. SCENE HEADINGS
2. CHARACTER NAMES above the dialogue
3. SOUNDS in the narrative
4. New CHARACTER NAMES the first time they are introduced in the narrative, and in the subsequent introduction of that same character if a new actor is being indicated (such as when a character introduced as a girl later appears as a woman)

Line Spacing

SINGLE SPACE the following:

1. Narrative
2. Between character heading and dialogue
3. Dialogue

DOUBLE SPACE the following:

1. Between scene header and narrative
2. Between narrative and character heading
3. After dialogue
4. Between paragraphs within the narrative
5. Before and after a CUT TO: or DISSOLVE TO:

Screenplay Margin and Tab Guide

If you are using a standard Pica typewriter format in a regular word program, the tabs for margins would be:

> 17—Narrative left margin
> 28—Dialogue left margin
> 35—Parenthetical
> 46—Character's name
> 66—CUT TO:
> 63—Dialogue right margin
> 75—Narrative right margin

The guide on page 24 shows the proper margins. A template designed to help you set margins is located in Appendix A.

Camera Directions

Camera directions, sometimes called camera angles (CLOSE SHOT, WIDE SHOT, HIGH ANGLE, CLOSE 2-SHOT, CAMERA DOLLIES LEFT, etc.), were once commonly used in a screenplay's narrative to tell the director how to shoot the script, but they are now considered old-fashioned and inappropriate. Unless you're going to direct your own script, don't pretend to be the director. Camera angles add clutter to the narrative, and are more likely to annoy potential directors than enlighten them. There's a better way: Let the emphasis of your description guide both reader and director.

Compare the following two approaches to a scene. First, the old-fashioned way:

```
EXT. FOOTBALL STADIUM — NIGHT

HIGH EXTREME WIDE ANGLE ON a football stadium, lit by
floods, in the middle of a dark city neighborhood.

LOWER WIDE ANGLE ON the stadium: the crowds have gone
home. Alone in the middle of the field, a single player,
MARK, the quarterback, kneels as if in prayer, his head
bowed.

PUSH CLOSER INTO LOW MEDIUM ANGLE and REVEAL that he's
leaning with one hand on a football.

WIDE ANGLE ON the center, BILL, coming out of the
tunnel.

                    BILL
          Come on, buddy. It's over.

MEDIUM ANGLE ON Mark, who doesn't answer or move.

CLOSE UP ON Mark's face: sweat drips down his nose.

                    BILL (OS)
          Mark, they're closing up. Let's go.
```

EXTREME CLOSE UP ON his eyes, which are closed. More drops roll down from them, not sweat, but tears. Suddenly the light dims. There's the sound of ELECTRIC BREAKERS being thrown.

> MARK (VO)
> It was the worst moment of my life. I'd just lost the Superbowl. Not my team. Me.

WIDE ANGLE ON stadium, as the huge floods go out, one by one.

Now here is the same scene without camera angles. Notice that it's clear we go from **HIGH EXTREME WIDE ANGLE** to **EXTREME CLOSE UP** without cluttering up the page with the camera angles.

EXT. FOOTBALL STADIUM — NIGHT

A bright green oval glows like an emerald in the middle of the velvet-dark city: a football stadium, lit by floods.

The steps are empty, the bleachers deserted. But out in the middle of the field kneels a single player: MARK, the quarterback. He bows his head, as if in prayer. One hand rests on the football.

BILL, the team Center, emerges from the tunnel twenty yards away.

> BILL
> Hey, Mark. Come on, buddy. It's over.

A single bead of sweat drips down Mark's nose. Then another. He doesn't answer or move.

> BILL (OS)
> Mark, they're closing up. Let's go.

Mark squeezes his eyes shut. At their corners, more drops emerge and fall: not sweat, but tears.

Suddenly the light dims. There's the sound of ELECTRIC BREAKERS being thrown.

> MARK (VO)
> It was the worst moment of my life. I'd just lost the Superbowl. Not my team. Me.

```
The huge floods above the stadium go out, one by one.
```

The one acceptable camera direction is POINT OF VIEW (P.O.V.). This is used when the writer wants the reader to "see" the scene through one particular character's eyes. It should be used only when this unique P.O.V. is crucial to the story.

```
GEORGE'S P.O.V. -- Counselor Johanson looks like some
giant extinct species of bird about to devour him.
```

Horror movies use point of view a great deal, for instance to give us the monster's P.O.V. of his next victim without yet showing the audience what the monster looks like, or to give us the frightened victim's P.O.V. as she stupidly goes alone into the basement. This strictly limits "our" vision to what a character herself can see, enhancing the sense of danger and claustrophobia.

The main point is that the way the scene is described should tell the reader what angles are indicated. And learning to focus on these telling details will make you a better writer. In all cases, remember that your screenplay should "play the movie" in the reader's mind. You want him to see the movie, not the set.

Montages

A montage is a rapid sequence of brief scenes or images that underscores the story or tells the viewer that time in the story is passing. For example, if the character decides to become a skier and the screenwriter wants to show the process of him learning, she might use a montage, which would look like this:

```
EXT. MOUNTAIN SLOPES — DAY

MONTAGE:
1) Larry stands on the skis for the first time. He
   falls.
2) He is now able to do a few simple movements.
3) He plows into a woman. She isn't happy about it.
4) He is getting better. He can now turn. He smiles with
   his success. A four-year-old girl passes him doing
   much better.
5) Larry brags in the bar about how fast he went today.
   Then he sees the woman he hit. She's unimpressed.
6) He is now getting much better. He flies down the
   hill.
7) He makes a perfect turn, just missing a tree.
8) He talks over his style with a trainer.
9) He tries a tentative jump. He makes it.
```

We've numbered the mini-scenes of this montage. However, you can also simply put a dash-dash before each.

Flashbacks

If your story needs a flashback, this is usually done by using a DISSOLVE TO: flush with the right-hand margin and placing the word FLASHBACK within the scene header like this:

                                               DISSOLVE TO:

    EXT. VIETNAM JUNGLE — NIGHT (FLASHBACK)

Once the flashback is over, it's important to let the reader know that we are back to the present. This is indicated by using another DISSOLVE TO: or CUT TO: (or even a CUT BACK TO:), and again addressing the time change in the scene heading:

                                                    CUT TO:

    EXT. CENTRAL PARK — NIGHT (PRESENT)

Sometimes a writer needs to show a quick memory flash. These are short bursts of pictures and sounds that show what the character is remembering. It's something like a P.O.V., only we see what the character is thinking instead of seeing. A memory flash is followed by a dash dash as follows:

    The huge Suspect doesn't even flinch. Rock aims but it's
    50 feet or more--too far.

    Ken is desperate, his busted face looks down the barrel
    of the gun.

    MEMORY FLASH--Ken sees his son's smiling face. Laughing,
    smiling, the boy plays with a toy gun.

    The Suspect readies an execution-style shot to Ken's
    head... BANG!

    Blood flows from the Suspect's ear. It was a clean shot,
    right through his head. He stands there for a moment.
    Amazed. He's dead, he just doesn't know it.

Telephone Calls

If you need to indicate a phone conversation in which the audience does not hear the party on the other end of the phone, then use ellipses to mark the moments when the off-camera party is speaking:

                        GRACE
                  (on the phone)
            No, you're lying. He really asked you to
            marry him? When?... You're joking!...
            What?

If we hear the other party speaking then indicate this by using O.S. (Off Screen):

> GRACE
> (on the phone)
> No, you're lying. He really asked you to marry him? When?

> SUE (O.S.)
> This morning. In bed.

> GRACE
> You're joking!

> SUE (O.S.)
> I said no.

> GRACE
> What?

Seeing both characters talking can become clumsy, as you cut back and forth between each scene. Instead you can shorthand the location shifts by indicating an INTERCUT in the scene header, and describing the action as if it were a single scene:

BUSY STREET — DAY

Bill dashes across the street to a corner phone booth. He jams coins into the slot and dials frantically, pressing his palm to his free ear to shut out the traffic noise.

> BILL
> Come on, come on, pick up!

INT. JOE'S APARTMENT — DAY

A messy bachelor pad. Joe lounges on his futon, munching potato chips as he answers the phone.

> JOE
> Yeah?

INTERCUT JOE'S APARTMENT AND PHONE BOOTH — DAY

> BILL
> Joe? Joe, you gotta help me!

> JOE
> Who is this?

```
Bill glances around nervously. No one's following him.

                    BILL
          It's your brother—who the hell do you
          think? Joe, I'm in trouble.

Joe sits up, pushing the chips aside.

                    JOE
          Bill? Where are you?
```

WAR STORIES

Robin

In every class I have taught, one student points out that Shane Black's *Lethal Weapon* script does both. This is true, and it is well known in the industry as the great exception, the one script that broke all the rules and got made anyway. Remember that crucial word: It was the *one* script that broke all the rules and got made anyway. In the four years I worked as a reader and script analyst, I read perhaps a hundred other scripts that attempted to copy Shane's flamboyant style, but not a single one of them copied his success.

Foreign Languages

When a character speaks a foreign language, which you are in fact writing in English so the reader can understand it, you indicate that it's a foreign language in the narrative or in parentheticals. If you are going to use subtitles, then point this out in the narrative or in the parentheticals as well:

```
The Nazi slaps Meyer, shouting at him in German
(subtitled):

                    NAZI
          I should kill you right now, but that
          would be too easy. Stupid Jew, you don't
          even understand what I'm saying, do you?

Meyer answers in English.

                    MEYER
          I understand you perfectly. And I know
          you understand me. So why don't you take
          a look behind you?
```

```
          The Nazi glances back. Three RESISTANCE FIGHTERS stand
          there, with their guns pointed at him.
```

Or:

```
          The Nazi slaps Meyer:

                         NAZI
                    (in German, subtitled)
               I should kill you right now, but that
               would be too easy. Stupid Jew, you don't
               even understand what I'm saying, do you?

                         MEYER
                    (in English)
               I understand you perfectly. And I know
               you understand me. So why don't you take
               a look behind you?

          The Nazi glances back. Three RESISTANCE FIGHTERS stand
          there, with their guns pointed at him.
```

This way we can read the dialogue unimpeded, knowing where subtitles will make it comprehensible on screen. Subtitles may not be indicated if the purpose of having a character speak in another language is to create a sense of mystery and confusion, to hide something from the audience or from another character who does not speak the language.

Credits

Generally, screenwriters do not indicate where and when opening or closing credits appear in a spec script. These are added to the shooting or editing script.

EXERCISES

1. Properly format a page-long scene that includes a flashback scene in which two people talk on the phone, one speaking in English, the other in Chinese.

2. Write a scene that "directs" the reader to see a wide master shot, a panning camera move and an extreme close-up, all without resorting to camera directions.

3. Write two short scenes that flow naturally into each other, where a CUT TO: is not needed. Then write two short scenes where a CUT TO: will emphasize a change of mood, time or location.

4. Write a conversation with parentheticals after every character heading. Then cut as many of them as possible, keeping only the ones that are essential, and write any other actions into the narrative.

3

Theme, Meaning and Emotion
So What's It About, Anyway?

Many new screenwriters are hesitant to discuss the theme of their script. Ask what their story is about and they'll answer, "It's about 110 pages." Theme goes by many names; it has been called meaning, the root idea, the universal value, the primary statement, the unifying objective, the moral, the premise, the central organizing principle and the story's purpose. Any way you say it, theme is the overall message, the abstract truth that is made concrete by the action of the characters. Sometimes the theme can be stated in a simple sentence, like, "A house divided against itself cannot stand," or, "You can't keep a good woman down," but often it's more complex. The great drama critic Walter Kerr wrote, "Themes are, almost by nature, difficult to define absolutely; they look to human nature in the round and, like a turning crystal, give off multiple reflections."

Every story is about something. Not as in, "*The Terminator* is about a woman trying to get away from a robot," or, "*Frankenstein* is about a scientist trying to stop a zombie," but as in, "*The Terminator* and *Frankenstein* are about humanity's sin of pride in creating dangerous monsters beyond the control of their human creator." Scholarly film critics spend their days writing long treatises extracting the theme from great movies like *Citizen Kane* (by the way, one of its main themes is, "A man who tries to force everyone to love him will die alone"), but for most writers theme is simply the relevant reason that made them want to write. In other words, it's the philosophical point of the story that they hope will generate a strong emotional and/or intellectual experience for their audience. Theme is simply the *truth* of the script.

FULL OF SOUND AND FURY, SIGNIFYING NOTHING (YET)

Let's start by looking at two student screenwriters' original ideas and see how they move from story to theme. The first student pitched, "I want to write a thriller about a female, rural cop who discovers that a seemingly senseless murder is related to a white supremacist group." The second, "I want to write about a chubby boy who dreams about becoming a great dancer and succeeds in spite of everything." As with most preliminary ideas, these focus on the characters and a general sense of the plot. At first this is just fine, but as the idea develops you will want to ask an important question: not "What is the theme?" but rather, "Why do I want to write this particular story?" Often, after a moment of uncomfortable silence, a beginning screenwriter's answer is, "Well, I just think it would be cool" or some similar flimsy response. But what makes it "cool"? What is it about these particular characters that appeals to you? Why *this* story and not *that* story? This often takes some soul searching. When you discover the answers you'll have identified the conscious or subconscious forces that brought you to these characters and this story. You have not arrived at theme yet, but you are heading in the right direction.

In the case of the white supremacist story, what interested the young screenwriter was the idea of an idealistic underdog who through brains and courage overcomes an intrinsic evil in society, in spite of prejudice against women and the doubts of her colleagues. Once the story's antagonist, the head of the supremacist group, was personified as a powerful man in local politics and someone with whom the protagonist had had a sexual relationship, the story took off. Building on that, every scene and line of dialogue will be focused around the concerns of regret, sexism and prejudice. With the dancer story, although a bubbly comedy, the student was attracted to a character whose dogged persistence overcomes personal limitations. Knowing this, the writer was able to dispense with whole rafts of irrelevant dialogue and scenes dealing with other issues, and focus the story on the essential conflict. The humor, instead of coming from random fat jokes, emerged from the hilarious situations in which this boy tries every possible ruse to get into a dance school and prove his worth. Notice that both stories revolve around an underdog who succeeds. It doesn't take years of psychoanalysis to find out that both screenwriters had experienced being an underdog. In fact, pretty much everybody has; that's why underdog stories resonate with audiences. Now the question is, how do underdogs succeed? Notice we are getting closer to theme.

As these student writers finished their first drafts they began to uncover their themes. The student working on the white supremacist story discovered that her theme was about how unquestioned love hides our better judgment, and how even the best of us hate to question our assumptions because we cannot handle self-doubt, yet only through self-doubt can we learn the truth about life. The other screenwriter found that his dancer story centered on our need not to be typecast by friends, society and especially ourselves. In both cases the themes spoke to the writers on a personal level. Some writers say that writing is like therapy because all writers are trying to find truthful answers to life's many questions. The answer the writer uncovers or perhaps invents *is* theme.

THEMES ALL RIGHT TO ME

Great movies stand the test of time not only because they mean something to the screenwriter, but also because they touch upon lasting and meaningful ideas that say something about our common humanity. For example, the theme of the movie *Social Network* is not about the development of Facebook. It is about how single-minded ambition destroys friendship and loyalty and leads to jealousy and guilt. It is about universal and unchanging truths about human nature. Add three witches and some swordplay to *The Social Network* and you have Shakespeare's 400-year-old *Macbeth* (well, at least if Macbeth had realized he was being a jerk by the end and had somewhat redeemed himself). Why does the ancient Greek tragedy *Oedipus Rex* still ring true two and a half millennia after Sophocles wrote it? Because its themes of fate wrestling with free will, of self-delusion and guilt colliding with self-knowledge and catharsis, still appeal to our modern confident-yet-insecure psyche. Once you have a basic theme, the first question you need to ask is, is it universal?

When it comes down to it, there are a limited number of universal themes to go around and different films often share similar if not the exact same theme: both *The Silence of the Lambs* and *The Exorcist* make the same thematic statement: "Courage and overcoming self-doubt are necessary for the destruction of evil." One of the themes of the Dustin Hoffman movie *Little Big Man* concerns lost innocence in the face of "progress," which is also the theme of the silly comedy *Dumb and Dumber*. The theme of the musical *How to Succeed in Business Without Really Trying*—that "only through hard work and love do we find happiness and true success"—is also found in the movie *Ghostbusters*.

The way to address this prefabricated theme problem is to construct your movie so that its theme is sufficiently specific and makes a statement that modifies the universal theme. James Cameron's *Titanic*'s central theme, the one that gets Celine Dion singing "My Heart Will Go On" (which by the way is why it's called the theme song), is that love conquers death, at least spiritually. You might think that this is the same universal theme as *Romeo and Juliet*, where similar "tragic young love" events transpire, but that's an error of not really looking at the specific story. *Titanic* is about a woman who lives to a ripe old age, never having forgotten the adventure of her love for a young man who died to keep her alive. *Romeo and Juliet* is not about the immortality of love but rather how two immature young people are destroyed by their rush to love; every important character and action reinforces the theme of how giving in to headstrong passions brings misery to all involved: "Never was a story of more woe / Than this of Juliet and her Romeo." The fact that Shakespeare makes their passion so attractive is what gives this theme its ironic power. So: similar protagonists and story elements, very different themes.

Similarly, "Courage overcomes evil" is too general—it applies to practically every action movie ever made, as well as many horror films, such as those noted above. Even the more specific theme we gave for *The Silence of the Lambs* and *The Exorcist* could be improved by making each still more specific: For *The Silence of the Lambs*, how about: "The courage to overcome paralyzing childhood fears is necessary to confront and destroy an evil threatening the lives of others." Or for *The Exorcist*, try "To defeat a supreme evil that threatens to destroy one's soul as well as the innocence of others, one must have the courage to overcome one's own self-doubts about faith." The theme of the science fiction film *District 9* speaks to how we only bring harm to ourselves when we ghettoize people we don't understand (or in this case, ghettoize alien "prawns" from another solar system). This same universal theme is one of those contained in Shakespeare's *The Merchant of Venice*: Shylock says, "If you prick us, do we not bleed? If you tickle us, do we not laugh? If you poison us, do we not die? And if you wrong us, shall we not revenge?" *District 9* takes the idea one step further, however, by stating that in order to understand another person (or prawn) you must walk in their shoes (or in this case be sprayed in the face with a grotesque extra-terrestrial liquid that slowly mutates your DNA and turns you into one of them). This nudges the original theme a little further, but is it unique? Not really. *Blade Runner*, about a cop who hunts down ghettoized "replicants" only to discover that he is one himself, has a similar theme. What modifies the theme in *District 9* is that its ghettoizing isn't done just by evil antagonists or violent tough guys, but also by nice people such as *District 9*'s bumbling protagonist (Wikus Wan De Merwe), a bureaucrat who accepts the assignment to relocate the aliens without making the slightest attempt to understand them, their culture, or their needs. He's just doing his job. *District 9* adds an important twist to its theme by addressing the banality of racism, to paraphrase Hannah Arendt; the film's theme makes us deal with the fact that *we*—the nerds, the average guys on the street who just go along to get along—are the problem.

Another example is *Eternal Sunshine of the Spotless Mind*. This is more than just a funny and fascinating script; it makes several important statements about love. It says that love is more than just attraction, or that "happily ever after" is never really going to be that easy. Okay, plays, poems, and movies have been saying something like this for thousands of years. It says that love is complex, again nothing new. But when Joel Barish (Jim Carrey) and Clementine Kruczynski (Kate Winslet) set out to erase each other from their memories, they discover that although there are numerous reasons why they are each less than perfect, yet there is something each sees in the other that makes them still want to be together. The theme says that true love is the ability to still long for each other, to still be infatuated, even after knowing all of each other's flaws. This excellent script finds a new way to tell the age-old story to reveal a universal theme and stand the test of time.

The key is to find a theme that is universal and says something about the human condition—and also that has specific meaning to you, and that you can reveal afresh in an entertaining and inventive way. You are an artist (yes, screenwriters are artists), and artists have something meaningful to say about how the world is and/or should be. You are going to spend months on this script, so make sure the theme is something you have a deep desire to communicate to the world. In short, the theme must reflect who you are.

WRITE FROM THE HEART

A screenplay has to be written with passion, or it will never engage the passions of the reader. The audience wants to be moved—hey, maybe that's why it's called a "moving picture." Those elements that contribute to an emotional experience are valuable; those that don't are either extraneous and dispensable or need to be reimagined so that they become part of the emotional experience. According to Aristotle, "catharsis" (emotional and spiritual cleansing) is the goal of drama and, in the case of tragedy, is produced by the strong emotions of "pity and fear." His treatise on comedy is lost, but it probably insisted on comparably strong emotions to create the catharsis of laughter. But why do we need cleansing, and of what impurities—and why do we need such extreme emotions to burn them away? To ask this is to ask why we need stories at all. Perhaps, we need to be cleansed of the aimless chaos of our lives. The characters and actions of real life are raw, in an unorganized state; a story structures life into a unified whole, and a unified theme. The great American playwright Arthur Miller wrote, "The very impulse to write springs from an inner chaos crying for order, for meaning…" A well-told story and theme let the audience find, if only for a few hours, some coherent expression of meaning. It can't just be an intellectual experience. The audience needs to feel the theme in their bones. They need, they crave, both understanding as well as emotion. Without either, we cannot have a good story, well told.

PAPA, DON'T PREACH

So what do we make of the famous dictum supposedly uttered by Sam Goldwyn (who founded several Hollywood studios including MGM—Metro-Goldwyn-Mayer): "If you want to send a message, call Western Union."? (For those of you too young to remember, Western Union was the email service of its day.) He meant that no one wants to be lectured or take medicine just because it's good for you. No one wants to go see a movie they "ought" to go see just because it has an "important message"; that's the humor Woody Allen exploits in *Annie Hall* when he obsesses about taking Annie to see Max Ophuls' *The Sorrow and the Pity*. As Annie says, "I'm not in the mood to see a four and a half hour documentary on Nazis." Few people are. People go to the movies to enjoy themselves. And yet, good movies always contain a strong thematic point of view, and if your script is going to be the basis for one of them, then you must make sure that you do not browbeat or try to indoctrinate the audience. Didactic screenplays sacrifice character and story to dogma and ideology. In other words, they become propaganda, stories in which the characters are only mouthpieces for the author's message. This type of a story, wrote Walter Kerr, the Broadway theatre critic, "is in a hurry; it has no time for the hesitant inflection of the human voice." So take your time and let the theme emerge though character and story. Whether it's a complex motif or a simple idea, the theme should be deeply embedded in the action, woven into the subtext, not stated openly, unless you can do this naturally and concisely within the context of a scene.

So develop your themes, but don't allow them to become political slogans, personal mottoes or life lectures. Allow your audience a chance to think, consider—but mostly, to feel. You do this by making your characters real. Let them have real feelings and motivations, and don't let them become puppets who only do what you, the author, want them to do in order to represent a cause or philosophical idea. One way to accomplish this is *not* to let the characters know what the theme is. In other words, as they strive to fulfill their goal they never (or at least not until the end) come to understand what their goal means to their (or your) philosophy of life. American playwright, director and actor Howard Lindsay is credited with saying that if your story contains propaganda the writer should not let the characters know what the propaganda is. Walter Kerr took Lindsay's idea one step further when he wrote that it would be best if even the writer isn't aware of what the propaganda is. In short, persuade, don't preach, and you'll stand a better chance of moving the audience—and a better chance of selling your script.

HOW TO REVEAL THE THEME

John Howard Lawson, the great screenwriter and first president of the WGA west (the union that represents Hollywood screenwriters), wrote that the unifying force of a script "is the idea; but an idea, however integral it may be, is in itself undramatic." There's the rub. Writers desperately want to make a point, but making a point risks being inherently undramatic and therefore uninteresting. George Pierce Baker, the renowned professor of dramatic literature at Harvard University who taught the Nobel Prize–winning playwright Eugene O'Neill how to write, said, "People rather than ideas arouse the interest of the general public," and that action "far more than characterization wins and holds the attention of the great majority." If we put these two thoughts together we find that theme by itself is useless unless it is supported by character, and characters are useless unless they are supported by action. In other words, the characters must do something and what they do must reveal the theme. Let's go back to *District 9*'s protagonist Wikus Van De Merwe, the bureaucrat whose job it is to relocate the alien "prawns." Notice that he is totally unaware of the theme of the movie, or theme of his life for that matter. He is simply trying to do his job, save his love life, save himself, and as he becomes an alien himself, to understand and save the aliens. His character and his desperate situation drive the actions of the story, but the result is theme. Once again Walter Kerr said it best when he wrote that it is better to make a character than make a point. If your characters feel real and take the right actions, you will make the point.

Coming back to the concept of catharsis: The actions the characters take at the end of the movie are the concluding building blocks that reveal the theme, and the result must have a profound impact on your characters and your protagonist in particular. For example at the end of *The Help*, the maid (Aibileen) is fired from her cleaning job and walks off into the distance, making a profound existential statement about standing up for herself in spite of a racist society. She sets out to tell her own story rather than allow other people to tell it for her. This is a universal theme, for there have always been voiceless and oppressed people—underdogs—for whom her actions represent courage and hope. But the theme is not clear until the end of the movie. The protagonist's final actions make the closing moments remarkable and moving, and the theme clear and memorable.

SOME CONSEQUENCE YET HANGING IN THE STARS

Having said this, we now remind you that, while it may be advantageous, it is not always necessary to know your theme in advance. Interesting characters and/or a good plot are enough to begin writing. Some writers insist that they simply write what moves them, and they do not attempt to understand their reasons for writing one way rather than another, at least on the first draft. They simply let it spill out. It is only later—not unlike their characters —when they look back to see what they've done and refine the writing that the theme emerges. Arthur Miller (*Death of a Salesman*) said that he often did not know the theme of his plays until the second or third draft. Other writers know exactly what their theme will be. The point is, not to let it prevent you from starting if you don't. Simply because it is your story and they are your characters, if you've created them well the theme will emerge organically.

A critic once supposedly complimented Robert Frost on his poem "Stopping by Woods on a Snowy Evening." The critic admired the way Frost's repetition of the last line, "And miles to go before I sleep," so simply and yet profoundly expressed man's melancholy awareness of life's inevitable journey toward death, and how that awareness both limited and gave meaning to the journey. To which Frost replied, "Really? I just liked the way it sounded." Whether this actually happened or not, the story contains an essential truth about writing, and about the problem of trying to teach someone how to write: sometimes great things simply happen by accident, and there's no way to predict or force them. The writer, acting on talent and instinct, may unconsciously create several layers of meaning where only one was intended, and these may in fact be discovered long after the piece is written. An experienced writer may be able to rely on her own instincts and know they won't lead her astray. But many beginning writers fail precisely because they don't yet have any instincts to rely on, and they end up frustrated with a story that meanders to a pointless, theme-less conclusion. Given that the best things often happen by accident and can only be discovered after the fact, it isn't possible to plan for and predict every layer of meaning in a screenplay. But it is possible—in fact, it is essential—to come to at least a strong initial sense of the intellectual and emotional ideas of your story, and to organize your various story elements around it.

FINAL THOUGHTS

Look at any movie of any quality, and you will discover that it coheres around a specific theme, a meaning that gives it emotional power. Now take a look at your script and your need to write it. There is a reason certain stories occur to you, just as there is a reason certain movies appeal to you. They may express your worldview, your sense of humor or pathos, or address deep personal concerns. Find out why you want to tell your story, what you're trying to say with it, and, whether in your first draft or your fourth, you will find a theme. Ultimately, the questions you must ask are: Why does this story need to be told? Why is it important? Why is it necessary? Most of all, why is it funny/sad/horrifying/thrilling/moving? When you have the answers to these questions you will have more than another knockoff action/SF/love story/horror script; you will have one with a universal theme, yet unique to yourself, that might just stand the test of time.

EXERCISES

1. Write three themes from your life that you believe would make great movies.

2. Write a list of your top ten favorite movies. Now identify each movie's theme.

3. Write a list of your top ten favorite movies. Now answer the following questions about each one:

    a.   Why does this story need to be told?
    b.   Why is it important?
    c.   Why is it necessary?

4

The World of the Story

Where Are We, Anyway?

"Where am I?" is one of the first questions readers ask when they start a novel or audience members wonder when the lights dim and a new movie begins. Like emerging from a long tunnel or the effects of anesthetic, we are disoriented, suddenly immersed in the light of a new and unfamiliar place. This is especially true of movies, where we sit in darkness while an immensely magnified "reality" unfolds before us. A movie's "world" includes the story's season, geographic location, physical environment and historical period. The world is as large as outer space and as small as a candle flame. It can be as simple as beginning a children's fable, "Once upon a time, long ago," or as complex as the vast milieu of *War and Peace*. In many ways, the world is like another character, with a distinctive appearance and identity, acting upon and defining the course of the story. The world creates the mood and defines the protagonist, the stakes and the antagonist. (Sometimes the world *is* the antagonist, as in *Alive* or in disaster movies.) There should be a sense that in this world, this story is the *essential* conflict, and that your characters are the *essential* people; conversely, we must feel that for this particular story and characters, this is the *essential* world. A screenplay's world is a critical part of its characterization and exposition. Yet it is also the one element that is most often taken for granted by beginning screenwriters.

Years ago, set designers for the theater simply painted the background environment on two-dimensional flats or backdrops. Doors, handles, windows, even furniture and trees were drawn or painted on, and the actors performed in front of them without interacting with them. These flats were made as generic as possible, so that they could be used time and again, no matter which play was being performed. Some screenwriters seem to approach the world of their story the same way. They treat the environment as decoration or ornamentation, not as a critical part of the story. They rely on dialogue to tell us the emotions and journey of the characters, almost ignoring the enormous emotional potential that the huge, glowing canvas of the screen presents.

Yet every story and every character would change if we picked them up and deposited them in a new environment. Imagine the Christmas classic

Miracle on 34th Street placed in the steamy South, or the chilly moral fable *Fargo* or the ice-bound vampire scarefest *30 Days of Night* set in sunny Hawaii. Their stories, characters and possibly even their themes would be transformed. Change the world and you change the story and characters. Look at how even the most well-known and dialogue-driven plays by Shakespeare are transformed when turned into movies, set in new and unexpected locations: the politics of medieval England become the harsh threats of modern fascism in the Ian McKellen version of *Richard III*, and the early Renaissance feudal struggle of *Romeo and Juliet* is transformed into an ultra-contemporary gang war in the Leo DiCaprio version. The plots and most of the dialogue are kept unchanged, and yet the change in world drastically alters the tone and character of the stories. So these are the critical questions a screenwriter must ask, right from the start: Have I chosen the right world for my story and the right characters for that world? How does this world affect and reflect my story and characters; how do my story and characters affect and reflect the world?

THROUGH THE LOOKING GLASS (STORY AND WORLD)

Audiences want to be transported to someplace new and wonderful, or be shown the familiar in an unfamiliar way. Obviously, a movie that takes place in a visually stimulating environment will be more eye-catching than one that does not. But spectacular settings alone do not create a meaningful world. A screenplay full of wild parties, stadiums jammed full of screaming fans and wonderful island sunsets might dress the scenes, but will not necessarily make for an interesting story. The setting of each scene must reflect an overall sense of the larger world of the story, and work to advance the latent emotions and thematic possibilities that world presents. Some films go so far as to get their title from their world: *Titanic*, *Halloween*, *Journey to the Center of the Earth*, *Escape from New York*, *The Abyss*, *The Hills Have Eyes*, *Wall Street*. The world is the playing field that defines the rules and the nature of the game.

When the world reflects the story, it assists by providing important ambiance, perspective, tone and context in which each particular scene takes place. In *Sling Blade*, for instance, each scene—from mental hospital to small southern town—strongly affects how Karl Childers talks, lives his life and makes decisions. The same is true for Forrest Gump, or for Bad Blake in *Crazy Heart*. In *Sense and Sensibility*, *Slumdog Millionaire*, *Winter's Bone*, and *The King's Speech*, for instance, the worlds dictate a code of behavior that directly influences each character's ability to speak and take action—and the consequence of each action is made clear by the setting within which the characters live. Their social life is visible in the texture of their surroundings (in other words, their environment), and everything from the carefully maintained homes to the rolling seaside vistas or crowded slums or bleak, rural Appalachia tell us what is and is not possible for them.

The world can also affect a story by supplying sources of conflict, throwing traps or roadblocks in the path of a character's success. And only the perfect character, with just the right abilities, can overcome them or reflect their larger meaning. In *Avatar*, the alien planet forces the hero to literally inhabit a different physical body, which in turn transforms his inner nature as the story progresses. In *Dog Day Afternoon*, the police corner two incompetent robbers in a Brooklyn bank. The mundane environment of the bank is simultaneously the source of their hopes (to get money) and of their despair: they are as securely sealed inside as the money they came to steal. The world here is a claustrophobic snare that forces the characters to confront themselves and their desires. In Alfred Hitchcock's *Rear Window*, Jimmy Stewart's character is trapped by a broken leg, which reduces his world to what he can see from his window. This limitation forces him to become a voyeur and distorts and enlarges his judgment and imagination until he isn't sure what is real any more. In *The Last Picture Show*, teenagers are entangled by the small minds and limited expectations of a tiny Texas town. The dusty streets, drab houses, cheap amusements and limitless, barren plains that surround them define the frustrations and futility of their lives. In *The Poseidon Adventure* and *Titanic*, a wrecked luxury ocean liner literally turns the characters' world upside down and forces them to fight their way to freedom. In *Saw*, the world is reduced to a single, abandoned bathroom in which the terror plays itself out. In each of these examples the world is the background for, as well as the source of, the essential conflict, trapping the characters into confronting their desires and limitations in a way they would not normally do. Without their worlds, their stories simply would not exist.

THE RIGHT (WO)MAN AT THE RIGHT TIME IN THE RIGHT PLACE (CHARACTER AND WORLD)

Characters grow out of a specific environment, which they understand and which defines and reveals their personalities. This is particularly true of the character's personal surroundings: their home, office, car, room, or any location directly related to one particular personality. Characters' tastes, lifestyles, incomes, jobs, educations and temperaments can be seen in their environment, the elements of which create a kind of indirect characterization. We know who they are because we see where and how they live.

Consider sound as part of your characters' world, as well. Where *Blow-Up* and *One Hour Photo* are intensely visual stories about voyeuristic protagonists, *The Conversation*, *Children of a Lesser God* and *Blow-Out* are about characters whose lives are defined by sound (or its absence). In Woody Allen's *Annie Hall*, the constant roar from the Coney Island rollercoaster above the protagonist's childhood home creates a funny metaphor for the noisy circus of his life.

You want to find those few significant details that depict and individualize the character. How is the personal environment in or out of harmony with the character? Look at Joan Wilder's apartment in *Romancing the Stone*: It is feminine, with a pampered cat, little bottles of airplane booze and Post-it notes reminding her of other Post-it notes to remind her of what she has forgotten to do. From this environment we can guess many particulars of her personality and life—that Joan Wilder lives alone (the pampered cat), she is a romantic (the feminine features of the apartment, contrasting with the masculine, elusive poster illustration of her book), she travels a lot (the tiny airplane liquor bottles) and has a hectic schedule and nonlinear mind (the Post-it notes on Post-it notes). And not a word needs to be spoken to give us all this. In *50/50*, right at the start we see Joseph Gordon-Levitt's character, Adam, decide not to cross the street when the Don't Walk light is on. He's a careful young man who takes good care of himself, which creates the irony of the situation when he's diagnosed with cancer.

A Stranger in a Strange Land

Often the world is a major source of conflict by being in direct contrast to the characters: rather than reflecting them, it clashes with them. When the protagonist finds herself a stranger in a strange land, suddenly ill-equipped to understand or handle its challenges, it is known as a *fish-out-of-water story*. Characters may travel to unfamiliar territory, or realize they don't really understand the place they've considered home, in which case they find themselves lost, "fish out of water." The whole premise of these pictures is to take a particular character and place her or him in an environment that is in direct contrast to his or her personality. In *Romancing the Stone*, the exotic and dangerous world of Wilder's dreams (hinted at by the poster) becomes real when she goes into the South American jungle. By leaving her cozy New York environment, she's become a fish out of water. But she's still exactly the right character for the story, because we've been clued in to her romantic personality—even her name indicates that there is a "wilder" side of her that will ultimately emerge. In *50/50*, Adam becomes a fish out of water when illness changes every aspect of his previously normal world; his girlfriend cheats on him, his intolerable and ignored mother becomes essential, and his sloppy, crude best friend turns out to be the most sensitive soul around. *Beverly Hills Cop* made a star out of Eddie Murphy with his turn as a tough Detroit cop pursuing a criminal to toney Beverly Hills.

In *The Devil's Advocate*, Keanu Reeves' character is a successful southern lawyer who takes his small-town wife to live in an expensive New York apartment building that just happens to be owned by the Devil. Not only is their apartment foreign to her, but the whole world of upscale New York, with its corrupt sensualism and deal-making parties, comes into direct conflict with her innocent personality. Her new world—the world of the Devil—literally causes her to lose her mind. The same is true of the foolishly idealistic American actress played by Diane Keaton in *The Little Drummer Girl*, who finds herself lost and betrayed in the labyrinthine world of Middle Eastern espionage. In *Crocodile Dundee* a big city reporter is plunked down in the strange environment of the rugged Australian outback, while the backwoods hero she meets there is later equally out of place in the urban world of New York City; similarly, *Coogan's Bluff* took Clint Eastwood's cowboy sheriff from Arizona into the wilds of the Big Apple. In *Being There* an illiterate, childlike gardener enters the foreign world of Washington, D.C., politics. In *Pretty Woman* a hooker finds herself in the contrasting world of the Beverly Hills ultra-rich. The most obvious fish-out-of-water story is of course *Splash*, which places a mermaid on dry land. In each of these, the screenwriter has created a character and a world that are in direct conflict; this is the lifeblood of a screenplay.

The world of the story, therefore, can have a variety or combination of effects. When you ask, "Is this the best location for a scene or story?," you're really asking a number of questions:

How does this world affect my characters?

How do my characters affect this world?

Does this world reveal the nature of my characters?

How is my story affected by this world?

How is this world affected by my story?

Does this world reflect the theme of my story?

How does this world affect the theme of my story?

Is this world visually interesting?

If you have a good answer to each of these questions, then you've probably found your world.

LAUGHING PAST THE GRAVEYARD (CONTRAST AND IRONY)

Contrast is at the heart of all art—in fact, of all perception. Put your hand in water and slowly warm it, and you may end up boiling yourself without realizing it. Thrust your hand into hot water and you take immediate notice, in the form of pain. We don't take notice of the myriad small sounds that drone around us constantly as "noise"—but when a sharply contrasting sound like a doorbell or a voice appears, it creates "information" and we take notice. The same thing goes for what we see. We crave contrast; without it, there is no way to establish perspective, boundaries or imagery. Contrasting objects define one another, create positive and negative space, foreground and background, information. How this information is presented defines the mood and effect of the image. Rembrandt and Caravaggio used exaggerated light sources to cast deep shadows, their dark backgrounds in sharp contrast to their subjects, in order to intensify a mood of mystery and contemplation. Picasso often flattened space and defined his subjects with hard outlines and bold color elements to emphasize design and subvert natural perspective. Rodin gave his bronze sculptures shimmering, faceted surfaces to intrigue the eye and emphasize the underlying form. Magritte and Dali used extremely naturalistic techniques to paint impossible or dreamlike images that challenged rational assumptions about our perception of the world. A screenwriter can create the same kinds of effects by contrasting the characters and/or the actions of the scene with each other, and with the world in which they exist. Visual—and aural—contrast can make a rather bland scene interesting. A man reading a book in a quiet room is bland. A man reading a book in a noisy construction site is intriguing.

When the screenwriter draws a sharp and deliberate contrast between apparent and intended meaning, we have visual irony. The most uninteresting scene can become powerful, even memorable. In *Harold and Maude*, a rather bland scene in which a casket is loaded into a hearse after a funeral is made extraordinary by having it take place while a marching band booms past. In *Jaws*, the fun of a summer beach contrasts with the terror of a shark attack only a few yards away. In *Blues Brothers*, a rather generic car chase is made original by having it take place inside a mall crowded with shoppers. All of these contrasts reflect what the movies are about. The contrast between the sorrow of a funeral and the inappropriate exuberance of the marching band perfectly reflects *Harold and Maude's* theme of life's joy overcoming death's shadow. The element of danger lurking beneath the surface of everyday life reflects the theme of *Jaws*, that human control is an illusion, masking a deeper, primordial chaos in the world and in our own subconscious. The *Blues Brothers'* car chase in the mall reflects the theme of joyous anarchy, of inspired insanity puncturing the humdrum commercialism of everyday life. In *Avatar*, a paraplegic soldier in a hyper-mechanistic mercenary unit is given the freedom to run again by becoming his Avatar in an alien, primordial world that he ironically at first helps to attack, and then in another ironic twist helps to defend by becoming the kind of legendary primitive warrior who can, essentially, tame the most terrifying of flying dinosaurs.

A student of ours wrote a screenplay about two medical students who fall in love. The writer had a scene in which one student asks the other for a first date. This scene occurred in a mental hospital hallway, and was rather bland; he asks her out, she says no. There was nothing to make the scene unique. While the world of the scene—the mental hospital—held possibilities, they were not used to full advantage. The environment did not reflect or affect the characters or action and so it did not help tell the story:

```
HALLWAY — DAY

Richard sees Leslie near the water cooler. He confidently
strides up.

                    RICHARD
          So, how would you like to go out tonight?
          We'll start off with a mud bath, maybe
          play some laser tag.
```

>   LESLIE
>   You're not my type.
>
>   RICHARD
>   Why's that?
>
>   LESLIE
>   I don't date patients.
>
> She walks away.

On the rewrite, the student writer took better advantage of the world to build a far more interesting environment. He moved the scene from the generic hallway to an operating room:

> INT. SURGICAL AUDITORIUM — DAY
>
> Doctors and nurses hunch over an operating table. The patient is receiving a lobotomy. They open his right eye and insert a never-ending needle through his upper eyelid and into his brain. The patient quivers.
>
> A gaggle of nearby interns watch the operation. Richard inches toward Leslie.
>
>   RICHARD
>   So, how would you like to go out tonight?
>   We'll start off with a mud bath, maybe
>   play some laser tag.
>
>   LESLIE
>   You're not my type.
>
>   RICHARD
>   Why's that?
>
>   LESLIE
>   I don't date patients.
>
> On the table, the patient twitches as they rotate the needle.

Not a single line of dialogue has been altered, but because the environment now contrasts with the action and creates a sense of irony, a bland scene has become interesting. The new location also allows the reader to understand the characters better. Richard is the type who'd ask for a date during a lobotomy, while Leslie's motivation for saying "no" is understandable: the guy must be a creep. A spectacular shoot-out between G-men and gangsters in Grand Central Station is not as interesting as when the shoot-out occurs with a baby carriage rolling through the line of fire (*The Untouchables*). The soldier who dies while charging the machine gun nest is not as thought-provoking as the soldier who is killed while reaching for a butterfly fluttering above the mud of the battlefield (*All Quiet on the Western Front*). Lovers who argue in the living room are not as provocative as lovers who argue during a wedding (*It Happened One Night*; *Arthur*) or a funeral (*Death at a Funeral*). Contrast and irony make for a visually interesting scene that can define the characters, reinforce and reflect the theme, and move the story forward in unique, dramatic and surprising ways.

Visual contrast and irony can also define the whole story. *Witness* would be a rather forgettable police drama if it were not located in a peaceful Amish community. The love story in *The Great Gatsby* wouldn't be nearly as interesting if it didn't contrast lavish flapper parties with poverty. *Phantom of the Opera* would be another typical horror movie if it weren't for the contrast and irony provided by its world. The disfigured recluse abducts the pretty soprano and takes her from the ornate beauty of the Paris opera house down into the maze of sewers beneath the streets; glorious art and noxious shadows are the two opposite, yet coexisting, sides of his world. Contrast and irony deriving from the world of the story can be the two elements that make a story different from all others of its kind, whether police dramas, horror thrillers or love stories.

Bouncing off the Walls (Interacting with the World)

The world of your story is carried by your narrative, and you need to exercise careful judgment in writing it. Hollywood readers often become impatient with the narrative and will skim through it or skip it altogether if they find it's either overwritten or if it adds little to the story. These problems can almost always be traced to one of two problems. Either the writer has added unimportant details, which do not advance the characters or story, or she has not created an exciting and relevant world for the story, but instead something generic that gives the characters nothing with which to interact.

The following scene is a section of a long fight sequence. Two cops fight it out in a parking deck. The screenwriter doesn't use the location to make the scene or fight interesting:

```
Buddy points the gun at Nick.

                NICK
        Just let me have Kevin. I'll leave you
        alone.

                BUDDY
        Oh, demands.

Nick upends Buddy. Nick smashes Buddy's hand against
ground.
```

```
The gun flips out of Buddy's hand. They both dive for
it. Buddy gets there first. He points the silver semi-
auto pistol at Nick's temple.

Nick is too exhausted to fight. He awaits his end.
Buddy's sweat drips down on Nick's face.

                    BUDDY
          Unmarked gun. Good-bye, asshole.

                    NICK
          Be good to my kid.

                    BUDDY
          I've been screwing your wife since you
          married her! What the hell makes you
          think Kevin is yours?

Nick snaps. He attacks with new life. They struggle over
the gun. Nick forces Buddy's arm up. BOOM!

BOOM! BOOM! BOOM! in quick succession, the gun empties.

Buddy slams the hot, metal barrel into Nick's face. Nick
is blinded by the blood. With one last burst Nick lands
a desperate swing on Buddy's jaw. He's out. Cold.
```

To fix this scene, the screenwriter took advantage of the environment. She added details—a Mercedes, an open, antiquated car elevator—which allowed the characters to interact with the surroundings. In other words, the location was used to individualize and move the story forward:

```
Securing Nick with his foot, Buddy reaches onto the
elevator and pushes the lever forward. The pulleys creak.
The ancient elevator pops up two feet. Buddy shoves
Nick's head under the elevator. With his free hand, he
grabs the lever and inches the elevator down toward
Nick's skull.

                    NICK
          I'll leave you alone.

                    BUDDY
          Oh, demands.

Nick digs his teeth into Buddy's ankle. With a scream,
Buddy slams the lever down. The elevator drops.
```

Nick jerks his head away just in time.

Nick upends Buddy and dives for the gun. They struggle. With a groan and jerk the elevator disappears down into the dark shaft.

WHACK! WHACK! Nick smashes Buddy's hand against the metal lip on the shaft.

The gun flips out of Buddy's hand. CLANG, Clang, clang. Each 'clang' softer as the gun falls down the shaft.

They continue to struggle, rolling in the grease spots. Suddenly, they roll off and disappear down the shaft.

CRASH! They collide with the thin metal grid on the top of the car elevator. They've fallen only a few feet.

The exposed cables slap against each other as the open elevator continues to descend.

Nick works his way free from Buddy. But with his first step, he crashes through the thin metal grid and lands on the hood of the classic Mercedes convertible below.

BUDDY -- jumps down, reaches over and opens the glove compartment, pulls out a silver semi-auto pistol and points it at Nick's temple.

NICK -- is too exhausted to fight. He awaits his end. Buddy's sweat drips down on Nick's face.

                BUDDY
      Unmarked gun. Good-bye, asshole.

                NICK
      Be good to my kid.

                BUDDY
      I've been screwing your wife since you
      married her! What the hell makes you
      think Kevin is yours?

Nick snaps. He attacks with new life. They struggle over the gun. BOOM! The first shot shatters the Mercedes's windshield. Little diamonds of glass shower down on them.

Nick forces Buddy's arm up. BOOM! BOOM! BOOM! BOOM! in
quick succession, the gun empties.

THE BULLETS -- cut into the elevator's worn metal cables.
They begin to unravel. An ominous rumbling comes from the
elevator, then it drops three feet. Other cables begin to
twist as the metal hairs splinter.

IN THE CAR --A snapped-cable falls on to the front seat.
Buddy slams the hot, metal barrel of the gun into Nick's
face. Nick is blinded by the blood.

POP POP like an assassin's distant gun, the cables, one
by one, twitch and snap.

Suddenly, ALL CABLES split.

They slingshot like massive rubber bands. Nick grabs
a cable and flies up, as the elevator, with classic
Mercedes aboard, plummets downward.

There is only the intense rush of air. And then an
EXPLOSION as it impacts five stories below.

Then ...

Silence.

Exhausted, Nick hangs from the oily, braided wire. His
hands slip. He's losing his grip. He looks down.

NICK'S P.O.V. -- Buddy hangs from his shoes.

It's clear to see that in the rewrite, the fight is directly affected by and uses the location. The environment causes greater obstacles and complications and, therefore, greater conflict and interest. The thematic elements of "falling" into corruption or "rising" to the occasion, the destruction of the emblem of ill-gotten wealth (the Mercedes), all reflect and strengthen the story and its theme.

SHOW AND TELL (WORLD AND EXPOSITION)

The world is a critical part of exposition. In a stage play, dialogue is the primary method of conveying exposition, because playwrights are constrained by the limitations and conventions of the theater. Twenty-five hundred years ago, the great Greek playwrights wrote their plays to be performed in massive open-air theaters that held up to 15,000 people. Viewed from the back rows, the performers on stage were hard to see, and the early convention of using masks eliminated any possibility of complex facial emotion. Actions were limited by space and the technical limitations of the time. All this forced playwrights to write rather obvious dialogue and verbal exposition. In comparison, screenwriters have it easy. We are allowed to focus the camera in on one small, revealing detail of the environment, blow it up on a screen forty feet across and show things about the characters and story that playwrights would find nearly impossible.

In the following scene, a student screenwriter describes Kasey, a thirty-year-old who still lives at home. She has just had a horrible fight with her father and is running away. She comes into her bedroom to pack her bags and is followed by her concerned brother. The screenwriter wants to communicate to the audience that Kasey has never grown up. This can be done in one of two ways: one, have Kasey do or say something immature, or two, have Kasey's environment reflect her immaturity. Notice that the screenwriter depends on the former, without even describing the surroundings, and the dialogue creates a rather obvious, talky and ultimately bland scene (along with being too on-the-nose; see Chapter 13, Dialogue):

```
INT. KASEY'S ROOM — NIGHT

Kasey storms in and packs her luggage. Norman follows.

                    NORMAN JR.
          Where are you going? You have no money.
          No place to stay. Kasey, you're just a
          child in a grownup's body.

                    KASEY
          Do me a favor and get that bastard. Why
          didn't you speak up? Why did you stand
          there and not say a word?

                    NORMAN JR.
          I don't know. I'm scared of him, too.

                    KASEY
          Screw off, Norman.

                    NORMAN JR.
          Kasey, I don't think you should do this.

                    KASEY
          Are you trying to tell me I can't take
          care of myself?

                    NORMAN JR.
          I didn't say that.
```

                    KASEY
          But you thought it.

                    NORMAN JR.
          You do act a little young for your age.

                    KASEY
          I do not. I am an adult!

                    NORMAN JR.
          You still play with dolls.

                    KASEY
          I collect them!

She gives him the finger and crawls out the window.

Here is the same scene with the environment carrying the weight of exposition:

INT. KASEY'S ROOM — NIGHT

Kasey struggles with the latch on her ancient Barbie
luggage set. She rips it open and begins dumping in
her meager belongings: party dresses, a diary, several
porcelain dolls. Norman runs in.

                    NORMAN JR.
          I'm sorry.

                    KASEY
          Do me a favor and get that bastard. Kill
          him if you have to!

She pulls her pictures of The Monkees and The Bee Gees
off the wall and loads them in to her Ken Doll shoulder
bag.

                    KASEY
          Why didn't you speak up? Why did you
          stand there and not say a word?

                    NORMAN JR.
          I don't know. I'm scared of him, too.

                    KASEY
          Screw off, Norman.

She gives him the finger, pulls the bows on her perfect
pink curtain sash, and crawls out the window.

Describing a key bit of the world allows the audience to see that Kasey is immature without the need for excessive dialogue. In the rewrite, the environment is now a critical part of the story. But again, don't add details that accomplish no purpose. If you find yourself doing so compulsively, go back and reexamine your outline and theme, because often overwriting the narrative is a symptom of not being sure what your story is about. It's the writer's equivalent of "vamping," where a comedian has run out of material but still has ten minutes left on stage.

BEEN THERE, DONE THAT (RESEARCH AND CONSISTENCY)

Finally, it is important to create a world that is true and consistent. A writer's imagination is wonderful, but often wrong. When it comes to environment, imagination is no replacement for solid research. If you're going to write about a place, then you must know the place. Research does not mean borrowing from other movies or novels that take place at the same location. It means doing detailed investigation into the place, people, time and culture. Lack of research can be particularly disastrous when the screenwriter tries to depict a culture or society that they do not understand and have not experienced. The writer who vacationed in Wyoming once may know enough to write about vacationing in Wyoming, but not necessarily enough to write a story concerning the local people, their lives, environment or personalities. Once a young screenwriter set her story in the crazy world of live television in the 1950s. It was badly written, full of inconsistencies, misinformation and stereotypes. When questioned about her research, she admitted that she had watched every episode of the *Dick Van Dyke Show* ever made. This isn't doing research.

Books and newspapers are good for research, but going to a place or conducting personal interviews with people who are from a given world is even better. If you're going to write about cowboys, then you'd better talk to a few cowboys. Once, while in the midst of doing research for a cop movie, Bill was pulled over by a state bull, fifteen miles an hour over the speed limit. He immediately saw it as an opportunity to do research. While his record was being checked, he told the police officer that he was writing a screenplay about a policeman. Twenty minutes later, he had the cop's life story, two jokes that cops tell about citizens, and got off with only a warning. On a recent cruise, Robin shared a table with a psychiatrist. Within half an hour the fellow wanted Robin to write a script about one of his more interesting cases. People love to talk about their lives, professions, problems, dreams and where they come from. Imagination is still very important, and no screenwriter can work without it, but proper research gives the imagination something with which to work. A frame of reference sets the imagination free.

Research can include:

Time	Customs	Architecture	History
Place	Weather	Social rules	Landscape
Location	Local language	Work rules	Culture

FINAL THOUGHTS

The world is a necessary part of story, character and theme. It affects and reflects each of these, and yet a screenwriter must not linger in its description. Just like the poet, the screenwriter must find those few, perfect words that can bring the setting vividly alive for the reader. Use only those words that reveal the essential details that are deeply characteristic of and relevant to the action. The inconsequential must be cut. The screenwriter's goal is to present a clear, sharp, focused version of the world that allows the reader to understand and move on without pausing, but to not be so brief as to become generic. A successful world is full of particulars. Find those that affect and reflect character, story and theme, and you'll have found your place in the world.

EXERCISES

1. Describe a leaf floating on a lake. Describe only the leaf, but from your description we should know details about the lake.

2. Write a short description of a personal environment (such as a room, house, office). Now read the description to a classmate or friend. Can your listener guess at the character's personality and occupation by your description alone?

3. Write a brief description of a character from which we can guess the world she lives in.

4. Write a description of a building that hints at the theme of the story.

5

Character

Meet John Doe

All right, you have a great premise, your "world" is well thought-out, the story is coming along, and you have all sorts of exciting scenes in mind. And yet you can't help feeling that something is wrong.

More than likely, your problem is character. Not your own—the ones you didn't develop well enough in the beginning to carry your story. Often, new screenwriters spend too much time plotting out the events of a script without thinking much about the characters who create those events. They worry, "What happens next?" rather than, "Who is this guy, and what would he make happen next?"

"But wait," you say, "how do I even know who my characters ought to be until I know my story? Or is it vice versa? Is story more important than characters, or are the characters more important than the story?" Good questions all.

WHICH CAME FIRST, THE HONEY OR THE BEE?

Aristotle argued 2,300 years ago in *Poetics* (required reading at all film schools) that character is less important than story. He felt that a story should be conceived first and then characters fabricated to carry it out. His logic was that a dramatic story is an imitation of a course of action in life, not of any particular person: "The drama interests us, not predominantly by its depiction of human nature, but primarily by the situations and only secondarily by the feelings of those therein involved." More recent writers tend to feel that Aristotle put the cart before the horse. Without great characters, the argument goes, you don't have a story worth caring about. Early screenwriter John Howard Lawson pointed out that a story "may contain a duel in every scene, a pitched battle in every act, and the spectator be sound asleep, or be kept awake only by the noise." Or even worse, be heading for the exits.

In *The Art of Dramatic Writing* (also required reading in all film schools), Lajos Egri grumbles, "What would the reader think of us if we were to announce that we had come to the conclusion that honey is beneficial to mankind, but that the bee's importance is secondary, and that the bee is therefore subsidiary to its product?" According to Egri, the bee is the character, and its product the story.

The question for Aristotle is, how can a story be interesting without multi-dimensional characters to make us care what happens in it? And yet Egri seems to forget that without a well-constructed story, even the best characters will wander around as aimlessly as, well, bees. Both methods—putting story ahead of character, or character ahead of story—can lead to critical failure. Go too far one way and you end up with a formula Hollywood plot machine whose characters are mere puppets in the action; go too far the other way, and you get a French film (at least, the kind in which people meander through their day, talking endlessly, without any apparent point). Somewhere in the middle lurks the unique, involving story for which you're hoping.

So what's a writer to do? If they're both of equal importance, which do you concentrate on first? This is more than just a chicken-and-egg argument, it is at the heart of the storytelling process.

The answer must be to create both story and character simultaneously. They are forever tied together and define one another in the process of their creation. At its most basic, a story is characters in action, while characters are defined by the actions they take. You must know your characters as you plot their action, in order to know what actions they would naturally take in any given circumstance. And you must simultaneously know what you want your story to be about, because it provides the circumstances that motivate your characters' actions.

GEEZ, YOU ACT LIKE YOU'RE IN A MOVIE

Characters differ from one type of storytelling to another. In novels, short stories, cartoons, sitcoms and operas, not only does the writer approach a character differently, but the characters are different in kind. Each form of storytelling has limits and approaches as to how the characters are revealed. The novelist can delve into the personal history and thoughts of a character through inner monologue or third-person description. Operatic characters are revealed by the role of their voices—tenor as hero, basso as villain—and are allowed long expository arias.

Screen characters must reveal themselves through action, the outward manifestation of that which is within. They come to life not when they feel and think, but when they act—when they say and do things that reveal their thoughts and feelings. It is not enough for them to be, or to merely contemplate—at least not if they are major characters whose purpose is to push the story forward. For thousands of years playwrights have used the word "action" to define character and story. In a broad sense, action means simply "to do." Actions are the characters' deeds, their response to the existing circumstances of the story, which in turn affect the future course of the story. Therefore, the character who does the most defines that course.

But action alone is not enough to create a gripping story: it must have a goal, and it must encounter opposition. In other words, it must be *dramatic* action. There must be conflict and important stakes hanging on its outcome. There is no interest in watching someone run a race alone. The character—a young woman, let's say—is taking action, but there are no stakes unless someone is pursuing her, or she is pursuing someone else, or she is desperate to outrun her own best time for some reason with which we can empathize (in which case she is in conflict with herself). If there is inner conflict, dramatic action is its outward expression. Dramatic action can mean fighting to overcome the inertia of one's own fears or limitations, or it can mean resisting the flow of other characters' desires and actions. Dramatic action can mean acting when action is not allowed, taking a stance against authority, expressing an unpopular opinion. It can be shown in an armed encounter or a quiet kiss, as long as it is an act of intention and as long as it has consequences.

Dramatic action, then, occurs when a character decides to do something either because of or in spite of the consequences. This is also the problem with trying to write your characters as "real people." While everyone takes dramatic action now and then, most of us go about most of our lives trying to avoid conflict. We receive an unjustified parking ticket and we pay rather than go to court. Our boss insults us and we bear it rather than confront him. We stay at home rather than face the raging storm outside. Most real people try to maintain the status quo, occasionally want or feel deeply about something, but only rarely do anything about it. This is deadly on screen, because until we can see characters do or say something that changes their circumstances or their world, there is no way to get a handle on them, or care about them. Unlike real people, screen characters are willing to force the issue, to engage in conflict, to take dramatic action—which is why we pay to watch them. They are metaphors. They do what we only dream.

Therefore, screen characters shouldn't necessarily feel like real people, but rather they should feel real within the context of the world, the theme, the goals and the conflicts you've created for them. All characters are abstracts from reality, and in movies their personalities, actions and placement within the story reflect and are determined by the function they serve.

WHAT ON EARTH IS HE DOING HERE? (CHARACTER FUNCTIONS)

It's not enough to ask, "Who are your characters?" You must also ask why they're in the story at all. How do they—who they are, what they are—reflect and express the central theme? What drives them? What are the sources of conflict between them? How much do we really need to know about them? Most importantly, are they essential to the story? Why are these the best, indeed the only, characters with which to populate this particular story? *A character without a function does not belong in your screenplay*. Each must serve a unique purpose, and have a unique temperament and focus, a reason why the story would be less effective, or even collapse, without him or her.

The Tweedledee and Tweedledum Problem

In acting there is a movement known as a double gesture. This is when an actor gestures with both hands in exactly the same way: both hands pointing, both hands pleading, both accusing. This is considered a weak gesture, because both hands are expressing the same emotion. One of the first things actors learn is that a single gesture or two contrasting gestures are more powerful than a double gesture. The same is true in writing. If two characters have similar functions and personalities, then a strong case can be made for eliminating one, combining them into a single character or figuring out how to differentiate them (unless you're creating a specific, usually comic effect, like having twins who always speak at the same time, but these are usually really one character). For example, suppose you're writing a Western. You've got two bad guys, train robbers. Both are mean, quick to kill and cunning. Because they are similar, chances are you could eliminate one train robber and in the process make the story stronger, or you could give each a unique function and temperament. This could be done by making one of the bad guys the chief antagonist and the other his sidekick. Now the chief bad guy becomes the brains of the operation, while the other does the dirty work. This leads to conflict because one wants to hit the train and get out fast, while the other is having too much fun intimidating the passengers. Now both bad guys have separate purposes and temperaments; they come into conflict and move the story forward in unique ways.

Another important reason why no two characters should have similar temperaments, desires or functions is that such characters are not apt to clash, so there will be less conflict (see Chapter 7, Power and Conflict). In order to avoid this problem, make sure that there are never two characters who consistently sympathize or agree. Again, such conflict should not be arbitrary or imposed upon them, but grow out of their natural differences and the different purposes they serve in the screenplay.

When determining the differences and functions of each of your characters, think about what actions they will take to move the story forward, and why. Is the character a mentor, who provides advice and wisdom to your protagonist? Is she an ally who helps carry out the protagonist's (or antagonist's) plan? Is he a false ally who appears to act on the protagonist's behalf, but in fact is betraying her to the antagonist? Is he a "threshold guardian," whose purpose is to warn the protagonist away from his course of action, or even impede it? Does the character drive a subplot? Or does the character represent us, the audience, as a "fly on the wall," watching and interpreting the actions of the protagonist? (Many of these functions apply across genres. See Chapter 11 for more on specific character functions in different kinds of stories. For another excellent and much more complete analysis of character functions in a "hero's journey" or quest story, see Chris Vogler's *The Writer's Journey*.)

The Main (Wo)man (Protagonist)

The protagonist is the central character, the hero, the Big Enchilada, the principal figure around whom the screenplay is written and the one with whom the audience can identify or empathize. The word "protagonist" comes from ancient Greek drama and referred to the first actor to engage in dialogue or action (literally, the first combatant), but it soon came to mean the principal player. This remains true today. Because of this, the protagonist is introduced early on, although many movies actually start with the antagonist instead, to set up the stakes and the problem that the protagonist must face. Some movies also keep the audience waiting on purpose, to create a sense of suspense or anticipation: when will we finally meet the guy everyone's been talking about? In such cases, even though absent physically, the protagonist may be present in the form of the anticipation his impending approach inspires in others. This is a classic technique in Westerns, detective and action movies. Others may introduce the protagonist as a surprise: the world is in chaos, no one knows what to do, when suddenly the hero rides into town.

The vast majority of movies have a single protagonist, but occasionally there are two who work in tandem, as in *Butch Cassidy and the Sundance Kid* or *Thelma & Louise*. These are known as "buddy movies." Even more rare are "ensemble movies" such as *The Big Chill, Gosford Park, Love Actually* or *Crash,* in which there are many protagonists. Buddy and multi-protagonist movies generally have one protagonist who is more important than the others. For example, in *Butch Cassidy and the Sundance Kid*, Butch is the more important of the two because he is the main decision-maker. Sundance is the muscle. In *Lethal Weapon*, Danny Glover's character is more important than Mel Gibson's because the enemy is from Glover's (Murtaugh's) own Vietnam war past, and it's his daughter's life at stake. Buddy and ensemble movies can be difficult to write, so if you are writing your first screenplay, you may want to start simple, with a single protagonist story.

Often (almost always in crime or action thrillers) the antagonist will initiate the conflict or create the situation that forces the protagonist to respond. In other words, the protagonist enters a situation created by the antagonist: for instance, in a detective story the killer may already have taken action by committing a murder, and now the detective reacts by determining to solve the crime. The antagonist may or may not specifically target the protagonist, but once the conflict is engaged it becomes personal. The murderer may not even know about the detective, but once he does, the story focuses on their conflict. James Bond only takes action in reaction to a plot already initiated by the evil mastermind, who usually does not start out by targeting Bond, but is forced to do so once Bond goes after him. In *Avatar*, the corporation's plan to rape Pandora of its natural resources is already underway when Jake gets recruited, and at first he's fighting for the wrong side. It isn't until halfway through that he switches sides and takes the fight to his former commander.

It's often said, inaccurately, that the protagonist has to drive the conflict from the start. This is occasionally true, but more often the protagonist needs to be forced into reacting, may (often does) have second thoughts about getting involved, and then eventually drives the conflict. For instance, in *Casablanca*, usually considered one of the two or three greatest films of all time, Rick (Humphrey Bogart) famously refuses to take action or "stick his neck out for anyone" until two-thirds of the way into the film. It takes him that long to react to what's happening and overcome his personal demons, which represent an internal conflict he's fighting rather than the external confrontation with Major Strasser and the Nazis. However, by the time Rick does decide to enter the fray, the audience is cheering for him and, having defeated his internal antagonist (himself), he is the one who drives the conclusion of the larger conflict against Major Strasser. Other characters may make the situation intolerable, they may abuse or prod, but the main action, and therefore main conflict, is ultimately the protagonist's. What you do *not* want is a protagonist who remains passive or reactive throughout.

Even when the protagonist's main action seems to be running away from something, he or she should also eventually be running toward something. In *The Fugitive*, although Dr. Richard Kimble is running away from the federal marshal, he is simultaneously running back to Chicago, acting to solve the murder of his wife and prove his own innocence. In *North by Northwest*, the classic Hitchcock thriller about a businessman who is mistaken for a spy, Cary Grant is not just running away from James Mason and his thugs, but pursuing his goal of freeing Eva Marie Saint. In *Eternal Sunshine of the Spotless Mind*, Jim Carrey's character is running away from the pain of his past relationship with Kate Winslet, but also running toward trying to recover what he's erased from his mind (their love). The difference may seem subtle, but it can distinguish an interesting protagonist from one who seems to be nothing but a victim. A protagonist may be a victim or at least an underdog, and often is; this is often how the folks in the audience feel and why they relate to the protagonist. But the whole point of the story is for the protagonist to eventually be willing to fight back, seek revenge or move toward a definite goal, so that the audience is empowered by vicariously participating in the protagonist's action.

Lastly, the audience must be able either to identify, or at least empathize with or relate to, the protagonist. You want them to root for the protagonist. If the protagonist is too headstrong, aggressive, powerful or self-absorbed, the audience will lose interest unless you give them a reason to remain engaged, some deeper merit to the character that shines through. Then, even apparently despicable protagonists such as Steve Buscemi's Nucky Thompson in *Boardwalk Empire*, Jane Fonda's prostitute in *Klute* or even Jack Nicholson's loathsome writer in *As Good as It Gets* will engage the audience's sympathies and they will root for them. Even if you are writing about an extraordinary hero, there must be something to which everyday people can relate. This is done by giving the protagonist a vulnerability: he or she is an underdog in the contest with the antagonist. This vulnerability may reveal itself as a comic or character flaw, or it may be shown in the virtue of the protagonist's goal or the difficulty of the struggle to attain it.

But this is only half the equation: the audience must feel the same emotional investment in the protagonist's success as the protagonist does, and this investment comes from understanding and approving the protagonist's struggle. Empathy comes when the protagonist's motivation is clear, laudable and plausible. The audience should be able to say, "If I were the protagonist, in this situation I would have similar feelings and wish I would have the courage, strength or motivation to take the same actions."

When the protagonist takes dramatic action—as he or she must—it must be action with consequences, especially for the protagonist, but that also affect others. Your protagonist should have more to lose or to gain than anyone else in the screenplay, except for those who depend on him or perhaps the antagonist. Only a weak or selfish protagonist fights for his life or well-being alone; these are low stakes, unless you're writing a light comedy, or the character is alone in his or her jeopardy (as in *The Naked Prey, 127 Hours,* or *The Most Dangerous Game*). The protagonist should also fight on behalf of others whose lives or well-being will suffer without his taking action. Obviously, these others have as much to lose as the protagonist, but the responsibility is the protagonist's alone, and his or her success or failure is proportionately increased by the stakes that the other characters represent. In the classic Western *High Noon*, the townspeople are faced with having their town overrun by a gang of outlaws, but it's Gary Cooper, the protagonist, who puts his life at stake to stand between the opposing forces and save the townspeople. Even in a light comedy like *Liar, Liar*, Jim Carrey's stakes (he might lose his family) are multiplied by the potential unhappiness of others (his family might lose him). In *Dodgeball*, Vince Vaughn's need to triumph over Ben Stiller is not only personal, but affects the happiness of the entire community of his gym. The protagonist who takes action against a sea of troubles but has nothing personally at stake in the outcome is not as interesting as the protagonist who stands to lose his own life, love or honor. The protagonist who fights only on his own behalf is less interesting than one who risks sacrificing herself on behalf of others.

The Heavy (Antagonist)

The antagonist is the person, place or thing standing in opposition to the protagonist, in the way of his or her achieving the goal. The antagonist can be a human, animal, an act of nature or can even be something supernatural. It can also be the protagonist's inner conflict or character flaw, such as alcoholism or self-doubt (see Power and Conflict, Chapter 7). The antagonist must appear more powerful than the protagonist and be in a position in which compromise is impossible. If the antagonist is weak, the conflict will also be weak.

A common mistake young screenwriters make is not fully developing the character of the antagonist. An undeveloped antagonist is boring. In good scripts, the antagonist (or the circumstance of conflict) is at least as complex as the protagonist, if not more so, which is what makes their contest so involving. As noted, the antagonist's plan is often what sets the stage for the central conflict. Professor Moriarty is more than the equal of Sherlock Holmes, and more complex in his motives. In *The Hurt Locker*, Jeremy Renner's addiction to the adrenaline rush of war is really his "antagonist," and its seduction is what drives and defines him. The screenwriter must find the antagonist's character arcs, dominant emotions, history, traits and "positive" motivations (the rationale by which he or she justifies his or her actions), or else fully define the circumstances that create the conflict for your protagonist. The antagonist is most effective when he is the dark doppelgänger of the protagonist, his shadow self, and whom he is necessarily forced to confront because of his own nature: in *Star Wars*, for instance, Darth Vader is Luke Skywalker's father. In *Casablanca*, Rick is his own worst enemy, his inner shadow-self created by heartbreak and self-pity. The antagonist is often the one character who reflects the personal aspects of the screenwriter that she likes least about herself, and therefore is the most difficult to create—unless the writer can look into her darkest and most contrary impulses. So get inside what's hidden in your own heart and mind, and then have fun with it. And remember—that shadow self has its own reasons for being there. From the shadow's (the antagonist's) point of view, it's acting correctly. Even Darth Vader or Goldfinger—even the shark in *Jaws*—all think they're doing the right thing from their point of view. If the screenwriter does not find the strong motivations behind the antagonist's actions (or the rationale for the antagonistic circumstances confronting the protagonist), the end result will be a cheap, dull stereotype. A great screenplay always has a fully developed, interesting antagonist.

Right Hand (Wo)man (Supporting Roles)

Supporting roles are exactly that: characters who support the main characters. They are intrinsic to the story, but are not the main focus or as fully explored as the protagonist or antagonist. However, even though supporting characters are not the main focus, considerable time should still be spent in developing them. The same steps taken to develop a protagonist or antagonist must be taken with the main supporting roles, although their motivations and actions can be less complex. Supporting roles take action to support the protagonist or antagonist, or act within a subplot that supports or contradicts the main plot. A good example of the former is found in *The Sting*, where all the supporting roles have unique characteristics and all have a part in helping Robert Redford and Paul Newman pull off their elaborate caper. Even the thugs who work for the antagonist are colorful and complete. Steve Carell's pals all conspire to help get him get laid in *The 40 Year Old Virgin*. Another example of characters who create a subplot that mirrors the main story is found in *Casablanca*, where the young Bulgarian bride is willing to sacrifice herself (by sleeping with Captain Renault) in order to gain safe passage to America for herself and her unwitting husband.

A Cast of Thousands (Minor and Background Characters)

Not all screen characters must be fully developed. The function of minor characters is either to fill the world of the story, or to push the story forward at a given moment and then disappear. Full character development is not needed because it would pull attention away from the main characters and upset the balance of your story. But that doesn't mean they should be faceless; even a walk-on should be given one simple dominant trait or emotion to individualize him, keep the story interesting on all levels and provide a specific visual description. Minor characters are like the spice in the meal of the story; if they aren't individualized and entertaining, they and the story will become flat. They might have a particular mannerism, special look, skill or speech pattern, anything to make them unique.

It could be argued that in crowd scenes or scripts with large numbers of cops or soldiers or students, there are plenty of minor characters who seem interchangeable. But in such instances, they are in fact there to fill the world with a single recognizable human element, and can be thought of as a single character. For example, the generic (non-starring) crew members in *Star Trek* are "expendables" with no real personality or contact with the main characters; they're all pretty much the same, except insofar as their deaths or the threat to their lives increases the stakes. But they fill the world and create a revenge or hostage-saving motivation for the central characters. They represent a life that must be saved or avenged.

Keeping Focused

When determining how much detail or emphasis to give any particular character, an analogy may be helpful: movies are pictures, and in every picture there are areas that are in focus and others that are less so. The same is true of the characters within the movie. The leading roles (protagonist and antagonist) are in sharp focus; they are the clear focal points of the movie. The supporting roles are slightly less in focus, the minor roles begin to look fuzzy, and finally the background characters stand on the perimeter and are barely discernible. Or you can look at it from the point of view of complexity, starting from the protagonist and antagonist as the most complex and well-rounded characters and going down to the simple and uncomplicated presence of the background characters or extras. The point is that each character must be clear and lively for the reader, but the secondary characters cannot pull the focus away from the main characters, just as extras should not "steal the scene" from the stars.

WHAT'S THE SITUATION? (CHARACTER AND CONTEXT)

Whatever their function, in order for characters to take dramatic action, they must be in a situation (story) in which something is at stake, and also in which there is more than one option for them, so they can make decisions.

Dramatic action can only happen when the characters have choices and are willing to make those choices. The more important the choices, the higher the stakes, and the more important and interesting the character. A character who is faced with and makes difficult social, moral or ethical choices can't help but be fascinating.

Let's look at character Bob Jones, a forty-year-old businessman. Average height, middle class, decent, Bob has three young kids, a mortgage, a receding hairline and is stuck in a rut. He can't advance in the company because he can't work weekends. His routine is set, and he lives with it. Bob is not a worthy screen character. Why? Because he just exists, he doesn't take action.

But what if one day Bob is robbed. After filing the police report, he's late for work. His boss reads him the riot act for being late. What does Bob do? He goes back to his cubicle and finishes his work. He swallows his pride, glad that at least he didn't lose his job. He is safe. How about now? Is Bob a worthy screen character? The answer here is, "It depends." True, he takes action, he keeps his job, but he makes no decision to take dramatic action, or action that will change his circumstances. This kind of character only works if his refusal to take action is limited and later reversed (as in the sequence from *Saving Private Ryan* where the young translator's fears paralyze and prevent him from rescuing his friend from a German soldier; his cowardice later leads him to take action by executing the German). Or, alternatively, the refusal to take dramatic action over the course of the entire story might reflect the theme of the film. For instance, in *Remains of the Day*, the butler's tragic inability to seize the opportunity for love condemns him to a life of loneliness. These passive characters are tragic and express life's limitations, which is why they usually turn up in subplots, their lack of courage to act contrasting with the protagonist's willingness to do so. They are reasonably common as protagonists in European films (*La Dolce Vita*, for instance), but are rare as protagonists in American movies (other than in small independents like *The Low Life*) because they express a distinctly "can't do," and therefore un-American, attitude.

Going back to poor old Bob—what if, after being humiliated by his boss, he quits on the spot, just up and quits? Tells his boss where he can go, cleans out his cubicle and walks. Now Bob is looking more like an American protagonist. He has taken action, but more, he has taken a dramatic action that has great consequences. Notice that in either case, what Bob does (his action) or doesn't do defines his character more than the fact that he is forty, a businessman with a mortgage and a receding hairline. A perfect example of this kind of character is found in *The Truman Show*, where a boring businessman suspects that his whole world is a fraud. He quickly begins to take dramatic action, investigating his house, setting up verbal traps for his wife and neighbors. Eventually, he uncovers the truth and takes the most dramatic action of all, leaving everything he knows in order to find the real world outside.

Don't Just Stand There! (Action/Reaction)

The necessities that make for good dramatic action are that the character must eventually initiate action, not simply react to others or the environment, and the action should cause circumstances to change or another character to take action. While most characters, even the protagonist, may start out by reacting to what's going on around them, strong characters at some point will instigate their own courses of action to change their world; weak characters will remain merely reactive to changes caused by others. For example, let's take Sally, a young woman on her way to her father's funeral. Her father, a respected leader in the community, molested her as a child. Her mother never believed her. Sally enters the funeral parlor alone, breaks down in tears, beats on his dead carcass and, sure that no one else can hear her, spits out her pitiful accusation at the corpse. Unless this leads to some later determination to change her life, Sally remains a weak screen character, because she is simply reacting to the situation in a way that has no consequences. We may feel sorry for her, but not care much beyond that because she isn't doing anything about her pain. But what if, as the funeral starts, Sally insists on giving a eulogy in which she tells the entire congregation about what her respected father did? Or what if Sally walks up to the casket, but this time her mother is with her? What if Sally opens her purse and takes out a large set of scissors and, to her mother's horror, slowly unzips his trousers, performs a postmortem amputation and hands the item to her mother? Her action fundamentally changes her father's corpse as well as her relationship with her mother. In these last scenarios, Sally doesn't merely react. She makes a conscious decision to take dramatic action with deep consequences. Note that the final one is more visceral, visual and personal, and therefore—although definitely more objectionable—it is stronger cinematically. (It can be funnier, too, as in graphically disgusting comedies such as *There's Something About Mary*.) It is important to have your characters take dramatic action, and the more gripping, even visceral, the better.

Let's look at another example. Let's say Jack is a hard-working cop, who one day finds out through the grapevine that his wife is sleeping with his best friend and partner, Larry. Jack beats up Larry and then divorces his wife. While his reaction of anger leads him to alter his life, Jack is still a less-than-interesting screen character, because what he does is mundane and predictable. Beating up Larry and divorcing his wife are both reflexive reactions, more than decisive actions. But what if Jack decides to seek a calculated revenge. He sets out to wine, dine and sleep with Larry's wife. True, now Jack acts, but it still isn't very inventive. But what if Jack—without letting Larry know he's aware of the affair—finds some excuse to move in with Larry; maybe he arranges with their captain to have them both assigned to a long stakeout. And then, by "casually" talking about how he met his wife, how much he loves her, what they've planned to do when they retire, Jack slowly talks Larry out of the affair. And then Jack returns to his wife, never mentioning what he knows or has done. This character not only acts decisively, but in an unpredictable and therefore fascinating way. Or, what if—let's say they live in Miami—Jack invites Larry to join him and his wife scuba diving off his boat one day. He rigs their regulators so they'll run out of air without knowing it, and then, while they are down in the water, he gets back on the boat and leaves them there, miles from shore? What if, for good measure, he knows there are sharks in the area, and pours buckets of blood he's hidden onboard into the water to attract the sharks to his unwitting victims before he leaves? Not very noble or pleasant, but it is a conscious and inventive plan. In short, the most compelling screen characters move under their own power, they don't only react to the power of others.

Made You Look! (Cause and Effect)

The strongest dramatic actions from a story point of view are those that cause another character to take action. Cause and effect, stimulus and response are the building blocks of any story. For example, let's go back to our businessman Bob with the receding hairline. What if Bob went home and told his wife that he quit and she accepts it. His act stands alone, it is a cause without an effect. On the other hand, if Bob goes home, tells his wife, and she sets out to sleep with his boss because his boss still has an income, or applies for Bob's old job herself, now it is a more effective dramatic action on the wife's part. Bob's action has motivated her to take action. Action causing action (as opposed to reaction) is at the heart of all stories.

Yet, an action will not be credible unless there is a deep, personal and understood motivation behind it. Emerson said, "Cause and effect, means and end, seed and fruit, cannot be severed; for the effect already blooms in the cause, the end pre-exists in the means, the fruit in the seed." In story terms, this means that there must be a strong foundation within the character that makes this particular action possible, justifiable, even inevitable. In order to know the causes, you must not only look to the circumstances surrounding your characters, but to their own personal reasons for acting the way they do. Like seeds awaiting rain and sunlight, the characters' personalities and needs are the origins of motivation, which grow into dramatic action when the situation is right.

There are countless motivations: revenge, injustice, ambition, haunting memories, sick relatives; that's the easy part. The hard part is knowing why one character will act upon the motivation while another will not—why does one of two brothers seek revenge for the murder of their father, while the other just wants to let it go? If you, the writer, do not understand why your characters act upon their motivations in the ways they do, then their actions will never appear integral or justified. You'll have one-dimensional characters who take action, but for no compelling reason. This is just as pointless as a character with plenty of motivation who does nothing. (Unless you are after exactly those qualities, in which case you'd have created either a hopeless scatterbrain or a resolutely passive-aggressive character, and neither is attractive.) More often in novice screenplays, characters appear and do things for no reason because the novice writer hadn't bothered to set one up. In other words, the writer didn't really get to know the characters. In order to do so, you've got to spotlight those elements that define and differentiate your characters.

TURN ON THE SPOTLIGHT (CHARACTER ELEMENTS)

The spotlighted elements of a screen character are those that reveal unique personality, and the needs and desires that cause the character to take action. You have to get inside your character's head and figure out why she is doing what she's doing in the context of this particular conflict. To know a character well enough to make a strong evaluation, we have to know all the elements that cause the character to make decisions and take action. In order to gain that understanding, a screenwriter can make a list of the character's traits by asking a series of questions about the general qualities of the character: physical, sociological and psychological. The list creates a thumbnail sketch of the character. A list of questions might look something like this:

GENERAL

What are the character's hobbies?

What are the character's mannerisms?

What are the character's tastes?

What are the character's political views?

What is the character's career?

What is the character's education?

What is the character's occupation?

What is the character's financial situation?

PHYSICAL

What are the character's medical problems?

What does the character wear?

What are the character's age and sex?

What is the character's appearance?

What is the character's health?

SOCIOLOGY

What are the character's hopes, ambitions, fears?

What are the character's morals?

What is the character's class or status?

What are the character's family relationships?

What is the character's nationality?

What is the character's religion?

PSYCHOLOGY

What are the character's ambitions?

What are the character's disappointments?

What are the character's inhibitions?

What are the character's obsessions?

What are the character's phobias?

What are the character's superstitions?

What are the character's talents?

What is the character's philosophy?

What is the character's temperament?

What was the character's childhood like?

There are some screenwriting teachers who even recommend writing long and detailed biographies of their characters, all the way back to their birth, histories that take every facet into account. The problem is that such lists or biographies can go on indefinitely, each question leading to new ones, one past event suggesting another. But it's all wasted time if it doesn't somehow affect your screenplay. Making a list or biography ceases to be helpful if it becomes overwhelming; it can paralyze and deflect you. And, frankly, an exhaustive biography is neither realistic nor necessary. The sum total of a character is too much for any writer or audience member to completely comprehend. Even a commonplace character is too complex to be presented effectively and convincingly in his or her entirety; perhaps James Joyce's great novel *Ulysses* came closest, and it isn't even remotely filmable (just check out the one attempt that was made).

We do not recommend this approach to anyone. Sure, it sounds convincing theoretically to say, "When you know what your character did in first grade, you'll know why he's doing something now." But in practice it's utter nonsense—unless one specific and still powerfully present thing happened back then, such as your character having accidentally shot his father's head off with what he thought was a toy gun. That might be worth including if it affects his current state of mind, but not whether he'd finally gotten potty-trained before kindergarten. The goal of a screenwriter is not to reproduce a total living person, but to create characters who give the impression that they are living people within the confines of a particular story. You must be selective.

The litmus test is simple. If a particular element of a character's history directly affects the character's actions during the two-hour course of the story—during the present—then it is important and should be included. Everything in a movie is present tense: the action, the narrative, even flashbacks are told as if they are happening now. The same is true of your characters. If something in the past is haunting a character, then it is present tense, because it is currently haunting and affecting him and will be referenced either in a scene or line of dialogue.

On the other hand, if a part of the character's history—no matter how colorful—isn't directly affecting the here and now, then it doesn't belong and must be cut. For example, a recent student screenplay had an important speech in which a lawyer regrets that years ago, during his first case, he failed to get a conviction. The murderer left the jail and murdered again. Yet, at no time in the screenplay did this memory affect his judgment, give him pause or make him take a different course of action than he would have without it. It was a fine little speech, well written, but it did not affect the present course of the story and so should have been cut, not only from the screenplay, but from the character. It was useless clutter.

A screenwriter must turn the spotlight only on those characteristics critical to the story, those things that create a unique identity and set of needs and desires. So once you've begun your list or biography, exercise your judgment and ask only those questions whose answers will show up in your script.

Character vs. Characteristics

One important distinction to make, however, is between what your characters appear to be, and who they are on a deep level. Characteristics and character are two different things. Sometimes the two coincide: the friendly old grandpa is just that, he looks like a friendly old grandpa, and guess what, that's who he is. However, what if he has all the characteristics of the friendly old grandpa—white hair, kind face, nice old pocket-watch, and so on—but in fact it turns out he's a ruthless, even evil mastermind? Max von Sydow plays this kind of character in *Minority Report*, as does James Cromwell in *L.A. Confidential*. In *Gremlins* and other similar fantasy comedies, what at first appear to be sweet, cuddly little critters turn out to be horrible little monsters. In other words, the characteristics are the surface appearance, which can either accurately reflect the inner self or be a mask disguising it. The more a character's true self is hidden or distorted by the mask she wears, often the more complex she can be and the more interesting the revelations as the story progresses.

Something's Missing (Needs, Motivations and Goals)

In order for desire or needs to exist—something that predisposes a character to act upon a given motivation—there must be something emotionally important missing from the character's life, something either taken away or not yet attained, but greatly desired in either case. What is missing ties directly into the character's goals and what the character is willing to do (action) in order to achieve them. The greater the missing element, the greater the need. The greater the motivation, the greater the resulting action.

The key to understanding motivation is to look at it from the character's point of view and not the writer's. A strong character is always attempting to change a negative into a positive from his or her perspective. In other words, the character is energized by certain specific needs and desires, which motivate him or her to try and find a positive action to counter a negative situation. Whether an event, action or situation is "negative" or "positive" reflects the character's beliefs, not necessarily the writer's. This applies to the protagonist, antagonist, in fact all the characters.

This means that a character can commit an evil act based on a strong "positive" motive. For example, you're writing the role of an antagonist, a terrorist who hijacks an airliner. A weak writer simply makes the terrorist "evil" just because he is. Reason, desire, need, motivation are glossed over in some brief exposition about him being insane, or wanting to make a vague and clichéd religious/political statement, or by showing him taking random cruel actions. A stronger writer attempts to find the negative that the character hopes to turn to a positive through the terrorist act. What has happened to the character to make him think that hijacking a plane was the right thing to do? Instead of being a cliché, the character acquires emotional weight and reality when he has an exact and comprehensible reason for an action, however misguided, which he believes will positively affect the world from his point of view.

One classic example of such a character is found in *Medea*, the great Greek tragedy about a woman who murders her children because her husband has abandoned her for a younger princess. In Medea's mind, there are several positive reasons for murdering her children: (1) it is better than letting her children starve to death in exile, and so it is actually a loving act; (2) it will punish her husband, which is better than having him go unpunished; and (3) it is better than letting her children live and be a constant reminder of what their father did to her. It is perhaps the most horrible action a person can take—to murder one's own children—but in Medea's mind, it is a positive action taken in the face of a negative situation.

Of course, such actions usually result in other negative consequences. Although characters may believe that their destructive means will justify their hoped-for ends, they may in fact discover that they reach an end more in keeping with their chosen means: they are themselves destroyed. More recently (by 2,500 years or so), in what is generally considered to be one of the two or three greatest films of all time, Orson Welles' *Citizen Kane*, the protagonist destroys himself and poisons his relationship with everyone for whom he cares through his vanity and ambition. In the *Godfather* series, Michael Corleone has first his brother-in-law and then his brother killed for betraying "the family." It is an intensely ironic, even perverse enforcement of family loyalty, but in Michael's world, it's better than letting a disloyal family member go unpunished. In the end, Michael discovers that his wife has had an abortion rather than give him another son, his young daughter is shot to death in front of him, and he eventually ends up alone, without any family at all. Many of the best *films noir* feature this kind of self-destructive protagonist, such as *The Asphalt Jungle*, *Out of the Past*, and *Night and the City*. In *It's a Wonderful Life*, George Bailey attempts to kill himself rather than face the disappointment of his family and a jail sentence for bank fraud; on a deeper level it is his disappointment with his own life and the unrealized dreams that he has subordinated to his responsibilities to his family. Now he feels he has failed even in those. It's his response to a negative situation of unbearable pain. But here there's a difference: he isn't really guilty of the bank fraud and he hasn't failed in either his responsibilities or his life. In fact, he's a great guy, and his motivations are later altered by seeing how valuable, how wonderful, his life really has been. On a more comic note, in *My Best Friend's Wedding*, Julia Roberts' character aims to prevent her best friend (a man) from marrying another woman, which appears better to her than letting her own long-denied love for him go unrealized. Finally she realizes that her course of action is wrong: it's too late, she blew it, and she's only brought pain to everyone and made a fool of herself. The Diablo Cody–scripted *Young Adult* has a similar, though darker, plot: Charlize Theron's beautiful but unhappy Mavis becomes a near-psychotic stalker when she learns that her high school boyfriend, now happily married to someone else, is about to become a father.

All well-written characters, at any given moment—even when they know they're doing something wrong—think their action, given the situation, is the right or only thing to do. They may be totally misguided, they may end up doing more harm than good, even bringing destruction down upon themselves, but their original impulse comes from a desire to turn what they perceive as a wrong into what they perceive as a right, a negative into a positive.

This brings up an important truth that flies in the face of a lot of screenwriting "musts": It is not necessary for us to "like" your characters. Rather, we need to be fascinated by them, to understand why they're taking the actions they do, and that we get caught up in their story because we want to know what on earth will happen.

That Can't Be Me! (The Limits of Self-Knowledge)

Aristotle speaks of a character flaw as being an "error," a "defect in judgment" or "shortcoming in conduct," especially in the greatest (i.e., tragic) characters. Similarly, screenplays are not about well-rounded people who have perfect 20/20 vision concerning their lives, the lives of others or their situations. The character's point of view, like that of the camera angle, is always limited and clouded by personal prejudice, fears, hopes and desires. The characters are flawed, and too immersed in their own life to have any objective perception. Characters must feel their way, learn, adjust, fail and grow. Hamlet is capable of revenge, but he doesn't know that about himself; Charlie Sheen's character in *Wall Street* is greedy, but again (at least in the beginning) he is not aware of it; Bill Murray's character in *Groundhog Day* thinks of himself as a hotshot reporter who doesn't need anyone else—and who goes to great lengths to let everyone around him know as much, regardless of their feelings—but soon learns to despise himself and tries to become worthy of love. Even Superman overestimates his power, underreacts and makes mistakes. These mistakes are caused by a lack of self-knowledge, overcoming which is at the heart of the story.

The key is to find the most critical, appropriate and characteristic flaw or blindness. In the case of your protagonist, this flaw is an exception to the character's more dominant traits, at odds with them. For example, John is a loving husband, an insightful stockbroker and fair businessman, but he loses his temper behind the wheel of a car. Valerie is a good lawyer, a strong advocate of women's rights, but is intimidated by her father. A mother may be a good provider and a caring wife, but she is a workaholic. A cop may enjoy his work, be fair and understanding, but he takes great risks. People do not know their own limits. All characters have limits: limited self-endurance, limited mental power, limited understanding. These limitations are known to the author but not to the characters, or else they do secretly know them but are afraid to confront them. In other words, the screenwriter must know the characters better than the characters know themselves and force them to confront their flaws. If a flaw is great enough to destroy all hope of success, it is called a tragic flaw. When it is a comical and/or harmless shortcoming, then it is called a comic flaw. In the antagonist, however, the flaw may in fact be the most extreme example of the character's dominant traits, and the source of his undoing: for instance, he may suffer from overwhelming pride, that blinds him to defects in his plan, or be insanely jealous, which compromises his judgment in taking action.

The actions that the characters take and the results they get eventually reveal their own true natures to themselves and expose what has been motivating, crippling or nurturing them. Once this is known, the character flaw can be recognized and corrected and the character made whole (or, in the case of a tragedy or of an antagonist, the revelation may bring only pain and defeat). With this the conflict ends, the goal is attained or lost forever and resolution quickly follows.

Getting Your Ghost (Unfinished Business)

A common variation on or aspect of the character flaw is what John Truby and others have called the "ghost." This is something that haunts the character from his or her past, some baggage or unfinished business that is so compelling that it cripples the character until it is addressed. In *Hamlet*, for example, there is a literal ghost—the ghost of Hamlet's father—and the need to avenge his murder is what both causes the action of the story and cripples Hamlet, who is torn by the conflicting desire to take murderous action and his own gentle, irresolute nature. In modern dramas (including comedies) the ghost may also be the unresolved death of a loved one (*Marathon Man, The Fugitive, The Descendants*), but it can also be an unhappy breakup (*Liar, Liar*), a lost opportunity for love or success (*Jerry MacGuire, Dumb and Dumber, Eternal Sunshine of the Spotless Mind*), having been humiliated or disgraced (*Rambo, The Verdict, The Fugitive* again) or some other debilitating factor from the past that preoccupies the character until, over the course of the story, he or she is able at last to put it to rest. In *Ghost*, what haunts the protagonist is why he was turned into a ghost himself and how to resolve his interrupted relationship with the woman he loves. *The Sixth Sense* and *The Others* offer variations on this concept of the protagonists as their own ghosts.

Sometimes the ghost is known only through exposition; sometimes there may be a prologue in which we see the ghost created (as in *Cliffhanger, Braveheart* or *The Fugitive*). Usually it is part of your protagonist's makeup, but good antagonists may also have ghosts, such as Captain Ahab having lost his leg to Moby Dick, or the Phantom of the Opera having had his music, his physical appearance and his lover stolen away from him. This element can make an antagonist more complex and understandable, even sympathetic, to an audience. Whatever your character's ghost may be, it must relate both to the central conflict faced by the character and to the theme of your story, or it will not feel integral or even necessary.

Characters that do not have a flaw and/or a ghost are as interesting as distilled water. Understand the characters' positive motivations and negative situations in relation to their character flaws and past baggage, and you are well on your way to creating an interesting character.

Should I Stay or Should I Go? (Internal Conflict)

Internal conflict is a contradiction in a character's life that he or she must work out, overcome or rise above. Conflict with oneself comes from a moral struggle, a debate over which action to take, anything that makes the character doubt him or herself (for more on internal conflict, see Chapter 7, Power and Conflict). The internal conflict is most effective when caused by two powerful, positive desires of nearly equal strength, but which are opposed to each other. For example, in *Baby Boom* Diane Keaton wants to be a good mother, but also feels that she must work hard to shatter the glass ceiling at work. These two desires, to be a good mother and to be a success, are opposed to each other and cause internal conflict. In *Donnie Brasco* and *The Departed*, both about undercover cops, the protagonists find themselves in the dilemma of being committed to wiping out the Mob, but also of betraying those criminals to whom they've become attached in their undercover lives or else facing their own destruction.

Like the ghost and character flaw, internal conflicts must grow naturally from the characters' own natures, or those conflicts will not be strong enough to motivate them. For instance, say Jack is a good cop. He voluntarily works in a dangerous neighborhood because he feels that there he does the most good. Jack also desperately wants children, but his wife refuses to have them until he quits the force or takes a safer desk job. Jack knows she's right, yet the good citizens of the neighborhood need him. Jack has an internal conflict between two positives: helping the neighborhood or having children. He is also the cause of the conflict: because he is a good man, he chooses to work in a bad neighborhood.

Internal conflict can also occur when characters' needs and goals come into conflict with their flaws. Suppose that when Jack was a child, he and his mother were homeless. The experience never left him, making him fear losing his job. His wife wants him to transfer to a safer job so they can have children, but he is afraid to ask, afraid that he will be fired and lose his security. Maybe his wife makes him feel guilty because he grew up homeless and should know better than to keep working at a job where he might be killed and leave his new family homeless. The internal conflict is brought on by several positives (or at least what the character perceives as positives): his desire for a child, his need to keep his job, and his concern about not wanting to leave his family homeless.

Just to up the stakes, let's give poor Jack a drinking problem. His wife won't have children now until he also stops drinking. This would appear to be a conflict between a positive and negative: having children or drinking. But Jack's alcoholism is not the internal conflict, it is a result of it. The conflict of fear and desire motivates his drinking, which only compounds his problem. But even the drinking makes sense to him. It's how he escapes his pain. So once again it is a positive. It is important that the screenwriter not confuse a character's action with the internal conflict. The character's action is often the result of the internal conflict, not the conflict itself.

You Can't Always Get What You Want (Need vs. Desire)

As John Truby has pointed out, a powerful source of internal conflict can come from the fact that often what the protagonist consciously *desires* may be something quite different from what he subconsciously *needs*. A good example of this is *As Good as It Gets*, where Mel's crabby desire to be left alone is in conflict with his deeper, romantic nature and need for love and human contact. Or say a protagonist begins with a burning desire to get rich in order to prove himself and win the affections of a beautiful but materialistic woman (because of his ghost or initial character problem: that his father died a poor, unloved man). But what he really needs is to be happy with who he is, with or without riches, and to marry the unselfish girl next door. His realization of what he needs will come after he's foolishly pursued the false goal of his desire and found it lacking. Along the way he acquires the self-empowering understanding that his father died unloved because he was unloving, not because he was poor. Once his illusions and misleading desires have been stripped away, he is free to find the true happiness that has been under his nose all along. The result is a happy ending. This, by the way, is why the guy always ends up with someone like Doris Day when he's been distracted all along by someone like Veronica Lake. Though more beautiful, Veronica represents the fool's gold of desire. Doris—pure and virginal—is what the hero really *needs* to be happy (again, Hollywood is into moral tales). Turn this around, have the protagonist never achieve wisdom or achieve it too late, and you have a darker ending, as in *Basic Instinct*, where the hero ends up taking lust over love (clearly the wrong "pick") or is destroyed, as in *Dangerous Liaisons*.

The conflict of need and desire can be one of the most powerful tools you have in constructing your character, creating new levels of psychological depth, but it always depends on the story you're telling. Sometimes need and desire coincide, as in *Rocky*, where his desire to survive a title fight on his feet mirrors his need to prove he's not just a bum.

SWF, 30–40, Loves Long Walks in the Park (Character Traits)

Along with determining your character's internal conflicts, positive motivations and self-knowledge issues, you must define a dominant trait and emotion. Listen to people describe other people. Almost always they will describe one dominant trait and/or emotion.

"Emily, the wacky pregnant woman in the office."

"Tybalt, the hothead who's always picking a fight."

"Beth, the basket case who can never find her purse."

"George, the quiet guy who never says good morning."

"Wanda, the spaz who's good with numbers."

When we describe a person it comes naturally to hit upon a dominant emotion and/or trait. The key for a screenwriter is to find the traits and emotions that are essential to pushing the story forward.

A dominant character trait is the defining quality that makes this character unique in your story, and also makes the character appropriate for his/her role in the screenplay. It can be that the character is a real problem-solver, silly, clever or cool; it can be something subtle or even extraordinary. But this trait always differentiates the character from all the others and defines his/her purpose. Look at *Jaws*: each of the characters has a dominant trait. Quint (Robert Shaw), the old shark chaser, is independent, self-reliant and obsessed; Hooper (Richard Dreyfuss), the academic, is cocky and self-assured; Brody (Roy Scheider), the sheriff, is a down-to-earth man of the people forced to take action against the danger posed by the shark in order to save swimmers from death and his community from financial ruin—and he's afraid of water. Each is unique, and perfectly suited to tell this particular story.

The dominant emotion is the overall mental state of the character. All characters have a wide range of emotions, but there is usually one strong feeling that defines each character. A character's dominant emotion could be jumpiness, depression, coolness, defensiveness, rage, etc. In *A Time to Kill*, Matthew McConnaughy's defense lawyer is cool and business-like, while Samuel Jackson's vengeful father is impassioned and cunning. In *Adaptation*, Nicolas Cage plays the dual roles of Charlie Kaufman and his twin brother Donald. Charlie is tormented and self-doubting, while Donald is cheerful and optimistic; in the end, when Donald dies, Charlie's character transforms to incorporate his brother's better qualities. About the only dominant emotion that doesn't work well in a movie is self-pity. Characters who indulge in self-pity generally take no action and, as we know, a screen character who takes no action is boring and undefined. An exception might be a subplot or comic character whose self-pity affects the actions of others by negative example—for instance, the long-suffering Jewish mother or jilted girlfriend who appears in some Woody Allen films, who drives the protagonist to exasperation. Remember, we're talking dominant emotion: George Bailey is surely self-pitying at the beginning of *It's a Wonderful Life*, but is forced to snap out of it and revert to his dominant emotion, which is love for others.

THE ARC OR THE COVENANT (CHARACTER ARC VS. CATALYTIC CHARACTER)

Change is a fundamental law in nature. Everything is in motion: the seasons change, the fields die and are reborn, mountains are washed away. The same is true with human beings. Lovers come together and divorce, children become adults, the weak grow strong and the strong weak. The change or growth in a character during the two-hour course of a motion picture is called a character arc, which dramatizes the writer's thematic attitudes about life's journey. Emotionally, intellectually and spiritually, such characters grow, learn and "become," and in the process express some truth about human experience. Lajos Egri says, "There is only one realm in which characters defy natural laws and remain the same—the realm of bad writing." Notwithstanding this pronouncement, not all good characters, or even good protagonists, have an arc. There is a class of characters, sometimes known as "traveling angels," whom we call "catalytic" characters: they do not change, but their steadfast presence and the unbending moral covenant they represent changes or affects the world around them. We'll examine each in turn.

The Irresistible Force (Change)

A character arc is almost always caused by conflict. People seldom grow without ripping themselves apart, questioning and reinventing themselves and their world. For example, the college years are often a time of tremendous growth because college is a competition. It is a time full of highly charged circumstances, anxiety, excitement, deadlines, mental and physical tests and discoveries and sheer exhaustion. There is seldom time for meditation, reflection or revision. College is full of conflict, both positive and negative, and when there is conflict there can be growth; students go in as teenagers, as kids, and come out (hopefully) as informed adults. Other stressful situations that can transform people are war, marriage, divorce—in short, many of the situations you find in the movies, because screen characters also grow through conflict. When you build a character you must create not only who the character "is" at the start, but who the character will "become" after living through the conflict of your story.

Here are a few examples of characters with an arc: In *Shine*, David Helfgott starts as a shy, odd man who in the end performs in front of huge crowds. In *Cop Land*, Sylvester Stallone starts off as a quiet cop who turns a blind eye to corruption but in the end proves himself a good policeman interested in equal justice. Over the course of the terrific Argentine film, *The Secret in Their Eyes*, Ricardo Darin's Detective Esposito goes from being too intimidated by his own low social class to confess his love for beautiful, upper-class prosecutor Irene Hastings, to being at last confident and capable of wooing her. In *Men in Black*, Tommy Lee Jones begins as a dedicated alien hunter and in the end wants his memories erased so that he can forget about the aliens and have a normal life. In *Animal House*, John Belushi starts as a drunk fraternity member and ends as a U.S. Senator. (Of course, whether this is really an arc or just a change of clothes might be debatable.)

The kind of story you're telling will determine the extent and speed of the characters' arc—their change—and how it occurs. We don't all change at the same rate, or to the same degree. Sometimes change occurs at a moment of great crisis, and other times steady conflict brings on a gradual transition. Change can be as broad as a pig becoming a hero in *Babe* or as subdued as John Lithgow's hardline local preacher in *Footloose*, who, after first condemning dancing, quietly, privately, ends up slow-dancing with his wife. Sometimes the smallest change is the most powerful.

At the end of the movie we should be able to look back and see why and how this character became who he is now. It should all make sense. Although not always obvious in the beginning, the small seeds that make the arc possible must be planted early on in the character's development, so that by the end the change is not only possible, but appears to have been inevitable.

The Immovable Object (Conviction)

Characters who do not change—well-written characters, at any rate—must also appear to have an inevitable quality to their natures. This comes from the fact that they live by an unshakable covenant, a set of beliefs or a code of honor that allows them to persist as rocks of stability in the face of a morally unstable, ever-changing universe. They are the immovable objects who turn the tide one way or the other by their presence and conviction. Sometimes these changeless characters have important secondary roles, such as being allies or mentors (Yoda, for example) who cause growth in the protagonists they are assisting or teaching. But often they are the protagonist. Most of Clint Eastwood's classic characters—Dirty Harry, the Man With No Name in the Sergio Leone Westerns, Blondie from *The Good, the Bad and the Ugly*— are the same from beginning to end. The same is true for (among others) many John Wayne, Humphrey Bogart and Sly Stallone characters—Rooster Cogburn, Sam Spade, Philip Marlowe, Rambo—as well as characters in the superhero mold such as James Bond, Superman and Batman. These protagonists cause change in the world around them and in those with whom they're in conflict by preventing their wrongdoing, bringing them to justice, getting them killed, showing them the error of their ways or by doing all of the above. These characters are usually loners who rarely age or die because they are more icons than real people. They may be put through hell, beaten up or nearly killed, their new lover slaughtered in front of them, but in the end they survive with their world and world view intact, thanks to their efforts. This is why, under the grateful gaze of the townsfolk, the heroic cowboy rides off alone into the sunset; there's no way to imagine him settling down.

This is also why these kinds of characters work well in sequels, because their essential nature remains intact. Some attempts have been made to take catalytic characters and have them age or change (such as Philip Marlowe in *Poodle Springs*, Robin Hood in *Robin and Marian*, Peter Pan in *Hook* or James Bond as a senior citizen in *Casino Royale* or showing a soft side in *License to*

Kill), but these were doomed to failure because they betrayed the essential expectations and nature of the protagonist. Such characters have a kind of contract with the audience: we are comfortable because we know who they are, what they are and what they will and will not do. That's why we go to see them, to have a predictable wish-fulfillment. If you break the contract, you alienate your audience. This is also why characters with strong arcs usually don't fare as well the second time around: because the "contract" with the audience from the previous film, which was the satisfying completion of their arc, must now be denied or undone in order for them to have another one.

The unchanging character is a staple of television shows as well, because they allow a recognizable, ongoing situation or franchise to continue over tens or hundreds of episodes. The character you know and love this show or this season isn't going to change on you; look at *Seinfeld, Perry Mason, The Simpsons, M*A*S*H, The Mentalist, House*—take your pick.

WRITE YOU ARE (BUILDING CHARACTERS)

Building a character is an arduous process. It begins with the first inkling of an idea, grows through research, exploration of motivations, and continues unabated to the last draft of the script, as the story nourishes the characters and as the characters enact the story. But all this work can still lead to weak characters if they lack believability. Believability comes only when a character—any character in the screenplay—comes from the screenwriter's own makeup. The writer must invest a part of him or herself in every character in order to make them real. Their life comes from yours, so you must have a level of intimacy with your characters. You must recognize them as aspects of yourself and listen to their voices from within. This is true no matter how different from you the character might be; as with theme, the character wouldn't have occurred to you if there wasn't something in you that responded to him or her, positively or negatively. If you're honest with yourself, you know that inside you are a hundred different fantasies or tendencies, not all of which you'd boast about publicly, but which you can tap to create believable characters. Inside everyone are memories or fantasies of power, revenge, sexual irresistibility, past humiliations and so on. This is what we mean by writing from yourself—not that all your characters should be imitations of the person you show to the world, but that they should reflect some facet of the rich cast of inner characters who make up your complete identity. Even if it's some part of your personality that appalls you, you must find and draw on that part of yourself that will bring reality to the character.

One excellent technique for discovering the part of yourself who is to become a character is to ask the "magic if": What would I do if I were this character in this situation? Constantin Stanislavski, the great Russian director and acting teacher, proposed the "magic if" as the key to all great characterizations. It works for writers, too; after all, screenwriters "act" on the page. If you can find the similarities between your own impulses and those of your characters, you can make the characters more real, because no matter how large the difference between you, there is common, human, shared experience. The shy writer must find within himself the tragic lover in order to write a Romeo. The passive writer must find the bully within herself in order to create a wife beater. The headstrong writer must recall his tentative childhood in order to write about the first day of grade school. No worthwhile character ever came from a writer whose inner life was withheld from the character's creation.

There comes a point in writing a screenplay when the characters become personalities. Writers often say that after long hours of struggling to find the right words to put in their characters' mouths, the characters begin to speak for themselves. A line of dialogue is written and the screenwriter wonders where it came from. It is almost as if someone else took control of the keyboard and wrote the line. This is the magic moment when the characters come alive. Of course, it's still the writer who creates that life, but this is the moment of true connection with one of those inner voices.

Precisely because of this connection, it is imperative that the writer should never lose aesthetic distance. The screenwriter creates characters, but he doesn't live their lives. One young screenwriter, while receiving critical notes about his protagonist, became more and more frustrated until he blurted out, "But that's not what I would do!" With this statement he confirmed that he had fallen into a classic pitfall of beginning screenwriters. On the surface it would seem that this was good, that a "magic if" had come up and the writer was appropriately defending his character's actions. But, in fact, the problem was that he had created a protagonist who was exactly like himself, although the character's world and situation was nothing the student would ever have experienced himself. He had not connected with the right parts of his personality to create a separate character, and therefore the character didn't work in the situation. The sympathetic/empathetic emotional rapport between the writer and the protagonist was so great that the character, for all practical purposes, had become the writer. When this happens, the screenwriter is no longer writing characters, but recording diary entries. Diary entries may be fascinating to the writer, but they will bore the audience. Screenplays are not diary entries. A producer we know was once invited to a college writing class; asked what advice she'd give the young writers, she declared with real passion, "Just remember, no one gives a damn about your life story." What she was saying was not that you shouldn't write what you know, but you shouldn't slavishly depend on it. No one cares about your life story unless it's really, really interesting, or unless you can alter the truth until it becomes truly entertaining. After years of reading bland, pointless "my girlfriend broke up with me in high school and boy did it hurt" screenplays, this producer was giving some valuable advice. Use that hurt, but create a story a wide audience would care to see.

Time and again, young screenwriters create secondary characters who are more interesting than the main characters. This is because they are so close to the main characters that they lose their sense of proportion and balance. They see the story through their protagonist's eyes, and since from the writer's perspective, he or she is normal, the protagonist will become bland

and normal as well. The writer feels more free to change and develop secondary characters, who are less like the writer and seen from an outside perspective. Screenwriters must try to achieve a similar distance from their protagonists, because judgment is only possible when one regards the characters from a distancing frame of reference. In short, it is acceptable to imagine yourself to be the characters in your story, to use the "magic if," as long as you never lose perspective about your characters, especially your protagonist. If you discover that one of your secondary characters—an ally, say—is not only more interesting but also better carries the thematic material of the story, you might decide you've got the wrong protagonist in the first place and that this other character is really whose story you're telling. In this case you might consider recasting the story from the point of view of the better character.

However, it should also be noted that being the "most interesting" character is not what defines a good protagonist. Often, secondary characters are more interesting because they can be more oddball or extreme: In *Star Wars*, Han Solo and Yoda are more interesting than Luke Skywalker; in *Jaws*, Robert Shaw's shark-hunter Quint is more interesting than Roy Scheider's Chief Brody; in *Inglorious Basterds*, Christoph Waltz's "Jew Hunter" is more interesting than Melanie Laurent's Shoshana (who is actually the protagonist); in *The Terminator*, Kyle Reese is more interesting than Sarah Conner; in *Lethal Weapon*, Gibson's Riggs is more interesting than Glover's Murtaugh (who is, again, the protagonist). This is not always the case; in *Terminator 2*, for instance, Sarah Connor now becomes more interesting than any of the other characters. What makes a good protagonist is less how distinctive he is, but instead whether his need and desire and willingness to engage in the central conflict is the most compelling, and whether his success or failure has the largest consequences for the world of the story.

Name That Character

Characters' names can provide insight—often humorous—into their nature, and reflect their attitude, class and heritage. A name provides a first impression that can influence the reader's attitude about a character. Name a character Adolph and we will immediately think of Adolph Hitler; name her Jacqueline and we'll associate her with Jacqueline Kennedy Onassis. The Bond movies have great fun with their character names: Oddjob, Pussy Galore, Plenty O'Toole, Goldfinger, Dr. No and so forth. In most cases the associations are subtler. In *Unforgiven*, the protagonist is named Will Munny, reflecting his active nature (he *will* take action) and the source of his dilemma and motivation (money), while the antagonist is named Little Bill, suggesting that he is the protagonist's flip side (both are named William) as well as his own connection to money (dollar bill). Jason Bourne evokes the idea of rebirth, as *The Bourne Identity* is about his recovering his memory and his past. Sometimes a name suggests rugged strength, like Shane or Matt Helm; sometimes it evokes other qualities: Scarlett O'Hara, Hans Kreuger, Tinkerbell. What you want to do is find just the right name to evoke your characters' inner nature in the same way that your narrative describes their appearance, so make sure you pick exactly the right handle. Find a unique combination of words and sounds that are easy to remember and fit the character—or contrast with him or her, creating an ironic distinction. Look to popular culture, song titles, people in the news, anything that might have created a larger social association for a particular and appropriate name. Phone books and graveyards are all great sources of inspiration, but baby-name books are even better. One last caution: do not, ever, give two characters names that are so similar that the reader gets them confused with each other, like Garry and Barry, or Jim and Tim, or even Harriet and Hazel. There are enough names out there for you to create some variety. (The best baby-name book is *The Baby Name Personality Survey* by Bruce Lansky and Barry Sinrod, published by Meadowbrook Press. This book not only lists thousands of possible character names but identifies the images that are often associated with those names. Another wonderful baby-naming book is *Proud Heritage: 11,000 Names for Your African-American Baby* by Elza Dinwiddle-Boyd, published by Avon Books.)

Screenplays often have an abundance of characters, too many for a reader to keep straight. If you name the minor characters, readers tend to think these characters are important or are going to resurface later as a twist in the plot. Soon they become confused by having to keep up with all the names. When readers get confused, they seldom take the time to go back and reread; they just throw the script in the rejection pile. Therefore, it's best to refrain from naming characters who appear only once or twice. For example, a scene takes place in a mini-mart. The protagonist is drilling the night shift clerk about a recent murder. If this is the only scene in which the clerk appears and/or he is not central to the understanding of the story, you might give the character a descriptive nickname rather than a real name. Nicknames like CARROTHEAD or NIGHTSHIFT LOSER will give a good picture of the clerk while also letting the reader know she won't have to keep track of this character later.

On the other hand, it is best not to give minor characters generic names like COP #1 and COP #2, which can drain the emotional charge of your story by making the characters seem like items on a laundry list. Instead, give each minor character a name that will place an image into the reader's mind. FAT COP, SMILING COP, BULLDOG COP are better names for distinguishing such minor characters.

Casting Call

If I were to refer to Karl Childers in *Sling Blade* or Randall P. McMurphy in *One Flew Over the Cuckoo's Nest*, few people would know who I was talking about, but if I said Billy Bob Thornton in *Sling Blade* or Uma Thurman in *Kill Bill* or Jack Nicholson in *One Flew Over the Cuckoo's Nest* or *Chinatown*, the reference is clear. It is often the case in Hollywood that the actor makes the role. Therefore, one trick to creating a realistic character is to write with a specific actor in mind. Directors often talk of "casting to type." This means that they are trying to find the actor who exactly fits the needs of the role. Casting to type can also work in reverse; when creating a character, you can "cast" to your mental image of the character. The person you cast should be close to the age, style and temperament of the character you've created. If the character is soft-spoken and easy going, you might cast a young Jimmy Stewart in the role. If the character is manipulative and vindictive you may think of Richard Nixon. If you are writing the role of a mobster, you might imagine Harvey Keitel playing the role and/or scene. In the end, whether Harvey Keitel plays the role is unimportant; the substitution was effective in creating a vivid image of the character for the writer.

As suggested in the paragraph above about character vs. characteristics, often the best way to create surprising and unique characters is to invert this strategy: cast someone "against type." This means that instead of modeling your firefighter character after a ruggedly handsome actor like Brad Pitt, you might cast Jonah Hill or Zach Braff, and imagine how aspects of their personality might still work for your story. Instead of casting Kristen Stewart as the vampish "black widow" in your thriller, you instead cast Kristen Wiig as an unlikely—and therefore more dangerous—antagonist. James Woods was the original casting choice for *Rambo*, not Sylvester Stallone; Tom Hanks was originally pursued for the roles of the twin writers in *Adaptation* before Nicolas Cage was cast; imagine how different and surprising they would have been. Remember, both Napoleon and Alexander the Great were little guys; it didn't stop them from being great warriors, and in fact, being short might have fueled their fire. Look beyond the obvious and you might get a much more interesting set of characters. Of course, there's also a danger in doing so: look at how terribly miscast Seth Rogen and Jay Chou were in *The Green Hornet*.

In order for either approach to work, the writer must have a vivid image of an actor's look and personality, and be able to hear how that particular actor talks. This technique works not only with stars but also with real people. Character models are all around us. Every person is a potential model for a screen character. Life is full of raw material.

Tall, Dark and Handsome (Stereotypes)

F. Scott Fitzgerald observed, "Begin with an individual and you find that you have created a type; begin with a type, and you find that you have created—nothing." The danger of casting to type with actors familiar from other roles, or even with people you know in only a superficial way, is that you can end up not with a type, but with a stereotype. A stereotype is a character that reflects a common prejudice or attitude towards a certain type of person, without adding to or improving it. Such characters reiterate generalized clichés and are tagged with stock conventions. In short, they are the result of lazy writing. To avoid stereotypes you must ask: how can I make this character distinctive? How and why is this character different from his or her type? The difference between a stereotype and a real character is that between a character you have borrowed without alteration and one you have re-created. The existing character from another film that you are using for a model may fulfill the same functions you are after in your screenplay, but you shouldn't reproduce exactly his or her actions or mannerisms. This is plagiarism, not borrowing. Find or create those elements that can make your character fresh and unlike any other, including your model.

Know Your Characters

You've seen enough real people and movie characters that you can hear them, see them, imagine them playing the role you are writing, but that isn't the same as knowing them. It all goes back to investing your own emotions and inner self in a character. When you create characters, you must synthesize different parts of people you have met, known or studied, with elements of your own nature. It is this that allows you to really know the character. One student screenwriter created a rather plain, stereotypical character. When questioned whether he really knew the character, he answered, "Oh sure, I'm using my roommate from college." The problem is that you can live in the same room with someone for years and not really know them. Knowing a character is more than understanding their mannerisms, moods or traits. Knowing a character means that you do not have to stop and think about what they will do or say in a given circumstance; there is no moment of doubt about the next action, because the character is acting as you would. As we've discussed, this isn't to say that you should turn the character into a copy of your normal self, doing what you would normally do; rather, you should think of what you would do *if you were that character in that situation*, taking into account the traits, desires and flaws you've given him or her.

A PIECE OF SUGAR (THE SHORTHAND OF DOGS, CATS, CHILDREN AND TUCKING IN BLANKETS)

One last thing. There are certain techniques and character traits that screenwriters use to make their characters likable, no matter how apparently awful. These techniques are so familiar that they verge on cliché, but they work, and there's always a way to reinvent them and find a way to make them feel unique and fresh. Basically, they boil down to associating your character with innocence.

One technique is to have your character like dogs and/or children (or come to like them, as in *Jurassic Park*). Other unusual animals will do, such as apes, elephants, even iguanas (in *Free Willy*, you have the double whammy of a child liking an unusual animal). Even better, have a dog or other animal like your protagonist, proving that underneath it all there is something in his/ her character worthy of selfless love.

Another technique is to have the character "nurture" others, caring for others even when they stand no chance of being thanked. This is the purpose of that hoary cliché of having the protagonist tuck in someone's blanket while they sleep—usually a child, certainly someone without power, thereby doubling the "nurturing" message that the protagonist is a good egg. Again, this effect is intensified by flipping it around: the small child will tuck in the snoring and exhausted brute warrior who has to look after the tyke, although he professes hating to do so. This shows that the big guy isn't such a brute after all, if a little kid can warm to him. Even better if it's a sickly child. A classic example of this appears in *As Good as It Gets*, where the apparently loathsome protagonist, Melvin, unaccountably attracts the affection of a small dog, even after Melvin has dropped him down a trash chute. Later, Melvin arranges medical care for a sickly child. The same strategy is used in *The Accidental Tourist*, where the affections of a dog and a sick child humanize William Hurt's icy protagonist.

The reason these techniques work is because dogs and children usually represent innocence, while nurturing represents altruism or selfless love. While dogs or children are vulnerable (powerless), they bestow moral power upon those they care for, or who care or sacrifice for them.

This does not work with cats. Cats are usually seen as knowing, sexual and selfish, distinctly not innocent, so a character who likes cats is usually despicable (see Blofeld in the Bond movies) or at any rate suspicious. For another example, look at the cat character in *Babe*. If the protagonist has a cat, even when it isn't explicitly evil, it will usually get him or her into trouble, as with Ripley's cat in *Alien*, Cinderella's stepmother's cat Lucifer in Disney's *Cinderella*, Mr. Jinx in *Meet the Parents,* or Julianne Moore's cat in *Assassins*; this may serve the plot, but does not help to humanize the character. This does not apply, by the way, to kittens, which are just cute, or big cats such as lions or tigers, which are generally associated with nobility and power. Additionally, anyone who owns an evil or aggressive dog is necessarily a villain, because the subtext is that he/she has corrupted the innocence of the animal.

A character can't kick a dog or a child unless he's a villain or unless the dog is a corrupted agent of the antagonist, but cats are fair game. Especially snotty, fluffy ones. Small, yappy dogs are an exception, but then the character must feel badly and do something to make amends, like adopt the beasty.

FINAL THOUGHTS

What a Character! One of the first books on screenwriting was *The Photoplay Handbook of Scenario Construction*. It was published in 1923, in the time of silent films, a time before the word "screenwriter" had even been invented. The advice given in this early screenwriting book still applies:

> "Our ultimate purpose, as a photoplaywright, is to arouse the emotions of the audience—to make them weep, to grip their hearts with pity, to thrill them, to make them laugh, and fear, and shed tears of joy. We strive to do these things by means of the actions of the people we create. We make our characters struggle and suffer and win and lose in their fight for happiness. Every act of every character may be regarded as an effect."

This was true in 1923 and it is still true today. Strong, well-developed characters who take action make the story. There may be a limited number of stories out there, but character is inexhaustible.

EXERCISE

Use the following headings to create a character worksheet for leading and supporting roles. Provide each element fully and with specificity, in order to create an interesting, well-developed character.

CHARACTER'S NAME: _____

IMPORTANT GENERAL QUALITIES OF THE CHARACTER: _____

_____

THE CHARACTER'S FUNCTION (PROTAGONIST, ANTAGONIST, MENTOR, ALLY, ETC.): _____

THE CHARACTER'S ARC (IF ANY) OR CONVICTION (IF ANY): _____

_____

THE CHARACTER'S DRAMATIC ACTION: _____

THE CHARACTER'S NEED: _____

THE CHARACTER'S DESIRE: _____

THE CHARACTER'S POSITIVE MOTIVATION: _____

LIMIT OF CHARACTER'S SELF-KNOWLEDGE: _____

THE CHARACTER'S DOMINANT TRAIT:_____

THE CHARACTER'S DOMINANT EMOTION:_____

CRITICAL ELEMENTS OF THE CHARACTER'S HISTORY:_____

THE CHARACTER'S INTERNAL CONFLICT: _____

THE CHARACTER'S FLAW: _____

THE CHARACTER'S "GHOST" (WHAT IS MISSING): _____

CHARACTERISTICS THAT REINFORCE THE TRUE CHARACTER:

_____

CHARACTERISTICS THAT MASK OR CONTRADICT THE TRUE CHARACTER: _____

PART TWO

STORY STRUCTURE

6

Historical Approaches to Structure

From Aristotle to Brutus

In Hollywood, story structure (or plot structure, as it's sometimes called) is spoken of with nearly religious reverence by development executives, script gurus and writing professors. This is because all good movies depend upon well-structured screenplays. Structure is the ground plan of the protagonist's journey, how the different parts of the screenplay (character, world, action, events, dialogue, theme) fit together into a unified whole. But figuring out how to organize these fluid, ever-shifting elements in a strong, coherent fashion is one of the most daunting challenges facing the writer. The result, as with most things regarded with awe, is that structure has acquired an aura of mystery, of hidden truths that may only be perceived by the initiated. Not surprisingly, many schools of thought have arisen regarding structure, sects that vigorously expound and defend their particular oracles. Writing professors and professional screenwriting theorists like Syd Field, Robert McKee, John Truby and many others have come up with a wide range of theories, formulas and templates (three-act, four-act, seven-act paradigms, twelve-step programs, twenty-two–point story frameworks, numbered plot points), some helpful, some impossibly complex. Many of these formulas are based on classical drama, others on psychology or mythology.

STRUCTURE STRICTURES

Let's look at some of the basics of how Hollywood often structures movies by using artificial guidelines called formulas. We do this because every screenwriter must have a working knowledge of at least some of the major story structure paradigms out there, in part because some of them contain helpful, even essential truths along with their arbitrary rules, and in part because their terminology has become a kind of convenient shorthand when people in "the business" need to talk about story structure. It's practically impossible to get through a story meeting without someone referring to a "plot point," a "problem in act two" or the exact nature of the "inciting incident." You'll need to know what they're talking about and respond in kind, even though, hopefully, after reading the next few chapters you will have a more organic understanding of how your screenplay is actually structured.

We'll start with the basic ideas and people that all students of screenwriting must know in order to understand how those in Hollywood view plot. These ideas and people include Joseph Campbell's *Hero with a Thousand Faces*, William Wallace Cook's *Plotto*, Georges Polti's *The Thirty-Six Dramatic Situations*, Lajos Egri's *The Art of Dramatic Writing*, the traditional three-act structure as represented by Syd Field and other teachers, and plotting using page numbers. We begin with the first screenwriting guru, Aristotle (if only he knew...).

ARISTOTLE AND *POETICS*

All screenwriting students must begin their study of structure with Aristotle's *Poetics*, the first known treatise on how to plot a dramatic story. Aristotle (384–322 B.C.), a philosopher in ancient Greece, remains one of the most influential forces in Western thought. His writings focused primarily on such issues as logic, biology, metaphysics, ethics and politics, but he also dabbled in the arts and wrote two treatises on plot. *Poetics* deals with the structure of tragedy, while its companion piece examined the structure of comedy; unfortunately, as it has come down to us, *Poetics* is incomplete and fragmented, while the treatise on comedy has been lost altogether (although a few of its principles are included in the *Poetics*). Because *Poetics* lacks cohesiveness, many feel it was written over a long period of time or abandoned for some reason. Some suggest that it may be merely a student's notes, taken while attending one of Aristotle's lectures. Complete or not, it has remained the first authority on the techniques of dramatic structure and has guided Western drama for hundreds of years.

With typical Greek rationalism, Aristotle approached dramatic storytelling as a science. He sought the universal elements that comprise a dramatic story. Aristotle identified six essential components of drama:

1. *Plot*—the arrangement of incidents
2. *Character*—the personalities
3. *Diction*—modes of utterance
4. *Thought*—the ideas or themes behind the story
5. *Spectacle*—the performance, set, costumes and effects
6. *Song*—(ancient tragedies were sung and so this section, while appropriate to them, is largely irrelevant to modern writers, unless you're writing an animated feature like *The Lion King* or an actual musical like *Evita* or *Chicago*).

Aristotle defined plot as an "arrangement of the incidents." These incidents, he said, must have "unity." Unity means that there is a cohesiveness, a synthesis, in which character, thought, diction, etc., come together to bear on a single subject or "spine." Unity also comes from the "likelihood" and "necessity" of each incident. In other words, the incidents must be both probable and essential to the story. This probability does not come from real life but from the internal logic of the story. A story, he said, does not slavishly copy nature but rather imitates it, and so it is not what is being imitated—nature—that determines the need and order of incidents, but rather the requirements of the story.

Unity also comes from the cause-and-effect relationship between incidents. Each incident must be related to the ones preceding or following it. Stories in which the incidents do not have a cause-and-effect relationship Aristotle labeled "episodic," the lowest form of storytelling, "in which the episodes or acts succeed one another without probable or necessary sequence." Episodic storytelling has been a common problem through the ages for playwrights and screenwriters alike, especially when they're attempting to dramatize long, picaresque novels, biographies or true stories. The problem is that in a true or picaresque story, the main characters may move from one incident to another, meeting and leaving other characters who will never be seen again, and all without any sense of singular motivation, theme or necessity. People's lives happen by accident. Drama doesn't. While a true story's incidents may in and of themselves be fascinating, if they're connected only because "that's the way it happened," or because the writer hasn't found a coherent cause-and-effect relationship to drive the narrative toward some necessary resolution, then the whole story will fall apart, or as Aristotle would say, it will lack unity.

An interesting way to put this in perspective is to look at sitcoms (though Aristotle, of course, didn't know about them). Each individual episode is usually a coherent cause-and-effect narrative. But if you look at the twenty-episode season as a whole, then the sense of unified storytelling often disintegrates. The season is by definition episodic. With rare exceptions, each episode is independent, has little relation to the preceding episode, and does not affect the next. Sitcoms are written this way so that the episodes can be rerun out of order in off-season or syndication without affecting viewer pleasure or understanding. This may be advantageous to the networks but it's a disadvantage to "story," as defined by the overall life of the show, because the characters are never allowed to learn, grow or change from one episode to the next.

Aristotle next points out that not only should the incidents have a cause-and-effect relationship, but they must also have "order and magnitude." When the incidents have a proper order and magnitude, they form a beginning, middle and end. Aristotle has a habit of pointing out things that seem obvious, but that are, in fact, deceptively difficult to achieve. "The beginning is that which does not itself follow anything...but after which something naturally is or comes to be. The end...is that which itself naturally follows some other thing...but has nothing following it. The middle is that which follows something, as some other thing follows it." Sounds easy enough—but where does a story truly begin, so that nothing of dramatic importance happens before that particular moment? How do we know where a whole course of action truly ends? How do we chart a journey of cause-and-effect to get inevitably from one incident to another? From this we see why screenplays (especially action stories) often begin with a spectacular event to kick things off, toppling the dominoes of the succeeding scenes in an order of growing magnitude, and ending in a similarly spectacular fashion, so there's a clear conclusion to the domino effect.

Let's look at the rather simple structure of an ancient Greek tragedy.

> **Beginning**—The protagonist lives a good life, but he has a great character flaw. At the end of the beginning, there is a reversal of fortune. This reversal is not simply a fall from fortune but a fall brought on by the character's own flaw.

> **Middle**—The protagonist fights against his change in fortune but at the end of the middle recognizes his error. He changes from ignorance to knowledge, but it is too late.

> **End**—In the end there is a catastrophe that brings on great suffering, which results in catharsis ("soul cleansing"), if not for the protagonist then for the audience. The world, which had been thrown into chaos, is restored to order.

Aristotle was attempting to synthesize the parts that make up a Greek tragedy. When all these parts came together into a unifying structure, he called it "form." All good plots have an arrangement, a sequence of incidences that link together to create a form. This form, Aristotle said, should guide all other elements: "One should first sketch the general structure, then fill in the exact occurrences and amplify in the details."

In keeping with his concern about episodic writing, Aristotle insisted that a drama must be limited in scope and "easily embraced" within a single viewing. A plot that imitated an entire life would lack form: "The infinitely miscellaneous incidents in one man's life cannot be reduced to a unity." Only when we look at one small part of a life can we find a sequence of incidents that have a cohesive beginning, middle and end. Unity depends on order. Order must be of a limited length. Thus, the proper length of a story depends on editing unimportant incidents that do not form the unity.

For Aristotle, plot defined the story. He wrote that "most important of all is the structure of the incidents. For Tragedy is an imitation, not of men, but of an action and of life, and life consists in action...without action there cannot be a tragedy; there may be without character." In other words, since drama can only imitate action—what happens—then action defines drama, rather than character. It didn't matter to Aristotle why a character would be motivated to take a certain action, just that he took it.

Poetics is the first known guide to formula storytelling. It's a short work, only about 15,000 words, but it has had a huge impact since its rediscovery in the sixteenth century. What made *Poetics* so powerful was that Aristotle was a systematic critic. He generally didn't care if a particular story was good or bad, but rather questioned how the story worked. His appraisal was not primarily a value judgment but rather a technical evaluation. While Aristotle's "scientific" approach to plot was immensely perceptive regarding the drama of his own time, it started us down a path of mechanical formulas that have culminated thousands of years later with competing plot systems and a variety of computer programs, all purporting to take the pain out of plot construction. (For more about the ideas expressed in Aristotle's *Poetics* you might read *Backwards & Forwards* by David Ball and published by Southern Illinois University Press.)

PLOTTO AND *THIRTY-SIX DRAMATIC SITUATIONS*

The next major influence on modern Hollywood screenwriting was Georges Polti's *The Thirty-Six Dramatic Situations*, published in 1921. Inspired by the writings of the eighteenth-century Italian playwright Carlo Gozzi, Polti claimed there were a limited number of human emotions and therefore a limited number of story ideas. He asserted that all plays, novels, short stories—and screenplays, for that matter—are variations on only thirty-six plots. He included categories such as "Fatal Imprudence," "Daring Enterprise" and "Murderous Adultery." According to Polti, there are no new ideas. A few years later, in 1928, William Wallace Cook also attempted to categorize plots in *Plotto*. This book was supposed to help the writer construct a plot by stringing together hundreds of possible "interchangeable clauses." *Plotto* lists hundreds of plot twists and story beats, along with an intricate cross-referencing system that is difficult to follow at best. These books mark the next step in attempting to organize plots. Both failed, but again were spiritual precursors to a growing number of computer programs now on the market that claim to do the same things.

LAJOS EGRI AND *THE ART OF DRAMATIC WRITING*

In the 1940s, Lajos Egri wrote *The Art of Dramatic Writing*. It is an essential work, and many of the ideas in this book owe a great debt to it. Unlike Aristotle, who emphasized plot over character, Egri argued that plot grows naturally out of premise, character and conflict—in other words, that it is a result, not a precondition, of the other elements of drama. This is one of the few books on dramatic writing that does not have a chapter on story or plot. As a result, many in Hollywood think it's a great book but not a useful tool in constructing a story; it's the attractive fork in the road they'd like to take, but just don't have time to. Most screenwriters are in too great a hurry to find the "hook," the exciting one-sentence element that will catch a producer's fleeting interest, and then to slap together a formulaic, plot-driven script before the "heat" of the idea goes cold. Or else they've been given a high-concept assignment by a producer, with no time to think about anything but nailing together a script to service the supposedly salable elements, whether these be the hook, or a star with a scheduling window of opportunity. But these scripts, if made, usually fail on the screen, because their characters are ill-conceived puppets going through the motions. It's hard to care about a puppet…unless, let's say, it's on a wonderfully character-driven journey to become a little boy. Egri's methods are perhaps better suited to the artistry of theater, where the primacy of a catchy plot idea is less of a concern, but they cannot but help to build more involving, character-centered screenplays.

JOSEPH CAMPBELL AND THE HERO'S JOURNEY

The next major player in Hollywood story structure, although it wasn't his intention, was anthropologist Joseph Campbell. Campbell generated unprecedented interest in mythology and storytelling with his books and his enormously popular series of interviews with Bill Moyers on PBS. Campbell was not a plot guru. Building on the work of Swiss psychologist Carl G. Jung—who sought to understand the universal story archetypes and mythic characters that seem to pop up in varying cultures—Campbell took it a step further by outlining a basic, ageless pattern of storytelling. His book *The Hero with a Thousand Faces* details how the plot structures of most heroic quest myths were similar no matter the country, culture or century from which they came. Campbell argues that all storytellers—from the ancient Greeks to Kenyans to Chinese to Hollywood screenwriters—follow the same basic formula as they retell these heroic stories, in spite of their infinite surface variations. This ancient structure involves the twelve stages of the "Hero's Journey:"

1. THE ORDINARY WORLD
   A myth begins with the hero in his own element.
2. THE CALL TO ADVENTURE
   A problem or challenge is presented that will unsettle the ordinary world of the protagonist.
3. THE RELUCTANT HERO
   The hero balks at the edge of adventure. He faces his fears concerning the unknown.
4. THE WISE OLD MAN
   The hero acquires a mentor, who helps the hero make the right decision, but the hero must undertake the quest alone.
5. INTO THE SPECIAL WORLD
   The hero makes the decision to undertake the adventure and leaves his own familiar world behind, to enter a special world of problems and challenges.
6. TEST, ALLIES AND ENEMIES
   The hero confronts allies of his opponent, as well as his own weaknesses, and takes action while dealing with the consequences of his action.
7. THE INMOST CAVE
   The hero enters the place of greatest danger, the world of the antagonist.
8. THE SUPREME ORDEAL
   The dark moment occurs. The hero must face a crucial failure, an apparent defeat, out of which he will achieve the wisdom or ability to succeed in the end.

9. SEIZING THE SWORD
    The hero gains power. With his new knowledge or greater capability, he can now defeat the hostile forces of the antagonist.
10. THE ROAD BACK
    The hero returns to the ordinary world. There are still dangers and problems as the antagonist or his allies pursue the hero and try to prevent his escape.
11. RESURRECTION
    The hero is spiritually or literally reborn and purified by his ordeal as he approaches the threshold of the ordinary world.
12. RETURN WITH THE ELIXIR
    The hero returns to the ordinary world with the treasure that will heal his world and restore the balance which was lost.

The most famous example of a movie that follows this formula is *Star Wars*. Here is how Luke Skywalker's (the protagonist's) journey follows Campbell's ancient story line.

1. THE ORDINARY WORLD—Luke Skywalker is a bored farmboy on a distant planet.
2. THE CALL TO ADVENTURE—Princess Leia and the rebel forces who resist the evil Emperor are in trouble. She sends a holographic request for help to Obi Wan Kenobi, who in turn asks Luke to join him.
3. THE RELUCTANT HERO—Skywalker refuses to join Obi Wan. He has too many responsibilities on the farm, but when he goes home, he finds that his family has been slaughtered by the Emperor's storm troopers.
4. THE WISE OLD MAN—A wise mentor, Obi Wan Kenobi, prepares Luke for the battle ahead. He gives Luke a light saber that once belonged to Luke's father, a Jedi knight. He tells Luke of the dark side of The Force.
5. INTO THE SPECIAL WORLD—Luke decides to leave his ordinary world and set things right.
6. TEST, ALLIES AND ENEMIES—Luke enters the dangerous world, meets strange creatures in the "threshold" area of the bar, joins forces with Han Solo, runs from the Emperor's storm troopers and enters the fight, flying off into space to rescue Princess Leia.
7. THE INMOST CAVE—Luke enters the Death Star, the home and ultimate weapon of the evil Emperor's main warrior, Darth Vader.
8. THE SUPREME ORDEAL—Luke, Han Solo and Princess Leia are trapped in the giant trash crusher of the Death Star; Luke is sucked under water by a strange creature. They are then saved by an ally, R2D2.
9. SEIZING THE SWORD—Luke rescues Princess Leia and seizes the plans of the Death Star.
10. THE ROAD BACK—Luke is pursued by Darth Vader.

11. RESURRECTION—Luke is almost killed by Darth but fights back and wins. Luke destroys the Death Star.
12. RETURN WITH THE ELIXIR—Luke is rewarded for all his hard work. The world is back in balance.

When Hollywood discovered *The Hero with a Thousand Faces*, many producers, directors and writers were overjoyed: they had finally found their plot-structure bible. Now they could plug any idea into this simple blueprint and come up with a pretty good story. But others were not so thrilled. Many felt that too many producers, anxious for a quick fix, saw Campbell's formula as the *only* way to structure a screenplay, no matter what type of story was being told. Campbell's structure might work great for *Star Wars* and other quest stories, but it offers little insight into stories like *'night Mother*, *My Dinner with Andre* or *Lost in Translation*.

For more information on Joseph Campbell's work we recommend Chris Vogler's excellent book *The Writer's Journey*. Vogler reworks Campbell's twelve-step "Hero's Journey" paradigm into a model that is useful to contemporary writers. This book is essential reading, but Vogler himself (leery of having his analysis misunderstood as another formula) is the first to warn that these steps may not occur in the same order as he presents them. Even worse for those seeking the holy grail of structure, he warns that the "Hero's Journey" paradigm doesn't fit all story types.

THE THREE-ACT STRUCTURE

Most modern screenwriting theorists preach some interpretation or version of what is known as the "three-act structure." Inspired by Aristotle and Campbell, there are several different versions of this formula out there. We'll try to present here a version that remains true to all of them.

"Act One, Act Two and Act Three" is really just a different way of saying "beginning, middle and end." Each section involves different elements:

Act One—The Situation

Act Two—The Complications

Act Three—The Conclusion

If a producer says that your second act is weak, he means the middle of your story, the complications, needs work. Acts are structural divisions used to divide a screenplay into workable units, not divisions marked by an intermission (or indicated in the script). But they have a concrete reality in the minds of those concerned. (To add to the confusion, sitcom and hour-length television writers use the word "act" in the same way as playwrights, as a formal break in the story marked by an intermission or, in their case, a commercial.)

The three-act system attempts to pinpoint the exact structural moments in the story where something important occurs. These moments are called *plot points*. Plot points are structural reference points that can take many forms: a character's realization, a decision, a twist or turn in events or the climax. Two points are generally thought of as essential: the point that begins Act Two, and the point that begins Act Three. To understand the three-act structure, it is necessary to identify the exact plot point where each act ends and the next begins—in other words, to identify where the beginning begins, the beginning ends, the middle begins, the middle ends, the end begins and the end ends. Confused? Read on; it gets simpler.

Let's examine the structures of two completely different movies: *The King's Speech*, the biopic for which David Seidler won an Oscar for Best Screenplay, about Prince Albert the Duke of York trying to overcome his stuttering, and *Rambo: First Blood*, the Sylvester Stallone action-adventure flick of a few years back. *The King's Speech* and *First Blood* (as unlikely as it may seem) share similar three-act structures, just as a grand cathedral and a plain boxlike office building can share the same structural skeleton.

Act One

The following are elements and plot points contained in the beginning: the opening balance, an opening event, a disturbance, a major dramatic question, and a decision.

Opening Balance Most screenplays begin with a world in apparent balance. The lives of the characters have achieved a certain equilibrium, which must be disturbed if there is to be conflict. *First Blood* starts with John Rambo, a Vietnam vet with special guerrilla training who is now a warrior without a war, unable to identify with the country he's worked so hard to defend. He is backpacking through the great Northwest looking for inner peace, and hoping to find an old war buddy. *The King's Speech* begins with Prince Albert ("Bertie," played by Colin Firth) attending the 1925 British Empire Exhibition at Wembley Stadium with his wife Elizabeth (Helena Bonham Carter).

Opening Event An opening event is a unique moment in the characters' lives. It can be an unusual incident, special occasion or a crisis. It could be a wedding, a funeral, a homecoming, preparation for a party or anything that makes this moment a little more special than the normal humdrum of the characters' lives. Both *First Blood* and *The King's Speech* begin with events. In *First Blood*, John Rambo discovers that his buddy has died of cancer caused by Agent Orange, a defoliant used in Vietnam. In *The King's Speech*, Bertie struggles to address the large crowd at the Exhibition. Elizabeth is agonized by witnessing his difficulty in performing this aspect of his public duties.

The Disturbance The disturbance is a plot point that disrupts the opening balance and gets the main action rolling. The opposing forces, protagonists and antagonists, are placed in a situation rich with possible conflict. In *First Blood*, after learning of his friend's death, John Rambo wanders into a small town. He's looking for a meal and a place to bed down for the night when the city's chief of police (who represents the country's indifference to Vietnam vets) lets Rambo know he's not welcome. The cop escorts Rambo to the city limits and tells him to keep walking. The police chief disturbs Rambo's search for inner peace. In *The King's Speech*, Bertie's problem with stuttering leads him to consult a series of upper-class but incompetent speech therapists, until Elizabeth essentially forces him to visit an unorthodox, lower-class Australian, Geoffrey Rush's Lionel Logue, who practices speech therapy without having had formal training or accreditation, but who has a reputation for success. Logue insists that he and Bertie start out on a first-name basis and disregard their class difference.

Screenwriter/theorist Robert McKee and others refer to this plot point as the "inciting incident." It is supposedly the single event that sets the story in motion. The disturbance or inciting incident, depending on whose interpretation of the three-act structure you follow, has been variously identified as the end of the first act, or perhaps a midway point in the first act. Either way, it is the plot point at which the protagonist is confronted with the challenge that eventually will define the story's spine, its central conflict.

The End of the Beginning (End of Act One)   The disturbance has caused the basic situation to deteriorate. This deterioration continues until the protagonist takes action. The beginning of a formula screenplay ends when the protagonist makes a major decision to act, a decision that results in more conflict. This decision now defines what the screenplay is about. It states the protagonist's goal and the *core action* of the plot. In *First Blood*, the end of the beginning occurs when John starts to walk away from the small town but then stops. He fought for this country, his friends have died for this country and he can't even get a meal. He decides to walk back into the small town and have dinner. Having dinner may not sound like a "major decision," but after the police chief told him not to show his face there, it becomes a decision (a declaration, if you will) that will lead to great conflicts, complications and death. In *The King's Speech*, Bertie is appalled at Logue's irreverent manner and at first refuses to continue treatment with him. He's convinced that it's all hopeless—until he learns he has no choice, that his father thinks Bertie's older brother, the Prince of Wales (who is in line to be king) is morally corrupt. "Who," he asks, "will stand between us, the jackboots, and the proletarian abyss—you?"

The Major Dramatic Question   The disturbance and the protagonist's decision cause a major dramatic question (sometimes called an M.D.Q.). This is the "hook" that keeps people in the theater for two hours because they want to know the answers, or the outcome. It's not the overall statement or theme of the screenplay, but a question that arouses curiosity and suspense. In *First Blood*, the M.D.Q. is: "Will John Rambo earn the respect he (and all Vietnam vets) deserve?" In *The King's Speech*, the question is: "Will Prince Albert accept help from a lower-class Australian and overcome his stutter in time to take the throne and inspire the English people as World War II erupts?"

How Long Should Act One Be?   If you know what kind of decision your protagonist makes at the end of the beginning (end of Act One), then you can also predict how long your beginning will be (this is why it's called a formula; decisions are made without the screenwriter having to think about them). If the protagonist makes a morally correct decision—"I will fall in love" or "I shall save my father from alcoholism" or "I must stand up for all Vietnam vets"—then it's not necessary to have a long beginning. Rambo makes morally correct decisions, so the beginning is rather short (in this case, Act One barely lasts longer than the opening credits). If the protagonist's decision lacks moral fiber—"I'll steal the money" or "I shall leave my family" or "I will cheat on my fiancé"—then the beginning needs to be long enough to make the audience feel that, in a similar situation, they too might make the same decision. In *The King's Speech*, Bertie's difficulty in accepting Logue's help, and his self-doubt when confronted with the possibility of having to be the public voice of the Royal Family, reveal that his character has not yet matured and so the movie has a long beginning and a late *point of attack*, also known as the *point of no return*.

The point of attack or point of no return is the moment in the story in which the main fuse is lit, the clouds of conflict appear and the primary action of the story clearly declares itself. *First Blood* has an early point of attack, when Rambo refuses to be run out of town or intimidated by the Sheriff. In *The King's Speech*, Europe is on the brink of war and the point of attack could be defined as when Bertie realizes he must be able to address the nation over the radio. Some formula writers believe that the point of attack should fall about 10 percent of the way into a screenplay. This is called the 10 percent rule. Others feel it happens 25 percent of the way in, so that the first and third acts are roughly equal quarters of the script, with the second act occupying half the length. The only thing we insist on is that you know what it is, that it presents the protagonist with an irrevocable and unavoidable course of action, and that the event or need that defines it becomes the protagonist's central motivation.

Act Two

The plot points contained in the middle are: conflicts, crises, obstacles, complications or reversals; rising action; and the protagonist's "dark moment."

Conflicts, Crises, Obstacles and Complications/Reversals The middle of the three-act screenplay is made up of the roadblocks that ensure that the protagonist's course of action is not clear sailing, for clear sailing is the death of drama (and comedy). Until the final climax, there's always another conflict, crisis, obstacle and/or complication. In *First Blood*, John meets stiff resistance as the police chief has him arrested and tortured. John escapes, but the police chief calls in the National Guard and their tanks to try to stop him. In *The King's Speech*, Bertie fails terribly at reading a speech his father has prepared for him, and thinks he's doomed to failure—until he at last listens to a recording of his voice that Logue made, having forced Bertie to recite a passage from *Hamlet* while listening to Beethoven through earphones. To his amazement, Bertie learns that he had recited it perfectly and without a stutter. Then he has to overcome his consciousness of class and the various burdens he carries from his childhood that left him feeling inadequate, including other physical disabilities, the death of his beloved little brother, and being treated harshly by his parents.

Rising Action   In the middle of a screenplay, the world is unstable. This insta-
bility is governed by *rising action* that makes each conflict, crisis, obstacle
and complication more powerful, more dramatic and more important than
the one before. In other words, the middle of a screenplay must follow the
path of most resistance. There may be moments of apparent success, but they
always lead to an even greater undoing. The middle of a screenplay is a series
of actions that result in the failure of the protagonist.

The Dark Moment   The end of Act Two (end of the middle) occurs when
the hero totally fails, the quest collapses, the protagonist's shortcomings have
tripped her up and the goal becomes unattainable. This is the *dark moment*.
It's the ultimate obstacle—the antagonist has won and the battle appears to
be over. Rambo's dark moment is a literal moment of darkness. Pursued by a
growing military force, he takes refuge in an abandoned mine. The National
Guard use bazookas to close the entrance. Rambo is caught. He will surely
suffocate. In *The King's Speech*, as his now-deceased father had predicted,
Bertie's older brother has proven too weak for the throne and abdicated,
leaving Bertie as the new King. He must address the nation—and it's at this
moment that he discovers that Logue has been treating him without any formal qualifications. He thinks Logue has betrayed his trust, at the very moment
he needs him most. He's terrified of being known as "Mad King George the
Stammerer, who let his people down so badly in their hour of need."

Act Three

The plot points contained in the end are: enlightenment, climax, and catharsis.

Enlightenment   The beginning of Act Three (the end) is enlightenment.
Enlightenment occurs when the protagonist understands how to defeat the
antagonist. Enlightenment can come in many forms: the protagonist may
join forces with another, there may be a revelation that sheds new light on
the problem or the protagonist, by falling into an emotional abyss, may now
be able to see her error. In *First Blood*, enlightenment occurs when John finds
an air shaft that leads to the mountaintop and gains a position of superiority over the armies below. In *The King's Speech*, Bertie becomes so angry
with Logue (who's casually sitting on the throne in the Cathedral where
Bertie's about to be crowned) that he loses his stammer: "I have a voice!" he
exclaims—and suddenly realizes that it's all thanks to Logue's help.

A good enlightenment involves several elements. First, it must be
something the protagonist (and audience) could not have understood before
enduring the conflicts and trials of the middle. What this often means is that
the protagonist comes to realize that what she wanted, or thought she needed,
was in fact a false goal; now she understands what her true need and goal
should be. Second, the enlightenment must be delicately set up earlier in the
screenplay. Ancient playwrights, working within a universe of divine fatalism,
used to depend on the character of a god, lowered from above, to set everything straight. This is called *deus ex machina*, which translates as "god from
a machine." Today, the idea of divinely ordained and immutable fate doesn't

hold, just as divine—or unbelievably coincidental—intervention to set things straight doesn't work. So the term has come to mean when a writer hasn't logically set up the enlightenment or the ending of a screenplay, and has to cheat his way out. If you've ever seen an old melodramatic Western, then you understand. It's the dark moment: the wagon train circles, the Indians attack, the settlers run out of bullets, and then, suddenly, without anything to indicate that they've been alerted, the cavalry arrives. This is *deus ex machina*.

Climax Armed with enlightenment, the protagonist is renewed and ready to defeat the antagonist. The outcome of the story becomes clear—although there should be enough doubt as to who will win to maintain suspense—so the pace should increase as the rising action drives toward climax. The climax, in a formula three-act screenplay, is usually defined as the moment the antagonist is defeated. The climax can be a violent, horrible moment as in *First Blood*, when John finally shoots the corrupt police chief, or a more profound moment as in *The King's Speech* when, after having taken the throne, Bertie must now come to grips with the threat of Hitler's Germany and bravely addresses the nation with an inspirational speech over the radio. This pays off his earlier terror and inability to read the prepared speech his father had given him to practice for reading over the radio.

Catharsis After climax is catharsis. Catharsis is a final purging of the character's emotions, restoring the world to balance and hinting at what the future might bring. There are two requirements of catharsis. First, it must not linger. Once the climax is over and the antagonist defeated, the story is essentially over and the audience wants out. Second, the ending must be consistent with the beginning. Although the ending may not be predictable at the beginning, by the end, in retrospect, it must appear to have been inevitable. In *The King's Speech*, the catharsis occurs after the speech, when Bertie's daughters tell him how splendid he sounded, and Logue gives him a simple nod of approval— at which point he goes with his family to the palace's viewing balcony and waves to his cheering people, having become the king they need. In *First Blood*, Rambo's former commanding officer takes him into custody and will make sure he will receive a fair trial for the trouble he has caused. John feels purged; he has stood up for his rights, defeated his antagonist and made an important statement about how we treat our veterans.

The King's Speech and First Blood, although wildly different, follow the same three-act formulaic structure. The fundamental elements (event, disturbance, decision, conflict, crisis, obstacles, complication, dark moment, enlightenment, climax and catharsis) all occur in the same order.

The following graph maps the structure of the standard modern formula (top) and Joseph Campbell's elements of universal myth (bottom). Notice the similarities.

Structuring by Numbers

Some modern theorists proclaim that specific moments in the plot must occur on particular pages. This method of screenwriting is much like the

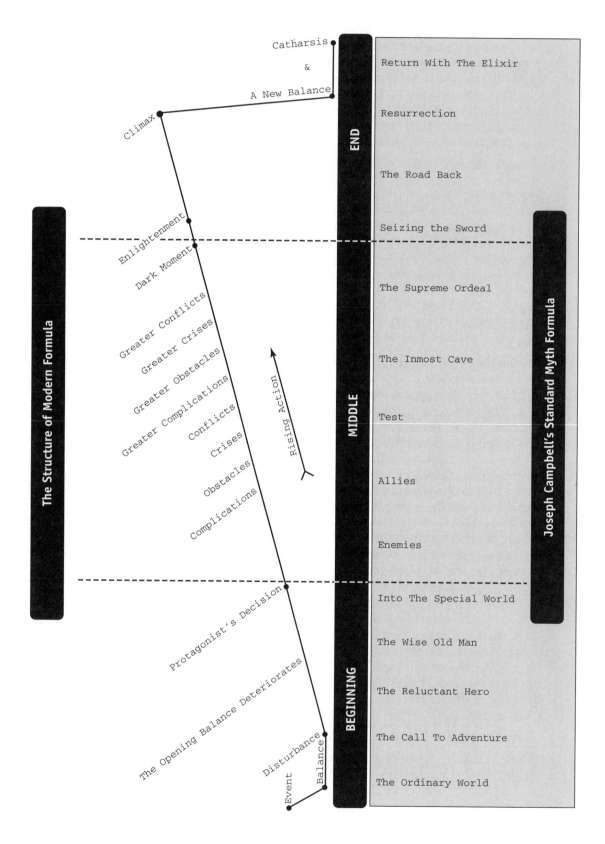

The Structure of Modern Formula

Joseph Campbell's Standard Myth Formula

Catharsis
&
A New Balance

Climax

Enlightenment

Dark Moment

Greater Conflicts

Greater Crises

Greater Obstacles

Greater Complications

Conflicts

Crises

Obstacles

Complications

Rising Action

Protagonist's Decision

The Opening Balance Deteriorates

Disturbance

Event

Balance

END

MIDDLE

BEGINNING

Return With The Elixir

Resurrection

The Road Back

Seizing the Sword

The Supreme Ordeal

The Inmost Cave

Test

Allies

Enemies

Into The Special World

The Wise Old Man

The Reluctant Hero

The Call To Adventure

The Ordinary World

painting-by-numbers you did as a child. Those who follow this model insist that the first "act break" must occur roughly half an hour in, or at the end of 25 to 35 pages. The second act ends by page 85 to 95, and the third by page 115 to 125. As with all the formulas in this chapter, some Hollywood screenwriters have met with a great deal of success by following such tight page number formulas, but the disadvantage is that this rigidity can (and often does) result in mechanical storytelling. Here is an example of what one of these page number formulas might look like. (There are several different samples out there and they don't all follow the same page count.) This one assumes that your screenplay will be 115 pages long.

ACT ONE

Pages 1–11: THE INGREDIENTS—These pages will ask the central questions: What is the ordinary world, who is the protagonist, who is the antagonist, what is the theme, what does the protagonist want and what does he need?

Page 12: THE DISTURBANCE—A new opportunity or problem presents itself to the protagonist.

Pages 13–29: THE CRISIS—Causes the protagonist's life to become unglued.

Page 30: THE CATALYST—Something happens to force the protagonist to act or set a new plan or goal.

ACT TWO

Pages 31–45: THE STRUGGLE—At first the new plan is working out, but the stakes get higher as the antagonist reacts. The road becomes more difficult.

Page 37: THE REVERSAL—First major plot twist or reversal.

Page 45: THE POINT OF NO RETURN—Something happens so that the protagonist cannot return to where he/she was in the beginning.

Pages 46–59: THE STAKES RISE—Complications and stakes make the goal now almost impossible to achieve.

Pages 60–84: THE LOSS OF HOPE—There is a major setback; at this point, the protagonist stops acting on behalf of others or on behalf of what he falsely thinks he needs and starts acting on what he really needs.

Pages 85–89: THE DARK MOMENT—The protagonist at last knows the true nature of the antagonist but, although he now knows the truth, his renewed action again seems doomed to failure.

ACT THREE

Pages 90–95: THE SECOND REVERSAL—The protagonist recovers, often through the aid of an ally, and suddenly the goal is again possible.

Pages 96–111:   THE FINAL PUSH—The conflict intensifies as the protagonist now has the energy or knowledge to defeat the antagonist.
Page 112:   THE FINAL OBSTACLE—The hero achieves the goal.
Pages 113–115:   THE DENOUEMENT—The final catharsis, resolution and look at what the protagonist's new life will be like.

Some page count outlines suggest that a major plot point or twist should occur every fifteen pages, others say it should be every ten pages. We may be fortunate because these page count methods of structuring a screenplay have not yet become so specific that they tell you whether the particular plot point should happen at the top, bottom or middle of a given page. All of this leads to the question: Should all movies follow the exact same formula, right down to the same page count? If so, can't computers do the job?

AUTOMATED STORY DEVELOPMENT

For the last few thousand years, technology has played a minor role in story-telling. Quills, paper, typewriters and computers have slowly replaced the oral tradition, but until recently they have not played a role in the building of a story. This is no longer the case. In the last few years, story creation software has evolved at an amazing pace. Some programs are designed to simply spark a writer's creative juices, others are designed to actually structure a story. Among the many proliferating programs designed to help screenwriters are:

- *Plots Unlimited*, which is inspired by William Wallace Cook's *Plotto*.
- *Collaborator*, which is based on Aristotle's six elements of drama.
- *StoryLine Pro and Blockbuster*, which are based on the teachings of story consultant and script doctor John Truby, who uses a 22-step plot, a deviation from the basic three-act structure.
- *Dramatica*, which is derived from a unique story-building theory called "story mind," which has a four-act structure and is extremely complex.
- *StoryCraft*, which is based on the ideas of Aristotle and Joseph Campbell.
- *StoryWeaver*, which is meant to be an intuitive approach based on Dramatica.

Where will all this formula structuring lead? Recently scientists have built computers that can structure stories on their own. One example is Brutus, the joint creation of Selmer Bringsjord of Rennselaer Polytechnic Institute and David Furuchi of IBM Research. Brutus is a story computer that pushes the limits of artificial intelligence. Brutus is coded with a number of plot structures, story tricks and a working database of literature that allow it to build a basic short story. Brutus, like some screenwriting theorists, reduces plot/structure to pure reason and logic. The result is a less-than-inspiring, computer-generated, formula story, but Brutus is only round one. Computers can now beat humans at *Jeopardy*, so how long will it be until they can construct a better story? The answer is never. Computers lack the human passion, love, talent and self-awareness that allow for the interesting, unpredictable structure of a good, human story. The late great Davey Marlin Jones, playwriting professor at UNLV, said, "A computer could never write as well as a human—it didn't have a bus door slammed in its face this morning."

FINAL THOUGHTS

Form vs. Formula So which of the story structure gurus are right? The answer is...none of them. Or all of them might be, if their models or systems help you to organize the morass of shapeless information with which you begin. Aristotle, Campbell, Cook, Polti, Egri or their modern counterparts Field, Truby, McKee, Vogler and all the others have perceptive ideas and helpful suggestions, and all are worth a look. But the problem remains that a system that works for one story might not work for another. There's no easy, paint-by-numbers, one-size-fits-all formula when it comes to creating a strong, original story, and the unfortunate reliance on formulaic thinking in Hollywood is largely responsible for the current lack of structural innovation and the cookie-cutter quality of so many American studio movies. This is not to say that standard formulas should not be studied, but no one formula or theory will answer all your story-structuring questions. The same is true of the various story design applications: These programs can be useful if they actually help you get into the writing of your script, and if the formulas they use are right for your kind of story. They may not be, and often they become just another form of procrastination, where the would-be writer gets caught up in fooling around with the program's elements and never actually gets to writing the script. There's a great moment in *The Sopranos* where Christopher (Michael Imperioli) has decided to become a filmmaker and buys some screenwriting software, then becomes frustrated when it won't write his script for him. You know who never had the advantage of these programs? Shakespeare, Orson Welles, Billy Wilder, the Epstein brothers, Frank Capra...you get the point.

It's interesting to note that few Hollywood screenwriting gurus have ever sold a movie (even Aristotle never wrote a play, but rather based his *Poetics* on existing tragedies such as Sophocles' *Oedipus Rex*). This is because the ability to structure a story and the ability to analyze the structure of a story are two totally different talents. They come from different parts of the brain. Plato pointed out in his *Apology* that writers are unable to give an exact account of their process. The same is true with top-notch screenwriters; unlike the story computer Brutus or screenwriting gurus, good writers seldom have an analytical understanding of what they do or how they do it. Instead they have a practical understanding of dramatic techniques, the basics of several different storytelling methods (like Aristotle, Campbell and the others), and the ability to use a technique or follow a formula if it works, or to abandon all formulas if they don't.

Isn't there one basic overall guide to help a young writer structure a movie? Isn't there one general theory that will show the common structural elements that all movie plots have? Yes, there is. It's not a cold formula, but rather the natural order that comes from characters and their conflicts. These conflicts organically build in the form of beats, scenes and scene sequences, the natural building-blocks of a good story. In the next two chapters we'll examine how these elements combine to create a natural, nonformulaic approach to structure.

EXERCISES

1. Try working out your story idea using the three-act formula. Add one short sentence to each part of the structure.

> *Act One*
> Opening Event:_____
> Basic Situation: _____
> Disturbance: _____
> Decision:_____
> Dramatic Question: _____
> *Act Two*
> Conflicts: _____
> Crises: _____
> Obstacles:_____
> Complications: _____
> Dark Moment:_____
> *Act Three*
> Enlightenment:_____
> Climax: _____
> Catharsis: _____

2. Try working out your idea using Joseph Campbell's "Hero's Journey."

> The Ordinary World:_____
> The Call to Adventure: _____
> The Reluctant Hero: _____
> The Wise Old Man: _____
> Into the Special World:_____
> Test, Allies and Enemies: _____
> The Inmost Cave:_____
> The Supreme Ordeal: _____
> Seizing the Sword:_____
> The Road Back: _____
> Resurrection:_____
> Return with the Elixir: _____

3. Try working out your idea by chaptering and titling each sequence, with no fewer than seven and no more than sixteen sequences.

7

Power and Conflict

Fighting for the Gun

Looking at dramatic writing empirically, we see that Shakespeare wrote without acts (the five-act structure you find in his plays was imposed by editors years after his death). A hundred years ago, plays commonly had four acts, then three and now most modern plays have only two or one. TV movies have seven acts, while most television shows have from two to seven acts. Of course, each school of thought has ways to prove that, in fact, these various acts are false subdivisions, and that on a deeper level all drama follows their particular model. But all you have to do is go to a movie to realize that movies have no acts at all: we never go to commercial, the curtain never drops.

In film, each moment flows into the next, each scene builds on the last, each grouping of related scenes adds up to larger movements within the story, and finally each larger movement combines with others to form the story as a whole. Each transition from beat to beat, scene to scene, sequence to sequence, presents either a success or setback in the protagonist's power struggle with the antagonist, moving either toward eventual success or failure for the protagonist. There is, of course, a beginning, a middle and an end, but there are no two or three or twelve or twenty main "plot points" that can reliably be found (or planned) in every successful film. Every scene must be, in a sense, a plot point, something in which crucial events and conflict occur, or that scene does not belong in the script.

This isn't to say that structure isn't essential. It is. But it's not a matter of specific page numbers, acts, paradigms or numbered plot points. To demystify it: A screenplay's structure is simply (a) the plan for how its story events and conflicts are arranged into a unified, satisfying journey, and (b) how the different elements of its story (plot, character, conflict, theme) fit together. The key words are "plan," "fit" and "unified." Once your theme, story, world and characters have been identified, you must have a plan, the elements must fit properly and the whole thing must be unified.

So let's look at what a movie really is: a continuum. And the first organizing factor in the structure of this continuum—of its screenplay—is the nature, levels and orchestration of its conflicts. Conflict is at the core of every screenplay, every scene, every character and every moment. A screenplay is

WAR STORIES

Robin

Even though plot points can be identified, they can almost always be shown to be arbitrary. As an exercise, I often challenge my screenwriting students to find the first-act and second-act plot points in a good screenplay, and then show them with equal certainty that, in fact, the plot points are randomly one, two, up to six scenes away in either direction from the ones they identified.

essentially the history of a particular conflict. The story begins with the first inkling of conflict and traces it through a series of peaks as the conflict grows to a climax. Only the final scene, after climax (catharsis), is allowed to be played without conflict—and in some films, not even there. In short, as UCLA screenwriting professor Richard Walter says, "No one wants to watch a movie about the village of the happy people"—unless something really unhappy is about to happen to it.

MAY THE FORCE BE WITH YOU (POWER AND CONFLICT)

In essence, conflict is the result of a struggle for power. We all desire power over our enemies, over our lives, over our destiny. Professor Howard Suber, also of UCLA, puts it in a nutshell: *"All conflict is about power,"* who's got it, who wants it, who or what helps them get it and who or what gets in the way. And therefore, so is all drama, whether tragic or comedic. (Professor Suber's insights and classroom discussions about the fundamental nature of power relationships in drama inform much of this chapter.)

If there is no power struggle, there is no conflict. If there is no conflict, then there is no story, because everyone has what they want or is unwilling to try to get it. To this we might add that a power struggle can also mean aspiring to empowerment. Movies from *Spartacus* and *Big Night* to *Rocky* to *Finding Nemo* to *Precious* are about characters trying to empower their lives. And of course, in following their efforts, the cathartic effect empowers the audience. In human relationships, conflict can be physical or confrontationally verbal, but more often it takes a subtler form. Some of the most devastating sequences in *Hamlet* or *Schindler's List* are very quiet, but boiling with conflict nonetheless.

Let's examine the nature of conflict and power, their forms, the mechanics of how they build a story, the techniques screenwriters use to create them; in short, how conflict and power inform everything from the overall story to each individual scene and sequence.

The Nature of Story—Conflict and Power

Conflict is a defining characteristic of existence, from the Big Bang itself to the birth of stars and mountain ranges, from the Darwinian struggle of predator and prey, species against species, to the difficult relationships between great nations, parents and children, men and women, young and old. It includes all races, all regions, religions and cultures. It is the chaotic cauldron of creation and destruction, its resolution the foundation of order and balance.

The simplest and most visually gripping form of human conflict is physical violence, which is the reason so many movies resort to it. If things are getting slow, a good brawl, gunfight or car chase is a quick way to liven things up. It's active, raw and visceral, an obvious power struggle with an obvious resolution—whoever is stronger/smarter wins. At its lowest common denominator, the fascination with raw conflict is exploited by "tough man" contests or exploitative talk shows, the louder and angrier the better.

And yet, although entertaining to watch in a mindless way, raw or violent conflict alone won't make a good movie. As an example, El Salvador once broke off diplomatic relations with Honduras after massive riots crippled the World Cup Regional Soccer Finals. The extreme conflict during the first two games caused the third game to be played while two thousand police kept control of the fans. On its own, this was fascinating to watch on the evening news, but it was still just raw material, meaningless conflict. For it to become meaningful, the soccer riot would need to be focused on the story of a particular character or set of characters whose dreams depend, for example, on winning the game in spite of the most adverse circumstances. Their victory would be proof of the triumph of civilized human competition in the face of uncivilized rioting. In other words, it would have to move from the general turmoil reported on the news to a personal story with meaning and purpose, a story with which an audience can empathize.

The Mechanics of Conflict and Power

The first steps in building a story are to understand the dynamics of dramatic conflict, and then to apply them in creating characters and circumstances that promote a power struggle, which is the source of conflict. In essence, a power struggle is made up of three elements: *a goal, an obstacle and an inability to compromise.*

Movies are not about people who have idyllic lives; they're about people whose lives are incomplete and who therefore have needs and desires, as we all do. But for there to be story, the need or desire cannot be easily achieved, or the movie will end before it begins: success is predetermined. There must be a barrier, an obstacle or opponent (or a series of these) preventing the protagonist from obtaining what she wants, and finally there must be something that causes an inability to compromise in the struggle to defeat or overcome that obstacle or opponent.

This is different from how most real people act. For example, statistics show that when a woman is involved in an abusive relationship with a wife beater, most will return to the man a shocking seven times before they take action to end the relationship. That's reality—these women continue to compromise their safety. But reality of this sort doesn't make for a good movie, because in a movie—if the woman is the protagonist—she must take action to end her abusive situation. When Uma Thurman's protagonist in *Kill Bill* gets abused, she takes action to gain power and end the relationship, rather definitively (by slicing to pieces everyone responsible).

Compromise for a main character cannot be an option, because it is the end of conflict. If the protagonist or antagonist is willing and able to compromise in any way and does, the conflict is over and so is the story. However, if the protagonist is willing or able to compromise in a positive way and doesn't, he will also lose sympathy. The only way to solve these problems is to eliminate the possibility of compromise altogether. Story occurs when there can be no mutual agreement, because the antagonist won't allow it and/or the protagonist's desire is too great. Often the lack of compromise is justified by using an event (a scene) to show why the protagonist and antagonist cannot find a middle ground and are irrevocably committed to confronting each other. The result is a power struggle. It's a simple equation:

Desire + Obstacle × Lack of Compromise = Conflict

Here are some examples:

1. *Desire*—She wants money for new textbooks.
2. *Obstacle*—He wants to balance the school's budget.
3. *Reason Compromise Is Not an Option*—The student test scores are the lowest in the state.

1. *Desire*—Kim desires the wedding of her dreams.
2. *Obstacle*—Her mother wants to choose the bridesmaids.
3. *Reason Compromise Is Not an Option*—*Bride* magazine will be there and will offer Kim a job if it goes well.

1. *Desire*—I must avenge my friend's death.
2. *Obstacle*—I do not know who killed him.
3. *Reason Compromise Is Not an Option*—I have been accused of the murder.

Notice that the third element is what makes the story possible. The desire and obstacle may be interesting, but the reason the story exists is because compromise is not an option.

However, compromise can be used in a subplot as a contrast to, or a motivating factor for, the main plot. For example, in a subplot of *The Godfather*, Sonny and Michael's sister Connie is married to an abusive husband; she'll complain about him, but will not leave him. Her compromising attitude contrasts with that of Sonny, who beats the guy up. And when it's revealed that the husband beat Connie in order to lure Sonny into an ambush, Michael (the protagonist) has him killed. There is no compromise allowed, even though the guy is the father of Michael's godchild. After he's been killed, Connie mourns for him, her attitude of compromise unchanging, but its presence has been the trap that springs the story.

What Doesn't Kill You Makes You Stronger

There is a tendency to equate conflict only with destructiveness, but in fact it is also the basis of creation. In a movie, conflict must result in growth or new wisdom (what James Joyce called *epiphany*). A world out of balance is restored to equilibrium, or at least is more profoundly understood. Success or failure depends almost by definition on a power struggle—the sickly patient battles against diseases, the seedling pushes its way to the surface, the oppressed rise up to correct injustice, a tyrant crushes the leader of the opposition and imposes servitude on his country, a serial killer destroys the cop who's after him, resulting in a darker understanding of the nature of the world. Conflict with positive results can be like exercise—when your muscles work hard against some form of resistance, the result is a lot of sweat, but also a stronger body. This kind of conflict arises from an attempt to effect change for the good, although it doesn't come easily in nature or in human character. Conflict with negative results can be like a cancer eating away at a healthy body; it consumes or destroys the good.

The power struggle at the heart of many movies has moral connotations: there is good power and evil power. Mr. Smith is good, the corrupt Senators in Washington, D.C., are evil. Silkwood is good, the nuclear power industry is evil. Little David kills Goliath and Moses defeats Pharaoh because they have the power of God (good) on their side, while the power of their enemies is worldly (evil or profane). The protagonist's acquisition of good power often comes from acquiring wisdom without loss of innocence, while the antagonist's bad power comes from the darker side of human desires. Spiritual or emotional enlightenment is positive, while carnal knowledge is negative. Love, morality and personal convictions are good, while selfishness and ruthlessness are evil. These polarities imply that at the heart of a story is a reversal. At the beginning, the world is out of balance because of the antagonist's exercise of bad power. When the protagonist overcomes the antagonist and the power polarity is reversed, good overcomes evil, the protagonist wins, the antagonist loses and we all go home happy that the world has such marvelous order. Or the protagonist loses, and we all end up miserable.

But not all movies are about a struggle between opposing moral positions, one of which necessitates destruction of the other; conflict and power reversal do not only apply to good against evil or positive versus negative. Antagonism can also occur between two good people or causes; likewise the term "antagonist" does not necessarily imply an evil element or character. To the ancient Greeks, who invented the term, the antagonist was simply "the opposing combatant." There was no thought of the antagonist being evil, corrupt or immoral. The antagonist was simply the character or force who stood in the way of the protagonist's action. The same still holds true.

For example, in a love story, boy meets girl, boy loses girl, boy gets girl (or in the modern version: girl meets boy, boy is gay, they become close friends). True, the lovers are in oppositional conflict with each other and there is a power struggle (often comical) to reach the same positive goal—love—but it is not a conflict between good and evil, although the conflict may have moral overtones, such as self-sacrifice vs. selfishness. The one who is in love is the protagonist, the one who denies love is the antagonist. Other examples might be dramas or comedies like *Driving Miss Daisy* or *Eternal Sunshine of the Spotless Mind* or *The Odd Couple*, where neither character is "good" or "bad," they're just very different and the differences, combined with their situation, cause a power struggle and conflict.

Feelings, Nothing More than Feelings ...

Many young screenwriters confuse conflict with emotional situations. An emotional situation can be a private outpouring of feelings, a special occasion or a vivid theatrical event. A screenplay can and should be full of emotional situations, but these must also involve conflict (or its eventual resolution) if the story is going to sustain itself. *Conflict isn't inherently present in a scene just because it's emotional.* Many emotional situations have no conflict. A wedding may be emotional, but is there conflict if everyone is happy? Is there a desire, obstacle and lack of compromise (for instance, Hugh Grant's hilarious discomfort and hopeless desire to be elsewhere in *Four Weddings and a Funeral*)? A retirement party may be full of emotional moments and surprises, as old friends celebrate the past, but is there conflict? Not unless someone wants something, someone or something stands in the way of his obtaining it, and there is no compromise (for instance, a story in which a man has been forced to retire, and this party is the scene where he rebels or decides to get even).

The Super Bowl has conflict, but the emotional award ceremony after it does not. A kiss may be emotional, but it lacks conflict unless someone doesn't want the kiss to happen (not necessarily one of the kissers, either—it could be their parents, as in *Romeo and Juliet*). Both of these events, without conflict, would only be appropriate in the cathartic final scene, where the conflict is resolved.

Or let's look at an emotional funeral. Everyone is crying. One by one the mourners get up and remember their dear, departed friend. We have tremendous misery mixed with fond remembrances. Later, at the grave, as the sun sets in streaks of blue and pink, a lone bagpipe blows a sad tune. The scene is very emotional, even visually compelling, yet in a screenplay it will not be interesting because no one has a goal, obstacle or a lack of compromise. Yet, if the eulogies turn to threats and accusations, if one person sees the other as a barrier or challenge to his goal, if just one of the mourners has an ulterior motive and someone tries to stop him, if there is a hint that this funeral is only the lull before the storm, now we have conflict. Now we have drama. Now we have an interesting scene. In *Four Weddings and a Funeral*, the death of a friend forces Hugh Grant's character to confront his own reluctance to commit to the woman he can barely admit to himself he loves; here, the protagonist is in conflict with himself. The core of a screenplay is conflict, not emotional moments. Both are needed, both are important, but the emotions must arise from or cause conflict, until the resolution in which balance is restored.

THE ORCHESTRATION OF POWER AND CONFLICT

The first step is to create characters and circumstances that involve or promise conflict. This means that the screenwriter must orchestrate (i.e., arrange or change) the conflict between the protagonist and antagonist so that it seems inevitable—they not only are the best two opponents for this story, but must seem like the only opponents possible. The second step is to arrange the types of conflict into a progressively rising and compounding series of power struggles as your scenes and sequences develop. Fundamentally, it is the orchestration of this progressively complex power struggle into sequences of rising action that defines the conflict and shapes the structure of the screenplay.

The David and Goliath Factor

The protagonist always starts from a position of disadvantage (less power). At the beginning, *your protagonist must be or appear to be weaker than the antagonist*. Both characters must have deep desires and strong justifications, but if your protagonist starts out stronger than your antagonist, your story will be boring because it is essentially over before it begins. The resolution can only go one way; your protagonist will win because he or she has the power to do so from the get-go. The antagonist must have so much power that your protagonist's chances for success are always in doubt until the climax. If your story is weak or boring, the problem can almost always be traced to a weak antagonist or a too-powerful protagonist.

No matter how strong the protagonist, the antagonist must be stronger in some way, have some crucial power that could spell defeat for his opponent. This is why Superman needs kryptonite; without it, the antagonist would have no chance. It is also why someone like James Bond is always up against an antagonist with such enormous intellectual, economic and military capabilities that he threatens to control or destroy the world. Only someone like that could put someone like James Bond at a disadvantage. But as with James Bond, each protagonist must have the raw material to learn or acquire the specific power he needs to overcome each specific adversary, which is why he will be the right protagonist for this particular conflict.

Circles of Influence

The world and the characters in a movie can be seen as going from the most personal to the most impersonal. Howard Suber illustrates these levels as concentric circles, with the individual at the center and society as the largest, outermost circle. These are the levels where different kinds of conflict originate.

The Individual   This is the person with whom we identify, the protagonist. (Even in buddy movies, usually there is one person who is more important.) Think of a soldier in Vietnam, as in *Platoon*.

The Family or Team This group is composed of people who inhabit the protagonist's home turf and its small constellation of personal friends or relatives. Family may be there at the start, or if the protagonist is a drifter, he'll acquire them early on. The family or team forms a unit that supports the protagonist; it may perhaps initially oppose what he wants to do—one kind of conflict—though the protagonist will win the family over in the end. Allies and mentors sometimes appear here. Think of the soldier's best buddies in the platoon, along with the good sergeant who offers mentoring wisdom.

The Community This group is a little less personal, but it comprises the protagonist's immediate world, where everyone seems to be on the same side. Think of the soldier's platoon as a whole.

The Society In the world of the story, society is impersonal. It is hard and cruel, caring nothing for the individual, and is ruled by powerful people who have been corrupted by their power. *It is this society that defines the world in which and against which the protagonist acts*.

In this case, think of the society as the corrupt military and the Vietnam War as the world. The evil sergeant is our antagonist because, although part of the community of the soldier's platoon, he embodies the soulless evil of war itself. And he kills the good sergeant, a member of his own community, the mentor with whom the protagonist identifies.

The Intimate Enemy

Often, the conflict is orchestrated so that protagonist and antagonist share more similarities than differences; they are intimate enemies. Even if the antagonist often comes from the outermost circle of the protagonist's experience (from the impersonal society) he often, paradoxically, will have originally come from the protagonist's past or inner circles of team or community. Because the protagonist and antagonist are similar and perhaps have shared experiences, they become more inevitable as adversaries. In fact, part of the antagonist's superior power position at the beginning may come precisely from the fact that he knows the protagonist well enough to use his weaknesses. In *Crimson Tide*, for instance, the antagonist is the captain of the sub, and we are told he is "one of the three most powerful men" on the planet. The protagonist is his lieutenant—in fact, he chose the protagonist to accompany him on this mission—and so they are of the same world and appear to share the same community. But the antagonist is again part of the "society" of war, while the protagonist is introduced as part of the "team" of friends and family, only to have to make a choice to stand against his former patron. The same situation happens in the first *Mission: Impossible* movie, in *Avatar*, and many other examples.

You and I Are Not So Different, Mr. Bond...

Intimacy between your protagonist and antagonist will help you ensure that they both want or need the same thing. Both want love. Both want the

Maltese Falcon. Both want the Grail. Both want to win the race. Both want the bomb, one to use it, one to stop him from using it. Both have become, at the end, almost equally powerful, with the protagonist winning (if he does) because he has the power of virtue on his side. This derives from the fact that the best antagonist is the dark doppelgänger, the shadow or mirror image of the protagonist—that's why they're inevitably drawn into a fundamental and personal conflict with one another (it's also why the antagonist is often the protagonist's own inner self—he's his own worst enemy). It's also why, incidentally, so many action movies have a final battle where the villain says, "I know you, you're the same as I am," and the hero says, "I'm nothing like you." With that, the hero kills the villain—his dark alter ego. Alternately, in the case of a tragedy, the protagonist loses because he is unable to overcome his internal obstacles, which fatally disempower him in his struggle with the antagonist.

The Ebb and Flow of Conflict and Power

Most stories combine more than one type of power struggle. Usually the screenplay adds in and orchestrates different levels of conflict over the course of the action in order to build a progressively more involving, multilayered story. Sometimes a different kind of conflict will be introduced, sometimes the same kind in a different context. This addition and progression is an important factor in story construction. As more types of conflict—more obstacles—are added, the overall intensity and complexity of the protagonist's struggle increases, until they are progressively overcome and finally eliminated by the protagonist in the climactic victory (in the case of a comedic ending) or until they relentlessly combine and compound to crush the protagonist (in a tragic ending).

TYPES OF STORY CONFLICT

There are essentially two categories of conflict: external and internal. External conflict is antagonist-driven or situation-driven, while internal conflict deals with the protagonist's own character flaw, ghost or personal dilemma. External conflict falls into four general groups: character vs. character, character vs. society, character vs. nature and character vs. fate, while internal conflict involves character vs. self.

Character vs. Character

Simply put, in this type of conflict two characters want something and believe only one can have it, or one character has something (or is about to have it) and another wants to get it from her (or prevent her from getting it). The protagonist is the one the audience wants to succeed in the struggle, while the antagonist is the one the audience wishes to fail. Often this interpersonal conflict involves a good protagonist and an evil antagonist, but as we've seen, this is not always the case. Almost every Hollywood movie has this kind of conflict, and it's worth noting that most love stories use character vs. character conflicts.

Character vs. Society

The old phrase "You can't fight City Hall" expresses our sense of powerlessness as individuals against the impersonal might of society. When an individual decides to challenge society against all odds, it creates conflict. The protagonist faces the obstacle of organizational opposition, and in a happy ending proves the theme that an individual can make a difference. In an unhappy ending, the protagonist may be crushed for his efforts, proving a darker theme that one person cannot defeat the system. "Society" can mean many things: another government, our government, the military, the IRS, the CIA, the Nazis, aliens from outer space—in short, "them," any of the huge, impersonal forces that can control, threaten or ruin "us," our lives or communities.

In order for character vs. society stories to work, society—the antagonist—must be given a face, a character or group that personifies the faceless threat. There are plays, such as *Waiting for Godot* or *Rosencrantz and Guildenstern Are Dead*, where the faceless universe remains a mysterious and irresistible force, but these are rare even in theater, and even more rare in good films. In films, we want to see the antagonist one way or another in order to emotionally understand its presence and threat. This antagonist represents all of society's dreaded power and can bring all of its resources to bear against the singular protagonist. *Dead Poet's Society, All the President's Men, Silkwood, Three Days of the Condor, Mr. Smith Goes to Washington, One Flew Over the Cuckoo's Nest* and *Gallipoli* are all examples of stories in which the main conflict focuses on character vs. society.

Character vs. Nature

This kind of story traps the protagonist in a battle with the environment. The geography or natural disasters become the obstacle (antagonist) as the protagonist tries to make it from point A to point B, to safety. As with character vs. society conflicts, the physical environment can be enormously powerful, impersonal and threatening. It creates a test of the protagonist's courage and abilities, but the question of whether a human being can succeed against the irrational forces of nature is seldom enough to sustain an entire movie. This problem is often addressed by having the environmental threat motivate character vs. character conflicts among a group who must make the journey together. The source of this conflict may in fact be the hubris of the one or more characters who got everyone into such a dangerous spot in the first place. (Most mountain climbing or dangerous-trek stories involve this conflict.) *Alive, White Squall, Jurassic Park, Into Thin Air, Volcano, Twister, Titanic* and *The Poseidon Adventure, 127 Hours,* even *2012,* all include character vs. nature conflict.

Character vs. Fate

To the ancient Greeks, Fate was a real force in the world, and most classical tragedies fall into this model. For instance, Oedipus was fated to kill his father and marry his mother. Even though his parents heard this prophecy and left him to die as an infant, he survived and unwittingly fulfilled it. There was nothing he or they could do about it, try as they might. Drama arises when humans, seeking to express their individuality and free will, come into conflict with the preordained plans of the gods. With the advent of realism and the notion that people create their own destinies, writers have become less concerned with fate, real or imagined. Hollywood has made a few movies with old-fashioned character vs. fate conflicts, but they are almost always based on ancient stories (like *Jason and the Argonauts* and the Steve Reeves *Hercules* films) and have plenty of other forms of conflict to sustain the story. Modern writers have replaced fate with other innate limitations: the characters' own fears and the limitations imposed by their sex or race or age or the constraints of the world in which they've grown up. An example would be *Norma Rae*, also a character vs. society story, in which Sally Field's character not only fights the male-dominated factory management but also her own quiet, shy nature and her lowly place in life in order to unionize a factory. In *American Graffiti*, the teenagers struggle with the limitations and low expectations imposed upon them by small town life. In the end, some succeed in overcoming their fate, while others give in to it. Unlike the ancient Greek tragedies, in modern movies fate is ultimately determined not by the gods, but by the protagonist's actions.

The Last Picture Show, The Adjustment Bureau, Bonnie and Clyde and *Butch Cassidy and the Sundance Kid* all have character vs. fate conflict.

Character vs. Self

Internal conflict—character vs. self—involves a character's struggle with an inner flaw (like fear, alcoholism, mental illness), a moral doubt (should I or shouldn't I?) or a psychic wound (such as responsibility for the death of a loved one). Internal conflict is present in almost all good films; the protagonist will start with some fear or failure of character that she must overcome in order to face the larger, external conflict presented by an antagonist. But, occasionally, a story deals primarily, if not exclusively, with this kind of internal antagonist, as the character grapples with an aspect of his or her own self. These internal conflicts, agonizing decisions, misgivings or self-hatred often result in a moral tale. *Dr. Jekyll and Mr. Hyde* is an obvious example, in which two sides of a man's character are physically separated into protagonist and antagonist. But, more often, the character's internal struggle with self is more subtle. In *Days of Wine and Roses*, the protagonist struggles with his drinking; in *How to Make an American Quilt*, she wrestles with her own doubts about love and marriage; in *Death of a Salesman*, he struggles to overcome his sense of being a failure; in *Charly* and *Eternal Sunshine of the Spotless Mind*, he is at war with the deterioration of his own mind. *Finding Nemo* is about a father overcoming his own agoraphobic fears in order to find his son. An internal power struggle can also happen if the character is facing a difficult moral dilemma. For example, suppose a soldier must choose between staying with the pregnant wife he loves or answering his country's call to duty; it's not clear at all whether love or duty is the right choice.

In a character vs. self story, the conflict is not on the surface and so can be harder to demonstrate in a filmic way. (Movies are pictures, and pictures can't always show what someone is thinking.) In theater, a character like Hamlet or Willie Loman (*Death of a Salesman*) can express their internal struggle through long soliloquies or monologues, but film has little patience for this. The conflict can be externalized by creating additional characters to reflect the inner conflict. In the delightful *Crossing Delancey*, a New York bookstore manager must come to understand her contradictory feelings about men and marriage. Her internal struggle is externalized by having her encounter a nutty singer in a deli who sings about love, having her grandmother harangue her, and having her date two men who couldn't be more different, the pickle salesman who represents the core decency of her nature, and the egocentric poet who represents her own petty intellectual ambitions and pretensions. Confronting the internal antagonist means confronting the protagonist's own demons, and in doing so, the protagonist either manages to overcome them or, as in *Leaving Las Vegas*, may be overcome by them. (For more on internal conflict, see Chapter 5.)

How Conflicts Combine

Action and adventure movies present conflict in its clearest, most visceral form—character vs. character violence—yet they can also be about internal and other forms of conflict. In *Cliffhanger*, Stallone's mountain-climbing protagonist Gabe is disempowered by the self-doubts and self-hatred from having failed to save the life of his best friend's lover (character vs. self). That best friend now hates him (character vs. character) and they must join up to rescue survivors of a plane crash. The survivors are high-tech thieves and killers, and while Gabe quickly escapes from them (another character vs. character level), his best friend does not, and his life now depends on Gabe. The antagonist has great power: intelligence, absolute ruthlessness and a team of trained assassins brought from the outside world (character vs. society). Gabe, alone on the snowy mountain, stripped even of protective clothing (character vs. nature), must somehow save his friend and defeat this antagonist. He is the perfect protagonist for this challenge because of his skills as a mountain-climber and the ghost he must put to rest. As he uses his knowledge of the mountains to his own advantage, he overcomes his fears, and is further empowered by the love and assistance of an ally, his girlfriend. Conversely, as the antagonist loses members of his team and becomes ensnared by the protagonist's superior knowledge of the mountains, the antagonist's power level progressively falls until, by the final showdown (climax), he is overcome.

In *Star Wars*, the idea of conflict as a moral power struggle is explicit: Darth Vader represents the dark side of "the Force," and therefore has negative power over the galaxy. The protagonist (Luke) starts disempowered: alone, without knowledge, without the power of The Force, but compelled to acquire it if he is to succeed. Helping him are mentors and allies. (There is also character vs. character conflict with these allies—Obi Wan, Princess Leia and Han Solo. These conflicts do not involve good vs. evil, but rather depression vs. encouragement, the desire to take action vs. obstinacy, greed vs. altruism.) Hindering Luke are adversaries in league with the antagonist (character vs. society) and/or Luke's own fears and limitations (character vs. self). It is only when Luke learns to channel the power of the good side of The Force and accept the help of allies and mentors that he wins: the power balance shifts from antagonist to protagonist as the story develops. When Luke is strong enough to overcome the obstacles that Darth Vader, the antagonist, represents, it is both a personal victory (character vs. character) and a victory over the forces of evil (character vs. society).

Clear conflict levels (different kinds of power struggle) are not limited to action films, however. They inform the structure of any good film. In *The Verdict*, Paul Newman's character is an underdog, alcoholic failure (character vs. self) who must fight virtually alone against an opponent referred to as "The Prince of Darkness," an unbeatable lawyer (character vs. character) with nearly infinite resources and a mighty law firm to back him. The antagonist ironically represents the institution of the Church (character vs. society), which has forgotten its values. In order to win, Paul Newman's lowly attorney must give up the vice of drinking in order to gain power, and overcome the obstacles such as lust that his opponent provides (character vs. self/character vs. character), as well as his own inclination to give in to the cardinal sin of despair (character vs. self). He gains the power of goodness by appealing to the innocent decency of the ordinary people on the jury, rather than the corrupted, institutional power of the judge (character vs. society).

The Piano, hardly a traditional Hollywood film, is set in the nineteenth century. It is the story of Ada, a mute, disempowered Scottish widow (character vs. self) who travels with her small daughter to New Zealand as a mail-order bride for a wealthy, respectable farmer she's never met. She also brings her prized piano; her music is her only way to express herself and provides a source of internal power. However, when the farmer arrives at the wild beach where she's been left, he refuses to bring the piano along (character vs. character) on the arduous journey to his home (character vs. nature). This takes away her "voice," a disempowering setback. It falls to an earthy, tattooed fellow who is more sexually uninhibited and in tune with things native to rescue the piano (power restored by another). He eventually seduces her by offering to "sell" it to her a few keys at a time in exchange for lessons. At first Ada resists the arrangement, resentful of having to buy back something that is already hers (character vs. self, character vs. character), but the exchanges quickly become lessons in erotic empowerment for her. Her husband tries to lock Ada in their house (a disempowering setback), but she regains power and achieves victory by escaping to the arms of her natural man.

Since the primary antagonist in each case is external, the protagonist's internal handicaps of fear, alcoholism, personal insecurity or resentment can be considered structurally as allies of the antagonist, who uses them against the protagonist. Defeating these internal opponents helps to disempower the antagonist.

The internal flaws or wounds also serve to engage our empathy for the protagonists by giving them personal vulnerabilities to which we can relate. By contrast, in the unsuccessful Christmas movie *Jingle All the Way*, an Arnold Schwarzenegger movie you probably never heard of, his character does not engage us. He comes into conflict with the postman (character vs. character), crowds at shopping centers (character vs. society) and winter (character vs. nature) in order to find the perfect gift—but there is no internal (character vs. self) conflict. Arnold might be mad at himself for not getting the gift earlier, but he has no doubt that he should get the gift and get it now. He has no moral debate, no internal conflict within his own psychological makeup.

It's not just that it's a comedy; successful comedies like *Annie Hall, Groundhog Day, There's Something About Mary, Dodgeball* or *City Slickers* have protagonists in hilarious conflict with themselves, as well as with others and their environments. There are some very successful comedies that do not involve character vs. self, such as the Pink Panther, *Dude, Where's My Car?* and Ace Ventura films, but in these cases the protagonists and their actions are so extreme and absurdly in conflict with everything around them that there is more than enough to generate humor. In *Jingle All the Way*, the protagonist is shown as just a regular guy, so without internal conflict he's just a regular bore.

All of the above examples are structurally "comedies" not because they're all funny, but because the protagonist succeeds. Most American films end this way, but many foreign films and a few of the best American films do not, and follow a tragic model. In the case of a "tragedy," the power shift is reversed: a protagonist with some power faces adversaries interior or exterior, and ultimately is left powerless.

Sometimes in a tragedy someone powerless will acquire power, be blind to what it means, and then lose it again, as in the *Godfather* series. In this case, Michael, the protagonist, actually has the power of innocence at the beginning but abandons it in favor of the corrupt power of "the family." The protagonist may also lose what it was he wanted the power for—love, happiness, belonging—as in the case of *King Lear*. In tragic stories, the protagonist's internal failing is usually a moral vice, such as pride or vanity, which is so embedded in the protagonist's character that it cannot be overcome, and this moral vice proves the character's undoing. It goes back to the ancient Greek notion of every great protagonist having a "fatal flaw," a *hamartia* that is more precisely translated as a crucial blind spot in their nature that prevents them from overcoming their Fate. Such characters are at war with themselves, unable to see the truth that is destroying them, and so their better instincts are defeated by the stronger, darker forces within their own psyches. In these cases, the *hamartia* is the primary antagonist, and the story becomes a conflict of character vs. self.

Take, for example, the brilliant Australian film *Gallipoli*. Here, society—represented by the murderous arrogance and institutional stupidity of the British military—defeats the protagonist, a soldier whose efforts to stop an order to send his unit and his best friend into certain death comes too late. The soldier is athletic, cocky and has an empowering friendship—his competitor, the only boy who can outrun him—but the overwhelming might and stupidity of the British military and the limitations of his own abilities combine to defeat him. This is a modern tragedy, in which the impersonal forces of war are too great for our protagonist to overcome. His own earlier arrogance (fatal flaw, character vs. self) about his athleticism comes back to haunt him when he cannot run quickly enough to save those he loves.

Upping the Stakes

In every struggle for power there is something to lose. When a screenwriter "ups the stakes" she is making the possible failure and its consequences as great as the story can handle. This can be taken to extremes, as in *Star Wars* where the entire galaxy is at stake, or it can mean a small loss that clearly implies greater repercussions. For example, the old sitcom *The Wonder Years* was full of power struggles that, if forfeited, implied a major loss that would affect the boy's relationships, friendships and loves for the rest of his life. The conflict must involve stakes that are high enough that an audience will care whether or not it is resolved. This is a huge problem for many first-time screenwriters: they make the stakes so low, so commonplace or negligible that they cannot generate enough interest to carry the story.

The Stakes	*Upping the Stakes*
The head of a small Savings and Loan is under great financial pressure. This will ruin his family. He is going to kill himself. He wishes that he had never lived.	If he hadn't lived (if he kills himself) not only would his family have been ruined, but the entire town and all its people would have been ruined by an evil banker.
An accident. A horse is badly injured by a logging truck. A woman takes the animal to a "horse whisperer" to be healed.	The daughter was injured and her friend killed in the same accident. The daughter has developed deep psychological scars that will not heal if the horse does not recover. The mother falls in love with the horse whisperer and must choose between her family and the man of her dreams.
When a big city detective discovers that there are corrupt murderers running the police department, he sets out to stop them or die trying.	An Amish boy witnesses the murder and must be protected. The detective falls in love with the boy's Amish mother. All of them now face death.

The stakes in a film work when the characters and premise contain enough potential conflict to justify them and when the conflict is orchestrated with progressive levels of complexity and intensity.

The Trap

The trap is the way you ensure the impossibility of compromise. *Publisher's Weekly* once released a list of children's book titles that were rejected. One of the titles was *The Little Train that Could but Chose Not To*. Inherent in this title is the reason it was rejected. The story lacked a "trap" to force the essential power struggle. In other words, the premise did not contain potential for conflict, because the protagonist was not motivated to engage in any; he was willing to compromise. Once the antagonist is in a position of power over the protagonist, once the protagonist is even aware of the antagonist (internal or external), they must be put on a collision course. This is set up with a trap: a situation, environment, time lock (an unavoidable deadline) or character trait that makes it impossible for the protagonist and antagonist to leave or back down to avoid conflict. They must act.

Often the trap is implied in the title. In *Jurassic Park*, the scientist physically cannot escape from an island full of cloned dinosaurs, although he might like to. In *Not Without My Daughter*, Sally Field's character cannot leave Iran (leave the conflict) until she rescues her daughter—not because it isn't physically possible, but because she is trapped by her love and moral responsibilities. The most famous example of a title expressing the trap is *High Noon*. In this movie, the trap is time: the bad men are arriving on the noon train and the sheriff is driven by his own moral code to confront them. Every good dramatic story has a trap. In the ancient Greek tragedy *Oedipus Rex*, the city of Thebes is racked by plagues, forcing the king to act now to find its cause and end it. In Ibsen's *A Doll's House*, Nora must act before her husband discovers the forgery, or face disgrace. In Walt Disney's *Bambi*, there's the fire, in *Alive* there's the threat of starvation, in *Juno* and *Young Adult* there's the impending birth of a child. The trap is an event, situation, time lock or character trait that forces a character to stand and take action.

Motivation

The ultimate trap is character. Powerful conflicts grow out of characters who have strong motivations and are not willing to compromise. Often, beginning screenwriters arbitrarily put their characters in direct opposition to each other without creating a reason. But coldly manipulating the characters into opposite corners of a boxing ring means that you are puppeteering them into conflict rather than generating the conflict out of deep motivations and needs. Say you're writing about a young daughter who wants to marry the boy she loves; she's our protagonist and it's a match made in heaven. A simplistic way to create conflict would be to turn the girl's father into an evil, power-hungry guardian who wants to control and perhaps destroy his daughter's life. And she just loves the boy because she does. Juliet in this mold would have been kept from Romeo because of simple, controlling selfishness by her father, and she would have no idea why she was in love with Romeo. It's the same as in old, programmed Westerns where the pure, honorable homesteader fights off the wicked land baron whose soul is as dark as midnight. This form of conflict descends directly from the Miracle and Mystery Plays of the Middle Ages, in which pure good faced pure evil. It's true that great conflict can be drawn this way, but a more satisfying conflict comes when two opposing characters both see themselves, their goals and desires as righteous, honorable and worthy of the good fight (whether they are or not is another question). This is how Shakespeare, although coming out of the Miracle and Mystery Play tradition, developed some of the elements even plays where it's not so obvious. For instance, in *Romeo and Juliet*, Juliet's father is a good man, trying to do the best for her within the confines of his prejudices and social constraints. Romeo has won Juliet over with his declarations of selfless passion and his claims that he is her soulmate. Her father's angry insistence that she marry the man of his choice rather than hers leads to her death, but this fact is not a reflection of his evil nature, but rather of his very human nature. The fact that she chooses Romeo reflects her trap: she cannot deny her own passion. Now instead of good vs. evil, Shakespeare has the most powerful form of conflict of all: good vs. good.

Good writers create powerful motivations that cause their characters to act, and draw them inevitably into opposition. The characters oppose each other not because the writer forces them to, but because the characters both desperately want the same thing or want to prevent each other from achieving their goals. They are not manipulated into conflict. Rather, because of the way the writer has created their backstory, orchestrated their needs and desires and motivated their conflicts, they simply cannot avoid it. The more complex your characters' motivations, the more interesting they and the journey of your story will be.

REVIEW
1. *Protagonist*—He, she or it must be in a weakened, inferior and threatened position at the beginning of the screenplay as a result of some internal failing or ghost. But the protagonist must also be capable of generating or eventually acquiring the power to overcome the obstacles presented by the antagonist.
2. *Antagonist*—He, she or it must not be weak or your conflict will be weak. The antagonist must be in a position of power from the start and unwilling to surrender power easily.
3. *Motivation*—There must be a strong reason(s) behind the characters' desire(s) and a definite need that must be fulfilled.
4. *Compromise*—Your protagonist and antagonist must be trapped in a situation in which there is no possibility of mutual agreement.
5. *Obstacles*—There must be a sufficient number of obstacles to thwart the protagonist, and they must grow in intensity.
6. *Emotion vs. Conflict*—The story must be built on one or more of the basic conflicts, not just on a string of emotional moments.

Other Aspects of Conflict (Conflict and Scene)

Every scene up to the resolution must contain conflict, immediate or imminent, which is related to the action or theme of the overall story. If the scene doesn't contain immediate conflict, there must be implied conflict waiting around the next bend. This threat can be used to charge an entire movie or a single scene with suspense. Let's look at a problem scene from a student screenplay about life on the home front during the Vietnam War. It's 1969 and Jon, Gina, George and Idemary are going to Lover's Lane:

```
EXT. LOVER'S LANE — NIGHT

Jon's Volkswagen follows a two-rutted road.

Here the road widens and splits into several parking
spots. Each occupied with cars and high school kids at
different stages of the mating ritual.

INT. JON'S VOLKSWAGEN — CONTINUOUS

In the front seat, Gina is passionately, if not rather
professionally, kissing Jon. He's too cool to respond.

In the back, Idemary leans in to kiss George. They
are less experienced. She takes careful aim. Docking
procedure commences. It's almost that romantic. George
is the Apollo spacecraft. Idemary is the Lunar Module.
One slip up and they'll crash into each other and tumble
into the sun.

                    IDEMARY
         I love you, George.

                    GEORGE
         I love you, too. But I'm not ready for
         this.

                    IDEMARY
         I totally understand.
```

This is boring because it lacks conflict! There is nothing to keep the reader interested. It's not that there is no immediate conflict—there is some nervous adolescent fumbling around—but it is extremely low-stakes. And there is no hint that any greater conflict is imminent. Now here is the same scene with both.

```
EXT. LOVER'S LANE — NIGHT

Jon's Volkswagen slows near a peeling "NO TRESPASSING"
sign. The warning has been riddled by shotgun blasts.

Jon veers off the blacktop and follows a two-rutted road
```

into the darkness.

Here the road widens and splits into several parking spots. Each occupied with cars and high school kids at different stages of the mating ritual.

Jon pulls up within a few inches of the cliff. A chunk of dirt breaks loose from beneath the wheels of the car and tumbles down a hundred feet, disintegrating as it hits the banks of the Wabash River.

INT. JON'S VOLKSWAGEN — NIGHT

George SCREAMS, alarmed.

>   GEORGE
>   Nobody breathe!

>   JON
>   Relax, enjoy the view.

George peeks out, unsure.

>   GEORGE
>   Perhaps if we all lean to this side,
>   we'll live.

>   IDEMARY
>   Isn't this romantic?

Idemary wants to be tongued. George considers his options. The cliff or Idemary.

In the front seat, Gina is passionately, if not rather professionally, kissing Jon. He's too cool to respond.

In back, Idemary leans in to kiss George. They are less experienced. She takes careful aim. Docking procedure commences. It's almost that romantic. George is the Apollo spacecraft. Idemary is the Lunar Module. One slip up and they'll crash into each other and tumble into the sun.

>   IDEMARY
>   I love you, George.

>   GEORGE
>   I love you too, I think...

```
                    IDEMARY
          Kiss me.


                    GEORGE
          I'm not ready for this.

     Idemary pulls a condom from her purse.

                    IDEMARY
          I am.


     George pulls back. The car shifts slightly as more dirt
     crumbles under its wheels, spilling down the cliff. Jon
     and Gina don't notice, but George throws open the door
     opposite and jumps out.
```

In the first scene, there is no conflict. Idemary wants it, George doesn't, and she understands. The scene is over before it begins. In the second scene, Idemary wants it, is not willing to compromise, and this produces immediate conflict. But more, there is also imminent conflict—the symbolic as well as real possibility that they may go over the edge. There is suspense as to what will happen next. The imminent conflict idea of going over the edge relates to the immediate conflict idea of going all the way, and it adds voltage to the scene.

Core Conflict

As we've said, economy is the rule in screenwriting. Enter a scene as late as possible, focus on the essentials and exit as soon as possible. The screenwriter must cut to the core conflict. All unnecessary elements must be lost—and the unnecessary elements are usually the non-conflicts. In the following scene, the writer wants to show that the father has a nasty temperament, but rather than cutting to the core conflict, he weighs the scene down with unnecessary details.

We have crossed out everything that does not advance the conflict.

```
     INT. FATHER'S NEW BUICK — NIGHT


     Norman looks out from the front seat at the remains of
     Flint. Beside him, Father's vitriolic chin dominates the
     front seat. In the back, Caroline and Belle are silent.


                    ~~FATHER~~
          ~~How is school?~~


                    ~~NORMAN JR.~~
          ~~Fine.~~


                    ~~FATHER~~
          ~~Grades?~~
```

                    NORMAN JR.
~~I've got a "C" in botany, but I think I~~
~~can bring that up by Christmas.~~

                    FATHER
~~Good.~~

                    NORMAN JR.
~~And the football team is doing well too.~~

                    FATHER
~~Good.~~

                    NORMAN
~~Father?~~

                    FATHER
~~Yes, son?~~

                    NORMAN
~~What did you get in Botany?~~

                    FATHER
~~I had a "C" at midterm, too.~~

AN ABRUPT SCREECH.

Norman's P.O.V.-- A car full of OLD LADIES from the
Saturday night Senior Citizen BBQ at the Episcopal Center
cuts them off.

Father slams on the brakes harder than he has to. The
HORN BLARES. Unconcerned, the guilty car drives off.

                    FATHER
          Wouldn't you know they'd be coming out of
          a church!

Father lays on the gas. Belle and Caroline, after having
been flung forward with the stop are now thrown back
from the acceleration.

Father swings the car around the side of the guilty
party. Pulling up parallel with the other car...

                    FATHER
               (to Norman)
          Roll your window down.

                         NORMAN
               Dad don't do this.

                         FATHER
               Roll Your Window Down!

          Norman cranks it down.

          The two cars continue side by side. Father beeps. The
          OLD LADY driving puts down her window.

                         FATHER
                    (yelling out the window)
               You're a very lucky person!

          The Old Lady driving the other car can barely hear.

                         FATHER
               ... I say, you're a very lucky person!
               Because of me, you're still alive! Or do
               you believe your God saved you just then?

          Norman sinks deep into his seat.

                         OLD LADY
               Jesus loves you!

                         FATHER
               I doubt that very much!

          The Old Lady shoots Father the bird.

          That's it! Father slams on his brakes and comes in
          behind the Old Lady's car.

                         FATHER
               Piece of paper and pencil!

          Father points to the glove box. Norman digs in and comes
          out with a half-chewed pencil and scrap of paper. He
          hands them to his Father.

          Father takes down the Old Lady's license plate number.
          But, he can't just do it, he must make a show of it.
          Letting the Old Ladies see what he's doing...

                         FATHER
                These people really think they'll get
                away with this.

When he's done, he smiles and waves at the Old Lady
as if his uncle might be the chief of police and he's
already planning what type of revenge to take.

In the back, Belle smiles at Caroline as if nothing
happened. Caroline tries to smile back but can't. She
manages only restrained shock.

Norman sinks deeper into his seat.

Father points at the glove compartment, Norman shoves the
license number in ... The box is full of little scraps
of paper with license plate numbers.

~~Norman rolls the window back up.~~

> FATHER
> ~~Is everyone buckled in?~~

> NORMAN JR.
> ~~Yes.~~

> CAROLINE
> ~~Yes.~~

> BELLE
> ~~Yes.~~

> FATHER
> ~~Good, because there are a lot of jerks on
> the road tonight.~~

> BELLE
> ~~So true.~~

> FATHER
> ~~Yes, so true.~~

And they continue on their way.

One technique to keep the conflict going from scene to scene is to cut out of a scene just before the conflict has a chance of exploding, thereby investing or carrying over that energy into the next scene. This second scene can therefore open with the conflict already in motion, rather than having to restate it all over again; this creates a sense of pace and urgency. So sometimes it's better to enter a scene as late as possible, just as the conflict begins or where it left off in the previous scene, and exit as soon as possible, before the climax, carrying the tension over to the next scene, until the conflict finally comes to resolution. *Smaller conflict resolutions will end scenes or scene sequences; overall conflict resolution will bring your story to its end.*

FINAL THOUGHTS

Power Structure   Look at your favorite films with an eye to the kinds of conflict they use, the nature of the power struggles they explore, and you'll come to understand how it all works. Screenwriting instructor John Truby perceptively calls the overall power shift through conflict and resolution a movement from "slavery to freedom" in the case of a happy ending, or "freedom to slavery" in the case of a tragic ending. This is another way to think of the journey from powerlessness to power or vice-versa. This is the arc of the story, the progression of the journey. The organization of the protagonist's conflicts, advances and pitfalls forms the structure of the screenplay. How to organize them is the subject of the next chapter.

EXERCISES

1. Rent a film you admire and analyze the movement of power throughout.

2. Write a scene in which there is only immediate conflict. Then write one that has only imminent conflict. Then write one that has both.

3. The following examples have a desire and obstacle. Create a reason that does not allow compromise to be an option:

> a. *Desire:* Sally wants a new job so that she can move on with her life.
> b. *Obstacle:* Her father, the boss, is the nicest guy in the world. It will break his heart if she quits.
> c. *Reason Compromise Is Not an Option:*

> a. *Desire:* Darla wants to confront her father's sexist, macho behavior.
> b. *Obstacle:* He tells her that he is dying.
> c. *Reason Compromise Is Not an Option:*

4. Take your own screenplay idea and see if you can find the protagonist's desire, the obstacle (the kind of conflict) and the reason compromise is not an option.

> a. *Desire:*

> b. *Obstacle/Kind of Conflict:*

> c. *Reason Compromise Is Not an Option:*

5. Take the story you're working on and identify the key elements of power, conflicts and rising stakes. Eliminate or combine any elements that do not contribute to these.

8

Beats, Scenes and Sequences

Flexible Structure

Once you've determined the nature of the conflicts and power relationships in your story, it's time to organize them into an appropriate structure. Again, this is not accomplished by adhering to strict plot points or page numbers, but by building the order and complexity of your conflicts and story events with the fundamental structural units of every screenplay. All movies (and therefore all screenplays) are made up of beats, which combine to form scenes, which are linked together into sequences. Each of these contains some aspect of the theme, the overall conflict and the power struggle. (See also Robert McKee's fine book *Story* for a good analysis of scenes and sequencing.)

Unlike the formulas of many screenwriting systems, the number of beats, scenes and sequences is not fixed but changes from story to story; so does the ebb and flow of the power relationship. The screenwriter who understands the basic nature of each of these—beats, scenes, sequences and power flow—and how they unite to form a story is free to choose the structure that best fits her screenplay rather than following predetermined guidelines that may or may not fit the story's needs. Let's look at each element, starting with the smallest structural building block, the beat.

FOLLOW THE BEAT

Just as a scientist comes to understand the structure of the universe by studying subatomic particles, so must the screenwriter understand the smallest structural unit of a story. A *beat* is a single unit of thought or action. It's a small section of dialogue or behavior that's accented by a particular emotion, subject and/or action. A change in emotion, subject or action marks the beginning of a new beat. But beats cannot stand alone, in and of themselves. The nature of a beat is that it not only represents itself but almost always is the motivation or cause of the next beat. When beats cause new beats, they link to form a beginning, middle and end, or in other words, a small story within the main story called a scene. For example, in the following series of beats, a nonreligious family has dinner with the daughter's new, very religious boyfriend. The moment is divided into five beats. Notice that each beat not only is a unit of action or thought but also causes the next unit of action or thought.

BEAT #1

Dinner is set. Extra table-leaves have been placed in the table to handle the guests. Everyone gathers around a meal of wiener wraps, pasty green bean casserole and piles of mashed potatoes that look like the mountains of the moon.

> MOTHER
> We're Reaaaady!

BEAT #2

Mother places the coffee mug in front of Father.

> MOTHER
> Terry, why don't you tell us a little about yourself.

> BOYFRIEND
> First, my name is Larry and I've got a paper route and I'm a member of my Sunday School bowling team and...

> MOTHER
> Oh! You play against other teams, like the PTA. Blue Devils?

> BOYFRIEND
> Sure do. We call our team "The Apostles."

> MOTHER
> You're such a busy child, with your paper route and bowling team.

> BOYFRIEND
> I'm also a junior member of the N.R.A.

> MOTHER
> Oh, Michelle, he even has time to advocate for women's rights!

BEAT #3

                    MOTHER
          This is such a special occasion. Why
          don't we make it even more special?
          Norman Junior, say grace.

The Son takes the fork out of his mouth.

                    SON
          What?

                    MOTHER
          You heard me, say grace!

                    SON
          But... I don't know...

Mother shoots the son the evil eye. Then, smiles
desperately at the Boyfriend.

                    MOTHER
          We're waiting.

BEAT #4

Father grunts and begins to eat.

                    FATHER
          Well, I'm not. Pass the salt!

BEAT #5

Humilated, the Daughter begins to cry. She avoids her
boyfriend's eyes as she chokes out the words.

                    DAUGHTER
          Dear God, thank you for this food we are
          about to receive. Forgive our sins as we
          forgive those who sin against us. Make
          us thankful for our family, friends and
          those we love.

The word "beat" is misleading. It seems to suggest a rhythmical unit of time, a common cadence or a brief pause. So why do we use the word "beat"? Why not "unit" or "section"? The theory as to how this musical term has come to its nonmusical structural meaning comes from when the disciples of Constantin Stanislavski (the head of the Moscow Art Theater and often called the father of modern acting) came to the United States in the 1930s to teach. Legend has it that the Americans were confused by the Russians' thick accents, and they mistook the word "bit" for "beat." If you say the line, "First you must split the scene into little bits," with a Russian accent, you'll find some truth to this theory. Whether it's true or not, looking at "beats" as "bits" makes a lot of sense. Scenes are made up of little bits; each bit is a new action that is motivated by something in one of the preceding bits. Each bit is logically interlocked with the bits before and after it to form the beginning, middle and end of a scene. In the example above, notice that each beat not only causes the next beat, but also increases the tension until it is resolved.

MAKING A SCENE

On a shooting-script level, a scene is everything that requires a new scene heading; that is, every time there is a change in location or time there is a new scene. But for the purposes of the spec screenwriter, a scene is the location for and the action of a particular event. It may be limited to one scene heading, just like a shooting script, but it may also effectively combine several, such as when a single continuous event takes a character from an interior to an exterior location without altering the nature or purpose of the action. For example, if you are writing about a principal who tells a student that he's kicked out of school, the scene starts in the principal's office. The young boy gets up and walks out. Pissed off, the principal follows the boy down the hall, telling him that he's washed up, kicked out for life. Through the cafeteria they go, the principal still hollering at the boy, and they finally end up out in the parking lot, where the boy turns and punches the principal in the nose. In a shooting script, this would be considered four scenes (principal's office, hallway, cafeteria and parking lot) but for the purpose of structuring a spec script, it may be considered only one scene because there is only one action—the principal telling the kid that he's through. (You still need to write each scene header.) A scene is made up of a group of beats that create the action of a particular event or, as Aristotle would say, an "incident."

The best way to see how scenes are constructed out of beats is to examine a few. Here are the opening two scenes from an action movie Robin wrote and sold. In these scenes we meet the antagonist and protagonist for the first time, encounter a "false" scene (an establishing shot) and see how beats link and build to form scenes with real and implied conflict:

```
INT. PRISON VISITING ROOM — DAY

A large, bleak room with several rows of tables and
chairs bolted to the scarred cement floor. PRISONERS in
blue outfits talk in hushed tones to their WIVES; one
talks with a seedy LAWYER.

One of two DEPUTIES stands watch, bored.
```

The SECOND DEPUTY escorts in another prisoner: JULIUS
KAISER--40, muscular, handsome except for the ragged scar
and powder burn on his cheek--a mob boss used to getting
his way. Or getting rid of those who won't give it to
him.

Kaiser takes a seat across from two waiting visitors: his
lieutenant, SALINAS--30, powerful, cheap suit, a face to
inspire nightmares—and the more expensively suited DR.
GREENE--short, fat, balding, habitually arrogant. Right
now his eyes are bloodshot from tension.

> SALINAS
> How you doing, chief--?

> KAISER
> How's Octavius?

Salinas and Greene exchange a glance. Salinas shrugs: not
his call.

Kaiser glares at Greene. Greene stammers. Spreads his
hands on the table. Hedging.

> GREENE
> Well... it's hard to know exactly—

> KAISER
> Don't screw with me.

His voice is calm, but his eyes bore into Greene's.
Greene blinks. Pulls his hands back.

> GREENE
> A week. Maybe two.

Kaiser nods. At least he's being told the truth.

> KAISER
> Have you made the arrangements I asked
> for?

Now it's Salinas who hedges. Not happy.

> SALINAS
> Yeah. But I gotta tell you, it's a risky
> set up. I don't see how we can pull it
> off.

> KAISER
> You let me worry about that. Bring
> your car around front. Keep the engine
> running.

Salinas stares at Kaiser. Not quite sure he heard right.
Then he and Greene go to the visitor's door, are BUZZED
outside.

The Second Deputy comes over.

> SECOND DEPUTY
> All right, visit's over. Let's go.

Kaiser remains seated, elbows on the table, head propped
on his hands. The Deputy claps a hand on his shoulder.

> SECOND DEPUTY
> I said--

Quick as a snake striking its prey, Kaiser grabs the
Deputy's hand, spins around behind him and has him in a
chokehold with one hand. The other hand has the pistol
from the Deputy's holster. Pressed against the Deputy's
spine.

The other Prisoners and their visitors duck down.

Through the security window, Deputies in the next room
scramble to full alert. SIRENS GO OFF.

> KAISER
> All right. Walk me out of here.

The First Deputy, hand on his holstered gun, cautiously
approaches.

> FIRST DEPUTY
> You're not going anywhere, Kaiser. Now
> just let him go, put the gun down.

Kaiser whispers into the Second Deputy's ear.

> KAISER
> You got a family? Wife, couple of kids?

> SECOND DEPUTY
> (nodding)
> Yeah.

Kaiser points the gun at the First Deputy. Shoots him right between the eyes. He falls dead. Visiting wives SCREAM.

> KAISER
> So did he, I bet. Let's go.

He returns the gun-barrel to the Second Deputy's spine.

> SECOND DEPUTY
> Open the door!

A beat. Then the visitor's door opens. More Deputies stand there, guns drawn. Hesitating. Kaiser whips the gun around and SHOOTS one of the other Prisoners dead. His visiting WIFE SCREAMS. Kaiser puts the gun at the Second Deputy's head.

> KAISER
> This gun has a fifteen round clip. I still have thirteen left. Not a lucky number. Maybe I should make it twelve?

The Deputies back off.

> KAISER
> Let me out and I'll let him go. But I even think I'm being followed, his wife and kids'll see him next at the funeral.

Kaiser walks the Second Deputy out the door.

EXT. ESTABLISHING, HOSPITAL, NEW YORK CITY — DAY

A small, upscale hospital in the big, bad city.

INT. HOSPITAL CORRIDOR — DAY

A quiet day in the hospital. A few NURSES go about their business. An Elderly Patient pushes a wheeled IV rack with a drip-bag, looking lost.

A laundry cart whizzes by him, going the other way.

JOEY LUPO shadow-boxes as he catches up. In his mid-twenties. Tough, Italian good looks. Long hair tied back in a bun. Hard muscles fill out his orderly's uniform. Tattoos and a new wedding ring punctuate his rough,

> scarred knuckles. Another tattoo of a ravening wolf
> crawls up his right arm.
>
> He scoops in more dirty linen from a wall bin. Then
> shoves the cart ahead toward the next bin, whistling as
> he goes...

The first scene begins with a scene heading indicating we're in a prison visiting room, daytime. The first paragraph sets the look and mood; we know by their generic names that the players described are extras, not important characters. In the second paragraph we meet the antagonist, Kaiser. (It is a common strategy in action movies to meet the antagonist first, thus setting up the eventual threat and stakes the protagonist will face.) Kaiser's demeanor is authoritative, his appearance marred by violence. His name suggests absolute power. (Note that his name is all-capitalized in the narrative because this is the first time we meet him; it will not be in subsequent scenes.)

Kaiser's entrance is the first beat, the first true action in the scene, and when he meets his "lieutenant" and doctor, we get our first glimpse of his allies and power base. Even in this prison context, Kaiser has absolute control over them. His dialogue is to the point: we know he's only interested in learning two things, the well-being of someone named Octavius (it is revealed later that this is his son), and whether the "arrangements" are in place. We learn that Octavius only has a week or two to live (the second beat, setting up Kaiser's urgency) and that in fact Kaiser's arrangements are in place (the third beat, concluding Kaiser's need for information). It isn't spelled out; only enough is revealed to create a sense of curiosity as to whom and what they are referring. Once he learns these two things, Kaiser takes immediate and ruthless action, seizing a gun and killing one deputy (the fourth beat), and then escapes from the prison (the fifth and final beat, ending the scene). His dialogue and action subtextually hit on the theme of looking out for one's children. Once Kaiser has completed the action of the scene—to escape—the scene is over. There is plenty of conflict, both actual—the killing and kidnapping of the deputies—and implied: Kaiser, a proven killer, has some other plan in motion.

The second scene, although it has a scene heading, is just an establishing shot and actually part of the third scene. It acts like a master shot to reveal the location and time. Because it is also daytime, as was the previous scene, we can assume it is probably the same time, if not shortly later. Although only one sentence, the narrative tells us that this hospital is an oasis in the harsh urban landscape. There are no real beats in Scene Two, because no character has taken action.

As we begin the second true scene, the header tells us we're in a hospital corridor in the daytime. (Again, the assumption is that it is the same time as the previous scene.) The narrative fills this out in as brief a fashion as possible; in three sentences we know the look and mood of the place. It's quiet, calm, in contrast to the tension and violence of the first scene. And since we've heard in the first scene that Octavius only has a week or two to live, we can assume that this hospital is our "world." The fourth and fifth sentences (involving the first two beats, the appearance of the cart, followed by the appearance of the protagonist) introduce the protagonist, Joey, and something about his personality and past: he seems easygoing, doesn't take his job too seriously. His physical description provides the essential details: what he looks like, that he may be a fighter, is probably a former gang member and he's just been married.

The last paragraph (the final beat as well) completes his action in the scene: to do his job as an orderly. Where's the conflict? Well, this is the calm before the storm. Remember, no one wants to see the "village of the happy people" unless something really unhappy is about to happen to it. The immediate juxtaposition with the prior scene implies that Joey will eventually have to face Kaiser, an effortlessly ruthless and violent man. Certain questions are also raised. Joey seems physically capable, but a bit lightweight. Will he have the intelligence and moral strength, given his obvious background, to meet the challenge? The question as to why he should, why he is the essential protagonist, is left to be answered a few pages later. Not all the information about a character has to appear the minute they appear, only what is necessary for the scene. From this, we see that each beat has a singular purpose. Each beat gives us information that builds the action into a scene.

Next, let's look at a short scene sequence from Clint Eastwood's *Unforgiven*, from an original script by David Webb Peoples. In this Western, a former gunslinger, Will Munny, is invited by a young, nearsighted, tough-talking wannabe gunfighter to leave his pig farm and go on one last adventure: to kill some cowhands who disfigured a whore after she laughed at one of them. Now the other prostitutes have offered a large reward for the death of these cowhands. Munny doesn't want to go; he's been reformed by his now-dead wife, and has given up killing and booze. But he needs money to raise his children, he's a lousy farmer, and so eventually he agrees to go. However, when he gets to the town where the whores live, he encounters Little Bill, a nasty gunfighter-turned-sheriff, who beats Will nearly to death on first sight. Here are a couple of scenes following Will Munny's beating at the hands of Little Bill.

```
INT. SHED — DAY

DAYLIGHT and the cut whore's face. Delilah is leaning
over Munny, wiping his brow. He is lying in the straw
looking up at her and he looks like shit... his face
ghastly pale and stubbled and covered with horrible cuts
and bad stitching... but his eyes are clear.

                    MUNNY
        I thought... you was an angel.
```

>   DELILAH
>   (embarrassed, getting up)
>   You ain't dead.

Delilah goes over to her horse and gets some packages
out of the saddle bags. Munny tries to sit up weakly.

>   MUNNY
>   Some big guy beat the shit out of me.
>   (feeling his sore face)
>   I guess I must look a lot like you, huh?

>   DELILAH
>   (angry, hurt)
>   You don't look nothin' like me, mister.

>   MUNNY
>   I didn't mean no offense.
>   (she doesn't answer)
>   I guess you're the one them cowboys cut.
>   (no answer)
>   Ned and the Kid, my partners, are
>   they...?

>   DELILAH
>   (coldly)
>   They went out scouting when they saw your
>   fever broke.

>   MUNNY
>   Scouting?

>   DELILAH
>   On the Bar T... looking for... them.

>   MUNNY
>   Oh... How long I been here?

>   DELILAH
>   (still cold)
>   Three days. Are you hungry?

>   MUNNY
>   Three days? I must be.

EXT. WOODS NEAR SHED — DAY

CLOSE on robins, four of them in the woods near the shed
and Munny is watching them where he sits wolfing chicken

hungrily, his back against the shed. Delilah is watching
him eat.

> MUNNY
> I thought I was gone. See them birds?
> Most times I wouldn't even notice them
> birds much. But I'm noticin' 'em real
> good 'cause I thought I was dead.

> DELILAH
> I brought your hat. You... left it down
> at Greely's.

> MUNNY
> That big guy lookin' for me?

As he looks over at her Munny's eye falls briefly on her
exposed ankle and Delilah feels the look.

> DELILAH
> Little Bill? He thinks you went north.

Munny can't help it and his eye flicks back to the
ankle.

> DELILAH
> Are you really going to kill them?

> MUNNY
> (unenthusiastically)
> Yeah, I guess.
> (suddenly)
> There's still payment, ain't there?

She nods and she moves so that more ankle is showing,
but Munny's eye is drawn to her breasts as she moves,
then he looks away quickly, guiltily and they sit there
silently until...

> DELILAH
> Them other two, they been takin' advances
> on the payment.

> MUNNY
> Advances?

He can't help looking at her body and she knows it.

> DELILAH
> (shyly)
> Free ones.

Her body is getting to him.

> MUNNY
> (stupidly)
> Free ones?

> DELILAH
> Alice an' Silky gave them... free ones.

> MUNNY
> (understanding, embarrassed)
> Oh. Yeah.

> DELILAH
> (shy, timid)
> You want... a free one?

> MUNNY
> (looking away, embarrassed)
> Me? No. No, I guess not.

And Delilah is hurt... crushed. She gets up and covers it by picking up the remains of the chicken and Munny is too embarrassed to look at her.

> DELILAH
> (covering her hurt)
> I didn't mean... with me. Alice and
> Silky, they'll give you one... if you
> want.

> MUNNY
> I... I guess not.
> (unusually perceptive suddenly)
> I didn't mean I didn't want one 'cause of
> you bein' cut up. I didn't mean that.

Delilah keeps her back to him.

> MUNNY
> (trying to get up)
> It ain't that at all. You're a beautiful
> woman. What I said before, how I might
> look like you... I didn't mean you was
> ugly, like me, hell no... I only meant
> how we both have scars.

He is standing weakly, supporting himself on the wall and
his speech is so sincere and Delilah wants to believe
it.

> MUNNY
> You're a beautiful woman an'... if I
> was to want a free one, I guess I'd want
> you more than them others. It ain't...
> See... I can't have no free one on
> account of my wife...

> DELILAH
> Your wife?

> MUNNY
> Yeah. See?

> DELILAH
> (after a pause)
> I admire that, you being true to your
> wife. I've seen a lot of... of men...
> who weren't.

> MUNNY
> (pleased and embarrassed)
> Yeah, I guess.

> DELILAH
> She back in Kansas?

> MUNNY
> Uh... yeah. Yeah. She's uh... watchin
> over my little ones.

And Munny gives her what for him is his best social
smile... sort of like a pig strangling.

These two scenes work as a pair; in fact—although there are two locations, an interior and an exterior, even a time lapse between them—they could be seen as a single scene. The main action or event of both scenes is that Will Munny comes back to consciousness after having been beaten and gets his bearings. But each scene works on its own, with a beginning, middle and end. The two scenes taken together also have a beginning, middle and end, working off of and enriching the meaning of each one separately. (Mr. Peoples uses a lot of parentheticals, which we advise against.)

The first scene starts with "DAYLIGHT and the cut whore" as Will Munny wakes up in a manger thinking that he's died, and that Delilah—the whore—must be an angel. Like many adventures set in the world of the Old

West, this is a moral fable, heavy with religious overtones. The first beat immediately and efficiently presents a subtext of false death and resurrection, down to the fact that he learns that he's been unconscious for three days (the period Christ supposedly spent in harrowing Hell before his own resurrection). In the second beat, Will inadvertently insults Delilah by touching his own cut-up face and saying that he must look like her, now. Delilah retorts that he looks nothing like her. But clearly we see that there is a bond between them, the reluctant bounty hunter and the injured woman who regrets the fact of the bounty in her name. Both are moral creatures, in spite of being a killer and a whore, and there is a tentativeness and mutual respect to their dialogue. In the third beat, Will learns that his friends are out preparing to earn the bounty, thus reminding the audience that the lethal plot is still in motion. In the final beat, just as elements of light and the "angel" begin the scene, the element of physical resurrection ends it; these work thematically, but also fit the emotional arc of the scene, going from the ethereal return to consciousness, to the solid fact of hunger.

The second scene picks up the action referred to in the first scene's ending dialogue ("Are you hungry?" and "Three days? I must be") by having Will already wolfing down some food. Note that we cut to this action already in progress; there was no need to have beats or scenes where the food is being prepared, or the small talk we can assume accompanied it. But the second scene contrasts with the first in that it is exterior, a hard transition from the darkness of the shed, signaling Will's shift from unconsciousness and awakening to full consciousness. Will's attention is on the small but real beauties of the day, its physical wonders: the food he's eating, the robins nearby, the sensual flesh of Delilah's ankle. Will draws explicit attention to the fact that something as insignificant as some birds mean something special to him now, because he thought he'd died.

Delilah returns Will's attention to the grim business by mentioning his hat, which he'd left at the whorehouse/saloon. He asks if the "big guy" is looking for him, and there is a subtextual resonance to his using these words. The "big guy" is his alter ego and antagonist, Little Bill, but is also the "Big Guy" in the religious sense. Delilah makes the issue of killing explicit, just as Will does with the issue of payment, keeping the plot clearly in mind. But both are uncomfortable with these grim topics, and besides, Will's sensual appetites have been awakened. He can't keep his eyes off Delilah's ankle, which leads to the flirtation as she offers him a "free one" and he refuses. She is hurt, assuming it's because she's now ugly from her wounds. But Will assures her this is not the case; in fact, they share a bond because they "both have scars." This a splendid bit of subtextual dialogue: they both have surface scars—of course—but they both suffer from deeper wounds of the spirit as well.

Will affirms her physical attractiveness to him, and then reveals the real reason he's not interested—he remains true to his wife. Delilah, not knowing his wife is dead, is simply charmed by his unusual faithfulness and asks about his wife. Will replies that she's watching over his little ones, thereby giving his dead wife the explicit role of an angel.

So we see that the first scene has four beats. It starts with the ethereal, the misperception of a living whore as an angel (beat 1), and then turns to the physical (beat 2), reveals what his friends are up to (beat 3) and climaxes with Will's expression of hunger (beat 4). This physical hunger—for food, beauty, sex—starts the second scene (beat 1), which then shifts back to the practical, the reason he's there (beat 2), then to the sexual offering (beat 3), which is refused, and the scene climaxes with Will's reference to the real angel in his life, his dead and sainted wife (beat 4). Each scene works on its own, but both combine to form a small, discrete sequence. Although not specifically about Will's goal of killing the cowhands, this sequence contains a small subplot—Will's flirtation with Delilah. The subplot gives a moral context to the main action of the plot: the possibility of redemption, of costs and payments in both the physical and spiritual worlds and of the price of divine judgment regarding the fate of the cruel cowhands and Will's soul as well.

Scenes are microcosms of the script as a whole. All of these subtextual and contextual issues run through the entire story and are returned to explicitly in later scenes, such as when Will and the Kid are waiting for their money to be delivered, and the Kid has an attack of conscience about having killed the man who cut Delilah's face. The Kid tries to rationalize it, saying, "I guess he had it coming." To which Will replies, "We all have it coming, Kid." This comment, by the way, states the movie's theme as clearly and yet subtly as any line in film ever has. When the money is brought by a whore, Will learns that it's come at a terrible cost: Little Bill has tortured Ned to death. And unlike the Kid, who flees, sickened at the carnage, Will reverts to his former, murderous nature and kills Little Bill. "I don't deserve this," says Little Bill, to which Will Munny replies, "Deserve's got nothing to do with it." It's all about the prison of a man's own character. Will's prison is to be an agent of death, whether he likes it or not, no matter what angels may be looking out for him.

A scene follows the same rules as the script as a whole. It has a beginning, middle and end, should be entered as late as possible and cut out of as soon as possible. There must be at least one main dramatic "question"—the purpose of the scene—with rising conflict and a climax. This climax should lead naturally into the next scene. While there are interstitial scenes with separate headers (such as establishing shots used to fix a location or to indicate a transition, such as getting into a car) these are not true scenes but rather parts of a larger scene.

SEQUENCES

Just as beats grow to form a scene, scenes are linked to form sequences. A sequence is a group of scenes that build toward a common goal. It's one section or movement of a movie that is linked by a common struggle, theme and/or action (not unlike movements in a symphony). Sometimes a sequence is a simple montage like the "training sequence" in movies like *Rocky* or *G.I. Jane*, where the protagonist must hone his or her abilities in order to achieve the goal. Other times the sequence is a major movement in the movie comprising numerous scenes linked together. There is the sequence in *High Noon* when the town clears out and the Sheriff is left alone to face the coming outlaws. There is the sequence at the end of *Sleepless in Seattle*, where Meg Ryan's character tries to get to the top of the Empire State Building to meet Tom Hanks, is delayed by traffic, and finally gets there only to discover that it looks as if it's too late. Interwoven with this, and generating more tension, is a matching sequence where Hanks's character goes there, waits and then leaves, only coming back because his little boy forgot his backpack. Note that the scenes in these sequences are not told one after the other, but staggered, going first to one sequence, then the other, weaving the two together into a larger sequence in which boy and girl finally meet at the top of the Empire State Building.

Rising Tension   Sequences are governed by rising tension, because either the stakes are rising (the Sheriff discovers he must face the outlaws alone) or more obstacles appear in the path of the character (traffic gets in Meg Ryan's way, delaying her) making the goal seem unattainable. In many films, the actions of the antagonist define the raising of the stakes. In *The Terminator*, for instance, the cyborg assassin first kills a loathsome punk (we don't care, we might even approve), then a gun merchant (again, not much grief there), then an innocent housewife (we begin to really care), then Matt, the boyfriend of Sarah's roommate (we begin to hate the Terminator), and then Sarah's roommate, shooting her in the back in gruesome slow motion (we are fully committed to hating the Terminator). The killings have been organized into a careful sequence of rising emotional impact, not simply thrown in randomly. In the climactic battle sequence, the Terminator keeps coming back, no matter how many times Sarah Connor and Reese "kill" it, its disguise of humanity—clothes, flesh, voice—stripped away until it is revealed as a stark image of death itself, a shining steel skeleton. It kills helpless bystanders, then kills Reese—the love of Sarah's life—and then threatens Sarah herself. Her need to destroy it (her stakes) is progressively heightened: at first the stakes are simple self-preservation, then revenge and finally the desperate need to survive in order to save the human race. So each sequence—just like a beat or scene—also has a beginning, a middle and end with the most important, the most tension, the highest stakes placed at the end.

Sequences Form a Story   Aristotle defined plot as an "arrangement of the incidents." As he pointed out, this arrangement has a cause-and-effect relationship. The same relationship that causes beats to become a scene, causes scenes to become a sequence and sequences to become a story. Each beat, scene and sequence has a purpose within the larger story or it is a meaningless link and must be cut. The number of beats, scenes or sequences changes from story to story. There is no overall formula as to how many there must or should be. The key to writing a good movie is finding the purpose and order of all the sequences.

Often beginning screenwriters discover that this is hard to do. Their story lacks structure because they cannot construct the sequences out of the random order of their scenes. They'll use a screenwriting guru's plot point formula only to find that between plot points they write mush, they're only filling in space between the major "tent poles." If each beat is necessary to the scene, and each scene is an important incident, then each sequence becomes a critical component of the story.

So, if formulas are so flawed, why do young screenwriters use them? They use them because formulas carefully label the plot points with easy-to-understand titles (opening event, inciting incident, etc.). These labels allow inexperienced screenwriters to get a handle on exactly where they are in the story. That's very comforting when you are trying to structure one. But following a formula is creating a structure without understanding why or how it works. By using sequences to construct a story, the writer—not the formula—has control over the material.

The best way to structure with sequences is to give each sequence a title. A hundred years ago, writers of Victorian melodramas used to give each act of a play an alluring title. This title was a mini-label that pinpointed the conflicts and purposes the characters had in that particular section. A screenwriter can do the same thing by titling each sequence (by the way, this can be done with each scene and beat) just for themselves. The mini-title focuses the action of the sequence around one central purpose.

Let's examine how this method might work using a full movie. Following is a step outline of the Kevin Costner film *Field of Dreams* (screenplay by Phil Alden Robinson) divided into scenes and sequences. We have given each sequence a title that identifies its purpose within the story. Notice that each scene builds to the next and that there are no sequences extraneous to the entire story. There are twelve sequences in *Field of Dreams*; your movie may need more or less.

FIELD OF DREAMS
Scenes and Sequences

SEQUENCE #1 "How I Moved to Iowa and Learned to Love Baseball"

>   MONTAGE--Photos and narration tell us about Ray's life,
>   why he loves baseball, how he met his wife, why he
>   became a farmer and his troubled relationship with his
>   now-departed father.

SEQUENCE #2 "The Voice"

>   SCENE 1: EXT. CORN FIELD — NIGHT
>   Ray hears the voice for the first time. It says, "If you
>   build it he will come."
>
>   SCENE 2: INT. KITCHEN — NIGHT
>   Ray is worried about the voice. Tells his wife about it.
>
>   SCENE 3: INT. BEDROOM — NIGHT
>   Ray hears the voice the second time.

SCENE 4: INT. KITCHEN — DAY
Ray tells his daughter that people who hear voices are sick.

SCENE 5: INT. FEED STORE — DAY
Ray questions other farmers about hearing voices. They think he's nuts.

SCENE 6: EXT. CORN FIELD — DAY
Ray hears the voice again. This time he gets mad. He sees the mirage of the baseball field.

SCENE 7: INT. LIVING ROOM — NIGHT
Ray tries to figure out what the voice means. He thinks that it might mean that if he builds a baseball field, Shoeless Joe Jackson will return.

SCENE 8: INT. BEDROOM — NIGHT
Ray worries that he is turning into his father. He lacks dreams. He and his wife decide to build the field.

SEQUENCE #3 "Building the Baseball Field"

SCENE 1: Montage--Ray plows under his corn field in order to build the baseball field. His neighbors think he's a weirdo. He tells the story of Shoeless Joe Jackson to his daughter.

SCENE 2: EXT. BASEBALL FIELD — NIGHT
The baseball field is done. "I have done something completely illogical."

SEQUENCE #4 "Waiting for Shoeless Joe"

SCENE 1: EXT. BEDROOM — NIGHT (FALL)
They wait for something to happen, but nothing happens.

SCENE 2: INT. LIVING ROOM — NIGHT (WINTER)
Christmas has come and still nothing has happened.

SCENE 3: INT. LIVING ROOM — NIGHT (SPRING)
Still nothing. They have gone over budget. They are running out of money. Suddenly, there is a man on the lawn.

SCENE 4: EXT. BASEBALL FIELD — NIGHT
Shoeless Joe Jackson has arrived. Ray introduces Shoeless Joe to his family. Shoeless Joe wants to bring the other players back with him. Ray decides no matter what the cost they're keeping the field.

SEQUENCE #5 "The Brother-in-Law"

    SCENE 1: INT. KITCHEN — DAY
    Mark, Ray's brother-in-law, offers to buy the farm to
    save Ray from bankruptcy.

    SCENE 2: EXT. FIELD — DAY
    The players return for a game. Mark cannot see them.

SEQUENCE #6 "The Second Message"

    SCENE 1: EXT. BASEBALL FIELD — DUSK
    Ray gets his second voice which says, "Ease his pain."

    SCENE 2: INT. HOUSE — DAY
    Ray tells his wife that he heard the voice again. He
    doesn't know what it means.

    SCENE 3: INT. SCHOOL BOARD MEETING — NIGHT
    Book banning is debated. Ray is preoccupied with
    understanding what "ease his pain" might mean. The
    townspeople want to ban a book by Terence Mann. At the
    mention of Terence Mann, Ray understands the voice's
    message.

    SCENE 4: INT. SCHOOL HALLWAY — NIGHT
    Rays tells his wife that he must find Terence Mann.

    SCENE 5: Montage--They research Terence Mann.

    SCENE 6: EXT. LOCAL LIBRARY — DAY
    Ray discovers a lot about Terence but he can't decipher
    how he figures into the voice's plan.

    SCENE 7: INT. TRUCK — DAY
    They find out that Terence was a great baseball fan.
    Wanted to play, but it never happened. Terence hasn't
    been to a game since the 1950s.

    SCENE 8: EXT. RAY'S FARM — DAY
    Ray comes to understand that he must take Terence to a
    baseball game. He simply does not know why.

    SCENE 9: INT. FARM HOUSE — DAY
    Ray decides he must go to New York to find Terence Mann.

SEQUENCE #7 "Finding Terence Mann"
    MONTAGE--Ray traveling to New York. He interviews people
    in Mann's New York neighborhood. He finds the door to
    Mann's apartment.

SEQUENCE #8 "Meeting Terence Mann"

SCENE 1: INT. APARTMENT BUILDING — DAY
Terence Mann slams the door in Ray's face. When Ray begs
him to listen, Mann gives Ray only one minute to talk.
Ray entreats him to come to a baseball game.

SCENE 2: EXT. STADIUM—HOT DOG STAND — NIGHT
Terence and Ray go to a baseball game. Terence still
thinks this whole thing is silly and that Ray may be
psychotic.

SCENE 3: EXT. BASEBALL STADIUM — NIGHT
Ray hears another voice "Go the distance" and sees the
stats for Archibald "Moonlight" Graham on the scoreboard.
Terence sees nothing.

SCENE 4: EXT. TERENCE MANN'S APARTMENT — NIGHT
Ray says good-bye. The mission is a failure, until
Terence admits that he too saw the stats for "Moonlight"
Graham. They decide to go to Wisconsin together and find
Graham.

SEQUENCE #9 "The Search for Moonlight Graham"

SCENE 1: MONTAGE--They drive to Wisconsin.

SCENE 2: EXT. GAS STATION — DAY
Ray calls his wife to tell her that everything is fine.

SCENE 3: INT. RAY'S FARM — DAY
His wife hangs up. Mark is back. He's going to foreclose
on the farm.

SCENE 4: INT. WISCONSIN county office — DAY
Ray and Terence find that Moonlight Graham is dead.
They discover that he was a wonderful doctor who helped
everyone, but they still don't understand why they have
to find him.

SCENE 5: INT. BAR — NIGHT
They interview people in a bar about Moonlight Graham.

SCENE 6: INT. HOTEL — NIGHT
They look over their research. They still cannot
understand why they must find this man.

SCENE 7: EXT. CITY STREET — NIGHT
Ray goes for a walk. He suddenly finds himself in the
past. He sees Moonlight Graham walking alone.

SCENE 8: INT. Graham's OFFICE — DAY
Ray asks Graham about his short major league career.
Graham played half of one inning. He never got to bat.
His great wish is to bat, just once, in a major league
game. Ray asks Graham to come with him back to Iowa. He
refuses.

SCENE 9: INT. HOTEL — NIGHT
Ray and Terence are confused about their purpose. Why
didn't Graham come with them?

SCENE 10: INT. FARMHOUSE — NIGHT
Ray calls home. The farm is in trouble. Terence decides
to go to Iowa with Ray.

SCENE 11: EXT. HIGHWAY — DAY
They pick up a hitchhiker, a kid who turns out to be the
younger incarnation of Moonlight Graham.

SEQUENCE #10 "Why Ray Regrets His Relationship with His
Father"

SCENE 1: EXT. HIGHWAY — DAY
The three of them head to Iowa. Ray tells Terence about
his troubled relationship with his father.

SCENE 2: EXT. HIGHWAY — NIGHT
Ray admits to Terence that he and his father fought over
his father's worship of Shoeless Joe Jackson.

SCENE 3: EXT. Ray's FARM — NIGHT
They get home--the ghost team is playing.

SEQUENCE #11 "Moonlight Graham Gets His Wish"

SCENE 1: EXT. BASEBALL FIELD — NIGHT
Terence and Graham are introduced to the ghost players.
They ask Graham to play.

SCENE 2: EXT. BASEBALL FIELD — NIGHT
The teams play ball. Graham has his chance to bat
against the big league players. He drives home a run.

SEQUENCE #12 "The Climax"

SCENE 1: EXT. BASEBALL FIELD — DAY
Mark comes to take the farm. Ray's daughter falls off
the seats. As he steps from the baseball diamond, to
help her, Moonlight Graham becomes the old doctor again
and saves her, but finds he can't go back. Graham, his
dream fulfilled, disappears into the field. Mark sees

> the ballplayers for the first time, and decides not to
> foreclose. The players ask Terence if he wants to come
> along. Terence gleefully goes with the players. Ray's
> father returns, is introduced to Ray's family, and Ray
> and his dad play catch.

These sequences add up to the largest sequence, the script as a whole, which might have the thematic title of "Ray Makes Peace with His Father."

THAT'S ANOTHER STORY: SUBPLOT SEQUENCES

The step outline is also where you'll want to think about your subplot(s). Many, though not all, films have secondary stories going, usually involving the secondary characters; these subplots either serve to reinforce or contrast with the main story line. For example, in *Field of Dreams*, the subplot involves Ray's tense relationship with his brother-in-law and the bankruptcy. In a love story involving two people who seem hopelessly incompatible, the subplot may involve a couple of friends (allies) who are perfectly, even nauseatingly, right for each other, thereby reinforcing the sense that our main characters will never get together. In the end, because the secondary characters' relationship was, let's say, based on superficial compatibilities but not true love, they may end up splitting just as our main characters embrace.

Or a subplot may involve the protagonist in another story line to complicate the events or deepen our sense of his character. For example, in *Casablanca*, the main plot is that of Rick and Elsa's relationship, but the subplot involving Claude Rains' Inspector Renault gives Rick another deep relationship that evolves over the course of the story. Rick starts off in an uneasy, amoral camaraderie with the French officer while he is agonizing over his reunion with the love of his life. In the end, he loses Elsa but sticks with Renault, in the "beginning of a beautiful friendship." This works, because the film is thematically not about the survival of true love, but rather about having to follow the call of duty. Another subplot involves Elsa and her husband, Victor, in which he learns about her infidelity with Rick and forgives her—where Rick can't. This proves he is, at this moment, a better man than Rick, deserving of her love. In the end, Rick regains the upper hand by sacrificing his own feelings—and Elsa—for the greater cause that Victor represents.

In the screenplay for *Titanic* there's a subplot (that was cut from the film for length reasons) in which Jack's love for the upper-class Rose is mirrored by that of his Italian friend Fabrizio (Danny Nucci) for a working-class Norwegian girl named Helga. Their early relationship is uncomplicated, where Jack and Rose's seems impossible; but at the end, when Rose chooses to leave her family and go with Jack, she ends up surviving, whereas Helga will not leave her family for Fabrizio and dies tragically, her love for him aborted.

In the detective thriller *Seven*, the subplot reinforces the tragic theme of pervasive evil. The main plot is that of Brad Pitt and Morgan Freeman's detective characters attempting to catch a serial killer who embodies evil. The subplot is that of Brad Pitt's love for his pure, lovely wife, who seems living proof that goodness exists in the world. In the end, the serial killer not only murders her, but their unborn child as well, and that act forces Pitt's character to commit the mortal sins of rage and murder himself. The subplot connects perfectly with the main plot.

There is no hard-and-fast rule as to how often a subplot element should appear, or how long it should last over the course of a screenplay. There may be one long subplot matching the main story point for point over the whole screenplay; for example, the subplot in *As Good as It Gets* involving the protagonist (Jack Nicholson's Melvin) and his gay neighbor reflects and reinforces the main love story. Or there may be several smaller subplots that appear, are resolved and vanish at various points in the screenplay. In *The Terminator*, for example, there is a short subplot at the beginning involving Sarah's roommate and her boyfriend Matt, a muscular but goofy guy who attempts unsuccessfully to scare Sarah (failing where the Terminator succeeds) and is totally incapable of defending himself or his lover from the Terminator (failing where Reese succeeds). Both face the same antagonist, but Matt and Sarah's roommate die, whereas Sarah lives, because she—with Reese's help—is stronger and more capable. The point is that the subplot should in some way deal with the same things as the main plot, either as a cautionary contradiction or as another level of reinforcement.

In planning out your subplots, you may wish to outline their sequence or sequences separately, so you can make sure they're properly constructed: that they have a distinct beginning, middle and end. Irritating "loose ends" can almost always be traced to incomplete or unresolved subplots. Again, you want to be sure that they thematically reflect or contrast with the main plot and don't wander away from it. Subplots should connect with the main story (share scenes or even the final resolution with it) at reasonably regular intervals so they remain integral to the main story. And however long or involved they are, subplot scenes and sequences should not all be jammed together. You don't want to lose sight of the main plot; split up the sequence(s) here and there to interweave subplot scenes with the scenes of the main plot. Where and how is your job, but one hint is that a subplot scene ending in a moment of crisis or high action may be a good jumping-off point into a scene of apparent calm or subdued action in the main plot. This will provide emotional and perhaps visual or aural contrast and give a sense of variety to the motion of the script.

FINAL THOUGHTS

Building Blocks   The smallest story unit is a beat, which constitutes a particular moment or action within a scene. A sequence of beats linked together—introduced, organized and ended properly—add up to a scene. An organized progression of related scenes add up to a sequence. Sequences combine to form the movement that is the screenplay as a whole. Each step of the way is informed and defined by the ebb and flow of the conflict, by the power struggles that result in the progressive empowerment (and occasional setbacks) of the protagonist and the progressive weakening (and occasional victories) of the antagonist. With all this in mind, in the next chapter we'll get into the most productive ways to map out your screenplay.

EXERCISES

1. Break the following scene into beats:

```
EXT. FRONT PORCH — DAY

The shoes belong to BELLE BURNAND, a flaky fifty-year-old
who is always in a quiet, personal hurry. Right now
she's balancing three shopping bags and a hatbox. She
hasn't got a free hand for the door.

                    BELLE
          Knock knock knock! Hands are full!

The door opens on Kasey's sarcastic smile. Belle
scurries...

INSIDE:

                    BELLE
          I'm sorry I'm late, I ran over some dog
          between the funeral and the shopping
          mall.

                    KASEY
          Your son is here.

                    BELLE
          Norman?

                    KASEY
          You only got one son.

Norman comes out of hiding from behind the door.

                    BELLE
          NORMAN! Look at you!

Belle gives him a huge bear hug. The bags are pinched
between them.

                    BELLE
          Oh, crushables! Crushables!

She unloads one sack into Norman's hands.

                    NORMAN JR.
          What's in here, a bowling ball?
```

           BELLE
As a matter of fact, yes.
She opens a package and hauls out a blue
and white swirly Lady Bowler II.

           BELLE
They've got this new PTA bowling team.
It gets me out of the house on Tuesday
nights and Saturday mornings. Now all I'd
need is something to occupy me on Friday
nights and I'd be able to avoid your
father in his retirement completely.

Belle takes some practice swings.

           BELLE
Oh! You won't believe it! They've changed
the supermarket again. Three times in as
many years. Meat against the back wall
now. Canned products where the vegetables
were. You know what I just don't
understand? The milk is right back to the
same place it was two years ago!

Belle stops talking long enough to catch Norman's
troubled look.

           BELLE
What is it? Your father home?

But before he can say it, Caroline enters. At first, she
doesn't see Belle.

          CAROLINE
Norman, did you tell your parents that I
was... Hi.

Belle stops mid swing.

           BELLE
       (dazed)
You brought someone with you.

         NORMAN JR.
Mom, I'd like you to meet Caroline.

Belle just stands there. A frozen stupid look on her
face. Caroline steps up to shake her hand but the
bowling ball is in the way.

> CAROLINE
> Mrs. Burnand, I've heard so much about
> you.

> BELLE
> Like what?

> CAROLINE
> Like... ah.

> NORMAN JR.
> I didn't give away any family secrets.

> BELLE
> Well, it's... ah...

> NORMAN JR.
> ... It's nice to meet you.

> BELLE
> Right. It's nice to meet you. What's your
> name?

> CAROLINE
> Caroline... Chrisler.

> BELLE
> Where did you meet my son?

> CAROLINE
> At the Campus Suicide Prevention Center.

This brings an anxious pause as Belle attempts to cover
her shock.

> CAROLINE
> ... I work there as a counselor. I'm
> getting my Master's in psychology. Norman
> used to do volunteer work there.

> BELLE
>   (dumbfounded)
> My Norman did volunteer work at a suicide
> prevention center?

> CAROLINE
> Yes. It's very rewarding.

> KASEY
> Well... that's interesting.

```
Belle takes control.

                    BELLE
          Kasey! Pick up your sister at school!

                    KASEY
          Yeah right.

Kasey heads for the door. Belle wants to talk to
Norman... alone. There is an uncomfortable lull. Belle
smiles at the stranger. Beat. Caroline gets the message.


                    CAROLINE
          Kasey, can I help?

                    KASEY
          Sure.

Caroline and Kasey exit to the car. Belle waits for them
to clear the door and then...

                    BELLE
          Don't tell me, she's pregnant!
```

2. Write a scene in which the location reveals the larger world of the story, and in which the character has an action that has a beginning, middle and end, and which reveals something about his/her character without telling us everything about his/her intentions.

3. If you are currently working on a screenplay, divide it into scenes and sequences. Give each sequence a title.

Sequence	Title	Scenes
#1		1. 2. 3. 4. 5. etc.
#2		1. 2. 3. 4. 5. etc.
#3		1. 2. 3. 4. 5. etc.
#4		1. 2. 3. 4. 5. etc.

9

Scene Cards

Mapping the Journey

New writers are often so anxious to start that they dive in with a basic idea, hoping to find their way as they go. This method might work for screenwriters with long years of experience who have developed an instinctive sense of how to create scenes and sequences into a coherent structure, but it's almost a surefire path to failure for beginning screenwriters. Finding your way as you go will only lead to wasted scenes, wasted rewrites and wasted time. Although it may seem frustrating and even painful, you have to take the time to work out a detailed step outline before you even think of typing the words "Fade In."

Think of your screenplay as a cross-country trip you want to take; you've only got a few days and you want to see as much as possible while still arriving at your destination on time. If you start driving with only a general sense of where you're going, you'll likely spend a lot of time getting lost, having to stop and ask directions, or doubling back because you missed a turnoff or a landmark you wanted to see. You might even run out of gas in the middle of nowhere, never getting where you wanted to go in the first place. If you don't want to take twice as long to see half as much as you'd hoped, you need to have a map and plan things out before you get into your car.

Your map in screenwriting is your step outline. It lets you plan the overall journey so that you can be sure you're traveling in the right direction and covering all the ground you need to, before you get lost in the details of the actual narration and dialogue. Once you're into the beats and scenes you're writing, it's hard to keep the larger plan in mind, and it's impossible if you haven't formulated the larger plan. You'll tend to wander from scene to scene, hoping your characters will more or less lead you to your story. They won't, they'll just wander with you.

The step outline also helps you maintain objectivity. At this stage, your story isn't locked in, and you can more easily make decisions about what is important and what can be done without. Once you've truly written a scene and given your world and characters a reality within it, it becomes much more difficult to change or eliminate them. You become emotionally attached to that brilliant bit of description or choice line of dialogue, whether or not it (or the character saying it) belongs in the script. The inevitable tendency—since everything to come is still vague and ill-defined—is to then warp the whole course of the story in order to keep these few cherished details, a classic case of the tail wagging the dog.

This is a particular trap for new writers who have not yet internalized the fact that a great scene or line of dialogue that doesn't fit the story only hurts the screenplay. Your story must track easily; each scene must tie directly into it, growing properly out of the preceding scene, and leading inevitably into the following scene.

Perhaps the simplest way to think of it is that creating your step outline is in fact writing your screenplay. In fact, the outline is where you do most of the hard work and where you should spend a great deal of your time. The more complete and polished your outline, the faster and easier your first draft will be. Instead of staring at the screen, tormented over what to write next or how to resolve the situation you've gotten yourself into, you'll already know the answers, and you'll breeze on through. Your step outline details the various destinations that together form the map of your journey. Once this is done—and not until it is done—the journey of the screenplay can begin.

IT'S IN THE CARDS

The most common way to compose a step outline is to use scene cards. These are nothing more than 3" × 5" index cards on which the writer jots a brief description of each scene, one scene per card. The cards are then pinned on a bulletin board or spread on the floor, arranged, rearranged, rewritten and modified until they form sequences so that, eventually, the full structure of the movie is realized. The number of scenes and sequences changes for every screenplay, but usually you'll need between forty and sixty scene cards and eight or more sequences to plot out your entire screenplay. Some gurus insist that there are only eight sequences in any good script, that break down to three acts: two for Act One, four for Act Two, and two for Act Three. Some insist there are seven sequences. Some insist there are twelve. We insist that each script is different, and you should write what works for your story. If you have less than eight sequences, however, your script will probably either be too short or will feel play-like because you've limited your location and scene changes; more than sixteen or so and the script will probably be too long.

The advantage of using scene cards instead of simply outlining scenes on a page is that they're easier to rearrange, they force you to keep descriptions brief and essential (there isn't much room on a card), and they allow you to step back and actually see the flow of the story. There are now a variety of writing and screenwriting programs that include a "corkboard" function with virtual "scene cards"; some of them allow you to export these into screenplay format as well. These virtual corkboards aren't bad, but you'll be limited by the size of your monitor, and so may sacrifice the ability to see the whole layout of your story, and so we still recommend old-school outlining with physical scene cards.

You'll need a place to display your scene cards. You don't want to have to take out your cards and lay them down every time you begin work. Instead, pin them up on a large bulletin board, ready to be worked on at a moment's notice. You never know when a thought or inspiration will strike, so scene cards should be ready twenty-four hours a day. Your finished scene cards board should look something like this:

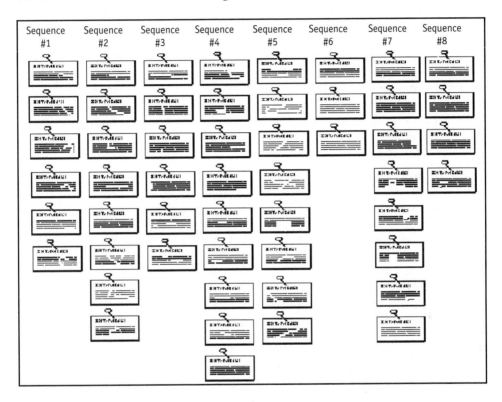

How Much Is Enough?

So, what exactly should be on the cards? Well, at first that depends on how much you know about the scenes you think you'll want. Scene cards are the map, but sometimes you may not have a clear idea of where you're going. If you are not sure (few screenwriters are at first), scene cards can be used to explore the story, as a brainstorming exercise. You don't need to start from the beginning. Just write out the scenes that you think you'll want, put them roughly in the order you think they'll go, and then start filling in the gaps both on and between the cards you have. If you only know that a certain event is going to take place, but haven't figured out exactly which characters will be there or what they'll say, you might simply write down the event: "Titanic hits iceberg," for instance. If you're still searching for your characters—as we all are—you might want to concentrate only on the action and conflict, and how they move the story forward. This will allow you to discover the characters as you go so that they will justify the action. But leave room for more information, which you'll add as you fill in the rest of the scenes and get a clearer idea of the story as a whole.

Some writers spend more time on their scene cards than they do writing the script. Through weeks of working, creating and rearranging, eventually you'll have all your scenes on cards and in proper order. A finished scene card contains the information needed to actually write the scene: information about where and when the scene takes place, who is involved, the event or action, the central conflicts, perhaps a thumbnail of the dialogue that will occur, and how the scene ties into the thematic arc of the story. You may also want to note whether certain characters or events relate to the main plot or the subplot. (Some writers indicate the subplot elements and characters in a different color, so they can get a visual sense of going back and forth between plot and subplot.) The scene cards should end up containing all the relevant information that will go into the scenes themselves. Think of them as rough first drafts of your scenes.

Your scene cards might include:

Location and Time   It's a good idea to top each finished scene card with a scene header (such as INT. LUNCH ROOM — DAY). This header forces you to think of each card as representing a scene that will happen at a particular location and a particular time. Locations are the larger world of the story (see Chapter 4), and you want to be sure that each scene uses the world to best effect. By indicating NIGHT or DAY on the outline cards (occasionally DAWN or DUSK, etc.) you can see at a glance whether the timeline flows logically, or whether there are too many consecutive scenes happening at night or during the day. (Robin once had a student whose script covered a week's worth of action, but somehow it all took place during what seemed to be the course of a single night.) Once you get into actually writing the scene, you'll use your narrative to amplify your descriptions of time and place; for example, you might describe the quality of the night or the golden light of the setting sun to create the proper visual impression and mood.

Characters   Obviously, you'll need to know who appears in the scene. It isn't necessary to indicate every single character, just those central to the action. Some writers jot each name in a color specific to that character, so they can see just by looking at their scene cards if they've left a central player out of the action for too long. We've both seen many student screenplays in which either the protagonist or antagonist mysteriously vanishes for twenty or thirty pages because the writer got lost in a subplot or irrelevant series of scenes and forgot whose story it was. Your story is about your main characters. Make sure they actually show up every so often.

Event/Action   Each scene card should describe at least one significant event essential to the arc of the story, keeping in mind how the event involves the actions or reactions of your characters. In his wonderful little book *Backwards & Forwards*, David Ball states, "When one event causes or permits another event, the two events together comprise an action." Each event flows into the next and defines or triggers a new action. This event-triggering action forms the step outline, which defines the journey of your screenplay. Instead of "the murder takes place," you'll eventually put something like, "Bill shoots Jenny in a jealous rage. Herbert runs for his life, shouting that he'll get even with Bill if it's the last thing he does." (Hopefully your card will say something more original than this, but you get the idea.) And this event, triggering Herbert's flight and threat, will in turn result in another event and action—in a new scene card. Events are what happen in the scene; the action is the characters' deeds, the tactics they use to obtain their goals and objectives.

Conflict Try to note the basic conflicts in the scene. If you can't find any, then you need to rethink or cut the scene. The outline is the place to figure this out, before you've lost sight of the problem in the wondrous camouflage of your narrative and dialogue. Recently, a student writer penned a screenplay in which the middle of the story was occupied by two lovers, who read poems to each other, ran barefoot on the beach and proclaimed their love, without any underlying conflict between them or from outside sources. The fact that the couple was in love was clear within the first eighth of a page, but since nothing dramatic (nothing that threatened or challenged their happiness) occurred for the next fifteen or so, there was no conflict and the story was dead. This could have been solved early on if the writer had attended to the issue of conflict in his outline. We're not saying he should have tossed in a fistfight for no reason; rather, he needed to work out the story better, both what happened in the scenes and how they related to one another, so that the love affair became an essential and exciting part of the larger dramatic (or comedic) arc—in other words, the ebb and flow of power and the conflicts that result.

You Don't Have to Include Minor Scenes Not all scenes must be included in a step outline. Most screenwriters do not include scene cards for establishing shots (interstitial scenes that reveal locations or simple transitions between locations). For example, if you need a short scene in which the characters walk from the car into a house, or get on to the airplane, it's usually not necessary to make a scene card. These are not true scenes, but rather extensions of other, more significant scenes. Only scenes that define action and the thematic arc of the story need to be included in the step outline.

The Whole Deck

Flexibility George Pierce Baker, Eugene O'Neill's professor at Harvard, said, "He who steers by the compass knows how with safety to change his course. He who steers by dead reckoning is liable to error and delay." Scene cards are the compass, but they are not the finished screenplay, so don't feel trapped by your first arrangement of cards. This is where you have the freedom to move things around and see how they work best. Even after you've begun writing you'll occasionally discover that a scene doesn't work or you get a better idea. So go back to the cards and try your changes out there before committing to them.

Below is an example of how the scene cards for an entire movie might look, in this case derived from the comedy/drama *Juno* by Diablo Cody (who won the Academy Award for Best Original Screenplay for this script). Note that in some places where there's a continuous action, even though the exact location may change within the house (for instance), we've counted it as a single scene. We've also "chaptered" each sequence of scenes with a title. Chaptering and titling sequences can help you sort out what happens where in the script, in a way that's more precise and relevant than abstract labels like "plot point one" or "the beginning of Act Two." It's not an exact science, but each sequence, like each scene, should have a beginning, middle, and end in which something important has changed for the characters.

JUNO

Sequence #1 - Sex and the Overstuffed Chair and Girl

1

EXT. HOMETOWN - DUSK

Opening event - Small Minnesota suburb.

Juno, a contemplative sixteen-year-old girl, drinks
from an absurdly oversized carton of juice, and
stares at an overstuffed chair sitting in the yard.

Juno VO: "Where it all began."

FLASHBACK:

INT. BLEEKER HOUSE - NIGHT

Juno walks up to a young boy, takes off her underwear,
and begins making love to him in the same overstuffed
chair.

EXT. HOMETOWN - CONTINUED

We are back with Juno and the discarded overstuffed
sex chair.

She considers it and drinks her juice.

A barking dog jars Juno back to reality.

Juno VO: to her the chair is magnificent.

2

EXT. LOCAL DRUGSTORE - FRONT COUNTER

Juno buys a pregnancy test "pee stick."

She tells the polyester-uniformed clerk that she
has had too much Sunny D so she needs to use the
bathroom, but he knows the truth.

With intense skepticism, the clerk gives her a hard
time. This is her third pregnancy test in two days.

3

INT. DRUGSTORE - BATHROOM

Hiding in the dark bathroom stall Juno clumsily
struggles to use the discount pregnancy test.

4

INT. LOCAL DRUGSTORE - FRONT COUNTER

Juno comes out of the bathroom and waits for the
results.

A pink "+" appears in the stick. Juno tries to shake
the Pregnancy Test to reset it, but it's not an
Etch-a-Sketch.

She buys a bag of Super Rope Licorice.

5

EXT. STREET - EVENING

Juno walks home. The high school cross-country track
team passes her. She is obviously not happy about the
pregnancy.

She stops at a low-hanging tree branch and makes a
hangman's noose from the Super Rope Licorice - and
eats it.

6

JUNO'S BEDROOM (intercut with) INT. LEAH'S HOUSE -
BEDROOM - NIGHT

Juno's room is decorated with punk posters; she has
a childish hamburger-shaped phone.

Juno calls her high school cheerleader friend Leah
and tells her she's pregnant. Leah suggests that
it's most likely "a food baby" - Did you have a big
lunch?

Leah brings up abortion - it's Juno's only option.

Sequence #2 - How Can a Boy Be a Father?

7

EXT. HOUSE - NIGHT

Leah and Juno struggle to drag the overstuffed sex
chair across the manicured suburban lawn. Leah wants
to know how Juno decided to go all the way with
Bleeker - Juno tells her about Spanish Class.

INSET - Bleeker passes Juno a note - She likes
what she reads. She obviously has a huge crush on
Bleeker.

Leah continues to push Juno for more information
about her love for Bleeker but Juno isn't willing to
talk about it in her fragile state.

8

INT. BLEEKER'S BEDROOM - MORNING

Bleeker is no older than Juno. His room has a cheesy
race car-themed decoration that hasn't been changed
since he was five.

He's just a kid - And a cross-country track runner.

He puts on long socks and short--too short--runner's
pants. With a microwaved croissant pocket he is ready
to face the day.

9

EXT. BLEEKER HOUSE - MORNING

Bleeker walks out of his house for his morning run.
He finds Juno sitting in the front yard in the
overstuffed sex chair smoking a pipe - Or at least
pretending to.

The high school cross-country team runs by, he's
late.

"I'm pregnant." He is dumbfounded. She suggests an
abortion. He's cool with that - Juno tries to be
cool too, but she is clearly disappointed.

Sequence #3 - The Life of a Pregnant Sixteen-Year-Old

10

EXT. HIGH SCHOOL HALLWAY - DAY

Juno rummages through her locker - drops something.
Steve Rendazo passes by and gives her a hard time,
but doesn't help.

Juno VO: Rendazo always wanted her. Boys like him
are really into cello-playing girls who will grow up
to be librarians. Leah is into paunchy middle-aged
teachers.

Sixteen-year-olds are really
screwed up when it comes to sex.

11

INT. HIGH SCHOOL - SCIENCE LAB - DAY

Juno and Bleeker are paired up with two other lab
partners - it's uncomfortable for them.

Before they can say anything they watch their lab partners fight about their relationship - one has a menstrual
migraine and the other is sick. They stalk off.

Relationships don't work.

12

INT. JUNO'S BEDROOM - AFTERNOON

Juno looks at a newspaper ad - "Pregnant? Need Help?"
Using her wonky hamburger phone, she calls the number
and inquires into an abortion.

Juno VO: she hates it when adults use the term
"sexually active." It's just so wrong.

INSET - High school health teacher, in slow motion
puts a condom on a banana.

FLASHBACK to Bleeker's face
during sex - it was obviously
his deflowering too.

13

NARRATED MONTAGE - JUNO'S FAMILY

We meet Juno's father for the first time. He is a salt-
of-the-earth, working-class HVAC (Heating Ventilation
Air Conditioning) repairman.

Juno VO: how her mother left and lives in a trailer
park in Arizona with replacement kids. And how she
sends Juno a cactus every Valentine's Day. It doesn't
help.

And how her stepmother's nail salon smells like methyl
methacrylate.

14

INT. DINING ROOM - NIGHT

Juno's stepmother asks Juno if
she barfed in her urn.

Inset - We see Juno hit with
morning sickness throwing up a
blue slushie in the urn.

Back to the dinning - Juno
denies it.

Sequence #4 - Juno Decides to Keep the Baby

15

EXT. WOMEN'S CLINIC - DAY

Juno tentatively approaches the clinic. There is a
lone abortion protester - A young girl who Juno knows.
The protester tells Juno that her baby has a beating
heart and fingernails.

Juno considers this but then pushes open the clinic
door.

16

INT. WOMEN'S CLINIC - RECEPTION - DAY

The lobby is cold. The punk receptionist sits behind
bulletproof glass. She offers Juno a boysenberry
condom - it makes her boyfriend's genitals smell like
pie.

Juno tries to fill out the admitting form but cannot
concentrate because the women in the waiting room are
nervously scratching and tapping. More tapping. More
scratching. Juno panics.

17

EXT. LEAH'S HOUSE - DAY

Juno confesses to Leah that she couldn't go through
with it. It was all just too disgusting.

Juno decides to have the baby!

She is going to give it away, perhaps to some nice
lesbians. Leah suggests that if she's going to have
the baby then she should find adoptive parents in the
local Penny Saver newspaper.

18

EXT. PARK BENCH - DAY

Juno and Leah look through the ads of the Penny
Saver. She is particular about whom she is going to
give the child.

Bingo! She finds the perfect couple in the Penny
Saver - Mark and Vanessa Loring. He is handsome, she
is pretty, they appear to be perfect.

Sequence #5 - Old Parents, New Parents

19

INT. BLEEKER'S BEDROOM - NIGHT

Alone in his room, Bleeker stares at a picture of Juno
in the high school yearbook - It's obvious that he
still cares for her.

There is a knock at the door: his mother calling him
to dinner. He's not hungry. She tells him that she
doesn't like Juno.

He cannot admit that he's still
in love with her.

20

INT. JUNO'S HOUSE - LIVING ROOM - AFTERNOON

Juno paces nervously - it's time to tell them. They
cannot figure out what's up. Has she been using drugs?
Has she been kicked out of school?

Juno tells her parents she pregnant.

Her father wants to know the father. She tells them.
They wish it had been drugs. That would have been
easier to deal with.

21

INT./EXT. LORING HOUSE - DAY

We see only the hands of Mark and Vanessa Loring as they make every
detail of their McMansion perfect. They want to make a good impression.

Juno and her father pull up in their old car. The house and neighborhood
are impressive. Juno and her father are out of place.

Vanessa is pretty and meticulous. She is desperate for a baby. Mark is
a cool guy. Also present is the Lorings' attorney.

Juno acts cocky, she doesn't
want to know about what's going
to happen to the baby after it's
born, she'll deliver it, give
it up, and it's over. And no
compensation. She just wants a
cool couple to love it.

22

INT. LORING HOUSE - DAY

During a break from the negotiations, Juno uses the
fancy bathroom. She has a sixteen-year-old's fascination
with Vanessa's stuff. She spritzes on some perfume.

Coming back to the meeting Juno runs into Mark. She
spies a guitar in one of the rooms. Mark shows her.

Juno knows a little about guitars and loves music -
she finds out Mark once played in a rock and roll
band. It's pretty darn cool for Juno.

Vanessa and Juno's father talk about Vanessa's Pilates
Machine - he's never seen one before.

Then they hear music coming from upstairs.

23

INT. LORING HOUSE - DAY

Mark composes commercial jingles
- he's given up his dream of
being a rock and roll star. Mark
and Juno play unplugged guitar.
He's teaching her a couple of
chords when Vanessa enters and
stops the jam session.

Unlike Mark, Vanessa is all business, desperate for a child
and doesn't want her more immature husband to blow the deal.

But a deal is made. Vanessa wants to be kept up on any
ultrasounds. She's worried that Juno might change her mind.
Juno's cool. If she could she would give them the child now.

Juno and her father leave. Vanessa breaks down in desperate
tears.

Sequence #6 — Babies Who Made a Baby

24

EXT. HIGH SCHOOL TRACK - DAY

Bleeker is running laps with a friend who tells him
that Juno is pregnant and everyone knows it's his.
Poor Bleeker's brain is on information overload. He's
much too young to be a father.

25

INT. HIGH SCHOOL - DAY

The school administrator is disgusted by Juno's
pregnant belly as she hands over a hall pass.

In the hall, Juno bumps into Bleeker. He invites her
to movies but she can't, because of her ultrasound.
He offers to come with her but she feels it's just
not right.

26

INT. DOCTOR'S OFFICE - AFTERNOON

THE ULTRASOUND: goo is poured on Juno's belly. Juno
and her stepmother watch the ultrasound - there it is,
a baby. Juno doesn't want to know the baby's sex.

Ultrasound tech, like the school administrator, can't
help but be disgusted by Juno's young age and large
belly.

Juno's stepmother comes to her defense.

27

INT. JUNO'S BEDROOM - DAY

Alone in her little girl bedroom, Juno lies on the
bed looking at the ultrasound. She makes a decision.

Sequence #7 - Juno Bonds with Mark and Bleeker

28

EXT. LORING HOUSE - ENTRY

Juno, unrepentant, arrives. Vanessa is not there but
Mark invites her in. Juno shows him the ultrasound.
He's interested but not fanatical like Vanessa.

They bond over their love for rock bands and gory
slasher movies. Mark is really a child.

29

INT. LORING HOUSE - AFTERNOON

Mark and Juno are watching a silly gory slasher movie when
Vanessa arrives. She is clearly uncomfortable about Juno being
there alone with her husband.

Juno shows Vanessa the ultrasound - she's thrilled.

Juno goes to leave. The entryway is piled with gifts for the
baby. Juno asks why they didn't have a baby shower. Vanessa
admits that they didn't because they are worried that she, Juno,
might change her mind.

The Lorings have gone through this before and the girl pulled out.
Juno tries to help, but nothing can relieve Vanessa's worries.

Juno leaves, Vanessa is panic-stricken.

30

EXT. JUNO'S HOUSE - NIGHT

Juno's Stepmom is worried about why Juno went to the
Lorings' home. Just mail them the ultrasound - after
all, Mark is a married man and there are boundaries.

They fight. As an act of revenge Juno dumps her blue
slushie in the stepmother's urn.

31

EXT. BLEEKER's HOUSE - NIGHT

Juno knocks, looking even more pregnant.

Bleeker's mother answers. Visibly annoyed, she
escorts Juno up to Bleekers's room.

32

INT. BLEEKER's BEDROOM - NIGHT

Bleeker is studying and sucking on orange Tic-Tacs.

Juno VO: on the night of her deflowering, Bleeker was sucking on orange
Tic-Tacs. It's the only thing she doesn't like about him.

Juno wants to know if he will still think she's cute when she's fat -
he thinks she's beautiful - Juno is caught off guard by his sincerity.
Bleeker says that after this is all over they could get back together -
Juno asks, were we together?

Testing him, Juno offers to set him up with another girl but he doesn't
like the idea - that girls smells like soup.

Sequence #8 - Will the Baby Kick for Neurotic Vanessa?

33

INT. LORING HOUSE - NURSERY - DAY

Mark and Vanessa have been painting the nursery. She
wants to know which is the right color, custard or
cheesecake. Mark doesn't care - they are both yellow
to him.

He thinks it's too early to paint, she obsesses on
every tiny detail.

34

INT. MALL - DAY

Leah and Juno walk through the mall. They see
Vanessa, playing with a friend's toddler in a play
area - she would make a good mother.

35

INT. MALL - LATER

Leah and Juno bump into Vanessa at the elevator.
Vanessa asks Juno how the pregnancy is going. Juno
lifts her shirt and shows Vanessa her popped-out navel.

The baby kicks - Vanessa wants to feel it, but when
she puts her hand on Juno's oversized belly, nothing
happens. Vanessa can't feel anything. The baby is not
moving for her.

In the middle of the mall Vanessa tries to get a
reaction from the baby by talking to Juno's belly.

She is thrilled when the baby finally kicks.

Sequence #9 - Bleeker and Mark Both Mess Up

36

INT. HIGH SCHOOL - DAY

Time has passed. Juno walks down the hall.

As the kids pass they are fixated on her enormous belly. Many are
disgusted.

At lunch Juno complains to Leah that for the first time in her life
she has to wear a bra and everyone in the high school is staring
at her.

Leah tells Juno that Bleeker is going to the prom with the girl who
smells like soup. Juno thinks it must be a pity date but she is
jealous.

At his locker, Bleeker is helping himself to orange Tic-Tacs when
Juno walks up. She asks him if he is really going to the prom with
the soup girl. He is.

Juno is pissed. Bleeker defends his decision and accuses her of
being immature. They break up - if they were ever together.

37

INT. CAR - DAY

Juno is so pregnant she has trouble getting in.

She puts on lipstick and adjusts her hair, makes
herself as desirable as a hugely pregnant sixteen-
year-old can be.

38

INT. LORING HOUSE - MUSIC ROOM - DAY

Vanessa is not home. Mark and Juno share music and
end up slow dancing together. Juno's belly bumps up
against him. She has a massive crush on him. And he on
her…

At this tender moment Mark tells Juno that he is
leaving Vanessa.

What about the baby? Juno is shocked - They fight.

Sequence #10 - Juno and Vanessa Hit Rock Bottom

39

INT. LORING HOUSE - KITCHEN - DAY

Vanessa enters with more baby toys. She bumps into
Juno, who is crying on her way out.

Mark enters - he says he has cold feet about the
adoption. Vanessa confronts Mark - will he ever grow
up? They argue - Juno storms out.

40

INT. CAR - DAY

THE DARK MOMENT: Sitting on the side of a lonely
stretch of highway, Juno cries. She tries to pull
her self together.

41

EXT. CORNER STORE - NIGHT

Juno contemplates her future. Then she is hit by an
idea.

She finds a crumpled up Jiffy Lube receipt in the
back seat and writes something on it. We do not see
what she wrote.

42

INT. LORING DINING ROOM - NIGHT

Depressed, Vanessa tilts back a glass of wine. Mark
enters. He says that their lawyer can represent both
of them in a collaborative divorce.

There is a knock at the door. They answer just as
Juno screeches away. Juno has left the note written
on the Jiffy Lube receipt.

Sequence #11 - Can Two People Love Each Other Forever?

43

JUNO'S HOUSE - NIGHT

Juno picks a flower from the unkempt garden out front and places it against her belly.

44

INT. JUNO'S HOUSE - KITCHEN - NIGHT

Juno tells her father that she is losing faith in humanity. She wonders if two people can stay together. Her father didn't.

Her father tells her that she needs to find the right person who loves her for who she is. She likes what she hears. She is in love.

Enlightenment.

45

INT. BLEEKER'S BEDROOM - NIGHT

In the middle of the night, Leah and Juno screech off in her old car - they've done something. But what?

46

EXT. BLEEKER'S FRONT PORCH - DAY

Next morning. Bleeker comes out of his house to find the words "Check the mail" scrawled in chalk on the front steps.

He checks the mailbox, it's full of orange Tic-Tacs. Bleeker smiles.

47

EXT. HIGH SCHOOL TRACK - MORNING

Bleeker sees Juno approach. Juno admits that she is in love with him. Every time she looks at him the baby kicks.

They kiss, oblivious to the gawking high school kids in the background.

Sequence #12 - Juno Gets Her Man, Vanessa Gets Her Boy

48

INT. JUNO'S BEDROOM - MORNING

She drives a toy car over her oversized belly when
suddenly, it's time!

49

INT. HOSPITAL ROOM - DAY

Juno is in obvious discomfort. She begs for a spinal
tap painkiller.

Juno gives birth.

50

EXT. HIGH SCHOOL TRACK - DAY

Bleeker is running in a track meet. He's winning.

Juno narrates that she decided not to tell Bleeker
about the birth right away because of the track meet.

After finishing a dash, Bleeker looks into the stands
and worries that she is not there. Suddenly, he
figures it out and runs towards the hospital.

51

INT. HOSPITAL ROOM - DAY

Juno is comforted by her father. Bleeker arrives -
still wearing his track uniform.

Juno VO: she and Bleeker decided not to see the
baby.

52

INT. HOSPITAL - MATERNITY WARD - DAY

A nurse swaddles newborn baby. Vanessa looks in at the
baby.

Vanessa holds her baby son.

53

INT. LORING HOUSE - NURSERY

Vanessa's perfect nursery is finished. It's yellow.
We see a rocking chair.

Juno VO: it started with a chair and ends with a
chair.

We see the Jiffy Lube note that Juno left. It's been
framed. It reads, "Vanessa, if you're still in, I'm
still in."

54

EXT. STREET -DAY

EPILOGUE: A few months later - a sparkling summer
afternoon. Juno rides her bike over to Bleeker's
house.

Bleeker and Juno share the afternoon and a song.

They kiss.

The high school runners pass by.

The End.

FINAL THOUGHTS

One Step at a Time. At UCLA film school, students have to turn out a first draft of a new screenplay every ten weeks (UCLA is on a trimester rather than semester system). Writing a 100- to 120-page screenplay in such a short time is a daunting challenge. After almost missing their deadlines on their first scripts, most students quickly discover that they are diving into their screenplays too quickly and spending too little time on their step outlines. Their panic over time—and the subsequent headlong rush into writing before their stories are thought out—usually leads to many false starts, endlessly rewritten first pages, and even failure to finish their first drafts at all. Robin once had a student who was confident in his ability to write quickly and who thought wasting time on a step outline would only slow him down. At the end of eight weeks the student came to Robin's office, distraught. He'd written almost 250 pages and still had no idea how (or when) he was going to end his screenplay. Finally beaten into submission, he retreated, spent a sleepless week coming up with a step outline that worked, and was able to go back and finish a 110-page first draft by the end of the term, one week later.

Perhaps the most important scene sequence is that which opens the screenplay. To this we've devoted the next chapter.

EXERCISES

1. Study the structure of an existing movie similar in genre or theme to what you want to write. Find one you can rent and watch it with pen in hand. Write down every important scene as you watch it on scene cards until you have "step outlined" the entire movie. When the cards are done, pin them up on a board and study how the story is organized. How many scenes are there? Are they all necessary, and if so, why? Why not? How do plot and sub-plot map out? Does the story follow a three-act structure, or does it employ another model? What structural lessons can it show you that might help you build your story?

2. Looking at the scene cards for *Juno*, identify a specific scene sequence and describe why it is a scene sequence and how it works within the larger story. Then write out a scene sequence for your screenplay, using scene cards. Do the scenes flow into each other properly and create a discrete unit within the larger story?

10

Entering the Story

First and Ten

This is a fact of life: if your first ten pages—roughly the first ten minutes of the movie—aren't what they need to be, your script has very little chance of being taken on by an agent or bought by a producer. "Hey, that's not fair!" you say. "That's less than ten percent of what I've written here!" True, but it's the most important less-than-ten-percent in terms of how your script will be read.

We reiterate—there are literally hundreds of thousands of scripts out there that need to be analyzed quickly and economically by tired readers, agents and producers; so don't hope they'll get to the good stuff on page 23. They won't unless there's good stuff on the preceding 22 pages.

"But," you complain, "you said a reader is paid to provide a complete synopsis of my script to his boss, so he'll have to read the great stuff on page 23!" Yes, but he won't read it carefully or with much enthusiasm. You'll have lost him. Not because he's a jerk (well, okay, he might be), but because he's looking for a good MOVIE for his boss to make. And he knows that a movie must have a gripping, irresistible opening, or it will lose its audience. If a movie based on your script would have people heading for the exits after ten or twenty boring or confusing opening minutes, your reader is going to assume you don't know what you're doing. And guess what? He'll be right.

The world, the protagonist, the antagonist, the tone, the theme, the stakes and the nature of the conflict all must be there within the first ten pages or so and in such a complete and compelling fashion that the reader simply must read on. As if that isn't hard enough, you must also make clear in the first few pages that, in this world, this story is the *essential* conflict, and your characters are the *essential* people to resolve it.

In order to see how so much can be done in such a seemingly short amount of time, let's take a look at two very different but effective movies, *The Terminator* and *Big Night* (the hit of the 1996 Sundance Film Festival) and examine how their first ten minutes work.

THE TERMINATOR: MAN VS. MACHINE

The Terminator is a Frankenstein story set in an action/adventure, science-fiction framework. (Mary Shelley's original *Frankenstein* was itself a kind of science fiction, in its own time.)

The world is the "normal," present-day city of Los Angeles, set in contrast to a potentially horrific future society in which machines have nearly wiped us out. The protagonist is an average, present-day working girl, assisted by a brave but virginal soldier from that future. The antagonist is an unstoppable robotic killing machine from this hellish future, disguised as a man. The tone is ominous and frightening, with moments of dark humor. The stakes are both global (if our heroes don't succeed, humanity will be wiped out) and also intensely personal (if our heroes don't succeed, they and their unborn child, the hope of the future, will die).

The nature of the conflict in *The Terminator* is the survival of the human race vs. the prospect of its complete annihilation. It is also about living, breathing people vs. a soulless killing machine. In the near future, government scientists (hubristic, faceless members of society) will create a "Frankenstein"—an intelligent, computerized defense system that will turn on its makers. Now, other fallible but courageous human beings—an everyday woman and a soldier who loves her—must fight their way back from the brink of this apocalypse. And all this is set up in the first few pages.

Let's see how *The Terminator* does this.

> MINUTE ONE/TWO: The movie begins at night in the blighted future, with human bones strewn among the wreckage of a ruined city. Terrifying machines crunch human skulls under caterpillar treads or fly through the sky shooting lasers at desperate human resistance fighters. A "crawl" (a written message superimposed on the screen) informs us that this is Los Angeles, 2029, but also that the battle of this story does not take place in the horrendous future we are looking at, but today.
>
> MINUTE THREE: The next scene, also at night, returns us to the present day. It takes us behind a schoolyard, where a dump truck is pulling in. Suddenly, flashes of static electricity frighten away the truck driver. There's a bright blast of light and a thunderclap, out of which appears a naked, perfect, muscular man, who kneels in fetal position on the pavement: the Terminator. He shows no pain or emotion. He stands up and walks to a view overlooking the lights of the city below.
>
> MINUTE FOUR/FIVE: He hears noise from several punk teenagers nearby and goes to them. They make fun of his nakedness; he repeats their words in a monotone,

and then demands their clothes. They refuse and attack him. One punk stabs him in the stomach, to no effect. The Terminator plunges his fist into the punk's chest, effortlessly lifting him off his feet and killing him. The others quickly give the Terminator their clothes.

MINUTE SIX: Down in a seedy alley, a bum is disturbed by a similar electrical disturbance. Another naked man, Reese, appears—but this time he drops hard to the pavement, in agony. He is muscular, but smaller than the Terminator. His hair is ragged, his skin scarred.

MINUTE SEVEN: Reese steals some filthy clothes from the bum. A police car appears, its searchlight finding him. The cops order Reese to stop, but he runs away. They chase him through the trash-strewn alley. He's fast, agile.

MINUTE EIGHT: More cops chase him; Reese runs into one who has his gun drawn and shoots, but misses. Reese snatches the gun away and points it at the cop, demanding to know what date and year it is. He escapes the cops by breaking into a department store. He's momentarily confused by the plastic mannequins. Then he steals some shoes and moves on. Coming back into the alley, Reese goes to an empty police car left behind in the pursuit, and steals the shotgun. Then he disappears into the night.

MINUTE NINE: Reese finds a phone booth and scans it for the name of Sarah Connor. He finds several, rips out the page. We then meet SARAH on her moped, a typical young woman, not gorgeous, but appealing. She's late for work as a waitress at a diner. We see her name again on her time card. She's harassed from the first moment, trying to get to all the complaining customers, knocking over a glass of water. A little boy makes her life even more miserable by dumping his scoop of ice cream into her apron pouch. Her coworker whispers to her, "Look at it this way: in a hundred years, who's gonna care?"

MINUTE TEN/ELEVEN: The Terminator, wearing the punks' clothes, punches out a car window and gets in. He rips open the steering column with his bare hands and hot-wires the car. He goes to a huge pawn shop/gun shop, and after selecting a huge arsenal of weapons, kills the owner. Then he, too, finds the list of "Sarah Connors" in a phone book, after first effortlessly yanking out the big bruiser who was using the phone booth.

Let's go back over this and see if we have our essentials: the best "world" for the story, an essential protagonist, an essential antagonist, a strong tone, a clear theme, high stakes and plenty of conflict.

In the first minute we see that the stakes are a future ruined by machines gone amuck, but that the conflict will take place today. The world of our story is clearly presented, as is the central conflict. The theme begins to emerge; the tone is appropriately dark and ominous. It's interesting to note that this prologue was not in the original script, but was added later. As the film progressed, it became clear that the audience would need to better understand both the two worlds and the stakes of the story early on, in order to fully identify with the dilemma of the characters.

Three minutes in we meet the Terminator, our antagonist. He is huge, perfect, without pain or emotion, though at this point we don't know he's a machine. He is shown to us in a superior position, looking down from a height over the sleeping city. And he kills the first human he encounters. Right away we know the Terminator is powerful, lethal and unstoppable. And he gets some cool, heavy-metal clothes.

By six minutes in, we meet our chief ally, Reese, in a roughly parallel way. Reese is fearless, but clearly human, battle-scarred and on the run. He does not emerge in painless perfection from the mysterious electrical cocoon or calmly look down on the sprawling city. Reese drops right into the city, into an alley no less, right into the grime of humanity. He looks as if he belongs there, too, especially when he puts on the bum's clothes. Unlike the Terminator, who seems to know exactly what date it is, Reese is unsure. He is a skilled fighter, but not superhuman. And he kills no one. His character is clear and distinct from the Terminator's.

The parallel structure is repeated as both Reese and the Terminator acquire weapons (the Terminator again killing to get them, while Reese doesn't), and both find Sarah Connor in the phone book. The comparison shows us that this ally, though tough and capable, is definitely up against a more powerful and ruthless antagonist. They think alike, and are both after the same thing: Sarah Connor. The larger, somewhat abstract stakes of a destroyed future are therefore made personal: one young woman's life is in danger.

But Reese is not the main protagonist. Sarah is. Although at first she seems to be the object of salvation, the "princess in the tower," Sarah is the one who undergoes the greatest transformation, from waitress to warrior to mother of the future. Reese and the Terminator are both outsiders to our "world," two sides of the same problem for Sarah—whether she will die or live to fulfill her destiny. Importantly, when we first meet her, she is "one of us," an ordinary person just trying to get by, someone in whom we can invest our feelings.

The conflict is clear. Two people must rise above themselves (gain power) and destroy (deprive of power) the flawless robotic emissary of a futuristic war machine if the human race is to survive. The imagery reinforces this conflict. From the death machines in the future, we cut to the seemingly innocuous machinery of the dump truck, and then the Terminator appears. The dump truck, with its frightened human driver, prepares us for the garbage-strewn alley into which Reese is "dumped" and alludes to the terror humanity is about to face. These, in turn, tell us that our human champions are severely outmatched—it's going to take every resource Reese and Sarah can muster simply to stop the Terminator.

By the tenth minute (page nine of the script), the dialogue subtly reiterates the stakes: "In a hundred years, who's gonna care?" The prologue has shown us that in a hundred years, the world may be a living hell. The first ten pages vividly present all the needed elements and leave us in no doubt that Sarah and Reese, in all their fallible humanity, are somehow uniquely indispensable in preventing that future from happening. We identify with Sarah, admire Reese, and are genuinely terrified by the Terminator.

All of the above clearly expresses and reinforces the theme, that is, by giving away power and responsibility to the machines we create, we may unleash the terrible forces of our own destruction. Only by retaining our own humanity can we survive. And it's all there in the first ten minutes: the best "world" for the story, an essential protagonist (plus a great ally), an essential antagonist, a strong tone, a clear theme, high stakes and plenty of conflict. What reader could put it down?

BIG NIGHT: SOUL VS. SUCCESS

Stanley Tucci and Joseph Tropiano's award-winning *Big Night* is about as different from *The Terminator* as it can be. It's a small, intimate character drama about two immigrant Italian brothers in the 1950s who are trying to open their own restaurant. The older brother, Primo, is the chef, a true artist unwilling to compromise his vision of what food should be to suit their middle-brow American customers. Primo longs to go back to the old country and hasn't learned much English yet. Secondo, the younger brother, speaks English better and longs to achieve the American dream of financial success, even if it means compromise. Serious tensions arise between the brothers because of their different visions and desires.

Such a film, about ordinary people living their lives, is perhaps the hardest kind of film to write because there are no special effects, gunfights, lurid sex or violence to juice up the conflict and distract from lack of character. There is nothing but character interaction to create the drama and stakes of the story. Because of this, such scripts often tend to wander, following their protagonists through the minutiae and random conversations of their day in an attempt to be "honest" and true to life. The problem, as we've said, is that movies are not true to life; they are true to its essence, as defined by the filmmaker. A character drama must be as concise and compelling in its first ten pages as any other kind of screenplay. So let's see how the first ten pages of *Big Night* accomplishes this. First we'll go over the main elements.

The world is a small New Jersey town in which the brothers have opened a restaurant, an ordinary slice of America in the 1950s. The protagonist is Secondo, the younger of the two brothers. Driven, ambitious, he longs for the kind of success that, to him, defines the American dream. The antagonist (not the bad guy, but the oppositional character) is his older brother, Primo, a brilliant chef who resents the crassness of America, longs for the Old World, and defines success in terms of artistic purity. It may at first seem that Pascal—the ruthless, successful restaurateur across the street—is the antagonist, but in fact he is a false ally, someone who pretends friendship while actually sabotaging Secondo. Pascal forces Secondo to recognize the truths that Primo represents. He is an example of the success Secondo thinks he wants, without realizing that such success comes at a terrible cost, a cost that Primo is unwilling to pay.

The tone is quiet and intimate, defined by the sleepy restaurant and the streets of this small town. Both the drama and the humor come from the complex reality of the characters, their immigrant background and their hopes and dreams. These also define the stakes: will Secondo succeed in achieving the American Dream? If he does, will it be at the cost of his own dignity and Primo's integrity? Such personal stakes are not heroic or larger than life; they do not affect the world at large. Rather, they represent the challenge common people face as they struggle to make a success of their own lives. The stakes are compelling not because we are in awe of them, but because we can identify with them.

Let's look at the first ten pages (minutes) and see how all of this is introduced, minute by minute.

> MINUTE ONE: The film opens at dusk. The restaurant's Spanish busboy, Cristiano, sits looking at the ocean, quietly eating a piece of homemade bread. He goes back to the restaurant; the kitchen entrance faces the ocean.
>
> MINUTE TWO: Cristiano enters to find Primo and Secondo in the kitchen, cooking risotto. He picks up some plates and goes through the doors to the restaurant. Primo asks Secondo to try it: "Prova?" ("Try it?" in Italian) Secondo tries it and approves. Primo asks in Italian if it needs more salt. Secondo insists he ask again, in English. They discuss the finer points of the ingredients, Primo cautioning his little brother to cut up the garlic the right way. He reverts to speaking Italian, and cleans the garlic smell from his fingers with a slice of lemon.
>
> As Cristiano comes back into the kitchen, Secondo tells him to get ready—the restaurant opens in five minutes. Cristiano comments in Spanish that it's a lot of work for not much money. He goes to wash the ashtrays, but the plumbing doesn't work well.

Secondo, nervous about the opening, gets dressed up in
a suit and tie. He picks up menus, labeled "Paradise
Restaurant." In the restaurant, he goes around fussing,
straightening the silverware, perfecting every table
setting. Original and interesting paintings hang on the
walls.

MINUTE THREE: Secondo downs an espresso (in the film it's
a shot of vodka). Then he carefully turns the "Closed"
sign to "Open." Stepping out the front door to the
street, he carefully adjusts the placement of the potted
plants outside. For a moment in the script we see his
dream of some wealthy patrons arriving in a Cadillac,
dressed in all their finery. But it's just a daydream,
and he goes back inside.

MINUTE FOUR: Later; Primo is still perfecting his seafood
risotto. Secondo is urging him to serve it already, as
the sole customers in the restaurant have been waiting an
hour. They smoke as they eat; as Secondo brings out their
dishes, they say it took so long they thought he had to
go all the way back to Italy to get it. Woman isn't sure
this is what she ordered: she doesn't see the seafood in
it. Then she asks for a side order of spaghetti. Secondo
tries to explain to her that they're both starch, but
she insists. She wants spaghetti with meatballs. Secondo
tells her they don't make meatballs; exasperated, she
finally just orders a side of plain spaghetti. But she
isn't happy.

MINUTE FIVE: Primo argues with Secondo about making
a side order of spaghetti: "Who are these people in
America?" Primo asks. Secondo insists that "This is what
the customer asked for--make it, make it, make it." These
are their only customers. Primo counters that the woman
is a criminal, a philistine. Secondo is sick of having
this argument every night. Furious, Primo throws a pot at
the door.

(The next five minutes contain roughly the same scenes in both the script and
the finished film, but their order has been changed around a bit. For the purpose of this analysis we'll stick to the film, since that is what the filmmakers,
who were also the screenwriters, eventually determined was the best way to
open the film.)

MINUTE SIX: There's a brief scene of the two brothers silently going to bed, side by side in their little apartment bedroom.

MINUTE SEVEN/EIGHT: The next day, Secondo visits his banker, PIERCE. He tries to seem cool and collected, talking about their renovation plans. Pierce abruptly tells him he's going to have to change the direction of the conversation right now: Secondo is behind on his loan payments. He'll have to do something, maybe sell his car. He worries that Secondo may not understand him; Secondo responds "I speak English." He tries to explain the situation, that he's doing everything he can, but Pierce insists there's no more time. They'll foreclose if they don't get a payment that month.

MINUTE NINE: That night while Cristiano puts the chairs on the tables, Secondo compares the day's meager receipts with the bills he must pay. STASH, a painter and friend, sits with Primo and finishes a meal. He compliments them on being the only restaurant where he can get rabbit, and apologizes that he can't pay with money; instead he gives them another painting. Primo laughs it off: "Please, money. What would I do with money?" Secondo hopes that someday Stash will become rich and famous so he can pay them with money. Primo is enthusiastic about the painting. Secondo just says, "Great, put it with the rest of them."

MINUTE TEN/ELEVEN: Secondo approaches Primo, who's alone in the restaurant, reading an Italian newspaper. He asks "How do you feel if we take risotto off the menu?" Primo pretends not to hear him, forcing him to repeat the question. Secondo tries to make it seem sensible: risotto costs them a lot to make and the customers don't really understand it. Primo at first seems to agree. Then he says, maybe they could instead serve "...what do they call them? You know...hot dogs? Hot dogs, hot dogs, hot dogs. I think people would like that. Those." It's an unkind dig at his brother, and he retreats: "If you give people time, they learn." Secondo angrily answers that they don't have time, and this is a restaurant, not a school.

Are all of our essentials present here in the first ten minutes? In the first two minutes, the world, tone and characters are clearly defined. We start with an immigrant worker, eating food and looking at the ocean over which the immigrants have come. We then meet our protagonist and antagonist in the restaurant itself, which forms the largest part of their world, the setting for the conflict between art and commerce, sustenance and failure. It's almost night, which is when the restaurant comes to life. The tone is set by the quiet location, the careful skill and clear tensions between the brothers as they prepare to open. The themes of becoming an American and preserving one's integrity are clear from the very first lines of dialogue, where Secondo insists that Primo speak English and Primo cautions Secondo to prepare the garlic correctly. The stakes of potential failure are quickly indicated by the failure of the plumbing and Cristiano's comment about working so hard for so little money. We also quickly see that while Primo is focused on the quality of the food, Secondo is focused on appearances: how the restaurant looks. They have called their little place "Paradise"—their piece of heaven.

By minute three, we see that the town is a typical small town, the period reminding American audiences (themselves mostly descended from immigrants within the last century) of their own families' experience. We also see that Secondo's dream of wealthy patrons is just that: a dream. Not long after we'll see it come true, but only for the crass restaurant across the street.

Four minutes in we see the essence of the brothers' conflict with each other and with the larger world, as Primo's labor of love takes second place to Secondo's desire to please the customers. Secondo wants desperately to fit in and succeed, while Primo couldn't care less and resents wasting his skills on "philistines."

In the next few minutes we see the source of Secondo's anxiety: he's going to lose the restaurant. The hard reality that he needs money contrasts with his brother's willingness to trade food for art—an even exchange for him, because he is an artist himself. It all comes to a head when Secondo suggests compromising their menu and Primo responds with bitter humor that instead of his masterful risotto, perhaps they should serve hot dogs. But throughout we can see that under the struggle there is a deep current of love between the brothers as they try to get along and help each other's dreams come true.

The script strongly and quickly brings a special world to life, gives us an intimate protagonist–antagonist relationship that reflects both the world and theme, and creates an appropriate tone with its loving details in the kitchen and hard realities outside the kitchen. The stakes are high within the context of the story: success in the new world or humiliation and bankruptcy. Each scene is filled with the conflict generated by those two potential outcomes.

These two examples, though wildly different in kind, are similar in how their first ten minutes are used to set up the rest of the story. "But wait," you say—"I've seen great films where we don't meet the protagonist or antagonist until well after the first ten minutes!" This is only apparently the case. It is true that not all stories require the actual presence of the protagonist or antagonist early on. In detective stories, for instance, we may not meet our antagonist in person until well into the story, even at the end. But we will encounter evidence of the antagonist, in the form of his or her crimes. In *Chinatown*, we don't meet Noah Cross until an hour into the film. But we do see a photo of him in the first ten minutes and, of course, we see plenty of evidence of his machinations, though we don't yet know he's behind them. In *Seven*, the horrible, perversely moralistic murders represent the antagonist—his presence is felt in every gruesome detail—though we don't meet him in person until better than halfway in, and even then we don't see his face. It isn't until near the end of the story that we meet him face-to-face, but the accumulation of details regarding his identity have kept him very much present in every preceding scene.

So the fact remains that whatever the genre, within the first ten minutes each element still needs to be addressed: world, essential protagonist and antagonist (or evidence of his work or crime, in place of his actual presence), tone, theme, stakes and conflict. No matter what kind of script you are writing, your main objective as you open your story must be to introduce all these elements in a clear, concise and compelling fashion so that after finishing your first ten pages, the reader's only thought will be to keep on reading and find out what happens next.

EXERCISES

1. Look at the first ten pages of your favorite movie if you can get the script, or view the first ten minutes if you can't. Can a short statement about each of the following be drawn?

The World: _____

_____

The Protagonist: _____

_____

The Antagonist: _____

_____

The Tone: _____

_____

2. Look at the first ten pages of your favorite movie and describe what happens minute by minute to draw the audience into the story and characters. (Remember one page equals one minute of screen time.)

MINUTE 1:

_____

_____

_____

MINUTE 2:

_____

_____

_____

MINUTE 3:

_____

_____

_____

MINUTE 4:

_____

_____

_____

MINUTE 5:

_____

_____

_____

MINUTE 6:

_____

_____

_____

MINUTE 7:

_____

_____

_____

MINUTE 8:

_____

_____

_____

MINUTE 9:

_____

_____

_____

MINUTE 10:

_____

_____

_____

3. Scene-card the first ten pages of your screenplay. Make sure each scene has a location that works with your "world," the right characters, a central event or action, conflict and something to indicate how the scene advances the thematic arc of the story.

11

The Structure of Genres

It's a Sci-Fi, Romantic Comedy, Western Thriller

Any discussion of film genres is bound to be controversial. Some respected screenwriters and film professors feel that there are no such things, and that the practice of categorizing different kinds of stories is deceptive. They emphasize—correctly—that all good films, no matter what stories they are telling, depend on the essentials (character, theme, world and so forth) and that attempting to follow the "rules" for any supposed genre can result in shallow, formulaic writing. Besides, once you've decided on your world, story and characters, then you've pretty much already defined the genre in which you're working.

But the fact remains that films are categorized into genres by everyone from producers to critics to audiences. It's how we bring order to the tremendous variety that movies offer us. It's the reason video stores have different sections, so that if you're in the mood for a laugh or a thrill or a dose of the weepies, you'll know where to look. When, as a writer, you make your choice of world and story—your genre—you set up certain expectations that must be satisfied, or the script will disappoint the reader. A suspense-thriller must be suspenseful and thrilling, a horror film must be frightening, a comedy must be funny, while a drama may not need to create any of these reactions.

There's nothing pernicious about it; genre is simply a parcel of film terrain to which audiences choose to return again and again. At first a genre is newly discovered territory, fresh and virginal. Then it gets developed, and eventually becomes overused and tired, its veins of valuable material tapped out. (This is when a genre also becomes so rife with cliché that it is ripe for satire, as Jim Abrahams and the Zucker brothers and their imitators have discovered—in such movies as *Airplane!*, *Naked Gun* or *Scary Movie*—creating a genre of their own that exploits this.) After a while, new filmmakers re-explore the old territories with fresh eyes and find new treasures there that others have missed or the passage of time has revealed, and the genre is revived.

Of course, many of the greatest films of all time are not easily pigeon-holed into a particular genre; part of their richness and complexity comes from the fact that they successfully mix elements of several genres at once. *The Terminator, Avatar, Butch Cassidy and the Sundance Kid, Sherlock Holmes* (the one directed by Guy Ritchie) and *Casablanca* are all good examples. In many cases, genre is simply a matter of emphasis. When a film contains both action-adventure and love story elements, it will be an action-adventure movie if the protagonist's struggle with an antagonist other than the lover is the central element; but it will be a love story if the romantic struggle is foremost, in which case the lover becomes the primary antagonist and the action is relegated to a secondary or subplot status. But it's important to know in principle what the expectations are in each area, more or less what will satisfy them, and why.

Writing students, in the throes of struggling with their stories, often beg to be told the "rules" of their genre, the magic key or formula which will suddenly make sense of it all. But it's not a matter of slavishly following a formula; every successful film script pushes and alters certain aspects of a genre, combines or even inverts them, follows certain rules and breaks others, in order to present something both recognizable and yet surprising and original. From the writer's point of view, it's a matter of understanding not the rules but the strategies that different genres employ to achieve their desired effects. Producers want more than anything to find a story that both falls within a recognizable and popular genre, and yet is in some way different from anything they've seen before. They want it because they know audiences also want it. In order for you to be in control of what you're writing to accomplish this, you must work from a base of understanding. If you know how and why a genre works—in fact, why it exists at all—you can more clearly decide which one your intended story falls into, and more clearly organize and innovate its elements.

A MOVING (PICTURE) EXPERIENCE

All films aim to evoke an emotional response in the audience: "make 'em laugh, make 'em cry." And at their core, genres spring from the same source as all storytelling: desire—the desire to experience love, to overcome fear (even the terror of death), to understand the meaning of it all (whatever "it" may be) or simply to escape the ordinariness of real life and experience places and thrills that only the imagination can provide. It's not an intellectual longing, or movies would be made from philosophical treatises. It's a deep, gut-based desire for a heightened sense of order, of connection, of adventure, of love or hate or hilarity or sexual passion—of power over the mysteries of life. As we've seen, all drama is about power. And movies, more than any other medium, empower their audiences because when people enter the dark dream-world of the theater, they can enter other worlds and vicariously experience the struggles and eventual successes or failures of the characters. They can come away unharmed, yet still filled with the emotional power of the experience. This is what Aristotle meant by "catharsis": we are emotionally purified by sorrow, by laughter, by sheer adrenaline—by having accompanied the fictional protagonists through their varied crucibles of intense experience and emotion.

Genre is simply the classification of these variations. There isn't room to cover every genre in detail, and our intention here isn't to provide a laundry list of descriptions and formulas; these can be found in other books, on the internet and elsewhere. Rather, let's step back and look at a number of genre categories from the point of view of their emotional intentions. We do not pretend to present a scientifically exact or complete taxonomy. In some cases we will examine a specific genre in detail; in others we'll simply examine the emotional and story strategies common to genres within a given emotion category. There will necessarily be many omissions, and some overlap as well, since different genres may employ similar strategies, or a film may employ the strategies of different genres. *The Terminator*, for example, successfully incorporates the action, horror and love story genres in almost equal measure. But although many different emotions may be aroused over the course of a given film, one will be primary, the one most intimately related to the theme and purpose of the story, to the catharsis at the end. This specific emotion guides and defines the film's genre.

Internal Consistency

Before we go into specifics, there are certain elements that apply across genres and which you ignore at your peril. First, it is essential that you create an internally consistent world, whether for a contemporary love story or an exotic science fiction/fear story. Each world has certain parameters that you must set up and to which you must remain true, or you will lose your audience. If you're telling a classic vampire story and set up at the beginning that the monster can be destroyed by sunlight or a wooden stake, your audience will feel cheated if you then spring the surprise that, guess what, this vampire is different. If you set up a world in which pain is harmless (as in a laughter film), you will shock and risk alienating your audience if the pain suddenly becomes real. So be careful to remain true to the new world you've created. You don't want to be like the writing student who wrote an outer space movie, went into detail about how this world had no gravity, but then had the space villain "fall" to his death at the climax. It's as annoying as the vampire who is not affected by a cross or sunlight: it breaks the rules of the story—not so much of the genre, but of the particular story—and each particular story world has its own internal rules. Either there is gravity, or there isn't. Either you can't hear sound in outer space, or you can. Discover or create these parameters, and then stick to them, or you will create plot holes, destroy the delicate illusion of reality, and lose your reader.

Another way to look at it is that once you have set up a certain "reality level," you must remain true to it. Movies, like poetry and other forms of fiction, depend on what John Keats called the "willing suspension of disbelief." If you're writing a horrific thriller and suddenly it veers into a slapstick comedy (an extreme example), you risk throwing the audience out of the movie. They will no longer be caught up in the world you've created, but suddenly distanced from it, since the world has changed. The contract you've drawn with them in your setup, enticing them into a willing suspension of disbelief, has been betrayed. There are exceptions, like *Something Wild*, which starts as a laughter film and ends as a dark thriller, or *Harold and Maude*, which also starts comically and ends up with a death and genuine pain; but these are rare exceptions and are not accidental shifts of reality levels. Such movies skillfully use the change of level and genre to challenge or give deeper meaning to the conventions with which they began. This is very difficult to pull off and probably not a good idea to attempt in your first few scripts. Get comfortable with creating solid, consistent worlds; then mess around with them once you know what you're doing.

That said, let's take a closer look at how genres work. The major emotion categories we'll examine here are courage, fear, need to know, laughter and love.

COURAGE

Action-Adventure, War, Western, Historical Epic and Heroic Science Fiction

One of the strongest human desires is to be brave, to have what it takes to save ourselves and our loved ones, even our nation, without sacrificing our dignity or morality. We want to have courage in the face of pain, but particularly in the face of death. It's been argued that the fear of death—that final, inevitable and most impenetrable mystery of all—is behind the belief in God, the creation of religions, the impulse to create art and even the act of war; for by creating something that will outlast us, or by killing a deadly opponent, in effect we have killed death itself, achieved a glorious immortality, at least in reputation. Of course, most of us aren't brave. We are terrified of pain and the oblivion that may await us all, of the fundamental uncertainty with which death confronts us, and we will do almost anything we can, from working out until our muscles scream, to plastic surgery or even going to Switzerland for sheep-hormone injections, to put off the final day of reckoning.

We want to defeat death. In art, we hope our talents and personalities will somehow survive and be immortalized and admired by generations to come. In religion, we hope to be resurrected, to go to heaven, be reunited with loved ones, be reincarnated or to have our consciousness merge in some meaningful, sentient way with the larger universe. In our recreation, we ride rollercoasters or go skydiving to experience the thrill of a near-death experience, knowing that we will safely return to our lives after having conquered death for just a moment. In our lives, our desire for immortality is why we look to see ourselves remade in the faces of our children; the intensity of sexual climax has been called "the little death" or "dying in each others arms." We equate the ecstasy of procreation with the moment of expiration, because the one cancels out the other. Our longing to see death defeated is also a great part of why we go to the movies.

Action-Adventure

Action-adventure movies are perhaps the most successful genre worldwide because they specifically address courage in the face of death. The Mel Gibson epic *Braveheart* (written by Randall Wallace) makes this explicit in the title. In such movies, the antagonist is a surrogate for death, an enormously powerful and lethal presence against which success seems hopeless. The protagonist is a surrogate for ourselves—an enhanced version, to be sure, smarter, stronger, better equipped—but basically someone through whose struggles we manage not only to fight the grim antagonist, but to win a new shot at life. (Throughout this section we will refer to both the protagonist and antagonist as male, for convenience, and because in this genre these characters have historically been almost exclusively male—although movies like *The Terminator* and *The Long Kiss Goodnight* provide welcome exceptions.) The emotional stakes are profound: death has been beaten back and the life force reaffirmed.

This type of movie is linear, meaning that once motivated, the protagonist's entire action is devoted to the eventual defeat of his antagonist. It is about a life-and-death struggle, and the test of courage is physical. It may also include a spiritual or emotional dimension, but essentially the danger to the protagonist and his world is physical death. If there is a love story or other subplot, it is kept strictly secondary, and usually involves nothing more than the lover warning the protagonist against the fight, standing helplessly by (often being captured) during the struggle, and then bestowing a congratulatory kiss on the victorious hero at the end; this is the elixir, of course, the promise of sexual intimacy and the restoration of the life force. In recent movies, the lover usually has been given some skills that assist the protagonist, turning her more into an active ally and involving her more in the central action.

Therefore, the most essential thing in an action-adventure movie is to be sure that the stakes—meaning the threat from the antagonist—are literally life-threatening, at least to the protagonist, and better still to the world itself. The antagonist must be identified with the forces of death and chaos. He must have not only the power, but the desire, to kill and destroy all that the protagonist holds dear. An obvious example is Darth Vader, the master of the Dark Side of The Force whose domain is the Death Star. In *Indiana Jones* the antagonist is the obsessed Nazi who sees God's Ark of the Covenant as the ultimate apocalyptic weapon; in *Spartacus* he's the dictatorial Crassus, who is willing to murder tens of thousands of slaves or other opponents who stand in the way of his totalitarian vision; in *The Terminator* it is an unstoppable killing machine revealed at the end to be a walking steel skeleton; in some of the Bond movies, he is the head of S.P.E.C.T.R.E., bent on enslaving the world, and so forth.

Enslavement or deprivation of free will, by the way, is the storytelling equivalent of death, especially to American audiences. It is a spiritual death, and may in fact be more frightening (which is why it appears often in the horror genre, in such films as *Invasion of the Body Snatchers*). In any event, the antagonist comes from and derives his power from the impersonal, larger forces (society) that now threaten the existence of the protagonist's community.

Because the stakes are so high, your world must create an intensified setting. Many action adventures take the hero on a journey to a strange and terrifying new location to confront the antagonist, along the lines of Joseph Campbell's "Hero's Journey." Death is by its nature otherworldly, and so in the classic myths and fairytales, the hero had to leave the bounds of the normal world in order to confront the demonic adversary and bring back the "elixir" or life force, which it guards. Similarly, in action-adventures, especially those with a science fiction element, the lair of the antagonist is often otherworldly. In martial arts movies, the protagonist must journey to a mysterious setting (usually Asian) where the forbidden fight is going to take place. In the Indiana Jones and Bond movies, we follow the hero to exotic locations where the normal rules of law do not apply. In *Armageddon*, the protagonists journey to the surface of an asteroid. In *Stargate* they go through a threshold portal to another planet. All of these are threatening, intensified and otherworldly settings.

Alternately, if the antagonist has brought the battle into the protagonist's "normal" world, the ordinary location must be reimagined to become a place of otherworldly terror. For example, in *Die Hard*, the mundane location of a high-rise building shifts from the known—the suite where the party is taking place—to the strange and unknown—the elevator and ventilation shafts, the basement with its high-tech safe and so on. We are forced into the hidden underworld, or else the normal world is disrupted and threatened with destruction, as in *Independence Day*. In Westerns, we are transported to a mythical setting in which the town and its community are transformed into the boarded-up battleground of the high-noon shootout. The same thing occurs in science fiction stories where we begin in a location other than present-day earth: we establish a mythical setting that nonetheless has its own normality. It is a surrogate for present-day earth, the real world, and is quickly threatened with destruction (e.g., *Star Wars, Star Trek, The Fifth Element*).

The protagonist with whom we identify belongs to the normal state of whatever world is created, to its community. In order for the protagonist to represent us, he must in most cases share our own fears, so we can empathize with his situation. *He must be an underdog*, because that's someone with whom we can identify. Therefore, the protagonist is usually given a "ghost," a personal shortcoming or fear that provides an internal obstacle; the protagonist lacks self-confidence on some level. This is the first level of his conflict. But he also has skills or potential that make him the uniquely suited character to challenge the death force. There is often a prologue scene or short sequence at the beginning that reveals the capabilities of the protagonist, and that later is usually related to the climactic confrontation, bringing the movie full circle. And when the protagonist finally masters the skills necessary to defeat the antagonist, when he realizes his potential and manages to overcome his fear, the awesome power of the enemy is diminished.

Whatever his internal doubts, the protagonist also hesitates to meet the challenge early on (as we would) because the danger is lethal and the antagonist appears unbeatable (as death does). So something beyond his own skills must motivate him to go to battle; the protagonist is never sufficiently motivated at the start to face death until he is personally and irredeemably engaged. In movies like the Bond series or war films, the protagonist goes to battle because it's his job or his duty. Or he may be incited by the desire for fame or glory or even money, at least at first. Very often, the initial motivator is that most basic and identifiable emotion of all: the desire for vengeance.

Revenge   Toward the beginning of many action movies, someone near and dear to the protagonist is killed or gravely endangered by the antagonist. In the simplest form of action movie—the "revenge" or "challenge" film—the point is to see the protagonist kick some butt, and the formula is that he is forced to accept a physically dangerous challenge in some form of prescribed contest because he is seeking revenge. Most martial arts, sword-fighting and boxing flicks and some old-fashioned Westerns fall into this category, but many others also follow the same basic pattern. In such movies, the protagonist is a martial artist of limited skills but enormous potential. He also has a close ally (usually a brother; in Hong Kong flicks, a master) of greater skill, but this ally is either murdered outright or recklessly drawn into a secret or illegal contest where fighters from various backgrounds come to prove their skills. The murderer is another fighter of great strength and wickedness, and either he or the promoter of the contest who backs him is the antagonist. The killing of the brother/friend/master solidly identifies this antagonist with the power of death. It also creates the ghost and the revenge motivation for the protagonist, because the death has been inflicted on someone close to him. In many such films, the protagonist is there when the ally is killed and the challenge is given, and the antagonist specifically points him out as the next intended victim.

In challenge films, that's pretty much all there is to it; the hero wants revenge, and the antagonist is an evil, two-dimensional killing machine. The protagonist could simply turn away from the antagonist and the threat of death, but his personal outrage and his pride won't let him. It is the nature of the world in such movies that the protagonist must accept the challenge on the antagonist's terms—in the formalized setting of the combat arena—in order to win honorably (which is why he doesn't simply pull a gun or ambush the bastard in an alley). Westerns use the convention of the shootout, in which the protagonist honorably waits to march alone into the street at the appointed hour.

Freedom   In more complex action films, revenge may have a prominent place, but it is superseded by larger motives, tied to the theme of freedom over slavery. In *Star Wars* or *Braveheart* or *Zorro* or *The Terminator*, for example, members of the protagonist's family are killed by the antagonist, launching our hero on a path of revenge. In *Spartacus*, Crassus brutally stabs a gladiator who refuses to kill Spartacus, his friend. But these protagonists soon see that their personal revenge is less important than the antagonist's threat to their world in general. In all these films, many other lives are at stake, and those who aren't killed will face enslavement if the protagonist does not succeed. He fights for the good of all, not just personal satisfaction, and our identification with him is therefore enhanced. Sure, we want to see him kick some butt, but we also identify with the dream of being the savior of those we love. Sometimes the stakes can be more personal and yet still more evolved than mere revenge, as in *Rocky*, where we identify with the protagonist's desire to realize his full potential.

The (Intimate) Enemy It is important to note that the antagonists in these films are more complex as well. For one thing, while the antagonist often represents larger, impersonal "societal" forces, he or one of his henchmen may sometimes paradoxically have a close personal relationship or history with the protagonist; they will be "intimate enemies" (see Chapter 7, Power and Conflict). For instance, in *Star Wars*, Darth Vader is Luke's father; in *Raiders of the Lost Ark*, the archaeologist helping the Nazis is an old competitor of Indiana's; in *On Deadly Ground*, Seagal's antagonist is his employer. While *Saving Private Ryan* returns somewhat to the clarity of older war films, where the antagonist is the obvious, impersonal enemy (the Nazis, the "Japs" and so on), in most war movies from the post-Vietnam era, the enemy, like the war, are often simply part of the world, and the antagonist is closer to home: he is one of us. He is an intimate enemy, as with Tom Berenger's evil sergeant in *Platoon*, Gene Hackman's submarine captain in *Crimson Tide* and the CIA operative in *Rambo: First Blood Part II*. Here, our own system of values has been poisoned from within, and the protagonist only faces the obvious enemy because of the corrupt motives of those who initiated the action, the intimate antagonist. It's instructive to note that even *Saving Private Ryan* contains an intimate enemy, the German prisoner of war who strikes up a friendship with one of his American captors. Captain Miller (played by Tom Hanks) lets the man go—only to be shot dead by him at the end.

Good antagonists also have depth because, from their point of view, what they're doing is correct. Sometimes they simply want to get rich, but often they have a larger end in mind. Whether it's Crassus or Hitler or Darth Vader or Edward Longshanks, each feels a moral imperative to impose a rigid, mechanistic "societal" order on their messy world. In *Rocky*, the antagonist Apollo Creed doesn't hate Rocky but sees fighting him as a way to achieve greater fame and fortune. In some ways, it could be argued that Creed isn't the antagonist, but that he is really just another aspect of the true antagonist, Rocky's own debilitating self-doubts. Creed is the "mountain" Rocky must climb in order to prove himself.

Even though the challenge and motivation are now in place, the protagonist—an extension of us—still does not have the ability to take on the antagonist. At this point a mentor arrives, sometimes a former fighter and now teacher, who offers to train the protagonist and give him the physical and spiritual skills required to win. In *Zorro*, this point is made explicit in the dialogue. The elderly Don Diego, the old Zorro (Anthony Hopkins) tells Alejandro, the future Zorro, that "there's an old saying: When the pupil is ready, the master will appear." In order to keep the story focused and increase the emotional desire to win, the mentor often is written as someone who has long been involved in the struggle against the antagonist. He recognizes in his student the one fighter who has the potential to defeat the antagonist once and for all. In James Bond films, it is M who knows that Bond is the only agent capable of defeating the adversary. In the first *Star Wars*, it is Obi Wan Kenobi, the aging Jedi knight who knows that Luke is destined to become one himself; in *The Empire Strikes Back*, Obi Wan is replaced by Yoda, who takes Luke's lessons further. In *Spartacus*, interestingly enough, the mentor is Batiatus, the "noble" slave trader who sees in Spartacus the potential to be a great gladiator and who brings him to his fighting school for training. Although Batiatus is amoral and addicted to luxury, his heart is on the side of the honest Republicans (Crassus' enemies) and he eventually ends up saving Spartacus' wife and child from being enslaved by Crassus.

The Team In courage movies, other allies should come from the protagonist's community, or be drawn to it as new members. Together they form a team upon whom the protagonist can depend, thereby increasing his power. During the central struggle, the antagonist may attack, kill and/or buy off these allies in response; these actions up the revenge stakes and thwart the protagonist's progress. *Braveheart* provides a good example, as William Wallace builds his "team" from first his hometown friends, then other Scotsmen, and then their Celtic relatives, the Irish. While these latter seem potentially untrustworthy, they prove to be faithful to Wallace, while the Scotsman he most admires, Robert the Bruce, is persuaded to betray him. And along the way most of Wallace's team are killed by Edward Longshanks, the antagonist.

In war films, these ally characters become the emotional core of the story: the platoon, squad or other group of buddies whose lives mean everything to the protagonist and whose deaths drive him to face death himself. Although set against a context of defeating a larger evil—the enemy—war movies focus their emotional impact by concentrating on the themes of looking out for the group and living up to personal responsibility. The mentor in such films is usually the sergeant or other older leader directly responsible for the protagonist and his friends; in the *Dirty Dozen*, this mentor role becomes so central that the mentor is the protagonist. The same is true in most John Wayne war films. In *Saving Private Ryan*, Captain John Miller is the team leader, but also clearly the protagonist; in this case the role of mentor, insofar as there is one, shifts to Tom Sizemore's battle-hardened Sgt. Horvath, who although lower in rank has equal, if not superior, experience and wisdom.

Because this is war, men will die, including members of the core team of allies. Who dies is determined by how each character is drawn. A mentor like Sgt. Horvath or the motley group of allies who make up *The Dirty Dozen* or *The Great Escape* seem incapable of existence outside the context of war; it's impossible to imagine them in civilian life, and so when they are killed off we are saddened, even angered, but generally do not feel betrayed or blindsided by the filmmakers.

Also, a character—ally or otherwise—who expresses a dream of settling down in some romantically agricultural setting is usually marked for death;

think of Sam Neill's character in *The Hunt for Red October*, for instance, who dreams of getting a ranch in Montana, or Captain Miller in *Saving Private Ryan*, who wants to see his wife's rose garden again, or William Wallace in *Braveheart*, who attempts to return to the family farm. Writer and teacher Cynthia Whitcomb put it this way: "Anyone who mentions dreaming of retiring to a farm in Wyoming is dead meat." The way we put it is that by dreaming of the farm, the character buys it. The hope for an idyllic, peaceful future gives us empathy for the character, but it is unrealistic within the context of a brutal world, and is therefore a sign of weakness. In a way, such a character's dream of pastoral peace is realized by sending them to the Elysian fields of heaven.

The Hero as Common Man   It's important to note that the protagonist invariably identifies with and is part of the rank and file, while the antagonist is associated with the impersonal "military machine." In *Braveheart*, the protagonist is in fact a Scottish nobleman, but is characterized as a humble farmer who rises to lead the rebellion. In *Spartacus* the protagonist is a slave. Schwarzenegger and Seagal movies are careful to have their protagonists working with and identifying with lower-level operatives (or children), who are invariably killed or kidnapped in order to provide revenge motivation. The same is true in James Bond films. In the *Dirty Dozen*, while the colonel who puts the team together is of high rank, he relates to his convict-platoon and has to constantly defend them against his higher-ups. Even in *Patton*, where the protagonist is a general, he is portrayed as a soldier's soldier who is happiest fighting in the trenches with his men; his internal antagonist is his own intolerant pride and his external antagonist is less the Nazis than the effete British general Montgomery, who is portrayed as a pompous creature of the Allied war machine.

Training   In order to defeat the antagonist, the protagonist must acquire wisdom, skills, tools and a belief in himself—bravery—and thus many action films involve us and maintain the story's credibility by showing us this progress in a scene sequence. The protagonist at first doubts the mentor, but finally agrees and goes into training. As we see him gain power, we more easily accept that he has a chance of winning. This sequence is occasionally leavened with humor as the protagonist comically stumbles here and there, to the benign exasperation of the mentor. But he improves dramatically, until he appears to be ready to face the inevitable confrontation. The training sequence is a staple of martial arts flicks and movies like *Rocky*, where we see the increasing physical power and skills of the protagonist, but we also find it in movies like *Zorro*, *Star Wars* and *The Terminator*. And good movies manipulate this sequence to achieve more than one end. In *Spartacus*, for instance, the training is intended to prepare Spartacus for the arena, but ironically ends up preparing him for war against Rome.

Not all action movies have this sequence, but they have something like it. In the Bond movies, training is replaced by an arming scene in which Q shows Bond the tools he'll be using. Similarly, in many Steven Seagal and Schwarzenegger films, the protagonist is already supremely trained, but must either acquire or improvise an arsenal with which to fight. Improvising weapons serves two purposes. It arms the protagonist and shows us that he is surprisingly clever; such "McGuyverish" improvisations appear in most Seagal and Schwarzenegger action-fests, but also in more serious films like *Braveheart* or *Saving Private Ryan*. In the *Indiana Jones* movies, training is replaced by a sequence in which Indiana learns more about the antagonist, gains some allies and travels into the antagonist's territory. In *Cliffhanger*, it's replaced by Gabe finding the tools and clothing he'll need to survive on the mountain and hooking up with his ally-lover, Jesse.

Similarly, instead of a formalized challenge and a known time and place for the final confrontation to take place, the protagonist must put together the pieces of the antagonist's endgame. He only learns through great effort where the antagonist's final actions will take place in order to prevent their success. Wherever this is becomes the arena for the final combat.

Attack and Counterattack   During all this time the antagonist has not been standing still, and all of the above must be interlaced with scenes showing him putting his plan in action. The Terminator arms himself, kills the wrong Sarah Connors and zeroes in on the right one; Edward Longshanks takes action to divide and conquer Scotland; Darth Vader prepares the Death Star to destroy the rebel stronghold; Crassus maneuvers for control of the Roman Senate and army. It's important that the antagonist's actions become increasingly lethal and ruthless, and that they increasingly affect those close to the protagonist, to increase the protagonist's personal commitment and jeopardy. In order to keep the central conflict going and the stakes rising, as the antagonist becomes aware of the protagonist's challenge to his power, he must take action to cause complications and setbacks for the protagonist. While at first his actions may affect unrelated, innocent people, as the protagonist begins to take action, the antagonist will increasingly focus his efforts on destroying the protagonist's morale and power base. He will attack the protagonist's close friends and allies. He may kidnap the protagonist's lover or child, or kill his mentor, or threaten innocent people who mean something to the protagonist, or buy off an ally or all of the above. He will do anything to ensure that the protagonist's initial efforts are defeated or his skills held ransom. And, of course, the antagonist—who is not bound by rules or honor—will not be above cheating, thus cementing our hatred for him and our rooting interest in the protagonist.

The protagonist often learns of some profound setback when actually involved in the final combat, and the distraction makes him vulnerable and almost succeeds in undoing him. In *Braveheart*, Longshanks buys off Wallace's allies with promises of land and money, a betrayal that Wallace discovers in the heat of battle. And Longshanks, like Bond villains or the villain in *Cliffhanger*, is not above killing his own allies if it means winning the battle. In a kung fu or boxing flick the antagonist may reveal that he's kidnapped the protagonist's lover or child, or he may throw blinding dust in the protagonist's eyes during the battle; in Westerns, he may cheat during the final shootout by having lackeys with rifles hidden on the rooftops.

The antagonist also has a team that forms part of his power base and helps enact his plan. A common element in courage stories is the antagonist's chief henchman (or woman)—the dark mirror image of the protagonist's best friend or ally—an enormously capable character who acts as a surrogate for or projection of the antagonist's power, especially if the antagonist is not physically imposing. Think of the character in *Die Hard* played by Alexander Godunov, or Oddjob in *Goldfinger*. These characters go all the way back to the story of David and Goliath, in which Goliath was the huge champion—the henchman—of the Philistine king. These allies of the antagonist are exceptionally lethal fighters chosen for their abilities; they provide both the antagonist's first demonstration of power and last line of defense. They also engage the protagonist in the greatest test of his physical skills before his final combat with the antagonist. Sometimes the henchman character will rebel against the antagonist as his plan starts to fall apart, and sometimes he will reappear after the protagonist has apparently killed him, to provide one final surprise obstacle. Sometimes the henchman is presented as a false ally of the protagonist, but is actually secretly in league with the antagonist. Occasionally the henchman will change sides and actually ally him or herself with the protagonist, if there is a sexual attraction (such as Pussy Galore, in *Goldfinger*), or if the henchman has an attack of conscience (such as Weps, Viggo Mortensen's character in *Crimson Tide*). Sometimes, even though he's changed alliance to the side of good, the henchman dies anyway as retribution for his former sins; sometimes he assumes the protagonist's struggle (such as Robert the Bruce, in *Braveheart*). Whatever the case, the henchman is nothing more than an aspect of the antagonist's power, and his or her death or changed alliance are part of the antagonist's disempowerment.

Victory over Death Eventually, the tide turns for the protagonist. Somehow the kidnapped child or lover escapes, the mentor manages to encourage him from beyond the door of death, or an ally frees the threatened innocent people and the protagonist is freed to dispatch the antagonist. Usually wounded during the time of his distraction, the protagonist must now call on the moral strengths instilled by the mentor and his own internal morality, until he is able to rise above his injuries. In the final battle, the antagonist must use all of his powers and wiles and force the protagonist almost to the point of defeat—but he will ultimately fail. The skills and powers the protagonist has acquired—plus the moral power he possesses by being on the side of the angels—ensure his success.

In challenge films, the protagonist will sometimes stop short of killing the antagonist, thus proving his moral superiority, but in most films the antagonist dies in some way that mirrors his own moral deficit. In *Zorro*, he's buried under a pile of gold bars; in *The Terminator*, he's crushed by a giant machine; in *Braveheart*, while Wallace is being tortured to death, Edward Longshanks is also dying, helplessly immobilized by the cancer from which he's been suffering all along, and which is emblematic of the cancer in his soul. And although Wallace is not there to see it, the false ally who has repeatedly betrayed him, Robert the Bruce, now takes up Wallace's fight and accomplishes his goal of freeing Scotland from English tyranny.

If there are others present at the protagonist's victory, they will applaud (there's sometimes a crowd of onlookers, gamblers at the fight, villagers, townsfolk, fellow combatants, whatever), reaffirming the hero's courage and the strength of the community, and the lover will bestow the life-affirming kiss. In movies where the protagonist dies, such as *Braveheart* or *Spartacus*, the kiss is replaced by the knowledge that the protagonist's lover is carrying his child, and therefore his life will continue in another form, long after the antagonist has gone to meet his maker. This also happens in *The Terminator*; the Mentor, Reese, dies, but Sarah, the protagonist, lives to carry his child. In *Saving Private Ryan*, Captain Miller dies, but in that moment he becomes a surrogate father to young Ryan (who is shown having only a mother) as he passes on the stern command: "Earn it." And we see that Ryan as an old man has not only earned the opportunity to live, but gone on to create a large family, helping to replace the lives that were lost in the war and to affirm the value of their sacrifice. Love is not the goal in these movies, but a result of the hero having proved himself. It is evidence of life conquering death, and the reward for the protagonist—us—having had the courage to fight the good fight.

FEAR AND LOATHING

Horror, the Supernatural and Dark Science Fiction

The flip side of courage is fear; courage is the overcoming of fear. Because of this, movies devoted to fear are almost equally as popular as those devoted to courage; there are obvious examples like *Frankenstein* or *Scream* or the endless variations on the zombie and vampire subgenres, but the fear category also includes such all-time blockbusters as *Jaws*, *Alien*, *Jurassic Park* and even *The Dark Knight*. Here, fear is primary, and death is much more personal, malicious and often serves no larger aim than simply to demonstrate its power over us. And if fear is the emphasized goal of a story, the strategy must change from that of a courage movie, or action-adventure. In a courage movie, the protagonist is an enhanced version of ourselves, whom we know from the start has the potential to defeat the antagonist; the thrill comes from identifying with the protagonist's courage. In a fear movie, we are overwhelmed by the face-to-face confrontation with our deepest and most irrational insecurities, and courage must be suppressed almost until the end of the movie. We include *The Dark Knight* because, even though Batman is a franchise character who we know will not die and an apparent "courage" protagonist, he is also a flawed hero plagued by internal fears and doubts. The persona Bruce Wayne adopts is not like those of Captain America, Superman, the Green Lantern or even Iron Man, as emblems of the invincibility of goodness and human capability. In the telling of his origin in *Detective Comics* #33, he realizes that in order to revenge his parents' death and fight the terror that afflicts Gotham, he himself must "strike terror into their hearts. I must be a creature of the night, black, terrible...a...a bat!" In effect, he has decided to appear like a vampire. In *The Dark Knight*, his own internal darkness becomes most horribly and threateningly externalized in the personification of chaos that is the Joker; in his challenge to sanity and reason itself, the Joker is actually rather similar to the shark in *Jaws*—he represents our darkest fear that the world is savage and irrational, and that we live in a bubble, an illusion of control and moral compass.

Terror and Horror

Terror arises from helplessness, so we must be (almost) helpless before the dread that arises from our subconscious, unable to clearly see that which is lost in darkness or only glimpsed at the edge of our peripheral vision. Horror results when that which we have only barely seen is brought into sudden focus and our worst imaginings are confirmed, leaving us paralyzed with the realization that death in its most cruel, brutal, intransigent form is in our midst, closing in on us as relentlessly as...well, as death. In order to experience this helplessness and paralysis, the protagonist with whom we identify must be more ordinary, much closer to "us," lacking the enhancements of the courage protagonist. The desire for revenge is often exploited as we come to hate the antagonist, but the thrill of fear comes less from revenge or from heroic conquest than from mere survival, from experiencing our deepest terrors in safety—and the more terrifying the better. The worse the fear we confront and survive, the stronger the cathartic release when it's over. As we see everything we most fear come true, we are both supremely vulnerable and yet invulnerable at the same time. Because of this shift of emphasis, the titles of such films (*The Stepfather, Dracula, The Birds, Jaws, The Thing, Psycho*) often name or refer to the antagonist rather than the protagonist, who is more often included in the titles of courage movies (*Spiderman, Patton, Rocky, Butch Cassidy and the Sundance Kid*). What we are after is less the rush of boldly going into battle than the exquisite anxiety of being pursued. Adrenaline is a "fight or flight" response to danger. Courage is "fight." Fear is "flight."

The Illusion of the Rational and the Failure of Law As with courage movies, the normal world is threatened, but fear movies go on to undermine that sense of normalcy by suggesting that just under the apparently safe surface of the world lies a festering, irrational chaos whose agents are specifically devoted to our destruction. It is the subconscious underlying the conscious, Satan's hell underlying and actively undermining God's placid creation. Courage is required when dealing with fear, but acting in a rationally courageous fashion, while denying the true nature of the threat, is foolhardy when dealing with the irrational. Those who attempt directly to confront or explain away the horror that has emerged are doomed to fail. In *Jaws*, the attempt to keep the presence of the shark quiet leads only to more death. Similarly, in *The Relic*, the mayor's insistence on keeping the museum open for a gala fundraiser—after the police lieutenant has warned him that the deadly killer may still be there—leads to chaos and many more deaths. Those in authority foolishly cannot believe that they are no longer in control. In movies like *Saw*, *Psycho* and *The Descent*, the problem is that the characters foolishly insist on trying to maintain control in the face of the uncontrollable, and refuse until it's too late to acknowledge that it's their own sins or deceptions that have put them in trouble. In films like *The Texas Chainsaw Massacre*, *Deliverance*, *The Strangers* and *The Hills Have Eyes*, it's the foolish belief that the world is a safe place and/or that strangers can be trusted (rural strangers are particularly not to be trusted in movies like these, because they are closer to "the natural" and therefore to the irrational). Perhaps more disturbingly, in movies like *The Shining*, *Invasion of the Body Snatchers* and *Scream*, it's the foolish belief that those who are not strangers can be trusted. But only by accepting and understanding the true nature of the evil can we defeat it. Often the protagonist understands it too late or not at all; sometimes confronting the dark forces of chaos leads to madness or even death. But even if the protagonist or his or her allies are destroyed, their self-sacrifice leads to the apparent salvation and restoration of the normal world. It must be only an apparent restoration, because once the presence of the irrational or supernatural is revealed and accepted as a fact, we can never truly go back to innocence and ignorance. The story has provided proof of the failure of sanity in the world, and perhaps most terrifyingly, in our own minds.

The loss of sanity or ability to find refuge is personified in those instances in which the protagonist himself becomes "infected" by whatever created the monster, and becomes or risks becoming one himself (as in most vampire or werewolf movies, *District 9* or *Invasion of the Body Snatchers*), or becomes host to it (as in the *Nightmare on Elm Street* and *Alien* movies). And there are some films like *The Fly*, *The Wolfman*, *Dr. Jekyll and Mr. Hyde* in which the protagonist becomes a monster early on and is his own antagonist. Or, as in *The Lost Boys* or *Wolf* or the *Blade*, *Underworld* and *Twilight* series, the protagonist becomes a benign version of the monster and must face a more dangerous and malignant antagonist (such as the James Spader character in *Wolf*, the "evil vampires" like Victoria in *Twilight*, or the Keifer Sutherland and Edward Hermann characters in *Lost Boys*). In these movies, death awaits if the protagonist cannot adapt to the loss of refuge or accept the failure of sanity; a new and positively altered reality, opening gates to previously forbidden wonder, awaits if he can. Love it or hate it, the *Twilight* series is an interesting hybrid of Young Adult romantic fantasy and fear genres, a potent emotional mixture that made it one of the most hugely successful series, both books and movies, in history.

Taboos: the Lust for Sex, Knowledge and Immortality   Related to this is another common theme in fear movies: that we, in our foolish, rationalistic pride, are to blame for unleashing the forces of chaos and terror, by overstepping moral boundaries. Transgression leads to retribution. In normal life, certain things are forbidden, defined by conventional morality and wisdom as taboo.

Taboos are related to our most primal, common desires and fears, which is why they are so powerful and also so naturally tempting—and why we can identify, even empathize, with the transgression. The most common and potent transgressions are sex and knowledge we shouldn't have; both relate to our fear of death, our longing to defy it, our hubristic lust to be immortal, like God. They're aspects of the same desire; it's not for nothing that the Bible refers to sexual experience as "knowledge." The Serpent convinces (the naked) Eve to take a bite of the fruit of the Tree of Knowledge by telling her, "You will surely not die, for God knows that in the day you eat of it your eyes will be opened, and you will be like God, knowing good and evil." And yet, when she and Adam have eaten, the result is shame over their nakedness, and the knowledge that they have condemned themselves to strife and mortality.

The same sexual/knowledge transgressions apply to modern fear movies as long as it is illicit sex and forbidden knowledge. The transgression may seem minor or egregious, but either way it unleashes a terrifying retribution. Two teenagers have illicit sex in a car by a lake (*Friday the 13th*); a scientist ignores the natural order of life and mixes or revives unusual DNA strands or otherwise perverts the natural order (*Species, The Relic, Jurassic Park, The Human Centipede*); a doctor tries to revive the dead (*Frankenstein*); a man finds a mysterious device and seeks to unlock its forbidden secrets (*Hellraiser*); a beautiful woman or a group of sexually free hippies foolishly travel through unknown countryside (*Psycho, Texas Chainsaw Massacre*); a normal group transgresses by entering off-limits or unknown territory (*The Descent, The Hills Have Eyes*) a woman goes swimming naked in the ocean at night, after having illicit sex (*Jaws*); in each case the transgression releases unexpected and drastic consequences. In *The Omen*, the sex/death equation is expressed as a father who substitutes an orphaned baby for his own, which was stillborn; by illicitly accepting the unknown changeling, without telling his wife, he has perverted the sexual contract of his marriage.

A World of Fear   In fear stories, the world of the story is either a supernatural or otherworldly place to which the protagonist has traveled, or the normal world, which the antagonist has invaded. The latter is more common, because we can best experience terror if what appears to be safe is proven to contain hidden danger. Our lovely new house is built on a cursed Indian burial ground (*Poltergeist*); we're at a sunny beach, when under the surface of the water a primordial predator attacks (*Jaws*); we're out for a boat ride, when previously docile animals descend from above like insane dive-bombers (*The Birds*); we're going about our work at a staid museum—albeit one full of dinosaur skeletons and arcane objects—when one of the specimens from the deepest Amazon comes to life (*The Relic*); we're enjoying casual sex with a beautiful woman in our hot tub or hotel bedroom when she transforms into an insectoid monster from another world (*Species*) or a ravening wolf (*American Werewolf in Paris*); we stop for roadside assistance and become barbeque fodder for a group of cannibalistic hillbillies (*Texas Chainsaw Massacre*). In *Blue Velvet*, we have a seemingly perfect, all-American little town in which sexual perversion and cruelty fester like the bugs that gnaw on the severed ear buried under a perfect lawn. In another successful hybrid, of family comedy and fear genres, the cuddly creatures in *Gremlins* are in fact monsters waiting to be unleashed.

Sometimes, as in *The Relic, King Kong, Alien,* or *The Exorcist,* we'll start in or go to an exotic location where the antagonist's reality seems more probable, a place of primordial, pre-rational assumptions: the deep jungle, an ancient archaeological site, an asteroid or a distant planet. But once the antagonist's exotic reality is transported to the normal world, our world, it will disrupt it and give expression to the moral or the theme: we shouldn't lust after the forbidden (*The Mummy, Hellraiser*) or try to improve or alter creation (*Frankenstein, Species, Jurassic Park*); we shouldn't break sexual taboos (*Friday the 13th* and practically all other "teen scream" films); we shouldn't assume that we are in control of the mysterious world (*Jaws, Alien, The Birds, Predator, The Descent*). Sometimes the unleashed "monster" acts out of primal instinct (*The Relic, Jaws, Congo, Species, Anaconda, Jurassic Park, Deliverance*), sometimes it has actually set a trap, with conscious intention (*Dracula, The Omen, Rosemary's Baby, The Hills Have Eyes*). But either way, things spin out of control, chaos reigns, and our normal assumptions about this world no longer apply. This model goes back to the Greek idea of "hubris," the foolish pride of thinking that we know and control our destiny, which inevitably results in the supernatural forces of the Gods destroying us. Illicit sex, knowledge and denial of the irrational are all present in the ancient Greek tragedies. In *Oedipus Rex,* the protagonist (unknowingly) kills his father and marries his mother, in the process bringing disaster to his city. He thinks he can solve the problem by uncovering the culprit, when in fact what he learns—that he himself is the culprit—destroys him. Medea kills her children after being abandoned by the man she illicitly "knew" and for whom she killed and dismembered her brother. In the *Bacchae,* the King is destroyed by his refusal to recognize Dionysus, the god of wine and primal lust, and his own mother rips his head off in a sexually orgiastic madness. In many ways, fear films are the closest to these classical models.

The Nature of the Beast and the Reality of Evil The antagonist in a fear film is an example of the worst that could go wrong in any given world, and in order to thoroughly destroy our sense of safety it must appear in a believable fashion from whatever the surroundings may be. It must be the right antagonist for this world, attacking its specific weaknesses, hypocrisies and taboos, and not be just some arbitrary monster. And the antagonist must be not only powerful and lethal, but from beyond the realm of normal experience or expectation or negotiation, a being driven to such extreme and/or irrational actions that the real world seems to warp and shift into the realm of nightmare.

Just as the antagonist subverts our sense of a normal and safe world, the antagonist also represents either a perversion of something normal (our neighbor, husband, nanny, sanity), an exaggeration of something in the natural world to which we have a reasonable aversion (such as bugs, slime, snakes) or an extreme personification of a recognizable supernatural force or "bogeyman" (ghosts, vampires, demons). In zombie and Frankenstein movies, the antagonist is a dead body brought to life; in Atomic Age horror flicks, it's either a horrific incarnation of radiation (*The Blob*) or something like a lizard (*Godzilla*) or bug or even a rabbit (*Night of the Lepus*) that has mutated to gigantic proportions (or that, as in the *Incredible Shrinking Man*, has become enormous in comparison with our protagonist's reduced size). In *Anaconda*, the monster is a super-snake, in *Jaws*, a super-shark; in *Alien*, *Predator, Invasion of the Body Snatchers* and *War of the Worlds* it's a malevolent extraterrestrial predator. In the *Friday the 13th, Halloween, Scream, Saw*, and *Nightmare on Elm Street* movies, we're in classic fairytale territory: be good or the bogeyman will get you. In ghost and Satanic stories, we enter the religious realm, which uses and reinforces cultural or institutional notions of good, evil and otherworldly retribution.

Fatal Attraction In movies like *Dracula* (and its progeny such as *The Hunger, Interview with the Vampire* and the *Twilight* Series), *Cat People*, and *Species*, we are confronted with an irresistible sexual power—we are attracted like moths to the flame that will destroy us. We long to be seduced, sucked dry (so to speak) and transformed, even as we are terrified of the prospect. We long for the sexuality and power of the wolf, even as we cringe from the blood-lust that accompanies it. The delicious thrill comes from flirting with the idea of unimaginable ecstasy, potency and/or potential immortality, whatever the cost to our souls. This attraction-repulsion is especially powerful, which accounts for the endless success and reinvention of the vampire story. Sexual obsession, and the fear of losing control of our lives to it, pervade films that are built on the fear model, even if they're not obviously "horror" flicks. These are sexual bogeyman (or bogeywoman) stories, such as *Fatal Attraction* and *The Hand that Rocks the Cradle*.

Scorched Earth Because the antagonist in fear movies is so overwhelming and terrifying, it must be destroyed completely. Where the antagonist is human, death in some grisly fashion is the minimum punishment. But where the antagonist is supernatural, it must either be dispatched in a prescribed supernatural way (a silver bullet, a wooden stake) or be disintegrated without a trace. This is why so many "fear antagonists" are destroyed by fire or sunlight, because these elements are metaphorically purifying and all-consuming. They are forces of light and heat, harnessed toward the destruction of darkness. An interesting variation appears in *The Wizard of Oz*, where water—the source of life—melts the wicked witch, the agent of death. As an aside, water as a signifier of the unconscious and the realm of sleep or death is more often associated more with the power of the antagonist (*Jaws, The Ring*, the bath scene in *The Shining*, etc.). But however it is eliminated, the antagonist must be so thoroughly erased that it cannot return. As noted above, once true evil has entered the world, it may be impossible to get rid of it completely, and some small trace of the antagonist may contaminate the protagonist or escape the flames (which, of course, provides fodder for sequels).

Who's to Blame The initial transgressor is often, but not necessarily, the protagonist. It can also be someone who stumbles innocently into a situation in which another has unleashed a demonic force, but who is then forced to deal with the consequences. This increases the sense of vulnerability; it's the difference between having a car accident due to reckless speeding or drunkenness and one in which we were innocent and simply blindsided. There is no way to prepare for or avoid this kind of evil, which is why it is so terrifying. In movies like *Fatal Attraction, Dr. Jekyll and Mr. Hyde, Frankenstein* and *Species* (and even *King Kong*) the protagonist must deal with a (sexually charged) monster he himself has created or unleashed, but in movies like *Dracula, The Strangers, Poltergeist* or *Phantom of the Opera*, the protagonists are simply innocents who have accidentally entered a realm of evil. In *Dracula*, the original transgression was Count Dracula's, when he cursed the name of God after his lover committed suicide. In *Rosemary's Baby*, Rosemary is just an ordinary housewife whose husband is the transgressor, betraying her into the hands of a Satanic cult, and ultimately of Satan himself. While her natural sexuality is nonthreatening, her unwitting sex with the Devil is her undoing. In *The Exorcist*, a priest doubts his faith—a form of transgression, it's true—but the demon he confronts was unleashed by the budding sexuality of a young girl. In *Night of the Living Dead*, the government is the transgressor: a group of people find themselves surrounded by flesh-eating corpses brought to life by a returning radioactive space probe. In *Jurassic Park*, the paleontologist played by Sam Neill is the protagonist, but the transgression is caused by the entrepreneur who re-created dinosaurs by perverse means, mixing dinosaur and amphibian DNA. Normal sexuality has been intentionally corrupted by this hybrid process: The dinosaurs are created asexually and intended to be sterile. This is also reflected by the protagonist's "perverse" avoidance of love and of children. It's only when he overcomes these unnatural aversions that he successfully escapes the perverse monsters.

The Savage Breast An interesting corollary to human responsibility for creating or releasing the antagonist is that the particular monster of the story may actually be quite sympathetic, a soulful beast whose destruction is almost as tragic as its creation. It is not its fault it's there, after all; look at Frankenstein's monster, for example, with his love of music and his pathetic, innocent attraction to the old blind man and the little girl; or King Kong, who falls tragically in love with Faye Wray. They are actually more innocent than the protagonists. Japanese audiences cited the betrayal of this principle for their disappointment with Roland Emmerich and Dean Devlin's remake of *Godzilla*. In the original movies, Godzilla was an empathetic, almost lovable creature whose destructive rampages were a response to human irresponsibility. The new mega-lizard and her ferocious brood were soulless and unmotivated by comparison.

Whether innocent or evil, the antagonist often proves his or her power—and raises the stakes—by killing off those who are progressively closer to the protagonist. Initially, those who die may be faceless strangers: the boat crews in *Dracula* or *The Relic*, the island workers in *Jurassic Park*, the beachgoers in *Jaws*. As the threat involves more specific characters, it will begin to affect those who have themselves transgressed in some fashion—who "deserved it." In *The Relic*, there's the security guard who has snuck off to smoke a joint and the ruthlessly ambitious scientist who tries to subvert the protagonist's funding. In *The Terminator*, it's an obnoxious punk. In *Jurassic Park*, we have the amoral scientist who's trying to sell the embryos and the immoral lawyer who represents the project. Sometimes these secondary characters die for the simple transgression of stupidity or curiosity: they go into the basement when they shouldn't. We take comfort from the fact that we're better than they are (even though we secretly know we may be just like them). But, eventually, the victims include true innocents or characters we like, such as the young couple or the child in *Night of the Living Dead*, Sarah Connor's best friend and her mother in *The Terminator* or the cops in *The Relic*, and we are left no refuge: this terror applies to us, too.

The Voice of Experience   Also, as with courage movies, there is usually a mentor in fear films, an older character who has some experience with the nature of the monster. He may be a kindly old fellow like the ancient anthropologist in *Wolf* or, because of prolonged exposure to or obsession with the antagonist, the mentor may seem to be a near-madman like Van Helsing in *Dracula* or Quint in *Jaws*. But he always possesses some wisdom or secret talisman that the protagonist must use in order to succeed. His wisdom will eventually be accepted, but often only after the veils of reason and disbelief have been stripped away. Often, the mentor character is destroyed in an act of obsessive hatred for the monster, a self-sacrifice that both saves and passes the mantle on to the protagonist.

Suspense (Terror) vs. Shock (Horror)   There are essentially two strategies to create a sense of fear and vulnerability, which are sometimes used separately, sometimes together. Movies can play on our fear of the unknown, creating suspense and terror, or they can actually show us something so shocking that we almost—almost—cannot bear to look at it, creating visceral revulsion, or horror. Terror may give way to horror when what might happen actually does happen, but it doesn't have to physically appear on screen for the terror to be generated. In fact, what we don't see—can't see—is often more haunting than what we do. Creating terror requires more skill than producing horror, because terror is about the suggestion of what might happen, while horror is a simple matter of showing us something revolting. This is why movies that depend exclusively on horror are usually lower-budget and lower-quality affairs. It's easier and cheaper to show torn flesh and fake blood than to generate a solidly suspenseful story. Movies like *Orgy of the Dead* and the *Friday the 13th, Nightmare on Elm Street, Saw* and *Hellraiser* series (and most zombie flicks) all rely on a "gross-out" factor—we see heads cut off, guts ripped out, people's skin flayed off, demons of revolting appearance feasting on raw flesh. The antagonists—while having some justification for their presence, such as prior mental illness, being summoned by some spell or religious transgression, or having been created by the characters' own dreams—exist mainly to exploit the voyeuristic desire to see someone (other than ourselves) gruesomely tortured and dispatched. Movies like *Rosemary's Baby*, *The Omen*, *The Sailor Who Fell from Grace with the Sea*, *Psycho* or *Hush, Hush, Sweet Charlotte* hardly show anything graphically disgusting, relying instead on the protagonist's growing terror as he discovers that what ought to be safe surroundings prove dangerous. Movies like *Night of the Living Dead*, *The Birds*, *Jaws*, the *Alien* movies and *The Relic* incorporate both. It's a matter of emphasis—are you after terror, or horror or both?

THE NEED TO KNOW

Detective Story, Suspense Thriller, Political Thriller

Fascination with the idea that just below or beyond normal appearances, a hidden truth is "out there"(as series like the *X-Files* or *Lost* or *Fringe* would have it) is the basis for films in the detective, *film noir* and thriller genres. The protagonist may be a cop, a private detective or just an ordinary person put into a situation where nothing is as it seems. These films draw power from our own sense of powerlessness in a world in which events often happen mysteriously and almost always beyond our control; we suspect there is more to any given situation than we are actually aware of. Give this suspicion a sinister twist and you have the makings of a criminal, supernatural or political conspiracy story. The antagonist is equally mysterious. All we have at the start is some faded and often confusing evidence, like the washed-out tracks of an animal in the woods or the Zapruder film of the Kennedy assassination.

The story, then, is about uncovering the truth, putting the puzzle together, discovering the antagonist and what his or her agenda really is. That discovery may or may not affect the success of the antagonist; in some cases it does, in others it doesn't (other than that the protagonist survives). In *Conspiracy Theory*, *L.A. Confidential*, *The Bourne Identity* and Guy Ritchie's *Sherlock Holmes*, for example, the protagonists manage to foil the conspiracy by uncovering the antagonist's identity and agenda. In *The Maltese Falcon*, it's a mixed success. Sam Spade gets justice for his murdered partner—he has the beautiful killer Brigid arrested and the Fat Man dealt a setback in his search for the jeweled bird—but Spade also loves Brigid and therefore loses her, and the Fat Man lives on to continue his search. In *Chinatown*, however, the antagonist wins. Jake—the detective—uncovers Noah Cross's conspiracy to steal water and control half of Los Angeles, but he can do nothing to stop it from happening, prevent Evelyn's death, or prevent Cross from taking custody of his daughter, who was conceived through his incestuous rape of Evelyn (his other daughter). Similarly, in *Body Heat*, *JFK*, *Three Days of the Condor* and the 2010 *Fair Game*, the conspirators/antagonists are too smart or powerful to be derailed or brought to justice. But from a storytelling point of view, it doesn't matter. The point of these films is that the dark truth has been revealed to us, the audience, even if it's at the expense of the protagonist. The mystery has been stripped away, and we are empowered by being "in the know," having our worst suspicions confirmed.

Suspense vs. Surprise

When constructing a need-to-know movie, you must understand and use the primary tools that create curiosity and fascination: suspense and surprise. Suspense comes from withholding information from the protagonist, though not necessarily from the audience. If we know no more than the protagonist does, then suspense comes from empathizing with his or her vulnerability as we watch events unfold. If we do know more than the character, then suspense comes from being helpless to assist or warn the protagonist of imminent danger, from the tension of waiting for an attack to take place. For example, we see a figure with a knife hiding around the corner as our protagonist approaches, unaware. Surprise, on the other hand, always applies to both the character and the audience. For example, the protagonist is walking down a hallway when someone unexpectedly bursts out with a knife. He—and we—react with adrenalized shock. Surprise is also a key element of a "reversal"—when someone we think is an ally proves actually to be an enemy, or vice versa, or when the innocent character seems to have escaped a pursuer but has actually run into a blind alley. A classic fear movie technique (which also applies to a need-to-know movie) incorporates both—we know there's a killer in the basement, but the character doesn't and goes down into danger unwittingly. Or he or she may suspect danger, but goes down anyway to investigate. Usually we see this from his or her P.O.V., which keeps our vision claustrophobically limited, blind to what is beside or behind us. We might also intercut this with the similarly claustrophobic point of view of the killer, who is focused intently on his prey. When the killer springs into the character's P.O.V., the suspense is ended by the surprise. Sometimes—and this effect has been overused to the point of cliché—the surprise is manipulated into a two-part sequence. The suspense of the approach to the basement and the first surprise frightens us, but is harmless: it's only a cat or a pigeon that has burst out at us. The resulting relief lulls us (and the character) into a false sense of security, and then the second surprise is sprung as the killer leaps out.

The key to making the elements of surprise and suspense work well is timing. This is not something you can leave up to the director or editor—you as writer must give them the plan, the effect you want, and the tone and order of events that will accomplish it. This includes determining the length of the scenes and sequences to create a slow build of tension or a rapid-fire series of shocks, whether to intercut one sequence with another in order to string it out and build tension, and determining how much to reveal or withhold, how much the reader should know at any given moment. It also includes finding exactly the right details and imagery to bring the scene to life. As with the audience member, you want the reader to experience thrills and chills as he reads the script.

Whatever the case, suspense and surprise create different effects, and should be used intentionally. If you want to create suspense, you must limit what your protagonist knows, but you may want to provide some clues to the audience. Contrary to what some screenwriting experts claim, this does not make the protagonist more stupid than the audience, it simply reflects his or her state of knowledge at a given moment. Great suspense, even dread, can be generated by letting the audience know about a threat of which the protagonist is unaware. Suspense can occur without direct audience knowledge of the antagonist's plans, but there must be an accumulation of clues and events to maintain the antagonist's presence and threat, or you run the risk of the story seeming random or arbitrary. Similarly, surprise must be used judiciously, because after a few unanticipated surprises the story can feel too coincidental; to avoid this, especially when dealing with a character reversal, you must plant seemingly innocuous clues that are both telling enough and yet misdirecting enough that they simultaneously set up and justify the surprise without giving it away. As far as the audience (and character) is concerned, the surprise works by suddenly casting what has come before in a new and unexpected light; for instance, the protagonist's brother seems like his closest ally and never leaves his side, but seems anxious and short of cash. He explains it away by saying it's just nerves and expenses for his upcoming wedding; but in fact he's deeply in debt to a loan shark and is setting up the protagonist for betrayal.

By carefully orchestrating suspense and surprise, mystery and knowledge, creating a world where everything is cast in darkness or where nothing is as it seems, you achieve the basic aim of the films that fall within these genres: to confirm the audience's suspicion that just because they're paranoid doesn't mean someone isn't out to get them.

The trick with a need-to-know movie is to find and exploit a suspicion or paranoia that enough people share. A movie that plays on our fascination with the hidden and our belief in conspiracy must have a mystery worth solving, or it won't be fascinating. And the world depicted—what we see—must either reinforce that sense of mystery, as in the dark, rainy cities of *film noir*, or contrast with it by its bland, apparent normalcy, as in a Hitchcock film.

The Detective Story

In a detective film, the problem initially seems to be pretty straightforward. We start with a crime, or the suspicion of a crime. There's a dead body, or someone comes to the protagonist and says that someone is missing or out to get him or her for some unknown reason. This is the first appearance of the antagonist, in the form of the evidence of his criminal activity or the suspicions of someone supposedly innocent. It is also the first piece of the puzzle that the protagonist must put together. But while it also seems to be the easiest piece, the most obvious clue, it must in fact lead the protagonist to new and progressively more shocking pieces of the puzzle. The initial crime is merely the bait, leading the protagonist into a labyrinthine web where nothing is obvious until the end.

The Cynical Believer   Why does the detective (protagonist) take on the challenge? It's not so much because he or she is personally threatened or someone close is threatened—although both may eventually become the case—but because the community is threatened in some way and it's the protagonist's job to protect the community, or at least avenge it. That's the kind of person the protagonist is, or he wouldn't be doing this kind of work. In order for the protagonist to have chosen the life of a detective, private or official, he must already be willing to take action against an antagonist. He (or she) is the perfect protagonist because of a base of prior experience, even cynicism, that has prepared him or her for the investigation. In Agatha Christie, Sherlock Holmes, and *Thin Man* types of stories, the protagonists take on the challenge as a kind of elaborate chess match or crossword puzzle, without much emotional involvement beyond the excitement of winning or solving it. The resolution comes in the form of an explanation, in which all is laid bare before the assembled victims and suspects, with the protagonist taking delight less in the meting out of justice than in the proof of his or her skills. The stakes are not life and death, but success or failure; the antagonist may attempt to kill the protagonist or escape, but rarely poses a real threat beyond the initial crime.

Code of Honor Things take on a darker, more personal tone in *film noir* and more hard-edged stories. In *The Maltese Falcon*, for instance, Sam Spade's partner is killed, and even though Spade didn't much like him, it's bad form, bad for business, for him not to take action—even if it eventually means sending his lover (the killer) up the river. In the Dirty Harry and Philip Marlowe movies, a private code of honor drives the protagonist, in addition to—or in spite of—other considerations, such as attractive women or official duties. These are moral men in an amoral universe, driven to try and bring some sense of justice or accountability to it. It's again about defeating death, but where in a courage movie death is overcome by action, in a need-to-know movie death is overcome by knowledge (though action may be involved).

Although capable, the detective protagonist still needs to be an underdog, which initially is indicated by a lack of knowledge. But he or she may also be alcoholic, divorced, disliked by superiors or disgraced through no fault of their own. Because of this background, and to maintain audience empathy, at some point early on there must be something about the particular crime or antagonist that gives the protagonist a moment of doubt—is he up to the challenge? Does she really want to get involved? Or the protagonist's boss may warn him away from the case, not wanting to open a can of worms or have to deal with the protagonist's unorthodox tactics. But this doubt or obstacle usually comes after the protagonist has taken some action that has resulted in him or her being entangled in the web. Whether he now needs to clear his name, or she has taken up her client's cause out of sexual attraction, or out of a personal code of honor or all of the above, the protagonist is hooked, overcomes whatever his or her objections might be, and doesn't back out.

Eventually the protagonist will uncover the truth, though in the darkest *film noir*, this may come at the cost of his life (as in *Kiss Me Deadly*, where atomic radiation is released), or of his freedom and innocence (as in *Seven*, a cross-genre fear/need-to-know movie, where he is driven to murder by the revelation that the antagonist has killed his pregnant wife).

For further exploration, P. D. James has written an excellent analysis of the genre, *Talking about Detective Fiction* (Knopf 2009), whose insights also apply to film.

The "Innocent Man"

Films like *Three Days of the Condor*, *The Manchurian Candidate*, *The Net*, *Breakdown*, *The Fugitive*, *Enemy of the State* or those in the Hitchcock model (*North by Northwest* is the classic example) follow a somewhat different tack. These are known as "innocent man" stories. Rather than having a detective whose life is devoted to solving crimes, here an innocent man (or woman) is suddenly thrust into danger, caught up in some mysterious conspiracy, and in order to survive, must figure out what has disrupted the bland, ordinary course of his or her life, and why. These stories share many elements with the fear movie genres: some dark power is at work in the world and has either specifically targeted the protagonist for destruction, or the protagonist has inadvertently stumbled across its path and plan. You want to be sure that something about your protagonist justifies making him or her the lead character in your story, something beyond simply being "innocent." Something in the protagonist's life and character must make him or her vulnerable to becoming involved. For example, in *Three Days of the Condor*, the protagonist is a low-level information gatherer for the CIA; his work is pedestrian, but his proximity to the sinister power of the organization puts him in jeopardy. In *The Manchurian Candidate*, the protagonist is a soldier whose service has subjected him to being captured and brainwashed by the enemy. Sometimes the protagonist "trespasses" in some way and unwittingly causes his own entrapment. In *Blow-Up*, he's a photographer with voyeuristic tendencies. In *Rear Window*, the protagonist's broken leg limits his world to his window and allows his own latent voyeurism to get him into trouble. In *The Net*, she's a computer whiz who becomes the victim of her own technology. In *North by Northwest*, he's an unattached playboy, the perfect fall-guy whom no one will miss or care about. In *The Fugitive*, he's a doctor devoted to saving lives and now accused of having taken one. In *Breakdown*, he's simply someone who is too trusting and not careful enough in strange surroundings.

Innocence and Paranoia   Like fear movies, "innocent man" movies play less upon the pleasure of watching a clever, tough protagonist unravel a mystery than upon our own paranoia, our sense of vulnerability to the faceless (societal) threats in our lives: foreign governments, our own government, the CIA, criminals in the garb of authority figures (sheriffs, cops) and so on. Some other examples include *Touch of Evil*, *Lone Star*, *Three Days of the Condor*, *North by Northwest* and *The Siege*. The protagonist is like us, an innocent, and therefore what happens to him or her could also happen to us. What would we do then, if only we were brave and clever enough? The story provides the wished-for answer: we would survive, perhaps sadder, but always wiser. The unknown threat provides the suspense; the uncovering of the mystery brings release and resolution.

Because need-to-know movies are based on a paranoid world-view, mentors and allies may exist, but they also carry with them the (often true) suspicion that they are in league with the antagonist, part of the conspiracy. In *The Truman Show*, for example, everyone in the protagonist's world is part of a conspiracy to control his life. Some appear to be friends in a real sense, but we're never shown for sure until the end. In *The Manchurian Candidate*, the protagonist has been brainwashed and can't even trust himself; in *A Beautiful Mind*, Russell Crowe's John Nash is subject to schizophrenic delusions. Whatever the case, you want the audience to feel that they never know whom the protagonist can trust, and the sense of jeopardy increases as the number of people the protagonist can trust decreases.

This is especially true of the love interest. In need-to-know movies, sexual intimacy can be used as a tool to leave the protagonist open to the danger of intimate betrayal; take a look at *Sea of Love*, *Basic Instinct*, *The Maltese Falcon* or *North by Northwest*. In *Sea of Love*, the protagonist's lover is also his chief murder suspect, but is factually innocent. In *Basic Instinct* and *The Maltese Falcon*, she's guilty. In *North by Northwest*, she is guilty of betraying and using the protagonist, but ends up redeeming herself. In *Body Heat*, which riffs off the classic *noir Double Indemnity*, the protagonist is a weak man irresistibly drawn into the web of a sexy black (about-to-be) widow. In all of them, the sexual attraction is intensified by the potential danger to the protagonist. This is what is behind the convention of the "femme fatale," or deadly woman. It's another form of the sex/death conjunction. Of course, the "fatal" partner doesn't have to be female; in *Gaslight*, for instance, Ingrid Bergman is nearly driven to insanity and death by the smoothly handsome Charles Boyer; the same applies to Julia Roberts' and Patrick Bergin's characters in *Sleeping with the Enemy*.

Sexual Danger (The Erotic Thriller)

Erotic thrillers operate on much the same basis, but here the focus of what's hidden and discovered is sexual transgression. This is woven into a story involving some other secret agenda—a plot at the protagonist's workplace to discredit him or her, or a serial killer who menaces a beautiful radio talk show host—but these films exist primarily for the purpose of exposing flesh. Because pornography has become readily available and does a much better job of this, the market for erotic thrillers has diminished, but some are still made, even by studios or other large companies (*Basic Instinct*, *Eyes Wide Shut*, *Sea of Love*, *Body Heat* and *Bound* fall within this category). If you have a strong main plot—a good murder mystery, for example—and if enough attention is paid to the basics, the sexual dimension can provide another watchable element and not cheapen the film. As noted, sex is a powerful force of motivation, transgression and betrayal. But if titillation is your goal, masked as a thriller—if what we "need to know" is how the actors will look naked—then you're probably not going to write a good script, or sell it.

LAUGHTER

Situational Comedy, Farce, Romantic Comedy

We use the term "laughter movie" here instead of comedy, because technically a comedy is simply a story with a happy or positive ending. What we're after is more specific. The goal of laughter movies is to get people to laugh. Sounds easy enough, but in fact it's one of the hardest results to accomplish. What is funny, anyway? How do you get millions of people to agree on it, and more importantly, to laugh? And if you fail to be funny in a laughter movie, the entire movie fails, because humor is its reason for being. This is why screenwriters who can consistently make people laugh are among the highest paid writers in the world.

The Gift of the Gods

Laughter is universal, and yet elusive; it's apparently inconsequential, and yet of profound importance to us, affecting everything from our health to our attitude about life. Laughter helps us cope with adversity and put problems that are beyond our control into perspective. It helps us survive. In Preston Sturges' wonderful *Sullivan's Travels*, the protagonist is a successful comedy director who longs to make an "important" film, a serious drama that will mean something to the masses. But when he sets out to shed his identity, to become poor and live like the masses in order to research his "important" material, he instead comes to realize that laughter is perhaps the greatest gift he can bestow, allowing ordinary, hardworking people to escape the heavy loads of their lives and experience joy, if only for a few hours.

No Joking Matter But how do you go about achieving the desired effect? The most common mistake novice writers make is to depend on jokes, verbal or visual; this approach almost always fails. Why? Because jokes are short, discrete units of humor that do not depend on a larger context. Imagine listening to someone tell unrelated jokes for two hours in a row, not all of which can be that funny to begin with; that's the effect you achieve by stringing them together over the course of a two-hour movie. It becomes tiresome. Some movies whose whole intention is to spoof other movies—such as *Airplane!* or the *Naked Gun* series—successfully depend on using one joke and visual gag after another, but these also depend on a general audience familiarity with the clichés and conventions of an overused, moribund genre that provides the coherent context.

In fact, humor arises from the same source as other human emotions: the situations in which people find themselves, their dreams, desires and personal quirks, and their conflicts. This is why the humor genre on television is called "situation comedy," or sitcom. Creating humor is a matter of creating situations in which people act or respond verbally in ways that make sense to them, but which are clearly and unintentionally inappropriate, overblown or harmlessly self-defeating.

So Funny It Hurts There's an old saying that comedy is cruel; comedians talk about "killing" an audience. It wouldn't really be funny to slip on a banana peel and smack into the floor, but watching it happen—without serious consequence—to a pompous school principal who's chasing after a student who's late for class can give us a primitive release because we identify with the student's plight, and because the principal's fragile balloon of self-importance has been punctured. The boring, normal course of events has been disrupted. We laugh because we're put in a superior position to the characters, knowing that their extreme emotions or actions are silly, or their self-images are deserving of comeuppance—and because we can observe and enjoy the characters' discomfiture, harmless pain, overreaction or embarrassment from the safety of the audience. We know from common experience how they must feel, but we are provoked to laughter by the simultaneous experience of feeling the character's distress along with the relief that it isn't happening to us. Humor often comes at someone's expense—someone else, that is.

The banana peel pratfall and other expressions of such primitively physical, slapstick humor tend to appeal more to men than women. Whether this is because men are less evolved is open to argument, but it seems to be an accepted fact: men like the Three Stooges and women do not, unless there's something seriously wrong with them (as Jay Leno says, "please, no outraged letters"). To indulge in a gross generalization, it may have something to do with the difference in response to the infliction of pain; perhaps because men have been taught to enjoy rough horseplay more, but also generally tolerate pain worse than women do, they're more reactive to its depiction and experience more of a release when the pain of horseplay has no serious consequence beyond making the characters look ridiculous. The simplicity and physicality of slapstick is also why it appeals to children and is a staple of cartoons—*Road Runner, Bugs Bunny*, take your pick—or family films like *Home Alone, Blades of Glory* or *Paul Blart: Mall Cop*. No sophistication is called for, and no matter how extreme the pain and destruction apparently inflicted, they always prove harmless save for the frustration they create for the character.

Humorous situations such as those in *I Love Lucy* have been popular with women and also involve a great deal of physical comedy that makes the female characters look ridiculous, but these situations involve embarrassment rather than pain. Embarrassment is in effect another kind of harmless pain, the depiction of which can be very funny. Another obvious example—perhaps because it's something women can viscerally relate to—is the pain of childbirth, which is often used to comic effect, sometimes combining the physical pain of the woman with the embarrassment pain of any men who might be in attendance. Here again there are no serious consequences, and the pain is recognizably a prelude to joy (the birth of a child).

So there are harmlessly painful situations that create humor for men and women alike. It depends on the context and how serious the plight of the character is. Pain is an aspect of chaos, a response to injury, and when chaos damages the order of the world, it can either have horrific or comic consequences, depending on whether it is dangerous or merely discomfiting.

But this is only part of the equation; there's another element that men seem to respond to more than women do: stupidity. Characters like the Stooges, or those in *Dumb and Dumber* and *Dude, Where's My Car?* generate humor through idiotic behavior and appeal to men. Where the character is smart, such as in Charlie Chaplin and Buster Keaton films—and where the situations involve more than simply the visual gag of poking someone in the eye—then even slapstick can appeal to both men and women. Watching three idiots slap each other around appeals to a male audience culturally conditioned to approve of rough-housing (and to take delight in female expressions of dismay, such as those of their mothers, sisters or wives). Watching the poor little tramp getting mauled by a health-spa masseur is something anyone who's ever tried to get in shape can identify with—because the tramp is smart enough to know he doesn't want to be there, any more than we would. He is a victim of a harmlessly painful situation, and we laugh for him in empathy. The Stooges, on the other hand, are cheerfully ignorant of the idiotic behavior that they themselves are perpetrating, and we laugh at them in contempt.

So, if you're going to use "foolish" male pain-infliction as the primary source of humor, you must accept that you have also probably narrowed and pre-selected your audience. The same goes for bodily function humor. Perhaps because of an historically macho culture, men simply find the coarseness—the social transgression—of farting, belching or vomiting funnier than women do. There's of course a certain sexism—or sex distinction—in these assertions, and with the general popularity of gross-out laughter films like *There's Something about Mary*, this distinction may be lessening. But there's still a great deal of truth to it; men and women can find different things funny or disgusting. It's the reason most standup comedians depend on the differences between the sexes as a source for their humor.

Serious Absurdity Only rarely are the characters in a laughter film aware of being funny, or their situation being preposterous, unless they are making an ironic commentary (as opposed to a joke). They are acting and responding honestly to events within the context of a given, usually distressing, situation. This is true even in slapstick: Moe, Larry and Curly are not joking it up, they're dead serious. So is Lucille Ball. The fact that she's serious about some patently ridiculous plan to get rich or make wine, or that the Stooges are serious about pretending to be surgeons or plumbers—and the progressively sillier lengths each of them goes to in order to maintain their plans—is the source of the humor. Charlie Chaplin's deadpan seriousness only accentuates the absurdity of the situations he finds himself in, whether it's slaving away to the point of delusion on an assembly line until he's chasing after a woman whose buttons look like hex-nuts (*Modern Times*), or belting his pants up with a rope (so he can dance with the girl of his dreams) only to discover that the rope is attached to a large dog (*The Gold Rush*). The more absurd the situation, the funnier it is when the character treats it seriously.

Their conflicts are humorous because their distress, actions and responses are somehow out of proportion with the situation, or else the situation is so absurd that it's hilarious to see them taking it seriously. A woman yelling at another woman to get out of her way can be serious and threatening. A woman yelling at a cow to get out of her way, however, is comic; the woman's action may be emotionally justified from her point of view, but is still inappropriate; it makes her ridiculous. Or perhaps something causes a burly weightlifter to scream in mortal fear; but if it's absurdly unthreatening—say a mouse running around his gym—then his response provokes laughter. Or say a character wanders through a urban shootout as if on a Sunday stroll, carrying his groceries. With bullets whizzing all around him, he doesn't even seem to notice until a bullet spills his milk—and then he's pissed off, because he has to go back to the market. Or perhaps a Wall Street banker, filled with pride at his high position in life, is reduced to despair when he becomes responsible for caring for his sick cousin's farm and cannot even milk a cow without soaking his five-hundred-dollar Gucci shoes. Our delight comes from his consternation, from his serious but inappropriate approach to the situation.

Even in spoof movies, the characters do not actually tell each other jokes, but rather play it straight in the face of grotesquely exaggerated, absurd and/or clichéd situations. Farce follows the same pattern, not in mocking other films, but by taking real-life situations to absurd extremes while everyone within them struggles to maintain an appearance of normality.

Comic Premise and Character   The first job for the writer whose primary goal is to inspire laughter, therefore, is to find a premise that has the potential to force characters into absurd, harmlessly painful or embarrassing situations, or to create characters who will by their nature act absurdly within normal situations. Either way, they are fish out of water, and the humor comes from the conflict of their inappropriate actions and attitudes with a given situation. Examples of normal people in absurd situations include: a trio of city dwellers who decide to get away from it all on a dude ranch (*City Slickers*); an ordinary guy who discovers that his world has been overrun by not-very-competent zombies (*Shaun of the Dead*); an adopted paleontologist who decides to find his real birth parents (*Flirting with Disaster*); a male nurse who has to deal with his paranoid, CIA officer, future father-in-law (*Meet the Parents*); a weatherman who finds he's been trapped in an ever-repeating *Groundhog Day*; an irresponsible lawyer who discovers that he has to tell the truth for one whole day (*Liar, Liar*); the women of a country who decide to stop having sex with their husbands until they stop fighting a foolish war (*Lysistrata*); an upper-class linguist who makes a bet that he can turn a guttersnipe into a lady (*Pygmalion, My Fair Lady*). Inappropriate or absurd characters within more-or-less normal situations can include: a dimwitted but self-important detective who goes after a world-class jewel thief (*The Pink Panther*); a manic private detective who will go to any length to retrieve stolen animals (*Ace Ventura*); an out-of-work actor who pretends to be a woman in order to get a part on a soap opera (*Tootsie*).

All of these were obviously ripe with the potential for situational humor, and relied on the exaggeration of a personality or situation to give it comic proportions. But sometimes the best humor comes from everyday situations, from simple recognition of the common annoyances and foibles of life. In *Parenthood*, for instance, Steve Martin's character does everything he can as a dutiful father to make his son's birthday party a success, including setting up a piñata. But the thing is impregnable, and he ends up—after trying everything he can think of—finally resorting to a handsaw to open it. The rest of the party is equally fraught with setbacks with which every parent can identify, and the humor comes from the exasperated extremes to which Martin goes in order to overcome them. In *LA Story*, Martin only slightly exaggerates the cultural stereotypes that people associate with Los Angeles. In one scene, he and some other Angelenos sit at a cafe, unselfconsciously ordering everything decaffeinated, from cappuccinos to coffee ice cream. Then an earthquake hits, and no one seems to notice. And when Martin's character expresses reservations about "making love" to the much younger, spacey babe played by Sarah Jessica Parker, she responds by saying that's all right, "we'll just have sex." Within the context of America's perceptions about Los Angeles, it's funny because it makes sense. In *Shaun of the Dead*, the protagonist learns that his best friend really isn't all that different once he's a zombie.

Outrage and Transgression In fear films, transgressions of taboo or social norms result in terrifying consequences. In laughter films, they result in hilarity because the initial fear associated with taboo violation is there, but not the serious consequences, and so we experience giddy relief. The transgressions themselves may also be of an embarrassing rather than dangerous nature. Sex and bodily functions, as noted, are both subject to taboos and are sources of embarrassment, although the level of the humor is unsophisticated and visceral. It can be at the simple level of a practical joke, as in *Dumb and Dumber*, where one fool secretly puts a laxative in the drink of the other in order to embarrass him in front of the girl they're both after; when we see and hear him noisily relieving himself, only to discover that the toilet he's on doesn't flush, it's the laughter equivalent of showing onscreen gore in a splatter film. But humor derived from upsetting "civilized" social norms can also reflect a deeper desire to see everyone cut down to size. Having someone fart or reveal his private parts on screen by itself crosses a social boundary; having it disrupt a stuffy social setting adds another layer of transgression. Audiences, especially American audiences, delight in the humiliation of hypocrites and the upper classes, of those who think they're better than the average person. If such transgressions happen to or occur in the presence of uptight, socially correct characters—or if such persons are shown in situations where they are exposed, naked, dirtied or performing a bodily function—it punctures the pompous conventions by which they protect and define their inflated self-images.

Cut Down to Size Humor of this sort is a great leveler, a reaffirmation of our democratic belief that no one is above ridicule. We love to catch powerful people "with their pants down." There's perhaps no better example in real life than the plethora of jokes emerging from moralizing politicians' alleged (and confirmed) infidelities and other sexual embarrassments. It's a case of the "Emperor's New Clothes." In the *Three Stooges*, the recipient of a pie in the face—other than one of the stooges—is usually a stuffy socialite. In *Dumb and Dumber*, we take secret revenge on all those officious cops who've given us tickets when one of them takes a swig from a beer bottle filled with urine. Even laughter movies of great sophistication take advantage of sexual/bodily function humor. Think of the scenes in Robert Altman's classic, *MASH*, where the arrogant, puritanical "Hot Lips Hoolihan" is revealed to be an adulterous hypocrite, first when we overhear her lovemaking on the PA system, and then when she's humiliated by being exposed before the entire camp while taking a shower. Her Bible-quoting, intolerant lover Frank is sent away in disgrace. We delight in their embarrassment because they've brought it on themselves by pretending to be superior. Humiliation is not limited to sexual or body-function taboos. It can be reducing a rapacious land-developer to poverty, a famous but arrogant athlete to public defeat, a pompous intellectual to admitting he was wrong; in short, anything that brings the self-impressed and mighty low.

Those who are perceived to be seriously damaging the social contract or who act malevolently against innocent people—criminals, dishonest politicians, corrupt bosses, lawyers—are also targets for humiliation (*Home Alone, The Apartment, Dave, The Social Network, Working Girl, Liar, Liar*). They too need to be brought to justice, usually by a character representing innocence, and with whom we identify: a child, an honest worker, a caring citizen, a smart dog. In these cases, public ridicule of those who have tormented or betrayed the protagonist (us) creates the same cathartic effect that death or imprisonment for the antagonist would in a serious movie.

Cynical Laughter   Darker comedies, such as *Bob Roberts, Network, Eating Raoul, Young Adult, Greenberg*, or *Dr. Strangelove*, usually reveal a more generalized and cynical attitude about human nature, and contain a comeuppance for the protagonists as well, that often occurs at each other's hands. The protagonist may actually kill the offending antagonist(s), as in *The Last Supper*, or get away with murder, as in *The Player*. In effect, everyone is corrupted and becomes an antagonist. To write such a film, you need to identify a theme and premise that are specific to the social foible you want to skewer—greed, hunger for power, lust—and then create a protagonist who has reason to obsess about it and strike out against it. However, the protagonist is drawn to fight the foible, as represented by an antagonist, precisely because he or she suffers from the same failing, and ultimately both are brought down. The humor in such movies is less cathartic than satiric and cautionary. The theme is that none of us is above sin or condemnation. This effect can be deliciously evil, playing to an audience's sophisticated cynicism rather than to its sense of the absurd. But you run the risk of alienating your audience if the effect is too self-righteous or bitter, or if you create a protagonist whose actions they ultimately cannot justify.

Laughing at Love (Romantic Comedy)

Boy meets girl, boy loses girl, boy gets girl; that's the timeworn formula for romantic comedy. Sometimes the genders will be reversed (or be identical, in a gay story), but the model remains. But what exactly does it involve, and why does it work? And does it still work, in a theoretically more advanced society? Sure it does.

As we've seen, humor comes from putting a character in an untenable situation, and from his or her inappropriate actions and responses to the obstacles or conflict that the situation presents. When that conflict involves the additional insecurity of trying to prove oneself lovable to another person, you have the basis for a romantic comedy. In most romantic laughter movies, the primary oppositional relationship is that between the two lovers. Structurally one is the protagonist and the other the antagonist; the untenable situation is that one would-be lover's greatest conflict (other than with him- or herself) is with the other would-be lover. In addition, the two potential lovers must appear clearly right for each other to the audience, while appearing clearly wrong to each other; either the protagonist, antagonist or both don't see this as working. (We will refer here to the "boy" and "girl" as protagonist and antagonist, and maintain this gender assignment except when referring to specific examples in which the gender roles are reversed; while we want to get away from the idea that only the male can be the protagonist in a romantic laughter film, it is too cumbersome and confusing to keep saying "him or her," or to alternate the genders in our discussion.)

"Not if You Were the Last Man on Earth"   This oppositional relationship is also why in movies—unlike life—romantic laughter films often start off with the eventual lovers actively disliking, fearing or avoiding each other, and having to overcome this initial antagonism in order to get together. There would be no conflict, and therefore no story, without it. This is a staple of Katherine Hepburn movies, whether the male lead is Spencer Tracy, Humphrey Bogart or Cary Grant, as well as others of that era (like *It Happened One Night*). Another classic example is *When Harry Met Sally*, and is taken to an extreme in *As Good as It Gets* and *What Women Want*, where the protagonists (Jack Nicholson's Melvin and Mel Gibson's Nick) are apparently vile misogynists, and the antagonists (Carol and Darcy, in both cases played by Helen Hunt) can barely tolerate them. Sometimes the would-be lovers appear impossibly mismatched because of class differences, as in *Pygmalion*, *The Prince & Me* and *Pretty Woman*.

There may also be other external obstacles, such as pre-existing relationships, competing suitors, delaying situations that arise, accidents of fate that disrupt or abort their initial union or internal obstacles such as the desire to remain single or a poor self-image. In some cases, where the "object of love" either doesn't know about the protagonist's affections or is so kind and sweet that she is not a good source for creating conflict, you can structure the story so that one of these other obstacles is more fully developed and becomes the antagonist. For instance, in *There's Something about Mary*, Ben Stiller's and

Cameron Diaz's characters initially like one another, but are separated when he accidentally catches his privates in his zipper on their prom night; when a wistful Stiller decides to find her years later, he hires a sleazy private eye. And when this character (Matt Dillon) falls in love with her, too, he becomes the antagonist. Cameron Diaz—"Mary"—is both too perfect and too unaware of what's going on to be the antagonist, and so becomes the MacGuffin (see Glossary): she and love are essentially the same thing. In *Sleepless in Seattle*, the potential lovers are separated by a continent; they are never in direct conflict with each other, and so the distance and the combination of their mutual internal doubts and hesitations becomes the antagonistic force. In *The Truth about Cats and Dogs* and *Roxanne*, which recast the classic story of *Cyrano De Bergerac* in modern times, poor self-image is the primary antagonist.

However, although these alternative antagonist structures can work beautifully, they are less common because in a romantic laughter film you normally want your two lovers to be the focus of the story and to be equally interesting and well-rounded—a balance that more naturally suggests a protagonist/antagonist relationship. We'll proceed on that model.

An old expression (slightly altered) goes: first you put the protagonist up a tree, then you throw rocks at him until he figures out how to get down. In laughter films, the more "rocks" the merrier. But there must also be an initial attraction, and the lengths to which the characters go to avoid admitting it to each other or themselves, and then to winning one another over after having made fools of themselves, create the humor of the story.

Boy Meets Girl, Boy Loses Girl, Boy Gets Girl When the protagonist meets the antagonist, he doesn't have the confidence or ability to win or keep her, so he does something to lose the object of his affections by some misguided action that proves he lacks the power of charm/wit/self-confidence/knowledge of what the antagonist or desired person wants or needs. The antagonist's superior power comes from the fact that she has what the protagonist needs to acquire: she is more centered, caring or decent. Look at the wholesome waitress Helen Hunt plays in *As Good as It Gets*, or Mary, who is practically a saint in *There's Something about Mary*. In *Jerry MacGuire*, the antagonist is the only honest, selfless woman with whom he works, the only one who sticks by him in his troubles. In *The Truth about Cats and Dogs* and *While You Were Sleeping*, where the antagonists are male, they are incredibly kind, decent men. Note that in *As Good as It Gets*, the antagonist cares for a sick child; in *There's Something about Mary*, she cares for a mentally disabled brother; in *Jerry MacGuire* she also has a goofy-looking little kid; in *The Truth about Cats and Dogs*, the male antagonist has a problematic dog. In all four, these "innocent" dependants are drawn to the protagonist in a way they never have been with any other person, and this acceptance is a signal to the antagonist that the protagonist is worthy. The antagonist is morally and emotionally where the protagonist needs to be; the protagonist is out of balance with the world and victory comes when the antagonist's power brings the protagonist back into balance. In the words of Jerry MacGuire, the protagonist needs the antagonist: "You complete me," he tells her.

Historically, in a male-centered culture in which one of a woman's primary powers came from withholding or allowing sexual intimacy, the female antagonist—like the dragon guarding its golden fleece—held the prize, the holy grail of sex: whether or not the protagonist gets to make love to her. (As noted, in the Greek comedy *Lysistrata*, this power alone brings a war to an end.) In recent years—as during the thirties and forties, when strong actresses were allowed to carry films—the playing field has become more level, and the roles occasionally appear reversed, with the man as the object of affection (as in *The Truth about Cats and Dogs*, *While You Were Sleeping* and *Young Adult*). Sex as an equivalent of the Holy Grail works either way.

But the raw desire for sex alone won't do, since it is too worldly and falls into the vice category of Lust. If that remains the protagonist's only goal, then he or she is doomed to comic failure. Sexual desire must be sublimated or combined with the higher level of true love. Through the advice of friends (allies and mentors), the failure of a series of inappropriate actions that backfire and embarrass or confound the protagonist, and through coming up against the powers of the antagonist, the protagonist is forced to learn how to be a better person and overcome his crippling self-doubts or character flaws. He acquires the power to "win" the antagonist over. Usually, the protagonist must also prove worthier than a secondary adversary such as a competing suitor or the snotty, inappropriate lover the antagonist is already stuck with. If such a relationship exists, the antagonist will be in it only out of a sense of obligation or some other admirable but ultimately insufficient reason.

Wrong Turns   The protagonist's internal flaws or self-doubts must cause him to take certain deceptive actions that he mistakenly thinks are appropriate, but that in fact are self-defeating. These actions and deceptions may be mean-spirited, foolish or well-intentioned, but in every case they backfire. In *The Truth about Cats and Dogs*, the (female) protagonist thinks of herself as a "dog"; because of this she is too afraid to meet the man of her dreams and concocts a scheme to introduce him instead to her beautiful best friend. In *While You Were Sleeping*, Sandra Bullock's lonely protagonist plays along with the misconception that she's engaged to a man in a coma in order to stay close to the family with whom she wants to belong. In *As Good as It Gets*, the protagonist is a true crackpot, who tries at first to get the attention of the waitress he fancies by cruel jokes. In *Working Girl*, Melanie Griffith's protagonist, a secretarial assistant, pretends to be an executive in order to get ahead in her work and with the man for whom she's fallen. In *Pretty Woman*, Richard Gere's billionaire tries to keep the relationship financial, even when he knows he's in love with Julia Roberts' prostitute. The deception may simply be that the protagonist will not admit to his true feelings. But slowly, his deceptions and defenses begin to erode by exposure to the antagonist and her positive actions. The protagonist learns from the antagonist how to cast away fears and become more real, more honest, more worthy.

The conflict comes from the fact that all these deceptions may either distance the antagonist in the first place, or if they attract the antagonist at first, the deceptions will later come back to haunt the protagonist and undo the attraction. In other words, just as the protagonist seems to have achieved success, this final and apparently fatal conflict will arise due to the protagonist's own prior machinations, which are now revealed. This also applies to alternative antagonist structures as well. In *There's Something about Mary*, Stiller's hiring of a private eye backfires and actually puts more distance between himself and his beloved, both through the machinations of the private eye and then through Mary's discovery of Stiller's surveillance plan.

"Fessing Up"   Once the deceptions are revealed and the plan unravels, the protagonist must come clean with a confession that everything he did was because of true love. The point is that true love can only bloom when deceptions are cast aside, when the protagonist reveals all and makes himself vulnerable in the presence of the antagonist. *This exposure is actually where the protagonist exhibits greatest power, because honesty is the one quality that will win over the antagonist.* Where courage movies depend on taking physical action and need-to-know movies on acquiring knowledge, romantic laughter films depend on "fessing up"—on honesty. Where fear movies are about transgression and retribution, romantic laughter films are about transgression and redemption.

The power relationships are the same in romantic movies as in any other kind of movie. The protagonist has the potential to win, but the antagonist appears too powerful. They come into oppositional conflict with each other, struggling to reach the same goal. But in romantic laughter films, we say that the protagonist "wins over" the antagonist rather than "defeats" her, because the difference is that a power equilibrium rather than a reversal is established at the end. The protagonist wins, but the antagonist doesn't lose, because the goal that they both need to achieve is positive for both and achieved by both; in fact, it depends on their mutual success, because it is true love.

LOVE AND LONGING

Romance, Melodrama, Platonic Love

Love is the most profound connection people can have with one another; in love, we lose our loneliness and sense of isolation in an impersonal or threatening world. The longing to experience love—to know that there can be one perfect union with another in which we can both lose ourselves and acquire the certainty that the world has meaning and purpose—is something almost everyone can identify with, and has led to some of the greatest stories and movies we have. They are stories of sacrifice and passion, of people who feel life's most exquisite pleasures and pains, who are allowed, as very few of us are, to become completely alive, perhaps for the rest of their lives, perhaps only for a brief but priceless moment. It doesn't really matter. Although it's more a buddy comedy than a love story, there's a wonderful moment in *City Slickers* when Curly—Jack Palance's old cowboy—describes having once long ago seen a beautiful girl, backlit by the sun; but he never even spoke to her, or saw her again. Billy Crystal's character is appalled—why didn't he? She could have been the love of Curly's life! To which Curly responds, "She is." Later, as a result of his adventure, Crystal's character comes to realize that his life has all the meaning it needs, because he has the love of his life, his wife and family.

Heart Beats

In a love story, this search for a perfect moment of connection and understanding becomes the main emphasis. Passion and the need for connection may be secondary or even absent in other genres; in a positive love story passion and the need for connection are expressions of the life force. We talk of "deathless love," of characters living happily ever after, not because they—us—will be literally immortal, but because we believe that if we can experience true love, we will have truly lived, and death will lose its power over us. The opposite is also true; in a negative love story, where the protagonist's love and longing remain unrequited, death's power is increased, and the results can be emotionally devastating.

Selfless Love   The longing for love can lead to empowerment and joy if it reiterates, responds to or positively alters the underlying morality and necessities of the world in which the characters live. The result is a love story with a happy ending. In *City Lights*, perhaps Chaplin's greatest film, a little tramp manages to scrape together the money to allow a blind flower girl to have an operation and restore her sight. But because he does not imagine himself worthy, he does not reveal his identity to her; the gift is entirely altruistic, a selfless act of pure love, and she mistakenly assumes that a wealthy man must have been her benefactor. In the end, however, the memory of his touch, from when she was still blind, reveals the little tramp's true identity to her, and we end with the knowledge that his actions have at last brought him the happiness he so richly deserves. His actions have positively transformed his world and that of the woman he loves. *Marty* is similar; two lonely underdogs find one another and against all odds redefine and improve their callous, cruel world.

Happy endings do not always mean that the lovers end up together. *Casablanca*, for example, has a happy ending that reinforces the moral necessities of a world in which good is at war with evil. Rick's reunion with Elsa allows him to leave behind the cynicism and pain that have paralyzed him, and allows her to unburden herself of the guilt of having abandoned him years before. But both come to realize that the greater cause in their world—as personified by Elsa's freedom-fighter husband, Victor—is more important than continuing their affair. Positive love is selfless, and Rick and Elsa's selflessness in spite of their longing reinforces the values of their world. They cannot be with one another, but that doesn't mean their love is lost; rather, they are able to sublimate it to a perfection that requires nothing more: "We'll always have Paris." *Forrest Gump* is another good example. In a chaotic, often absurd and cruel world, Forrest's decency and selfless love end up saving—at least spiritually—the victimized and tormented girl he's always loved. And even though Jenny dies, as with a courage film, the result of Forrest's actions is life-affirming: she has borne him a son, in whom her love survives. Perhaps the most successful example of selfless love—certainly at the box office— is *Titanic*. Here an apparently well-ordered world is thrown into chaos. Although he perishes, Jack's selfless love for Rose saves her "in every way that a person can be saved," and allows her to experience a fuller and longer life than almost anyone could imagine. All of these films have a bittersweet quality, but ultimately are still "comedic," in that life and the value of love have been reaffirmed.

It is important to note that much of what applies to romantic laughter films also applies to almost any comedic (happy ending) love story, whether or not its primary intention is to engender laughter. The difference is the degree of genuine anguish the characters experience before they succeed (remember, genuine pain is not funny), who or what is at fault for the deceptions the protagonist is driven to, and the degree of exaggeration applied to the situations and characters' actions. In a laughter film, the problems a protagonist faces are largely of his own making, and his efforts to overcome them become increasingly ridiculous. In a serious "comedic" love story, deceptions are imposed upon the protagonist by others or by circumstances, and evoke empathy rather than laughter.

This is clearly seen if we compare Jane Austen's *Emma* (or its modern derivative *Clueless*), which is clearly a laughter story, with Jane Austen's *Sense and Sensibility*, which is not (although it has comic elements). Both follow largely the same pattern: a young woman in the socially rigid society of early nineteenth century England falls in love with a perfect man, but is prevented by circumstances from having him until the end. In *Emma*, it's Emma's own foolish blindness to what she needs combined with her busybody mismanaging of a friend's love life that are the sources of the laughter. She's well off, and cannot leave well enough alone. Her misguided deceptions, plottings and denials are entirely her own fault, based on her own pride and social prejudices, and she must be comically humbled, her pride stripped away, before she can achieve the honesty and understanding that true love requires. *Sense and Sensibility*, by contrast, elicits pathos, because the protagonist is constrained into denying her feelings against her will; her once well-to-do family has fallen on hard times, and through no fault of her own she is left no choice by the social constraints of her day but to deny her feelings. She is ultimately rewarded with love for her constancy, discretion and virtue, while others who have acted against her are humbled for having imposed their prejudicial constraints and deceits upon her. Both examples use the same world and very similar kinds of characters (as far as appearance and social context go) to achieve very different effects.

Love stories with happy endings are usually set in a world where the normal order appears solid. At first this provides contrast to the inner chaos that the characters are experiencing and that throws them out of balance with the world. The happy resolution of their love, the new equilibrium of protagonist and antagonist, brings them both back into balance with the world and reaffirms its order.

Selfish Love: Romantic Tragedy However, the longing for love can be so great and all-consuming, where nothing else matters, that it comes into unresolvable conflict with the larger world. It is "star-crossed," against the will of the gods (whoever those might be), and therefore represents a kind of hubris or fatal pride. Their love burns too hot, the light so bright that it blinds the characters to anything but their own selfish desire, and as a result they are consumed by it. This is a tragic love story.

One obvious example is *Romeo and Juliet*; their love is the hot, pure desire of youth, innocent but nonetheless hormonal, lust sublimated into exquisite mutual worship. Because they cannot accept the realities of their world, they end up destroying those closest to them and ultimately themselves. The same thing happens in *The English Patient*, where Ralph Fiennes' and Kristin Scott Thomas' characters betray those closest to them, even their country in a time of war, in order to satisfy their blinding love, and both are destroyed. In both of these examples there are contrasting subplots that present "comedic" alternatives in order to reaffirm the proper order of their worlds. Romeo and Juliet's deaths shock their families into accepting peace with each other, and Juliette Binoche's nurse finds happiness and love with her Indian sergeant as the Allies achieve victory. But in the film (which reverses the emphasis of the Michael Ondaatje novel from which it's adapted) these are secondary to the themes of burning, destructive passion.

In spite of its having won the Oscar for Best Picture, many American audiences disliked *The English Patient*, and a comparison with the ever-popular *Casablanca* is revealing. In *The English Patient*, the main characters put their own consciously adulterous passions ahead of the cause of victory over the Nazis, while in *Casablanca* they sacrifice their personal feelings for the greater cause; and although they did commit adultery in the past, they were unaware of it (Elsa thought her husband was dead). *Casablanca* reflects an American sentiment that faithfulness and sacrifice for a larger, noble cause are always correct, while *The English Patient* represents a more European attitude that honor and fidelity are relative matters. Europeans live in a world where armies and allegiances shift back and forth across national boundaries, and where marriages have traditionally been financial rather than emotional arrangements, so that what matters more are personal passions and needs. These two movies demonstrate the difference between (and differences in attitude toward) honest and transgressional love.

Tragic (unhappy ending) love stories are often set in a world where chaos has been unleashed by war or other extreme circumstances; in stories like *Gone with the Wind*, *Anna Karenina* or *The English Patient*, the chaos of the world mirrors and intensifies the inner chaos of the lovers. As the world returns to order, the lovers remain out of balance, their love still chaotic or transgressional. They are like swimmers who have gone too far out to sea and cannot return to shore, and so they drown. In other movies, like Hemingway's *For Whom the Bell Tolls*, their love may be pure, in contrast to the chaos of the world, but it is unable to stand against the force of the whirlwind. The theme here is that two people's love for each other cannot save them from a world swept by hateful destruction.

Alternately, tragic love can be set in an ordered world, but be irrevocably transgressional from the beginning, as in *Brokeback Mountain* (homosexuality), *Othello* (miscegenation) or *Lolita* (pedophilia), or European films like *Swept Away* (adultery and class transgression). This is an unusual strategy in American films and usually gets a tepid or even angry response, because it goes against the largely positive and equalizing American psyche. To Americans, if the world is in order, then love must eventually reaffirm it, even if it is transgressional; look at *Mississippi Masala*, *The Adjustment Bureau* or *Moonstruck*, for instance. If love fails or goes beyond the pale, the story loses us. Europeans are generally more pessimistic and therefore more accepting of human failure.

Platonic Love   Not all love-and-longing movies are sexual. Some of the most powerful involve the love of a parent for a child (*Mask*, *Lorenzo's Oil*); one friend for another (*Brian's Song*, *Scarecrow*, *Midnight Cowboy*, *The Secret Garden*, *Enemy Mine*); a child for a special adult (*The Bicycle Thief*, *Cinema Paradiso*, *The Little Princess*); or a human, usually a child, for an animal (*The Black Stallion*, *Old Yeller*, *Free Willy*). Because these stories are uncomplicated by erotic passion, they have a different kind of purity. Depending on whether they are comedic or tragic, they are stories of the triumph or failure of innocence in the face of a cruel world, of selflessness in a selfish world.

To write such a story, instead of sexual attraction, you need to explore the impulse to care for another, the instinct to comfort the wounded or shield the weak; in short, that constellation of actions and emotions that we label altruism. You can approach this kind of story from two directions. As in a romantic love story, you can set it up so that one (or both) of the two main characters dislikes the other at first, but comes to love him or her in the end, as in *Enemy Mine* (where the human and alien start off trying to kill each other and end up as best friends) or in *Cinema Paradiso* (where the cranky old projectionist at first rejects the young boy, but ends up replacing the father the boy has lost). Or you can set up a situation in which two people deeply love one another but are separated, or in which their love is endangered by circumstances, as in *The Little Princess* (where the little girl and her father are separated by war) or in *Lorenzo's Oil* (where a fatal illness threatens to kill the little boy). The conflict and theme arise from the struggle to provide, to protect, to maintain connection when the chaotic forces of the world threaten to tear your characters apart. In a tragedy, these forces succeed, as in *Midnight Cowboy* or *The Bicycle Thief*; in a comedy, they fail, as in the *Black Stallion* or *The Secret Garden*. Even death does not spell failure if the survivor ends up empowered by the love he or she has experienced, as is the case in *Cinema Paradiso*, *84 Charing Cross Road* and *Brian's Song*. Although heart-wrenching, these have positive endings and themes, and are comedic.

Furthermore, most "buddy" movies fall into this category. *Lethal Weapon*, for instance, is about two mismatched cops who come to love each other over the course of the action. The aforementioned *City Slickers* is about platonic male-bonding, as are the classic *Diner* and the *Hangover* movies. Every version of Sherlock Holmes is essentially a buddy-love film about the mismatched, misanthropic genius Holmes and the good-hearted but less perceptive Dr. Watson. *Thelma & Louise* is about female bonding, about two women whose journey challenges their male-dominated world, even to the moment of their deaths. Kristen Wiig's brilliant *Bridesmaids* gives female ownership to previously male-oriented raunchy buddy-bonding.

FINAL THOUGHTS

Picking Your Poison　There are many other genres to explore, such as biographies and historical sagas, where the varied events of specific, real experiences are organized and focused around resonant, universal themes; or fantasy and science fiction, where, in the context of being transported to other worlds, we can both marvel at their strangeness and yet see our deepest moral and emotional concerns played out. We do not have space to pursue all these genres here; but hopefully the elements and strategies outlined above will give you a good sense of how and why different kinds of stories work the way they do, why they fascinate and move us, and most importantly, how to choose and create the kind of story you want to tell.

EXERCISES

1. Take two characters and create, in a paragraph or two, a romantic laughter film around them.

2. Now take the same characters and alter their world and circumstances so you have a romantic tragedy.

3. Now take the same characters and alter one of their personalities so that you now have a fear movie. The point of the above exercises is to see how you can, by altering one or two essential aspects, create a very different kind of film using otherwise similar elements.

4. Create a "trail of evidence" that reveals the nature and agenda of an antagonist in a need-to-know movie. Do not introduce or reveal the character in person.

5. In a paragraph or two, describe a courage character who has a specific arc. Now take that same character and see if you can re-create him or her as a catalytic character, again in a paragraph or two. Define the similarities and differences.

PART THREE

WRITING

Narrative

Dialogue

Rewriting

12

Narrative

Writing the Picture

A movie is a story told in pictures and sound. The narrative—also called the "narration," "business" or "description"—is where a screenwriter creates those pictures and sounds (other than dialogue). Set at the widest margins, the narrative occupies a position of authority on the page as it details the action, setting, character appearance and mood of each scene. At its simplest, it is a basic description of what the audience will see and hear. Yet, while the screenwriter must strive for simplicity, narrative should not be a mere summary or bland listing of scene elements. It must convey motion and emotion with an almost poetic economy and force and feed the reader's imagination. It is through the narrative that the writer tries to get the reader to experience not only the sights and sounds, but also the excitement of the story, so that the movie itself "plays" in her head.

KEEP IT MOVING!

Keeping the story moving, literally, requires brevity, clarity and pace. A novelist can linger on a moment or a physical detail and devote paragraphs or pages to full-blown descriptions. This is death in a screenplay, the equivalent of stopping the film projector on a single frame. There simply isn't the time or luxury. A screenplay's narrative must manage to convey a vivid sense of location, a hint of character and mood, and a lively account of the action, all with the fewest possible words. Only that which is relevant to the story and/or characters belongs. No repetitious words, no hyperbolic descriptions or phrases, no asides to the reader, nothing should interrupt the flow of the story (movie) as it progresses through time.

Narrative is a critical part of any screenplay, yet unfortunately it's often skipped by readers because most beginning screenwriters—and some experienced writers who should know better—don't take the time to learn how to write powerful, active, lean narrative. So the reader simply scans the narrative, focusing instead on the dialogue—which means the reader may be paying attention to the least important part of the screenplay. Let's look at what makes good narrative by starting with paragraphs and working our way down to phrasing and individual words.

Paragraphs

When readers open a screenplay to find large blocks of dense narrative dominating the page, they are immediately turned off. For one thing, lengthy paragraphs make the narrative hard to read. For another, experienced readers know that dense narrative is indicative of the writer spending too much time on unimportant details that must now be sifted through in order to get to the meat of the story. Lastly, one page of a screenplay roughly equals one minute of screen time. If the page takes too long to read, the reader will lose a sense of the story's movement. As a result, no paragraph in a screenplay should be longer than four or five sentences—short, uncomplicated sentences. The following is the kind of narrative that readers dread:

EXT. KONIGSBERG'S HOUSE — NIGHT

Konigsberg peeks outside to find that the fuse box--simple metal walls buckled from a massive blow--has been smashed. Konigsberg hears a MUFFLED SOUND, something hard to identify, that comes from behind him. He turns to find a DARK FIGURE in a knitted wool ski mask and surgical gloves holding a Louisville Slugger. Konigsberg quickly runs inside and locks the back door behind him, then frantically searches the kitchen drawers, from which he pulls out a silver semi-automatic handgun with a pearl handle. Then there's only silence. Only his hard breath. He slowly approaches the door and peers through the curtained glass. SMASH! The baseball bat shatters the window. A surgical glove reaches in and unlocks the door. The Dark Figure, bat raised, coolly enters and walks toward Mr. Konigsberg, who backs away in terror. The broken glass twinkles on the Dark Figure's ski mask. Konigsberg closes his eyes and with a flinch, squeezes the trigger of his pearl-handled semi-automatic handgun. CLICK! A dud.

There are several problems with this paragraph in addition to its length. First, it's in the wrong font: screenplays should be in Courier 12 pt. For another thing, there are sentences with subordinate and complicated clauses: "Konigsberg peeks outside to find that the fuse box—simple metal walls buckled from a massive blow—has been smashed." For yet another, there's way too much unessential detail, such as the description of the gun, which is repeated painstakingly. And we don't need to see him described as "Mr. Konigsberg." There is even another, greater problem; the scene shifts from exterior to interior without the change being indicated by a new scene header. This narrative should be trimmed and broken into easy-to-read paragraphs as follows:

```
EXT. KONIGSBERG'S HOUSE — NIGHT

Its simple metal walls have buckled from a massive blow.

A MUFFLED SOUND comes from behind him. He turns.

There's a DARK FIGURE in a ski mask and surgical gloves,
holding a Louisville Slugger.

INT. KONIGSBERG'S KITCHEN — NIGHT

Konigsberg runs in and locks the back door. He
frantically searches the kitchen drawers. Pulls out a
silver semi-auto hand gun.

Then, silence. Only his hard breath. He slowly approaches
the door and peers through the curtained glass.

SMASH! The baseball bat shatters the window. A surgical
glove reaches in and unlocks the door. The Dark Figure,
bat raised, coolly enters and walks toward Konigsberg.
The broken glass twinkles on his ski mask.

Konigsberg backs away in terror. He closes his eyes and
with a flinch squeezes the trigger. CLICK! A dud.
```

Shortening and dividing up the description makes it easier to read. A few incomplete sentences are okay, if they create the effect of a scene in motion. And by choosing the paragraph breaks carefully, the writer also helps to "direct" the scene in the reader's mind, by hinting at shifts from shot to shot.

Some screenwriters use "mini-slug lines" to refocus the reader's attention on what each character is doing within a given scene. When using mini-slug lines, the screenwriter places (in caps) the character's name, which is followed by a dash dash, and then the narrative. Mini-slug lines can lead the reader's eye and break the action into easy-to-read bits. However, if overused they can make a read feel choppy, even mannered, so they should be used with discretion. Here is the same scene using mini-slug lines:

```
KONIGSBERG'S HOUSE — NIGHT

KONIGSBERG'S P.O.V. -- The fuse box has been smashed. Its
simple metal walls have buckled from a massive blow.

A MUFFLED SOUND comes from behind him. He turns...

A DARK FIGURE -- Ski mask, surgical gloves, holding a
Louisville Slugger.
```

```
INT. KONIGSBERG'S KITCHEN — NIGHT

KONIGSBERG -- runs in and locks the back door. He
frantically searches the kitchen drawers. Pulls out a
silver semi-auto hand gun.

Then, silence. Only his hard breath. He slowly approaches
the door and peers through the curtained glass.

SMASH -- The baseball bat shatters the window. A surgical
glove reaches in and unlocks the door.

THE DARK FIGURE -- bat raised, coolly enters and walks
toward Konigsberg. The broken glass twinkles on his ski
mask.

KONIGSBERG -- backs away in terror, closes his eyes and
with a flinch squeezes the trigger. CLICK! A dud.
```

Sentences

The narrative describes the action and imagery with economy, so simple sentences (subject, verb, object) should dominate the text. Complex grammar will only slow the read and lessen the impact. These simple sentences should be written in present tense, in an active voice and with a minimum of adverbs and adjectives.

Present Tense

Keeping verb tenses consistent is never a problem for screenwriters because all narrative is written in present tense. Even flashbacks take place in the here and now: everything is written as if it were happening now, in front of our eyes, just as the film will be. This might seem rather elementary, yet a surprising number of beginning screenwriters make this simple mistake. As a reminder, here are several lines of narrative the wrong and right way.

WRONG *(PAST TENSE)*
```
Samuel staggered up the blurred stairs. The floorboards
creaked in the dark. He inched his way towards the
closed bedroom door.
```

RIGHT *(PRESENT TENSE)*
```
Samuel staggers up the blurred stairs. The floorboards
CREAK in the dark. He inches his way towards the closed
bedroom door.
```

WRONG *(PAST TENSE)*
```
Jack watched for unwanted eyes. The coast was clear. He
took the duffel bag from the trunk, walked over to the
```

```
edge and dropped it into the slow-moving river.
```
RIGHT *(PRESENT TENSE)*
```
Jack watches for unwanted eyes. The coast is clear. He
takes the duffel bag from the trunk, walks over to the
edge and drops it into the slow-moving river.
```

Even in (what should be rare) moments of poetic license indicating a character's internal state, such as "Beauty was in the eye of the beholder," the narrative should read, "Beauty is in the eye of the beholder."

An even worse problem is for a screenwriter to mix tenses. Here, the screenwriter suddenly switches from present to past tense.

STUPID *(MIXING TENSES)*
```
They kiss. And again. More passionate. Grace presses Andy
against the refrigerator. Barnyard animal magnets fall
on them. CRASH, a jar of pennies rains down. They didn't
notice, they were too busy enjoying each other's company.
```

Remember, present tense only. There is *no exception* to this rule.

Active Voice

Narrative should also be written in active voice. Active voice is easier to understand and more immediate than passive voice (present progressive, technically, but we'll call it passive for simplicity). It also conveys the sense of—guess what—action! The subject of the sentence performs the action of the verb on the object:

```
Jill slaps Jack.
```

Jill, the subject, performs the action "slaps." When the sentence is written in passive voice, the object receives the action of the verb from the subject:

```
Jack is slapped by Jill.
```

An active voice energizes the narrative by concentrating on verbs that emphasize the performer of the action. It is more direct and dramatic. And, of equal importance, it uses fewer words.

Right (Active Voice)	*Wrong (Passive Voice)*
Sam slams the car into reverse.	The car is slammed into reverse by Sam.
Oswalt takes aim.	The gun is aimed by Oswalt.
Sandra kisses her Mother.	Mother is kissed by Sandra.

WRITE ONLY WHAT WE CAN SEE OR HEAR

As noted, screenplay narrative can only describe what the audience can see or hear. Unlike the novelist, who can describe a character's thoughts, past events and future considerations, a screenwriter is limited to the present, and to what can be filmed. For example, in the following narrative, a student screenwriter describes a character's thoughts. How can this be filmed?

> The stone-faced members of the PAROLE BOARD huddle behind a huge oak table. Nearby, Nick waits for the verdict. He misses his wife and child. He wants to forget all this and relive happier times. He loved his wife and son so much; they were the light of his existence. Now they seem a world away.

From what we can see, how can we know that Nick is thinking all these things? We see an actor sitting there thinking, perhaps upset or wistful, but how does the audience know that he is thinking in particular about his wife, son and happier times? This is poor narrative because it describes elements that no director could possibly shoot, no actor could reasonably be expected to act. Both require specifics to shoot or play. Now here's the same narrative with visuals to help the audience "see" what Nick is thinking.

> The stone-faced members of the PAROLE BOARD huddle behind a huge oak table. Nick's haunted eyes drift down to his manacled hands; he clutches the tattered photo of himself with Kevin and Sally in happier times.

Notice that if the visual is strong, it's not necessary to even hint at what Nick is thinking. His thoughts are clear by the action alone. Or the context of a scene, in relation to the scenes preceding and following it, may provide the crucial information. For instance, a man may be staring wistfully out at the ocean and we know what he's thinking because in the previous scene his wife left him, in spite of his begging her not to. Or you could achieve a comic effect by having a chubby man in a running outfit staring soulfully across a park, and then cut to what he's looking at (a thin fellow on a bench, devouring a candy bar), at which point the chubby man's belly growls audibly (something we can hear).

The same goes for exposition. In the following, the screenwriter includes information we cannot see or hear.

> BETH enters; she is John's long-lost sister. Nearby, SALLY and JILL wave, they were once roommates in college and have remained close friends ever since.

If Beth is John's long-lost sister, that information must come out in the dialogue or be somehow revealed by the context or visual clues, and not be stated in the narrative. If Sally and Jill are best friends, you might write that they hug and treat each other like old chums, but the fact they were room-mates and have remained close since college must come out in the dialogue or be shown visually.

DESCRIBING CHARACTERS

When introducing a new character, a screenwriter is allowed few words of description in the narrative. You don't want to stop the action with a long delineation. For example, you could write, "CAPTAIN BARTS is five-feet-five, two hundred and twenty pounds, dark hair, blue eyes, short stubby features, etc..." and bore to death everyone who reads it, or you could just state, "CAPTAIN BARTS looks too fat to be a cop." Let the brief description be a stepping-off point. Just give the reader a first impression; any further character information will come from the dialogue and action. One way to do this is to contrast two character traits. For example, "SAM is a handsome man in spite of the burn marks on his cheeks"; "age is catching up with pretty SALLY"; "JUDD, a tall yet drooping basketball player, enters."

It's also best to concentrate on a character's visual appearance rather than digging into personality or character analysis. For example, you don't want to say "Beth is a strong woman with frank insights" or "Johnny treats people as if they were all his best friend, and he loves children even more." The problem here is that these elements of character must be shown to the audience rather than explained to the reader in the narrative. If Beth is a strong woman, show us: have her do something that lets us see that she is strong, or have her express a frank opinion. If Johnny treats people well, let his actions or words speak for his character. Here are some good examples of character description:

BLADERUNNER
```
The man facing him is lean, hollow-cheeked and dressed
in gray. Detached and efficient, he looks like a cop or
an accountant. His name is HOLDEN and he's all business,
except for the sweat on his face.
```

THE SILENCE OF THE LAMBS
```
She is tense, sweaty, wide-eyed with concentration. This
is CLARICE STARLING--mid-20's, trim, very pretty. She
wears Kevlar body armor over a navy windbreaker, khaki
pants. Her thick hair is piled under a navy baseball
cap. A revolver, clutched in her right hand, hovers by
her ear.
```

THE TERMINATOR
```
The man is in his late thirties, tall and powerfully
built, moving with graceful precision. His facial
features reiterate the power of his body and are
dominated by the eyes, which are intense, blue and
depthless. His hair is military short. This man is the
TERMINATOR.
```

DESCRIBING LOCATIONS

There are several mistakes beginning screenwriters make when describing the location. First, as we've seen, they overemphasize details of the environment at the expense of story or action. Second, they ignore it altogether. True, the description of the environment must be kept brief, but it can't be omitted. If the location is nonspecific, not only will the story appear generic, but it will be difficult for the reader to visualize. When the screenwriter doesn't tempt the reader's imagination, build a sense of illusion, the reader remains outside the story and reads it as if it's an essay, not a screenplay. Third, as a result of not having done proper research, inexperienced screenwriters create clichéd descriptions of locations that are instantly recognizable as having been cadged from other movies. Lack of research is the mother of cliché. If you really know your world, you'll be able to describe those things that make it unique and original.

So how much is too little description and how much is too much? The key is story and character. If a detail ties directly into the story, if it is needed to advance the audience's understanding of the characters and actions within the story, then it must be included. If it does not apply to character or story, it is extraneous and must be cut, no matter how dear it is to the writer's heart. Robin once had a student who spent six pages describing a location, without ever introducing characters or what the story was about. Each facet of the world was lovingly described and it was agony for the rest of the class (who were listening to it being read) to get through because everyone was waiting for the story to begin. Worse, once it did, very little of what had been described had any bearing on the specific actions of the characters. Chekhov, the great Russian playwright, said, "If you describe a gun hanging on the wall in the first scene, by the final scene that gun had better go off." In other words, if a detail of the scene is described, it must have some relevance to the story: it must be useful. If it isn't, then you've set up an expectation that is never met, disappointing the audience and muddling the story. Sometimes a whole world can be conveyed with a single word. The most famous example of this comes from the late, great Stirling Silliphant, author of such movies as *In the Heat of the Night* and *The Towering Inferno*. Once, when describing the environment of a bar, he simply wrote "shitty." While not strictly visual, no other description was necessary.

Picture-Making Words

The environment should have an effect on the reader. You don't just want the reader to understand your world, you want her to see and experience it, to lose herself in it. The best way to do this is to use picture-making words, words that place specific images in the reader's imagination. Picture-making words appeal to the senses, not to the intellect. Here is an example of a description lacking in picture-making words.

```
INT. LIVING ROOM — DAY

An eccentric lives here. There is a door into the kitchen
and windows to the front porch. It's an old scary place.
```

This description is made of up generalizations and gives the reader very little to see. For example, does the word "old" mean that the room is physically falling apart or is it of older style? The word "scary" tells readers what to feel rather than allowing them to feel it. The description informs the reader that an eccentric person lives here, but gives no indication of what might lead to that conclusion. It also consumes precious resources (words) by providing unimportant details like where doors and windows are located. It's a living room; we can pretty much assume there are doors and windows.

Strong descriptions of the environment allow the reader to see, hear and feel. Readers derive great satisfaction from creating their own mental pictures, drawing on their own memories and associations, but it's your job to guide them. This reader/writer collaboration happens when the writer feeds the reader's imagination. Rewritten with picture-making words and cutting unimportant particulars, the description might read like this:

```
INT. VICTORIAN LIVING ROOM — DAY

A faded shell of its former glory. Thin sunset light
leeches through the crud on the cracked windows. In the
shadows sits Spike, the family dog, fangs bared. But he's
dead and dusty. Stuffed, like the furniture.
```

From this description we can guess that the living room is scary and that whoever lives here is an eccentric. The writer concentrates on strong, specific picture-making words/images that allow the reader to feel the environment rather than coolly examine it.

Here is another example. This narrative was actually handed in during a graduate-level screenwriting class at UCLA. (The names have been changed to protect the innocent.)

```
INT. COURT ROOM — DAY

The Judge sits at his desk with several file folders
open in front of him. Jack is seated at a table, facing
the Judge. Tom, Jack's attorney, sits beside him. Dick
sits at another table facing the Judge. Dick's attorney
sits beside Dick.
```

We don't know about you, but we couldn't care less about what's going to happen next. The screenwriter wastes valuable words detailing the seating arrangement for the reader, but says nothing about the courtroom. How does the courtroom look? Is it packed with press-hounds and onlookers, or bleak and unattended? How does the room reflect what's about to happen? How do the characters look? Confident? Tired? Afraid? What do we see and feel? Anything would be better than this uninteresting laundry list of place settings. To give the screenwriter credit, he redeemed himself on the rewrite:

```
INT. COURT ROOM — DAY

Dark. Military. Cold. Flanked by his attorney, Jack faces
his Judge. On one side a door to freedom, on the other,
the door leading to hell.
```

Similes and Metaphors

A simile is a comparison of one thing to another using the words "like" or "as." For example, "The bridge lists like an old lady tipping under the weight of time," or perhaps, "The soldiers stand as stiff as ironing boards." A simile compares two unlike things and draws an analogy. It compares something the reader is unaware of in the scene to something she is aware of, images and things that draw on common experience. Similes dress up the description by giving it a pictorial appeal. Metaphors differ from similes by stating that one thing *is* another thing. For example, "Mary leaps around playfully, a young colt in spring," or "He's a tough old battleship, battered but still floating" or "There is a mummified Twinkie in the dead man's hand." You are not actually saying that the woman is a horse, the man is a boat or the Twinkie has gone through the ancient mummification process, but the analogies still work.

Here is a student's description without the help of metaphors and similes:

```
INT. JOHN'S ROOM — DAY

John enters. His room is a mess. Paper, garbage, clothing
are spread about. The bed isn't made, cookie crumbs are
everywhere and the lamps are broken, the window shades
bent.
```

This is a serviceable description, but it could be made shorter and more interesting by use of similes or metaphors:

```
JOHN'S ROOM — DAY

John enters his room, which looks like a wrecked garbage
truck.
```

or

```
INT. JOHN'S ROOM — DAY

John enters the wrecked garbage truck of his room.
```

The function of metaphor and simile is to evoke visual images and emotions in the reader. In order to work, the metaphor or simile must first be original. Clichés do not evoke emotions. Trite stereotypes evoke postcard pictures that bore the reader, if they evoke anything at all. "He's strong as an ox," "She's cute as a button" and the like are worse than no description at all. Second, the metaphor or simile must be simple, short and to the point. Gratuitous metaphors will only distract the reader and weigh down the description with unneeded flowery gymnastics. (For more on location and environment, and their effect on story, see Chapter 4.)

Trim Adverbs

An abundance of adverbs slows and weakens your narrative. An adverb is a word or group of words that modify a verb, adjective or another adverb. In the following sentence the adverb is italicized and the verb is underlined.

        Ben <u>enters</u> the bar *bravely*.

Adverbs are simple modifiers that add some particular quality to the manner, degree, amount of time or action denoted by the verb. You can tell a word is an adverb if it answers the questions: "how," "when," and/or "how many." Adverbs are easily identified, as many end in "ly" and all can be moved to different places in the sentence without changing the meaning. The problem with adverbs is that they are often redundant, adding clutter to the narrative, as in the following example:

        The old man inches *slowly* toward the electric chair.

In this sentence the verb "inches" already tells us how the old man is moving and so the adverb "slowly" is redundant. Often, adverbs can be replaced with a more powerful or descriptive verb.

        John speaks *loudly*.

Here the adverb "loudly" is unnecessary if the screenwriter comes up with a snappier verb:

        John bellows.

In the following examples, the left column has bits of narrative with the useless adverb in italics. In the right column, the weak verb and adverb have been replaced with a more powerful, more descriptive verb, making the adverb unnecessary.

Mary looks at John *closely*.	Mary inspects John.
Kathy *badly* plays a tune on the piano.	Kathy grinds out a tune on the piano.
Jake walks *quietly* down the alley.	Jake tiptoes down the alley.
The guards *quickly* stop the riot.	The guards crush the riot.

We're not saying that all adverbs should be cut. Skillfully chosen, they can add a great deal to any read. But the majority of adverbs are crutches for unimaginative choices of verb, are not needed and should be eliminated... quickly and expeditiously.

Trim Adjectives

Just as with adverbs, too many adjectives will weaken the narrative. Adjectives modify nouns: they answer the questions "which one," "how many" or "what kind." In the following sentences the adjectives are italicized and the nouns they modify are underlined:

```
Jack peers at the expensive, brilliant chandelier.

She smiles at the dark-haired, blue-eyed gentleman.
```

Adjectives are a necessary part of any narrative, but beginning screenwriters tend to pile them on, as in the following example:

```
LAGATTUTA, an old fuddy-duddy, trudges from his generic
door to retrieve the thin evening newspaper. His fidgety,
liver-spotted hands shake in the gripping, cutting
December cold. His old-man pants droop, barely held up
by timeworn, deteriorating, slim suspenders. His long,
flaccid ears look red and chapped in the icy, midwinter
sun.
```

The abundance of adjectives here slows the read and hampers the simple action of the scene, which is that Mr. Lagattuta walks out on his porch and picks up his newspaper. The rest is all mood and environment, most of it overwritten and redundant. The clutter of adjectives has also led the writer into using passive voice in the description of the pants and suspenders, further slowing things down. Mood and environment are important, but could be established with one-third the adjectives used above, allowing the action to dominate:

```
MR. LAGATTUTA, an old fuddy-duddy, trudges out to
retrieve the evening newspaper. His liver-spotted hands
shake in the cold. Timeworn suspenders barely hold up his
old-man pants. His flaccid ears look red and chapped.
```

One way to eliminate redundant or numerous adjectives is to find more descriptive nouns. A precise or colorful noun can reduce or completely eliminate the need for an adjective. In the following examples, the left column is burdened with adjectives, while in the right column, the adjectives and nouns have been reduced or replaced with stronger, more descriptive nouns (and stronger verbs, which can also help).

Jerry enters his cool, masculine, sexy apartment.	Jerry saunters into his bachelor pad.
May, an old, ugly and witchlike woman, looks angrily at the abusive young gang members who are yelling obscene insults at her.	May, a crone, scowls at the gang, who sling curses her.
Inside the old Studebaker, the fidgety kids squirm on the stark, barren and flat seats.	Stuck in the jalopy, the toddlers squirm on the benches.

As with adverbs, we are not saying that adjectives should be completely eliminated from a screenplay narrative. A scattering of adjectives can be helpful, but if they dominate they can make a screenplay appear to be all mood and environment and very little action.

They can also indicate a deeper problem, which is that you may be "vamping," using overdescription and repetitions to cover the fact that you're not sure what your next action needs to be. If you find yourself piling up the adjectives, step back and make sure you know what your scene is about.

Common Narrative Mistakes

Repeating Verbs—Don't repeat the same verb over and over, page after page. How many times can characters "run," "jump" or "look?" It's time to break out that old thesaurus and find a variety of action verbs—specific to the kind of running, jumping or looking—that place accurate, moving pictures into the reader's mind. When you finish the first draft, go back and highlight verbs you use more than twice per page and replace them. (A good thesaurus is *The Synonym Finder*, edited by J.I. Rodale and published by Warner Books.)

Improper Spelling, Punctuation and Grammar—We've said it before and we'll say it again: poor spelling, improper punctuation and bad grammar will sink a script. This is also true in the narrative. It's time to relearn all those lessons you thought you'd learned. It's not that you can't use incomplete sentences, or even "sentences" of a single word here and there, but these must be intentional and used for a specific effect, such as to create a sense of hurried activity or terse, tense action. (The best book is still *Elements of Style* by William Strunk, Jr., and E. B. White, published by Allyn & Bacon. This book is also available on the web. Good grammar and punctuation sites can be found on the web, such as the Purdue University Online Writing Lab (http:// owl.english.purdue.edu/).

Too Many Words—Be brief. When reading a screenplay, the reader should have the sense of moving along at roughly the same pace as the film itself would. So never use seven words when four words will do. Details are essential, but only those details that provide unique and necessary imagery and that advance the story or the characters.

Too Few Words (Nonspecificity)—This is usually the result of not enough research, or simple laziness when it comes to creating the characters and the world (see Chapters 4 and 5). There simply isn't any, or enough, description to allow the reader to visualize the story. And it isn't necessarily a matter of adding more words, but of finding exactly the right words.

Camera Angles—Don't include camera angles; as stated in Chapter 2, this is a big no-no. We don't care if you can find examples to the contrary, they're probably either very old, or production (shooting) drafts or were written by the director. Your narrative should achieve the visuals without telling the director how to shoot the film. Again, you want the reader to see the movie, not the set.

Overdescribing in the First Few Pages—Don't start a screenplay off with nothing but narrative, unless there is a long and involving action sequence that will keep the reader engaged. Even so, as a practical matter, if after your first few pages you don't have some dialogue, the screenplay will appear to be a difficult read. You want to try for a nice balance of dialogue and narrative. This is not a hard and fast rule; some wonderful screenplays do not have dialogue on the first few pages, but these are the exceptions and are usually the work of experienced writers who understand how to keep their narrative involving and related to the action of the story. With novice writers, pages of uninterrupted narrative are a sign of overwritten description that delays the action of the story and irritates the reader.

FINAL THOUGHTS

Make It Personal A writer can and must infuse the narrative with his own personality. Holding yourself back, looking at events from light years away in the name of objectivity, will only lead to boring narrative. It's totally acceptable to let your personality show; it's part of your style, your voice. A passionate, individual voice tells readers that you care about the characters and situations, and that you are also deeply involved in the events. If you're not involved and passionate, why should they be? Here is an example of a narrative in which the author shows his own personality by very nearly having a conversation with the reader. This is perfectly acceptable as long as it fits the mood of the screenplay.

```
INT. DAVE'S ROOM — NIGHT

Dave is a tall, owl-faced kicker with heart. People like
him at first sight.

DAVE'S P.O.V. -- Okay, the place isn't messy, but it
could be cleaner. The three-day-old sandwich is a bit
much. Dried tomatoes; gross.
```

After all, the narrative is the writer speaking directly to the reader. Dialogue is written for actors and the audience. Narrative is just you and the reader. It's a one-on-one relationship. If the reader feels connected to the writer, he'll stick with the narrative and read it with the same interest as he does the dialogue. But don't get too jokey or informal, because this will distance the reader, too; you'll be commenting on the story instead of conveying it. Remember, the narrative is where you create your world. It's where you play the movie for your reader. It's where you, and no one else, is in control.

EXERCISES

1. A strong verb doesn't require additional amplification. A descriptive noun needs fewer adjectives. In the following narrative, replace the adverbs with more descriptive verbs and reduce the number of adjectives by finding more powerful, visually specific nouns.

```
EXT. GRACE'S APARTMENT — NIGHT

A marginal, older, dilapidated neighborhood. A hard rain
falls. Bob pulls up in the rusty taxi. He checks the
address against the ripped slip of paper, then coolly
looks up at the cold stone apartment. The dim, gloomy
lights on the third floor are on. She's home. He slowly
climbs out, turns up his collar against the briskly
falling rain and quickly runs to the door.
```

2. In the following scene, the writer describes characters' thoughts that cannot be seen or heard. Rewrite the narrative using visuals and action to make the characters' thoughts clear (using a voice-over is not allowed).

```
EXT. GRAVEYARD — DAY

A shabby family gathers around a coffin. A child hangs
on to his widowed mother, wondering why his father isn't
there with them. Several older ladies dressed in black
cry, wishing they'd treated their dead friend better in
life, as a priest sprinkles the box with holy water.

Two hundred feet away, half hidden by a stand of trees
is Angel, silently watching. She knows that this is all
her fault. If only she were a better driver. She cries
when she thinks of all the trouble she's caused. If only
they would allow her to attend, she thinks.
```

3. Verbs in active voice show the subject acting. Verbs in passive (present progressive) voice show something else being acted upon by the subject. The following bits of narrative have lines written in passive voice. Find the passive clause and rewrite it so that the verbs show the subject acting (in other words, rewrite in an active voice).

    a. Nick and William shake on the deal. Nick's hand
       is squeezed by William. Nick fights back. William
       twitches, obviously in pain from the power of Nick's
       grip.

    b. The punk is thrown down by Anne, a woman half his
       size. Before he knows what is happening, he is
       handcuffed by Anne.

    c. Wine, candlelight, romantic music and the fake
       fireplace. Sally's tear is wiped away by Larry. She
       smiles.

13

Dialogue

You Don't Say

William Strunk, Jr., the great writing tutor, said, "Vigorous writing is concise. A sentence should contain no unnecessary words, a paragraph no unnecessary sentences, for the same reason that a drawing should have no unnecessary lines and a machine no unnecessary parts." Nowhere is this more appropriate than when it comes to screen dialogue. While stage plays depend almost exclusively on dialogue to tell and advance their stories, film is primarily a visual medium, as we emphasized in the previous chapter. The first filmed dramas were silent, of course, and contained no dialogue at all, at best a few interspersed cards to fill us in on the conversations. Dialogue is almost equally sparse in many of the most expensive contemporary blockbusters, whose huge set-pieces and elaborate special effects take the visual (nonverbal) storytelling side of the medium to new extremes. Words seem barely necessary, almost vestigial. In fact, many big-budget action movie screenwriters (such as Sylvester Stallone) have prided themselves on how little their characters actually say.

But this is a simplistic attitude. Film is about what we see, certainly, but it's also about what we hear. Not all screen dialogue can or should be reduced to the grunts, expositional fillers and ironic asides you find in action-adventure flicks. It all depends on what kind of movie you are writing. Many of the best dramas, especially those with lower budgets, depend heavily on dialogue to tell their stories. Dialogue is cheap. It's the least expensive special effect, although even in big action movies it can be the most memorable element: "Go ahead, make my day"; "Hasta la vista, baby"; "… you've got to ask yourself one question: Do I feel lucky? Well, do ya, punk?"; "Who are those guys?"

Dialogue is how we hear the mind, nature and feelings of the characters expressed ("Of all the gin joints in all the towns in all the world, she walks into mine …"; "Show me the money!"; "You're not too smart, are you? I like that in a man."). Both old masters like the Epstein brothers (*Casablanca*), Billy Wilder and I. A. L. Diamond (*The Apartment, Some Like It Hot*), Robert Benton (*Kramer vs. Kramer*) and Robert Towne (*Chinatown*), as well as those from more recent generations of screenwriters like Quentin Tarantino (*Pulp*

Fiction, Inglorious Basterds), Diablo Cody (*Juno, Young Adult*) and the Coen brothers (*Raising Arizona, Fargo, A Serious Man*), luxuriate at length in the humor and texture of their characters' voices. And Stallone's best screenplay, *Rocky*, is also his talkiest. However...

THE ROLE OF DIALOGUE

In screenwriting, the role of dialogue is much more limited and subjugated to other aspects of storytelling than it is in playwriting.

Screen dialogue serves three chief, simultaneous purposes:

1. It advances the story.
2. It reveals the characters.
3. It plays off of the visual world of the film.

To advance the story, dialogue reflects immediate circumstances and needs, addresses future considerations, and perhaps recounts events in the past. It reveals the characters by showing us their personalities through their unique voices. And it reinforces or provides contrast to what we are actually seeing happen on the screen.

In a movie, most information can be conveyed without dialogue. We can focus in on a newspaper article, show a particular scar or follow the smoke from a hidden gun. What we see can be more powerful than what any-one says, so a screenwriter should always try to *show* rather than *tell*. James Cameron's *Titanic* was much criticized for its mediocre dialogue, but became the most successful movie in history, until his equally dialogue-impaired *Avatar* came out. Reflecting on this, no less an authority than screenwriter William Goldman (winner of two Oscars and writer of *Butch Cassidy and the Sundance Kid, All the President's Men,* and *Marathon Man*) wrote that movie dialogue *"is among the least important parts of a screenplay.* Sure, intelligent talk is always better than dumb stuff [especially in witty comedies or dramas]. But for the most part, the public and critics have come to believe that screen-plays are dialogue. Wrong. *If movies are story, and they are, then screenplays are structure"* (Goldman's italics). It's Cameron's storytelling, his arrangement of character and story events and his use of astonishing visual imagery to convey the drama, that makes *Titanic* a good screenplay, in spite of some lousy dialogue. That said, however, it would have been a better screenplay with better dialogue.

One student screenplay concerned some college kids who discover that their weird professor has invented a time machine. In the first scene, at a bar, the students recounted the previous night's adventure, talking about how they broke into the professor's office and attempted to start the machine. The problem was that there was no need to express these events through dialogue. Since this was the event that started the story, the answer was to create an exciting scene in which the students crawled in the window, discovered the time machine and tried to start it, letting the audience see the action rather than hearing about it.

There are times in which dialogue can be used effectively to recount past events, such as the scene in *Jaws* in which Quint expresses his hatred of sharks by telling his experience of watching thousands of sailors being eaten alive when their ship sank in the Second World War. But in general, it is better to show us the scene, not tell us the story. In the following, the student screenwriter allows the characters to talk about the action rather than showing it.

```
EXT. FRONT YARD — DAY

Karoline and Casey walk up to the old Buick Roadmaster
parked in the driveway.


                    KAROLINE
          So this is a Buick.

                    CASEY
          The American Dream gone to pieces. I
          swear this thing is held together by
          rust.

                    KAROLINE
          Boy, it's old.

                    CASEY
          Yeah, how do you like those fins?

                    KAROLINE
          Neat.

                    CASEY
          We've had it for years.

                    KAROLINE
          Does it run?

                    CASEY
          Dad still drives it to work everyday.

                    KAROLINE
          You're kidding.

                    CASEY
          The man lives in the past. He actually
          thinks this car is cool.

                    KAROLINE
          It's junk.
```

```
                              CASEY
                If you want him to like you, say
                something nice about it.
```

What do we learn from this scene? That Dad owns an old junky Buick Roadmaster he's had for years. The car still runs, Dad thinks the car is cool, and Casey wants Dad to like Karoline. Little of this needs to be expressed directly in dialogue:

```
EXT. FRONT YARD — DAY

BANG, a backfire: Casey and Karoline wait as Dad
approaches in an ancient, rusted 1950s Roadmaster,
trailed by a glutinous cloud of smoke. BANG.

                    CASEY
      If you want him to like you, say
      something nice about the car.

The chromemobile pulls into the driveway. From its sad-
faced dented grill, faded two-tone paint flows back
through its baroque architecture to the massive jagged
fins and cathedral taillights.

As Dad gets out, Karoline attempts a complimentary smile.

                    KAROLINE
      Nice car. Cool fins!

Dad's face lights up. He pats the fender affectionately.

                    DAD
      Yep. They just don't make 'em like they
      used to.
```

In this shorter scene, most of what is talked about in the previous scene is now either obvious from or implied in the action.

No One Talks like That!

The second thing to understand is that dialogue is not real speech. Dialogue must *sound* natural, but it is not natural. It's an echo of real speech that has been carefully edited, refined and designed to appear as real speech. Record and listen to any real conversation and you'll find yourself wading through mostly garbled thoughts, lost trains of association and irrelevancies. Film dialogue is stripped of these and shaped to fit a character's background, needs and function. It is sort of like what you wish you'd said if only you'd had the time (or a writer) to come up with the perfect words.

Also, it isn't random. Every dialogue passage has a beginning, middle and end that follow the same rules as script and scene construction: get in as late as possible, keep it as brief and as colorful as possible, develop and intensify the argument, end with a climax of some sort (a "capper") and then get out. This is why we get conventions such as characters who answer the phone with a "yeah?" instead of a "hello?"—it's briefer and seems hipper—and why they never say "goodbye" before they hang up. It isn't how real people answer or say goodbye, but for the character, the essential dialogue is over.

When You Say What You Mean, Do You Mean What You Say?

Why do we talk? At the most basic level, we talk because we want. When Kurt Vonnegut taught creative writing, he said he "would tell the students to make their characters want something right away—even if it's only a glass of water." Generally, if we want nothing, we say nothing. As infants, we cry when we're hungry or wet. As we grow and our needs become more complicated, we're forced to learn speech in order to communicate what we want. The need for a bottle or a fresh diaper is replaced by the need to conquer, to acquire, to find justice, to protect our egos, to seek companionship. And our strategies to get what we want through speech become more complicated, too: when we fail to get what we want, we either become inhibited, or we learn to hide our agendas and manipulate our arguments in order to provoke, settle scores, find love, defeat our enemies and satisfy our wants without announcing them directly. We do this because sometimes, direct communication can get us in trouble. Simply and openly stating our desire ("I want to have sex with you") is often the surest way not to get it, and so we disguise our intentions and create indirect verbal strategies to get what we want. Sometimes, when our deepest wants go unfulfilled, they seep into our subconscious, coloring our speech with secondary meanings and concealed desires. These are the origins of subtext, of saying one thing and meaning another, which is the most sophisticated kind of dialogue.

Speech, then, is the result, the function, of characters who want. Know what a character wants, know what her fears, hopes and limitations are, and you'll understand why and how that character needs to speak. (For more information on character see Chapter 5.)

Get Off the Nose

When a character states exactly what he wants it's called *on-the-nose* dialogue. The character is speaking the subtext; there is no hidden meaning behind the words, no secret want, because everything is spelled out. But most interesting people, and certainly most interesting characters, don't do this. They approach their needs indirectly, because they are complex, and often because they don't consciously understand what their needs are. Dialogue must feel simple, but its simplicity is deceptive. Dialogue is like an iceberg: only one level of meaning can be seen "above the waterline," yet many other unspoken levels of emotion and intention are present beneath the surface.

These levels are provided not only by the lines themselves, but also by who speaks them and when and where they are spoken—in other words, by the context. The line "I hate you" seems simple, with few interpretations, until the screenwriter provides the context. Then it can take on many possible meanings. "I hate you," in the context of a grieving husband yelling at the grave of his dead wife, could mean, "I miss you." Spoken by an aspiring actress to her screen idol, it could mean, "I wish I were you." In *When Harry Met Sally*, this final line of the movie means, "I love you."

Dialogue reveals character and is therefore determined by it, by the nature of the characters you've created and the situations in which they find themselves. Is your character honest or dishonest? Straightforward or manipulative? Humorless or ironic? Is he relaxed, or under great stress? Is she acting and speaking casually because it is a casual situation, or because she is trying to remain in control of a desperate one? Is he being cruel because he wishes to be cruel, or because he is in love and afraid of rejection? Is she joking because she's happy, or because she's masking some internal pain?

On a deeper subtextual level, as with everything else in the screenplay, screen dialogue should reflect (reinforcing or contradicting) the overall theme of the story, what it's about (see Chapter 3).

There is a fine example of subtextual dialogue in *Big Night*, a terrific film about two immigrant Italian brothers in the 1950s who are trying to open their own restaurant. In the following conversation, Pascal, the ruthless and very successful restaurant owner from across the street, is paying them a visit, bragging about having bought a boat. Secondo is terribly anxious to impress Pascal and envies his success. Pascal has promised to help them by inviting a celebrity to eat at their restaurant that night, but in fact he has not done so, and intends to ruin Secondo and try to hire Primo for himself:

```
                    PRIMO
        Oh.  That mean you're gonna sail away?


                    PASCAL
        Maybe.  When the sky is red . . . you know,
        what's that rhyme?


                    SECONDO
        Oh, yeah.  When is the good one?


                    PRIMO
        Red sky at morning means it will rain
        outside.


                    SECONDO
        What about rain inside?


                    PRIMO
        Huh?
```

                        SECONDO
Nothing.

                        PRIMO
No, what do you mean?

                        SECONDO
You say, "rain outside," and I think for
you to say the word "outside" is funny.

                        PRIMO
Why?

                        SECONDO
Because it can't rain inside.

                        PRIMO
I didn't say "inside."

                        SECONDO
I know.

                        PRIMO
I say "outside."

                        SECONDO
No, I know.

                        PRIMO
So where is the problem?

                        PASCAL
Yeah, I don't get it.

                        SECONDO
No, it's just you don't have to say
"outside" ... because it can't rain
inside.

They all think about this for a second. A beat.

                        PASCAL
What the fuck--

                        PRIMO
I know it can't rain inside.

                        SECONDO
Forget it. Forget. Forget.

>   PASCAL
>   What the fuck is he talking about?
>
>   PRIMO
>   I am confused.
>
>   SECONDO
>   No, no ... I make fun.
>
>   PASCAL
>   You make fun of your brother?
>
>   SECONDO
>   No. It was a joke. I make like a joke.
>
>   PASCAL
>   I don't hear the joke.

At this point, Pascal ends the seemingly pointless argument by proposing a toast to the brothers' success that night, knowing full well that he has undermined any chance they have.

But the argument isn't pointless. Although all they are actually talking about is whether Primo should have said it rains "outside," the subtext is that Secondo is trying to embarrass his older brother and make himself look good in front of someone he's trying to impress. It is about Secondo's frustration and anxiety: who speaks the language better, who is smarter, who is more "American." And because it is a petty, mean-spirited jab, it instead comes back to embarrass Secondo himself—just as he will later find his dreams crushed, through his own blindness to the realities of the world in which he lives.

You're One of a Kind

As noted, character determines dialogue. So, just as there should be no redundant characters who fulfill identical functions in the script, each unique character must be given a unique voice. They should speak the language of their own world, their own experience, their own personality and regional idiom, distinct in some way from the other characters in the film.

HOW CAN I SAY THIS? (DIALOGUE TECHNIQUES)

Once you've created the perfect characters for the world and story of your screenplay, there are several basic techniques that can help you master your dialogue: cast your characters, write headlines, avoid conclusionary statements, show emotions—don't talk about them—replace conversations with visuals, and know how a character listens.

Casting Call

As discussed in Chapter 5 (Character), one way to create unique voices is to "cast" the parts as a casting director would. That is, write dialogue with a particular actor, celebrity or person in mind. Find a movie star, celebrity or person whose voice style is imprinted in your memory and can be easily "borrowed." Writers are always looking for "imprints," the words, inflections, tone and resonance that make a voice unique. If you simply cannot come up with a character's voice, then do some research: go out and listen to people. While keeping in mind that dialogue is not real speech, remember that good listeners write good dialogue.

Now write out your perfect cast list. Include only movie stars, celebrities or persons whose voices you can hear in your mind. Example:

Ben	Donald Trump
Sandy	Glenn Close
Mr. Walterton	Jeff Goldblum
Davey	Kevin Bacon
Sally	May (my next door neighbor)
Mark	Danny Glover
Mrs. Murdock	Hillary Rodham Clinton

Once you have your "cast," write each character's dialogue as if that particular cast member were playing the role. Think of the person's speech patterns and write using that voice. The reader should be able to mask the character's name and still identify who is speaking by how they speak. But lastly, be careful not to slavishly copy an existing actor or person's voice or your dialogue will feel mannered and derivative. Use it as a model, but then reinvent it to suit your own purposes.

In the Headlines

In a stage play, dialogue dominates. This is because, for thousands of years, the live set has been a place for characters to use language to explore the mystery, horror and comedy of life. Because the stage has much more limited visual possibilities than movies have recently come to provide, dialogue has always been the playwright's main tool. Through it, stage characters work out their problems, describe their world, take action and find compromises and new understandings. They talk their way through their stories, much the way patients undergoing Freudian psychoanalysis talk their way through their problems to slowly discover the hidden truths, the subtexts, to their lives. Freud called it a "talking cure." Play dialogue is the art of talking through to the truth.

In a screenplay, truth is equally important, but there are other, powerful tools available to reveal it. Where a stage character is reduced to describing a huge battle, for example, a movie can show us the battle in all its scope and terror. Screen characters can take unspoken action that is as revealing as any dialogue, often more revealing. And because on film we can see every detail of expression crossing the character's face, thoughts and feelings can also be played silently. As a result, screen dialogue is compressed, eliminated in favor of anything that can better be shown using the enormous visual and aural power of the movie. Because of the limitations of the stage, the playwright has license to present entire conversations, go into interior monologues, and recount events that cannot possibly be staged. The screenwriter, while freed to show almost anything of which her imagination is capable, cannot indulge this way without betraying the very nature, demands and possibilities of the medium. Dialogue can too easily become a crutch, rather than a tool; it is the screenwriter's job to fill the screen, and dialogue is only a small part of that. Dialogue should not be substituted for strong visual storytelling. It must be essential, not convenient.

Think of it as "writing headlines." Say only what needs to be said. There's no need, as there is in theater, to go into the extended details and description of the story. As noted, different types of movies require different approaches to and amounts of dialogue, but all are the same in that each passage of dialogue must be terse, strong, to the point. Even where characters are shown working through their feelings or talking through their therapy, every word must count, or it must be cut. The following dialogue might be fine for a play, but it lacks the compactness necessary for the screen.

```
INT. EMMA's GUEST BEDROOM — DAY

A Victorian bedroom, warm light, wood tones, a high
ceiling and the feeling of history. A perfect place to
read the New York Times Book Review. EMMA enters with
JILL, who carries an overnight bag.

                    JILL
         How's Herman? Is he still writing that
         novel?

                    EMMA
         Oh, he's dead.

                    JILL
         Oh. I'm so sorry.

                    EMMA
         He had prostate cancer. He died almost
         five years ago now.

                    JILL
         I haven't kept in touch. I should have at
         least written. I'm a terrible person.

                    EMMA
         I found him here. Slumped over a copy of
         Bartlett's Familiar Quotations. Sixteenth
         edition.
```

Emma sets out to tidy the place. Jill tries to lend a
hand whenever possible.

> JILL
> Emma, I'm imposing here. I should have at
> least called before I came.

> EMMA
> I'm all grown-up now, I can make basic
> decisions, like who I invite to stay in
> my house.

> JILL
> Are you sure about this?

> EMMA
> You're not uncomfortable sleeping in the
> room where Herman bought it, now are you?

> JILL
> (lying)
> No. Not at all. I'm fine with that.

> EMMA
> He was a good husband, I miss him
> horribly, although he did have a bad case
> of testosterone poisoning. Men have that,
> you know. It's quite common.

> JILL
> Yes, I know.

> EMMA
> You know, once in my life I'd like to be
> shot full of testosterone so that I'll
> know what it's like to be totally right!

> JILL
> I have to admit I often feel the same
> way.

Now, here is the same scene with over fifty words cut from the dialogue:

INT. EMMA's GUEST BEDROOM — DAY

A Victorian bedroom, warm light, wood tones, a high
ceiling and the feeling of history. A perfect place to

read the *New York Times Book Review*. EMMA enters with
Jill, who carries an overnight bag.

Jill spots a writing pad, inkwell and ink pen on the
desk. She opens the inkwell; it's dried out and crusted.
Emma notices.

> EMMA
> Herman's dead. Cancer. Five years ago. I
> left his things as they were.

> JILL
> Oh, I'm sorry. I'm so terrible, I haven't
> kept in touch.

> EMMA
> I found him here. Slumped over this.

Emma shows Jill a copy of *Bartlett's Familiar Quotations*,
still lying on the chair. She puts it on a shelf and
starts to tidy the place. Jill tentatively lends a hand.

> JILL
> Emma, I should have called, before--

> EMMA
> It's okay, I'm a big girl now. You don't
> mind sleeping in here?

> JILL
> No. Not at all. I'm fine with that.

Emma lets Jill's lie go. She picks up the ink pen,
touches the tip, tenderly.

> EMMA
> He was a good husband . . . but . . .

Jill raises an eyebrow. Emma laughs, puts the pen down.

> EMMA
> You know, just once I'd like to be shot
> full of testosterone so I'd know what it's
> like to be totally right all the time.

Jill laughs, too. The tension is gone.

The idiosyncrasies of the characters and particulars of the scene are kept, but the dialogue has been reduced. Notice that some of what had been talked about is now shown through visual elements in the scene—we see rather than hear that Herman was a writer and was reading *Bartlett's Quotations*. Each word is now justified by carrying only the information and emotion that can't be carried by the picture.

Leapfrogging One technique in writing headlines is "leapfrogging," skipping unnecessary lines to get to the important thought or emotion. We've already had an example of this in the previous scene. Notice that the first draft has the following lines:

```
                    JILL
          Is he still writing that novel?


                    EMMA
          Oh, he's dead.


                    JILL
          Oh. I'm so sorry.


                    EMMA
          He had prostate cancer.
```

In the rewrite, we leapfrog several lines that can be assumed, implied by the picture, or combined:

```
                    EMMA
          Herman's dead. His prostate. Five years ago. I left his
          things as they were.
```

Leapfrogging can also be done with entire thoughts. Here is the Emma–Jill scene cut again:

```
          She opens the inkwell; it's dried out and crusted. Emma
          notices. She shakes her head.

                    EMMA
            Herman died. Cancer, five years ago.

                    JILL
          I'm so terrible, I haven't kept in touch—

          Emma starts to tidy the place. Jill tentatively lends a
          hand.

                    EMMA
            You're okay sleeping here?

          Jill nods, hiding her discomfort. Emma picks up the pen.
```

```
                    EMMA
        He was a good husband ... but just once
        I'd like to know what it's like to be
        totally right!

   Jill laughs, the tension gone.
```

Now the scene is even closer to headlines, but still reveals the character and action of the story. Of course, you don't want to cut the dialogue to such bare bones that it becomes colorless and generic. The test is, does each word advance the story and/or reveal something new about the characters?

Don't Come to Conclusions

The problem with writing extremely lean dialogue is that it can lead to another type of "on-the-nose" dialogue: having the characters state a conclusion rather than having them reveal the specifics that lead to it. The writer puts generalized observations in their mouths, rather than colorful thoughts or details that reveal an unsaid truth. Conclusionary dialogue tells the audience what to think rather than letting them draw their own conclusions. For example, in the following scene two off-duty cops talk late at night in a bar:

```
INT. JOE'S TAVERN — NIGHT


A sweltering hole-in-the-wall pub. A bored COUNTRY BAND
plays a tired TUNE. Nick and Buddy suck down lifeless
beers.

                    NICK
        I'm a fool. She hates me.

                    BUDDY
        She doesn't hate you.

                    NICK
        No. She hates me. It's over.
```

The statements, "I'm a fool" and "She hates me" are both conclusionary, telling us what the character thinks in generalized language. They don't allow the audience to see or understand what brought the character to those conclusions. But the dialogue can become more interesting, without sacrificing understanding, by concentrating on details:

```
JOE'S TAVERN — NIGHT


A sweltering hole-in-the-wall pub. A bored COUNTRY BAND
plays a tired TUNE. Nick and Buddy suck down lifeless
beers.
```

>   NICK
> I got her a humidifier.
>
>   BUDDY
> For Valentine's Day?
>
>   NICK
> She went home to her mother.

From this bit of dialogue we can assume that she hates him and that he feels like a fool (or is a fool). The dialogue is still written in headlines (it actually uses fewer words), but the conclusionary statements have been replaced with details that provide the time frame, specific characterization and context.

Let's look at a second example. Here's a sample of dialogue that is full of on-the-nose, conclusionary statements:

> INT. HENRY'S BOARDING ROOM — DAY
>
> Henry calmly sucks down another Lone Star. Darla
> slams in while juggling her purse, several heavy,
> disintegrating grocery bags and keys. She makes it
> to the counter just as the bag rips open.
>
>   DARLA
> Christ, no wonder everyone hates you.
>
>   HENRY
> Haven't you heard, I'm loved by millions.
>
>   DARLA
> Says who? You can't name a single person
> who's read your books.
>
>   HENRY
> That's not true.
>
>   DARLA
> I never see them in stores. I've looked
> and looked and no one carries them.
> You're so self-important.
>
>   HENRY
> Drop it or I'll get mad!
>
>   DARLA
> You just think you're popular, but you're
> not. No one has read your work. No one!

This is horrible dialogue. Now, the same scene with the conclusionary statements replaced with dialogue that leads the reader to the same conclusions without openly stating them.

```
INT. HENRY'S BOARDING ROOM — DAY

Henry calmly sucks down another Lone Star. Darla slams in
while juggling her purse, several heavy, disintegrating
grocery bags and keys. She makes it to the counter just
as a bag rips open.

                    DARLA
          Christ, what were you thinking? Writing
          an attack on Miss America? No one's going
          to buy it!

                    HENRY
          I have a hundred thousand books in print!

                    DARLA
          Self-publishing doesn't count.

                    HENRY
          I have never self-published!

                    DARLA
          Who are you trying to kid? You've got a
          basement full of books that no one's ever
          going to read.

                    HENRY
          Just drop it. Drop it now!
```

We're not saying that you should never have a conclusionary statement, but reserve them for moments of great impact, or else (as discussed above) give them a subtextual twist.

Don't Talk of Love, Show Me!

Again, avoid conclusionary statements about the characters' emotions or state of mind in which they talk about their feelings rather than about the events or circumstances that have generated them. This goes back to the issue of subtext. If a character is shy or sensitive, talking about his shyness or sensitivity is the weakest way to reveal it. Better to see him struggling to verbalize whatever it is that's troubling him. In a screenplay, whenever a character stops to speak about his or her feelings, the story stops, too. When a character acts or speaks in response to his or her feelings, the story moves. A screenwriter should imply emotions while allowing the dialogue to advance the story.

For example, a woman who's worried that her husband is having an affair might bring up the subject of having another baby. This way she tests her husband to see if he's still interested in her without revealing her true purpose. The dialogue involves having another baby, but the emotion is, "I'm afraid you want a divorce." As in the example from *Big Night*, good screen dialogue uses what the characters are talking about to reveal what the characters are *not* talking about. This is known as "writing between the lines," because what is not said is often more important than what is.

Let's go back to our two off-duty cops, Nick and Buddy:

```
INT. JOE'S TAVERN — NIGHT

A sweltering hole-in-the-wall pub. A bored COUNTRY BAND
plays a tired TUNE. Nick and Buddy suck down lifeless
beers.

                    NICK
         I'm sick of how you look at Sally all the
         time.

                    BUDDY
         Why do I get this feeling that you think
         I'm after your wife?

                    NICK
         I can't prove anything, but it's just
         tearing me up inside.

                    BUDDY
         Relax, I got a wife.

                    NICK
         You don't love Amelia.

                    BUDDY
         Maybe not, but I don't hate her.

                    NICK
         God, sometimes you piss me off.
```

Again, this is horrible, on-the-nose dialogue that stops the story dead in its tracks. Because Nick and Buddy speak their emotions rather than revealing them through an action or subtextually charged dialogue, the story stops. Also as a result, their characters are undifferentiated. Here is the same scene, but now the emotions are made clear through action and indirect dialogue:

INT. JOE'S TAVERN — NIGHT

A sweltering hole-in-the-wall pub. A bored COUNTRY BAND
plays a tired TUNE. Nick and AMELIA, Buddy's wife, suck
down lifeless beers.

Nick glances gloomily at the dance floor: Buddy spins
SALLY around, cheek to cheek. They're not Fred & Ginger,
but she's the type of woman men love to dance with and
Buddy is loving it, all right.

DRUNK OLD-TIMERS watch Sally. She teases them with a flip
of her skirt as she sails past. They like that.

Nick tries to catch her eye, but she avoids him as they
dance nearby. He overhears Buddy's flirtatious banter.

> BUDDY
> ... then this taxi comes flying around
> the corner, misses the mother, but hits
> the baby carriage. Proceeds to drive ten
> blocks with the carriage lodged between
> the oil pan and the street. It was
> like the 4th of July, sparks shootin'
> everywhere!

> SALLY
> Ooh. I like sparks.

Buddy pulls Sally in close, pressing his chest against
her breasts.

Nick can't take it anymore. He walks out and taps
Buddy's shoulder.

> NICK
> I'm cuttin' in with my wife.

> BUDDY
> We're partners, Nick. Supposed to share
> things.

Nick gives him a cold stare. Buddy shrugs and
relinquishes Sally to Nick's arms. She's still talking to
Buddy.

> SALLY
> ... So what happened to the baby ... ?

```
Nick pulls her away, ending the conversation.

                    NICK
          Baby's fine. No big deal.

NICK'S P.O.V.-- Buddy swings and rocks over to Amelia,
by the bar. She smiles and stands expectantly, but Buddy
sits and orders a beer. She slumps back onto her stool,
disappointed. They say nothing to each other.
```

Now Nick's emotions and Buddy's intentions are clear without them having to talk about them, and their personalities are distinct. Try not to allow your characters to stand outside themselves and describe feelings they should be showing.

Are You Listening?

Writing dialogue isn't just about what the characters are saying, but what they are hearing and how they react to it. Seldom do characters hear exactly what another is saying. More often than not, characters (just like people) filter what they hear through their own needs, desires and wants. Characters ignore, interpret, misinterpret or read special meanings into everything. When writing dialogue, you must keep in mind not only what is being said, but also how it is being heard. These can be two very different things. Let's look at a simple exchange of dialogue between two characters:

```
John pokes around in the kitchen cabinet, frustrated.
Sally doesn't appear to notice.

                    JOHN
          Honey, where's the coffee?

                    SALLY
          In the fridge.

                    JOHN
          And sugar?

                    SALLY
          Right beside it, on the left.
```

This is boring dialogue. Why? Both John and Sally hear each other perfectly and respond obviously. The conversation is nothing more than an information exchange. But look what happens when the obvious is used to express the hidden:

```
John pokes around in the kitchen cabinet, frustrated.
Sally doesn't appear to notice.
```

```
                         JOHN
              Honey, where's the coffee?

     Sally ignores him.

                         JOHN
                Honey--

                         SALLY
              You don't think I know, do you.

     John looks some more, finds the coffee.

                         JOHN
              What, about the sugar?

                         SALLY
              Are you testing me?
```

Or perhaps:

```
     John pokes around in the kitchen cabinet, frustrated.
     Sally doesn't appear to notice.

                         JOHN
              Honey, where's the coffee?

                         SALLY
              The doctor said no more caffeine.

                         JOHN
              That's not what I asked.

                         SALLY
              Did you take your medication?
```

In the rewritten examples, a simple question is heard and interpreted to mean something quite different from its obvious meaning, adding purpose and richness to an otherwise mundane exchange, and moving the story along.

Don't Say That! (Dialogue Problems)

Just as there are basic techniques to writing dialogue, there are mistakes that must be avoided. The most common are: filler lines, speeches, raw exposition (including characters telling each other what they already know), clichés and didactic dialogue.

Filler Up   Filler lines are those words and sentences that take up space between real conflicts or ideas. Lines like "What do you mean by that?" or "What're you trying to tell me?" are filler lines. They are false prompts and can almost always be leapfrogged. Lines like "I can't believe you're moving to Alaska" or "So what do you think?" are clumsy ways to start a conversation and should be avoided—unless clumsiness is the effect you're after. The situation must be alive and full of energy and conversations should start spontaneously without false prompting. Another form of filler is the use of words like "So" or "Well" to begin a sentence. By the second draft, you'll discover that most of the "so's" and "well's" can be eliminated, as this example illustrates:

                    JOE
        ~~So,~~ are you going to the funeral?

                    ALLEN
        ~~Well,~~ I'm late for work.

                    JOE
        ~~Well,~~ I think you should. You need to end
        this part of your life.

                    ALLEN
        ~~So,~~ are you telling me or asking me?

Another type of filler to avoid is *name calling*. This happens when characters overuse each other's given names; again, these can almost always be cut.

                    CLARA
        ~~Sally,~~ you've never told him about this
        have you?

                    SALLY
        Oh, ~~Clara.~~ He thinks I'm brilliant at
        stretching the budget.

                    CLARA
        Thank you for paying the marriage
        counselor, ~~Sally~~.

                    SALLY
        No problem, ~~Clara~~.

Fillers indicate that the writer is still fishing for what the dialogue ought to be, or worse, obfuscating it. The English author George Orwell said that too many vague words will cloud a work and "fall upon the facts like soft snow, blurring the outlines and covering up all the details."

Speech, Speech! Monologues may be wonderful on the stage but they generally don't work in a movie. Some exceptions are voice-over narration or actual speeches being given in context, such as a lawyer giving her summation at the end of a trial, or William Wallace rallying his troops before the battle. Another example from the same movie—*Braveheart*—comes when

Edward Longshanks, having killed his son's lover, meditates on the best plan of action to follow to defeat Wallace. But these are the exception, and even these kinds of speeches must be approached with caution. In real life, people generally don't go on at great length without interruption, so monologues are a bit unnatural. This is true in screenplays as well. Long monologues often slow the pace because there is little interaction with other characters or little action being taken by the character who is speaking. Monologues are also visually boring. Whenever possible, try to break monologues up into shorter, more manageable dialogue passages. There's a famous story of a producer who took a ruler, slapped it down on a screenwriter's script, measured the length of a monologue written there, and said, "Three inches long! Cut it by two." This is a bit extreme, but you get the point.

Another "speech" problem occurs when the character works out his problems in complete, extended thoughts rather than through exploration and interaction with other characters. This form of dialogue (sometimes called a "false monologue") turns characters inward; it causes them to feed off themselves rather than relate to or act off of other characters. In the following example, two lawyers argue over evidence. Notice that they are not interacting but thinking everything out in complete thoughts.

```
                ZOOKER
      That was twenty years ago. People
      change. What's the truth today? I mean,
      you should've said something. Demanded
      proof. You can't blame someone today for
      how they acted twenty years ago. You
      should've objected!

                ACE
      Thank you for telling me how to do my
      job, but we adjourned before I could do
      so. They asked the question. A question
      I couldn't answer because I'm afraid the
      prosecution has exactly what I have.
      Proof!

Ace digs out a divorce decree.

                ACE
      I stole it from the county records when
      the trial began. Was bein' a good little
      lawyer-man, coverin' my client's ass. I'm
      good at that.
```

Now here is the same scene, broken into dialogue rather than speeches. Notice that it is more realistic and allows the characters to play off each other rather than feed off themselves.

```
              ZOOKER
That was twenty years ago. People change.
What is the truth today? You should've
said something--

              ACE
Thank you for tellin' me how to do my
job--

              ZOOKER
Demanded proof.

              ACE
We adjourned before I--

              ZOOKER
You can't blame someone today for how
they acted twenty years ago... You
should've objected!

              ACE
I couldn't! I'm afraid the prosecution
has exactly what I have. Proof!

Ace digs out a divorce decree.

              ACE
I stole it from the county records when
the trial began. Was bein' a good little
lawyer-man, coverin' my client's ass. I'm
good at that.
```

Now there's some reality to the scene, some believable conflict, and some energy.

Touché ... Cliché! A cliché is a commonplace phrase that has become overused and trite. "Beyond the shadow of a doubt," "beat swords into plowshares," "It'll all come out in the wash," "water under the bridge," "as close as peas in a pod," "You'll never get away with this," are all obvious clichés both on and off the screen. In movie talk, there are many more: "I'm too old for this [pick your expletive]," "Are you all right?" "Let's do it," "Run for it!" are examples of overused and essentially meaningless phrases which should be avoided. People do occasionally talk in clichés, but a screenplay deals with heightened language. A screenwriter should try to come up with new ways to re-express a familiar sentiment, rather than resort to shopworn phrases. The only exception is if you have a character like Polonius in *Hamlet*, whose superficial character is revealed by his reliance on clichéd truths and sentiments.

Get Off the Soapbox Characters who speak from a soapbox (unless, as in the case of Polonius, this is their nature) are usually the result of inexperienced writers who wish to convey a "message." This results in didactic or propagandistic speeches. Your message (which is, of course, your theme) should be subtextual, suggested rather than openly stated, dialectic rather than pedantic. If you must have a character talk about the theme, then it should come as a revelation, a discovery based on the action of the story. But allow the action to "speak first" and lead the character to his or her dialogue, as for instance, when Dorothy finally realizes that "There's no place like home," or when Jules explains the meaning of his salvation at the end of *Pulp Fiction*. Show and persuade your audience (and your characters), don't browbeat them. Dialogue is exploration and communication, not indoctrination.

I WAS BORN IN A LOG CABIN I BUILT WITH MY OWN HANDS... (EXPOSITION)

Exposition is dialogue that sets up or explains the story; it is like the getting-to-know-you conversation on a first date. It relates action that has happened, is happening or will happen outside the frame of the movie: everything that happens between the words FADE IN and FADE OUT. Most exposition is handled visually—we see what is happening, or what happened, through flashback or prologue scenes—but occasionally a screenwriter must use dialogue. Contrary to popular opinion, there's nothing wrong with verbal exposition if it's handled properly, but there are many pitfalls.

If the sole purpose of the dialogue or scene is to provide exposition, to "fill the audience in," then it will fail, because the scene becomes static; the action of the story pauses while we get information. Exposition must be woven into the action, so that it contributes to the forward motion of the story, or at any rate doesn't hinder it. Problems also occur when exposition is too obvious (relating things that are already clear to the audience, or having characters tell each other things they already know in order to inform the audience), or is too extended, containing unnecessary details.

You're So Obvious Phrases like "As you can see," "As you know...," or "As I told you...," "...remember?" and "Like I told you yesterday..." are sure signs that obvious or on-the-nose exposition lurks nearby. The characters aren't talking to each other, they're simply filling in the reader. Many novice writers fall into this trap, not knowing how else to reveal the information they feel the reader needs to know. Years ago a friend of ours at the Second City improvisation company did a skit called the *Obvious Exposition Players*. It went something like this:

```
            SON #1
How's Mom?


            SON #2
Considering the fact that she's nearly
seventy, she's doing just fine.
```

                    SON #1
```
If only she hadn't had that heart attack
last year.
```

                    SON #2
```
That was a bad one. Left her in the
hospital for three months.
```

                    SON #1
```
I took care of her, remember? I was there
every night till the nurse kicked me out.
```

                    SON #2
```
What about me? I was there every morning.
```

                    SON #1
```
You were. She's been a good mother.
Remember the time she lied about your age
so that you could join Little League?
```

                    SON #2
```
How could I forget? I'd never be a big
league pitcher if it wasn't for her.
```

                    SON #1
```
And I'd never be a barber if she hadn't
let me experiment on her head.
```

While this is a comic example of bad dialogue, it highlights a very common problem. Obviously, both sons already know everything they're telling each other. So why on earth would they speak like this? Only because the writer has forced them into it. If the information is crucial to understanding the story, then the writer must find more skillful ways of providing it.

    You're Missing the Point   The key to writing exposition is to make sure that it directly affects the current action. Unnecessary exposition can take several forms: it can retell things we've already seen on screen or already know from other dialogue, it can contain back story that is not needed to make sense of the story, it can describe things that are happening as the character speaks, and it can tell us things that are going to happen on screen anyway, or that have nothing to do with the resolution of the story. The question the writer must always ask is, do we need to hear this? For example, we absolutely need to know what Leonardo Di Caprio's character does for a living in *Inception*, because it's the basis of the plot. In contrast, we barely need to know what Leonardo Di Caprio's character does for a living in *Revolutionary Road*, because it's just an office job that he hates and that has little to do with the story. And was Cary Grant ever married before he was abducted in *North by Northwest*? What about Willy Loman, what does he sell in *Death of a Salesman*? These bits of "backstory" are not revealed because they do not affect the story. Necessary exposition contains information that affects our understanding of the present action, of the characters and the story. If it affects the story *now*, then it is necessary. You may want to develop and know many things about the past in order to have a clearer idea of how to write what happens in the script, but very little of it actually needs to be said on screen unless the character has an urgent and present need to say it.

Let's Put It This Way... (Dialogue Solutions)

Once you've determined that you need to use dialogue for exposition, you must find ways to integrate it with the natural flow of scene. Some methods include "hiding" the exposition by use of background action, conflict, humor, question and answer, conversation with a confidant and use of a narrator.

Listen to Me! The simplest and most commonly used method to hide or mask exposition is through conflict. Characters can either talk while they're in the midst of exciting action and/or they can disagree with each other. For instance, in *The Terminator*, Kyle Reese reveals the backstory of who he is, where he's from and what dangers are facing Sarah Connor, all during a desperate car chase in which they are directly reacting to the threat he's attempting to explain to her. At the same time, Sarah doesn't yet comprehend the reality she is facing and thinks Kyle must be insane; she pleads with him to let her go, bites him and tries to escape. They are in conflict with the antagonist, as well as with each other, and so the backstory exposition doesn't slow the story down; it illuminates what is happening to them, right now. This allows the audience to hook into the emotional conflict without focusing on the exposition.

Whatever the fight or argument, of course, it must be a natural part of the story and characters. This shouldn't be a problem because a screenplay is never about people who agree with one another, at least for long. Remember, drama is conflict.

You Must Be Joking If the audience is laughing, they're seldom aware that the scene (or line) contains expositional information. Take a look at any Woody Allen film. In his rants, he fills us in on who he is, what his relationships are with the other characters, what he wants or fears from them—but everything is couched in jokes and ironic commentary, which are essential to the nature of his character. In *Die Hard*, both Bruce Willis' and Alan Rickman's characters reveal details of backstory and plot through humorous exposition. But they do so because it is natural for them to speak this way. The humor must arise organically from the character and the conflict in the scene.

Cry on My Shoulder (Confidants) A *confidant* is a character who is basically there to give the main character someone with whom to talk. As the confidant is filled in, so is the audience. The trick is to make sure the confidant's reason for being in the story is more than just being a confidant; he or she should be a lover, ally, mentor, parent, someone who fulfills another function within the story. All characters must advance the movie and not just serve the writer's need to get out exposition.

Once upon a Time... Nowadays, narrative *voice-overs* (V.O.) are generally looked down on as non-cinematic. Movies have become more sophisticated in their storytelling techniques, and having some disembodied voice carry us through the movie can feel old-fashioned and clumsy. Gurus and critics complain that too often a voice-over is a crutch, a simple commentator who tells the story only because the writer doesn't know how else to reveal her exposition. However, when used effectively, the narrative voice-over can be a wonderful tool—just look at *Little Big Man, Annie Hall, Reversal of Fortune, Juno, Road to Perdition, Days of Heaven, Tree of Life,* the *Lord of the Rings* trilogy, or *Sunset Boulevard.* In fact, two of the top four all-time movies on the AFI top 100 list use extensive voice-over, including arguably the best American movie ever made, *Citizen Kane.* These work because the narrators are integral parts of the story, full characters who are rich in personal conflict and whose narration adds to the tone and quality of the story. The V.O. offers a sense of dramatic irony or perspective. In *Little Big Man,* the narrator is an ancient invalid being interviewed by a skeptical young reporter. His narration conveys humor, contempt and savage irony, which give both us and the interviewer perspective and a sense of undeniable truth as to what he's relating. In *Annie Hall,* the narrative voice provides a humorous and philosophical context. In *Reversal of Fortune, American Beauty* and *Sunset Boulevard,* the narrators are either dead or comatose, and their narration reinforces their themes of the subjective nature of knowledge, ambition and final judgment. In other words, the narrator is a real character in the story. Never use a narrator as merely a source of information, as a last gasp to clarify a story that is confusing and needs to be explained. If this is the case, you need to fix your story.

Shades of Things to Come One technique of writing "between the lines" that is particularly useful is *foreshadowing,* in which seemingly normal, everyday dialogue actually hints at either the future or theme of the story. Such foreshadowing dialogue is sometimes referred to as "signposts," which hint at and sometimes justify future events.

For instance, in *The Terminator,* look at how seemingly innocuous dialogue both foreshadows the story and reflects the subtext. Near the beginning, when Sarah is having a terrible day at her waitressing job, her co-worker jokes, "In a hundred years, who's gonna care?" Of course, in a hundred years the future of humanity will depend on Sarah. Later, when she and her roommate are preparing themselves for a date, her roommate looks at Sarah and exclaims, "Better than mortal man deserves." Reese, a man who drops out of the sky from the future, is surely more than a mere mortal man. And when Reese and Sarah are on the run from the Terminator, she asks him to tell her about her future son. Reese tells her: "He's about my height. He has your eyes." Reese at this point doesn't know he's going to be the father, but the screenwriter does, and uses this innocent bit of dialogue to foretell what is going to happen.

A good signpost foreshadows future events, yet does not spoil the movie by allowing the audience to predict exactly what is going to happen. Lines like, "I hear there's a storm coming. That creek may overflow. Someone could get killed," or "Be sure to look out for Dead Man's Curve, there's construction there, and I hear they're using dynamite," are both really bad signposts. They don't hint at future events, they force us to assume that the dangers referred to will happen. If these dangers do occur, the audience will have lost the pleasure of surprise, and if they don't, the audience will feel betrayed. The signpost must be integrated into and hidden in the dialogue. Often, if the writer wants to create suspense—there's a dead man's curve where danger may occur—it's best to reveal it visually. Dialogue about it is much clumsier and calls attention to itself.

The classic example of a visual signpost is the "gun on the wall," in which we see a gun in the background and therefore have been prepared for the fact that it will be used to solve some story problem, like killing the bad guy. Similarly, a mention of some characteristic—"He was a fireman when he was young, but he lost his nerve"—signals that there's probably going to be a fire later on which will test that character's courage. In *Pretty Woman*, Richard Gere tells Julia Roberts that he's afraid of heights. Over the course of the story he inches further and further out on his balcony, showing his growth, until at the end he must climb a fire escape to prove his love to Julia Roberts. If you do mention a distinctive character trait of this sort, you'd better use it later on, or the audience will feel cheated. Unnecessary signposts clutter the story with useless information.

Catching Red Herrings   The one exception to this is the "red herring," a signpost that leads the audience to think the story is going one way when it's really heading another. Usually a red herring is more than a line of dialogue, it's a whole character, even a subplot. But reduced to its essentials it's a false signpost by which the audience's attention and expectations are intentionally misled, turned toward future events, problems and/or solutions that in fact will appear elsewhere in the story. Dialogue can be an essential part of such misdirection. For example, in a murder mystery there might be foreshadowing comments that hint at several characters with motives for murder, or at one in particular who will later be revealed to be innocent. Red herrings can be great fun, but must be handled with care or the story will become confusing and contain too many coincidences. They can be either visual or carried in dialogue, but it's better if they're visual.

TECHNICAL DO'S AND DON'T'S

Let's move on to some of the technical aspects of writing dialogue, including punctuation, telephone conversations, foreign language and dialects.

Punctuation

Punctuation marks are used to clarify the dialogue's meaning. All the standard practices concerning punctuation apply to dialogue, although they can be tweaked for special effect.

Dash-Dash The dash-dash (--) or hyphen-hyphen is used to indicate when a speech or line has been interrupted:

>   FRED
>   If you ever talk to Kathy again, I'll
>   teach you a few things! Just look at her
>   and I'll--
>
>   SAM
>   Shut up and get out!

Ellipsis The ellipsis (...) is used to show a suspended sentence. The character may lose the train of thought, drift off or fade to another subject:

>   BUDDY
>   I'm not sure if you realize what just
>   happened. I started this conversation
>   because... look, I paid you a compliment.
>   Showed some interest and... but you're
>   really not interested.

Ellipses suggest a slower pace. Sometimes you can use a dash-dash when there's a rapid shift of direction within a line of dialogue:

>   SALLY
>   I can't believe it! I was just standing
>   there but--I mean he came out of nowhere,
>   and--damn, I think my arm's broken!

Italics and Capitalization Screenwriters will occasionally use italics to emphasize a particular line or word in a speech. But this feels like a kind of parenthetical (see Chapter 2), forcing a reading of a line, and should be used sparingly. Capitalization indicates that a speech or line is shouted:

>   BETH
>   You're talking about me? ME! In front of
>   my face? Fine! YOU CAN ALL GO TO BLAZES!

But neither italics nor capitalization are really necessary to these (or most other) lines:

>   BETH
>   You mean me? You are talking about me?
>   Me! In front of my face? Fine! You can
>   all go to blazes!

Following the overall rule of simplicity, it is better to avoid these devices unless the meaning is opaque without them. In that case, it's better to just rewrite the line in the first place.

Abbreviations Abbreviations are used in dialogue only if the character also uses the abbreviation. For example, if you want the character to say "TV" instead of "television," then the abbreviation is acceptable. Other abbreviations should be eliminated because we need to hear how a word will be spoken. Numbers should be written out. Instead of writing "15," write "fifteen."

Comma In dialogue, the comma (,) is used to show a slight hesitation. Hesitations occur naturally in speech, so it may be appropriate to indicate them. By careful placement of commas, a screenwriter can help the reader or actor understand the tempo of a given line of dialogue. But if you don't intend a hesitation, there's no need to use a comma in the traditional way; dialogue does not have to be the Queen's English.

Other Dialogue Issues

Screenwriting has evolved certain conventions or solutions when addressing common dialogue issues such as phone conversations, foreign languages and accents.

Phoning It In Telephone conversations are often used in movies, but in fact should be a last resort. The problem with the telephone is that it is visually boring. What do we see? Some guy with a phone pressed against his ear. Dialogue is therefore forced to carry the entire action of the scene. Whenever possible, eliminate phone conversations; it's much better to allow the characters to meet face to face. (For formatting information on this, see Chapter 2.)

"Speeka de Inglitch!" If a character is speaking in a foreign language, it will bore readers terribly if you attempt to write in the actual language, especially if they don't know the language you're writing. So keep it short, only a phrase or two, and then shift into English. Better yet, use English throughout, and indicate that they are speaking Swahili or whatever in the narration or parentheticals. (For formatting information on this, see Chapter 2.)

Accents When a character has an accent, then it should be noted in description or in a parenthetical, but not phonetically spelled out in the dialogue (you only need to mention it once). Instead, the dialogue should be written with the rhythm, tempo, words and slang of the dialect, leaving the exact sounds for the actor playing the role:

```
                    DARLA
               (with a southern twang)
          That's because men don't train boys to be
          men, mamas do. And whether you like it
          or not, a father trains a girl to be a
          woman, but they seldom finish.
```

This is the wrong way (obviously exaggerated):

```
                    DARLA
      That's cawse mayun don't trayun boys to be
      meyun, mawmuhs doo. And whither you lahk
      et owuh not, uh fathuh trayuns a gull to
      be uh wom'n, but they sayldum finish.
```

We have read many examples of this kind of thing, especially where the characters are mafiosi or southerners, and it is torture to get through. Also, if you are using a dialect to make a statement on the characters' intelligence or socioeconomic class, you stand a good chance of falling into the trap of stereotype. Further, do not assume you know how one part of the country speaks. Research is essential. While you want to cast your part, as noted, don't rely exclusively on what you hear on television or in the movies; the screenwriter you are imitating may have been lazy or incorrect in creating his dialogue, and the actor may not have gone through the trouble of hiring a dialect coach. Above all it's crucial that the screenwriter understand the sensibilities of the character: the forces that shape a region, its people and dialects. A screenwriter certainly wouldn't imbue a farmer from Warwick, Rhode Island, with the same tempo and rhythm as a farmer from Cuthbert, Georgia. They may both be farmers, but they've been shaped by very different socioeconomic, religious and historical forces.

FOR CRYING OUT LOUD!

Screen dialogue is not written to be silently read, it is meant to be spoken. The only way to know if your dialogue works is to read it aloud, or better yet, have it read to you. Playwrights, dependent on dialogue as their chief tool, have done this for centuries. Once you think your script is ready, make copies, invite a few friends over (preferably actors, but not necessarily), assign roles (including someone to read narrative), and listen to your script as it's read aloud. Don't be tempted to read a role yourself; you cannot be objective about your own reading and you'll be too distracted by performing to really hear the others. Keep quiet, and listen actively. Take notes and analyze. Does some dialogue seem to fall flat? Is the exposition too obvious? Have you indulged in conclusionary statements? Does it make sense? Above all, does the dialogue seem to drag or feel unnatural? These questions are phrased as negatives—what is wrong—because you're not looking for praise or for what is just fine. You're looking for what needs to be fixed. A reading can be a very painful and humbling experience when you realize that what seemed so perfect on the page is so awful coming out of an actor's mouth. But that's the point. You want to find out what works, and what doesn't. When the reading is over, ask for suggestions. If there's time, go back to problem lines and have your actors improvise dialogue; often a spontaneous expression will work beautifully. You might also record the reading on tape, so you can listen to it again if you want to; sometimes your first impressions may be wrong, or you may find new problems the second time around. Then write it all down. You should be armed with pages of notes and be ready to attack a new draft.

FINAL THOUGHTS

Yadda, Yadda, Yadda Throughout this chapter we've stressed that dialogue defines character and vice-versa. It's worth repeating—until you remember it! What a character says and how he says it reveals who he is. When Dirty Harry is confronted with a robber who has a gun pointed at Harry's favorite coffee-shop waitress, threatening to blow her head off, Harry doesn't plead or run or put his gun down and negotiate. He points his gun at the robber point-blank and calmly says, "Go ahead. Make my day." It's a simple line, but it tells us a world about him: he's fearless, he takes chances with his own and other people's lives, he has a grim sense of humor, a straightforward approach to a difficult problem and, most importantly, at some deeper level he just doesn't give a damn. The certainty of his character convinces the robber that Harry would just as soon see a friend die, if it would give him the satisfaction of being able to exact a lethal revenge. Brevity, keeping to the point, working on several levels of obvious and subtextual meaning—these are what you're looking for in your dialogue. Do ya feel lucky, punk? Well, do ya?

EXERCISES

These exercises include examples of problem dialogue. See if you can come up with specific solutions.

1. The following scene has several filler lines and extra words. How many words can you edit or leapfrog and still have the scene advance the story and reveal the characters?

```
INT. MICROFILM ROOM — NIGHT

Alone in the dark, Grace cranks the microfilm reader. The
screen scrolls, then stops and scrolls a little more. She
leans forward. She's found it.

GRACE'S P.O.V.: The newspaper byline reads, 'COP PLEADS
GUILTY.'

                    FAT TROOPER (OS)
          Grace!

                    GRACE
          I'm back here. In the microfilm room.

A FAT TROOPER runs in.

                    FAT TROOPER
          They want to see you, now.
```

                    GRACE
Why now?

                    FAT TROOPER
You're in big trouble with the higher
ups.

                    GRACE
Who?

                    FAT TROOPER
The Captain. The Chief of Police. The
Mayor. They're all upset.

                    GRACE
So, what are you trying to tell me? They
don't like my article?

                    FAT TROOPER
Well, you name it, they're pissed off
about it. They want to see you now.

                    GRACE
Send 'em in.

                    FAT TROOPER
ASAP.

2. In the following scene, characters express themselves through conclusionary statements. Rewrite, allowing for specifics to lead the reader to the conclusion, rather than making the conclusion for them. Use the same number of words, or fewer.

INT. COUNSELOR'S OFFICE — DAY

COUNSELOR JOHANSON looks like a giant extinct species of
bird of which he is the last surviving member. He looks
down on George, who is twenty, but looks fifteen.

                    COUNSELOR JOHANSON
You're flunking.

                    GEORGE
I know, but that doesn't mean I'm stupid.

                    COUNSELOR JOHANSON
I think you're stupid. So does your
mother.

```
                    GEORGE
          I hate my mother.

                    COUNSELOR JOHANSON
          I'm so tired of you, George. When are you
          going to grow up?

                    GEORGE
          I am grown up.

                    COUNSELOR JOHANSON
          You act like a child. You even look
          like a child! You're never going to
          get anywhere until you learn to be more
          mature.
```

3. The following scene has characters talking about their emotions rather than showing them. Rewrite the scene so that characters never talk about their emotions, yet allow how they feel to be clear.

```
          INT. CLASSROOM — DAY

          MARY, an assistant professor in her thirties, sits
          nervously waiting for GEORGE, her department chairman,
          in his sixties, to look up from her class evaluations.
          Finally he looks over his silly half glasses.

                    GEORGE
          I know you're nervous about this.

                    MARY
          Oh, terribly. All morning I've been
          feeling touchy.

                    GEORGE
          My daughter took an "Intro to Theatre"
          class from you. She says she really
          enjoyed it.

                    MARY
          I liked her. She always made me feel
          appreciated for what she learned in my
          class.

                    GEORGE
          Well, I've always felt that "Intro to
          Theatre" was superficial. I never had the
          patience for it. Too easy to teach. I
          like something more demanding.
```

>   MARY
> It's not that easy. I only have fifteen
> students, but I'm overworked.
>
>   GEORGE
> A working mother with two kids; you must
> be tired.
>
>   MARY
> Tired and sick. Half the time I don't
> even know what I'm doing.
>
>   GEORGE
> I thought as much. Did you know what
> you were doing when you gave my little
> sweetheart an "F"? That really pissed me
> off.

4. In the following dialogue the screenwriter has the characters talk about the story rather than enact it. Create a scene in which visuals and actions largely replace the dialogue.

>   GARRY
> You should really try to get along with
> your father. You know, you never miss
> your father until he's gone.
>
>   ROSS
> What a pleasant thought.
>
>   GARRY
> My father was always filled with grand
> delusions about me. Then one day I
> decided to come straight with him. I told
> him the truth about myself. Suddenly, all
> the games were stripped away. We really
> looked at each other for the first time.
> Naked! Only our true emotions on the
> table. He immediately grabbed his chest,
> fell back in his Craftmatic adjustable
> bed and died. How's that for a guilt
> trip?
>
>   ROSS
> You told him you were gay?
>
>   GARRY
> No, I told him I was an actor.

>   ROSS
> And he believed you?
>
>   GARRY
> Why shouldn't he?
>
>   ROSS
> If I knew I'd get the same result you
> did, I might try the same approach with
> my dad. Wonderful guy--not! When I was a
> kid, from the time I was five, I asked
> him for a baseball glove. Finally he got
> me one when I graduated from high school.
> It was for the wrong hand!

5. In this scene, the characters speak in short speeches rather than dialogue. Rewrite so that characters interact rather than speaking in complete thoughts.

>   DORIS
> Look, I know you mean well, but pouring
> him a drink is part of our evening
> ritual. It means so much to him when I
> pay attention to the little things. I
> think that's what a good wife should do.
> I just want my husband to be happy. Isn't
> that what you want for your husband, when
> you get married?
>
>   SHARON
> No! Just because he wants a drink, that
> doesn't mean you have to leap up, dump
> everything and run to get it. He's got
> legs. He doesn't even ask for the drink,
> he just sits there and stares at you.
> I'll never marry a man like that.
>
>   DORIS
> He's a man of few words. But he's very
> sensitive. For instance, his drink has to
> be just perfectly mixed or he won't enjoy
> it. He has wonderful taste buds. Never
> smoked. You remember how much I smoked,
> for five years. Thank God your father
> beat that out of me.

> SHARON
>
> Mom, we all get lonely. And Dad was a
> pig; I hated the way he abused you. I
> suppose his death was hard on all of us,
> but you can't marry this man just because
> he reminds you of dad. Mom, you may think
> this is love, but this isn't, and it
> never was. This is being a maid.

> DORIS
>
> Or a prostitute. Am I right? Oh come
> on now, you can say it if you want to.
> I've heard the word before. It's in the
> dictionary. Prostitute. Well, maybe there
> are some practical considerations. He's
> got money ... and did I tell you that he
> is a practical man? Nothing wrong with
> that. You're just upset because I found
> happiness. Learned to love again. In my
> own way. Sounds like the title of one of
> those trashy supermarket books doesn't
> it? But that's how life is sometimes.

6. Now take your rewrite of the previous scene and leapfrog as many words and thoughts as you can. Turn the dialogue into "headlines."

7. The following scene is full of obvious exposition. Rewrite the scene using conflict, humor or a confidant to replace obvious exposition:

> SAL
>
> So, when did you move to Cleveland?

> TED
>
> Almost two years ago.

> SAL
>
> You are kidding. I moved here two years
> ago myself.

> TED
>
> What are you doing now?

> SAL
>
> I work for a large investment banker.

> TED
>
> I'm a successful umpire.

                    SAL
          I love baseball. But I have no time to
          go anymore, let alone play. I used to be
          pitcher on the bank's softball team.

                    TED
          I'm getting a little bored with it,
          actually.

                    SAL
          How could you? Everyone loves baseball.
          My kids especially do.

                    TED
          I have no kids.

                    SAL
          I thought you were married.

                    TED
          I was. We divorced. My wife was very
          selfish; she didn't want to ruin her
          figure with children.

                    SAL
          I have three great kids.

                    TED
          That's great.

                    SAL
          One from each of my marriages. But the
          third time is a charm; my new wife is a
          wonderful woman.

14

Rewriting

Not So Fast, Bub

All right, you've finished your first draft and it's a thing of beauty. It's so hot that it's burning your fingers, and you just can't wait to send it out to agents, producers and anyone else you can think of, sure that big bucks and a major studio release are soon to follow. Of course there might be a detail or two that needs work, a few nagging doubts about that problem section in the middle; but no one's really going to care about those, if they notice any problems at all. So basically it's ready to go! Right?

Wrong. Really wrong. *Do not delude yourself into thinking that your first draft is good enough. It almost certainly is not.* There's an old saying: "All writing is rewriting." While this is an exaggeration, it contains a great deal of truth. The first and purest reason to rewrite is that, no matter how talented you are or how careful you've been with your outline and first draft, there are always things that need to be altered, cut or improved, things you forgot you wanted, things you were sure you needed but really didn't. No first draft is ever ready to be seen by anyone other than yourself and a few trusted readers, who will hopefully help point out all the various, previously unnoticed failings of your precious creation. And it's likely you won't catch all the problems on your second pass, either. Most professional screenwriters go through three to five drafts before they send their scripts out.

There is a practical reason for this as well: you will ruin your chances with your script in the real world if you send it out prematurely. Remember, you have exactly one shot with whomever you send it to. If they pass on it, that's it. Forever. Once you submit a script to a producer, studio or agency, it gets covered by the reader (see Chapter 1) and "goes into the system," which means that the reader's synopsis and recommendation are entered into a computer database. If you later realize that you needed to fix some things and try to resubmit it, whoever gets it—even years later—will simply type in both the title and your name (in case you get the tricky idea of changing the title) and take a look at the prior review. If it was a pass—which it probably was, or you wouldn't be resubmitting it—that's as far as it'll go. If they're friends of yours they may lie and tell you they'll look at it again, but they won't. No one is going to read your belated new draft unless Leonardo DiCaprio personally insists they do because he's dying to star in it even if it means working for scale. Ain't gonna happen. You blew your chance, at least at that place. And there aren't that many places.

So take a deep breath, take that brand-new, virgin first draft and give it to a few trusted friends to read. Then try to forget you ever wrote the thing for the next couple of weeks. Once you've had time to get a little distance from your writing, gather whatever comments and criticisms you can, reread the script carefully along the lines described in this chapter, and get back to work. Then rinse and repeat, until your script is as good as you are capable of making it, if not better. Take the extra time and effort or you will simply be throwing away all the time and effort you've already spent in writing the first draft.

IT'S GREAT! NOW LET ME FIX IT

There's a joke that goes: "A writer and a producer are lost in the desert, dying of thirst. The writer begins to hallucinate a beautiful oasis, with gorgeous, shady trees and a pristine pool of water. His imagination is so powerful that even the producer sees the mirage…in fact, it becomes real. The writer, over-joyed, runs to the water to drink, when the producer shouts, 'Wait!' He shoves the writer aside, unzips and relieves himself in the water. The producer then steps back. 'There,' he says, 'now it's perfect.'" The point is that even when you've written a fantastic script, even when it's been purchased and is set for production, it's still going to be messed with. Hollywood, a land of infinite ego and insecurity (two sides of the same coin), loves to rewrite. Movies are rewritten at every stage of the process, from the writer's many drafts, through development, during pre-production, on the set just before a shot, and even in post-production. (Editing the film is sometimes called the final rewrite and, in any event, scenes are often reshot or new ones added.) And usually the person, or persons, doing the rewriting is not the original writer. Some Hollywood screenwriters have made their reputation and a very good living on their ability to rewrite other people's scripts. These script doctors, some-times called closers, can receive huge sums (as high as $200,000 per week) to whip a script into final shape just before or during production.

There is a serious debate among working writers as to whether this is a valuable and necessary aspect of the business or an immoral act of can-nibalism, in which some writers, driven by money and the desire for credit, glom onto and deform other writers' work. Some writers have gone so far as to actually sign a pledge not to rewrite another person's script. Others laugh happily all the way to the bank.

The fact is that many good scripts—and the resulting films—are harmed by this process. But this doesn't always result in an inferior prod-uct. Sometimes the script just isn't quite there and no matter how hard the original writer has tried, it needs a fresh perspective. If you are that original writer, your only defense against having your project taken away is to figure out how to gain that perspective yourself, so that the producers do not feel another rewrite—or another writer—is necessary.

Don't Object (Be Objective)

Producers are continually hiring new writers to rewrite the scripts they have in development. A movie may have several dozen writers, but due to complicated arbitration rules set up by the WGA, only a few will receive screen credit. The rest will remain what might be called ghostwriters. Why do producers demand so many rewrites? Put simply, they lack objectivity. "The biggest problem is so many producers today are less sure of what they think and believe," says Lucy Stille, a Hollywood screenwriting agent. "...It's hard to stay with one writer if you don't know what you want." These producers are making one of the most basic mistakes when rewriting (whether you're doing it or hiring someone else to do it): they're trying to rewrite before they know what they want.

What do they want? They want what all producers, directors, actors and writers want, a great script. What makes a great script? How do you know that what you've got isn't already a great script? It's hard to know, to be objective. This is where craft, where knowing what belongs structurally and thematically, comes in. There's a story about three Hollywood script doctors who were doing an emergency group rewrite on a children's movie. They had been working on it for days, the deadline was closing, but they just couldn't make the story work. The problem was that the original script contained the character of an enchanting little horse, which no longer seemed to fit. They were pulling another all-nighter, it was getting near dawn, when one of the writers suddenly said, "What horse?" It occurred to them that they were trying to adhere to a scenario that no longer worked. The story had grown; the little horse, no matter how enchanting, was no longer needed. The solution had always been obvious, but they'd been too mired in the rewrite to see it. They cut the horse and finished the rewrite.

Good rewriting is a special talent. Writing the first draft can be magical and creative, but rewriting—whether your own work or someone else's—is more analytical. Rewriting is repair work; it is like editing a novel. It's asking the question, "What horse?" It demands objectivity, problem-solving skills and a detailed knowledge of technique. If you have these abilities, then you might be suited for this kind of work. But even if you're only interested in rewriting your own work, you must learn to be objective and capable of problem solving after the hard work of your first, second, or eighth draft is done. Being objective means that before beginning a new draft you have a clear idea of what needs to be repaired. Only when you are armed with a solid understanding of the script's problems and possible solutions should your next draft begin.

In this way, rewriting is much like writing in the first place: it requires a plan of attack. The problem is, after weeks or months of work on the same story and characters, a screenwriter's vision can become narrowed and weary, the creative answers elusive. What a screenwriter needs is "new eyes." This is the ability to see a script fresh, as if for the first time. There are three ways to gain objectivity: time, readings and notes.

Gimme a Break! (Time Is Your Friend)

Have you ever found an old short story or poem you wrote years ago, read it and disliked it? Here is something you thought was wonderful when you conceived it but now you see all its faults. Distance is one of the best ways to achieve new eyes. Heraclitus (ca. 470 B.C.), the Greek philosopher, said, "You can't step in the same river twice." Events move along, the world changes, and you're constantly changing and growing, too. This change and growth happens much faster than most of us realize. Parmenides (ca. 515–440 B.C.), Heraclitus' successor, was even more to the point when he said, "You can't step in the same river even once." The present is no sooner here than it's become the past. We're all being rewritten, all the time. And when you come back to your script, you'll be a slightly different person, with new eyes.

Take advantage of this. Once you've finished your first draft, totally divorce yourself from the screenplay, lock it up, don't even think about it. It doesn't take years; in fact it seldom takes more than a few weeks. You'll be surprised how quickly you'll have changed perspective and achieved a new objectivity. Between drafts, some writers work on another project, others simply take a vacation (even writers deserve vacations). Whatever your choice, this intermission will recharge your mind, reset the breakers on your imagination and let you work or play at something different while your subconscious works on your script. Then, perhaps two weeks later, open the script and read it. Suddenly faults will reveal themselves, hidden problems will become obvious, and the strong/weak elements of the script will no longer be cloudy. All those little nagging doubts you dismissed, the problems you hoped weren't there and just skipped over, will declare themselves and demand to be addressed. And probably you'll have come up with the solutions. Time is the best editor, distance the best way to achieve objectivity.

Hear, Hear! (Readings)

Objectivity can also be gained though a reading. Readings are easy; gather a few friends (actors are nice but not necessary), make copies, assign roles and listen as the script is read out loud, in your living room.

Here are a few tricks that will help you stage a successful reading. First, make it a party, treat everyone to pizza. Then, since screenplays have many roles, you'll want to double-cast. This doesn't mean having two people read the same lines at the same time, which only creates an unpleasant echo effect. Double-casting means that one reader will play multiple roles, unless you have a great many friends whom you can get in one room all at the same time. One way to do this is to assign the leading roles (protagonists and antagonists) to an individual while other readers will play multiple smaller roles. Next, do your readers a favor and highlight their lines for them; this way there won't be any uncomfortable pauses when someone doesn't pick up their cue or searches for their part. It's best to cast two readers for the narrative so they can switch off and keep it fresh. Also, your script should be read cold; in other words, without rehearsals. This is because the script should be clear and easy to understand on the first reading. Rehearsal will only hide problems. When a line goes wrong, when a scene fails, don't be tempted to blame the readers. The screenwriter who thinks, "It really does work, they're just not reading it right" is more than likely simply finding excuses for a script's faults.

During the reading, don't read anything yourself, not even the narrative. With your copy of the script in front of you, just listen, and make notes, right there on the script page: what works, what doesn't. When a reader stumbles on lines, note the line so it can be checked. Don't try to rewrite it on the spot or stop the readers so you can discuss a problem that has arisen. You'll lose the flow of the reading. Just jot down a few key words to remind yourself of what and where the problem lies. It's also a good idea to tape-record the reading, so that you can go back over it for anything you may have missed.

Basically, readings allow you to hear the script interpreted by someone other than yourself; everything sounds different in someone else's mouth than it does in your own mind when you're writing. Flaws, unintended but happy accidents, not-so-happy accidents, poorly written narrative, unclear plot points, boring stretches and rushed passages, all will become much more clear to you.

At some point during the evening, should one or more of the readers need to take a break or go to the bathroom, mark the place in the script where they feel they can put it down and take that break. It's probably a spot where the story has slowed down. A script should be a page-turner; there should never be a lull where readers feel it's okay to stop. During a reading, if possible, use the squeakiest chairs you can find. When readers become bored they will shift in the chairs. You can tell how bored they are by the number of squeaks. If no squeaking is possible, then just notice how many times they yawn and recross their legs. Mark which pages seem to take forever to read. Where does the action slow down? When are the characters inconsistent? Where does the story fail?

By the end of the reading, your script should be full of notations (use red ink—it's easier to spot your notes) and you'll be ready for the next draft. If you loved the reading, if you wouldn't change a thing, then more than likely you were not listening critically—so ask for and pay careful attention to the (hopefully constructive) criticisms of your readers. Invite people to stay and talk about the script. Friends will have a tendency to be kind, so let them know that they should not sugarcoat their comments. Promise them you won't be offended—and then keep that promise. Don't argue with them or justify your choices—just listen, and learn. Remember, this isn't about you, it's about the screenplay. Better to hear it now than in a rejection letter from an agent or producer. Sometimes they'll all agree that something is wrong and if that happens, they're probably right. (There's an old expression, "If everyone tells you you're drunk, then hand over the keys whether you agree with them or not.") More often, there will be some disagreements among your readers, and then you'll have to decide who's right.

But remember one important point—often people can sense a problem in a certain part of the story without being able to pinpoint the exact cause. They may agree something's wrong, but each of them points to a different part of the scene or line of dialogue as the culprit, when in fact the problem may be the scene's relationship to a scene just preceding or following it, or to some other unidentified flaw in the vicinity. In a scene with three beats (A, B and C), for instance, one reader may point to beat A, another to C, when in fact the problem is with beat B. It's all a matter of the context. Again, be objective. Acknowledge that something here needs work, whether or not it's the exact line or scene someone has identified. Then, when you're rewriting, step back and look over the problem area for the true cause of people's misgivings.

All of this may seem painful, but it is actually a positive experience because the problems you and your friends discover are also guide posts that will help point your rewrite in the right direction. (By the way, playwrights have been using readings to test their writing for thousands of years. Many theatre companies do weekly readings of new scripts, and some will even consider screenplays.)

Notes from the Underground

Where to find an honest opinion? Whom can you trust? Young writers spend much time trying to find mentors to guide them through the process. They want an authoritative voice to tell them they did well, or how to improve. The internet is now full of such advice, usually for a price; but who are those guys, anyway? Most of them have never written a thing. Everyone is willing to make suggestions, but a true mentor is difficult to find.

Once, during a class at UCLA film school, a professor made an offhand suggestion concerning a student's script. The student desperately seized the suggestion and rewrote. A week later the student returned to class, haggard and exhausted; he had pulled several all-night writing sessions to completely incorporate the professor's notion. The class read the new script aloud. It was worse. The professor said, "Naw, that doesn't work either." The student was stunned. Not all suggestions are gold. Just because someone makes a suggestion, even someone with years of experience, doesn't mean they're right. But how do you know who's right and who isn't? Exactly what will work, what will sell, what makes a script great? No one really knows. One reader will call you brilliant; the next will label you an amateur. As valuable as other people's opinions are, ultimately you must become your own mentor. Remember, it's your story, your inspiration—and your responsibility. Have confidence in what genuinely excites you about your script, because if it truly pleases you, it will likely please others.

Warning! Warning! Danger, Will Robinson!

An important caution: before you ask people for notes, be very clear with them that this is not an offer to share authorship with them. If they even hint at shared credit should you use their idea, don't listen! Your work is your work and you must never share authorship because someone has given a good note. This doesn't arise in classroom situations, but it can in the real world.

It's a fact that until a screenwriter sells his work, he retains the copyright and all rights therein are guaranteed. This means that if someone makes a suggestion on how to improve your script and you incorporate the suggestion, they cannot legally demand joint authorship. But that doesn't mean they won't try. There have been several court cases related to this situation. The courts have ruled that the only way an individual can claim to be a collaborator is if his or her additions to your script are independently copyrightable and the two parties (you and the actor, director, producer, any note giver) intended to be joint authors at the time the screenplay was created. This conflict doesn't arise often, but if an unscrupulous note giver confronts you regarding sharing credit because of a suggestion, stand your ground. The law is on your side. But it's always better to establish the ground rules first. (Of course, once you sell your script, this no longer applies.)

TAKING IT APART AND PUTTING IT BACK TOGETHER

Hearing the problems with your script is, of course, only half the battle. Now you have to figure out how to fix them. When a writer has trouble solving problems, it's usually because she is trying to solve too many problems at once. A rewrite is made up of hundreds of small obstacles and choices. So start your rewrite by attempting to separate and identify each problem so that you can solve them one at a time. Here are the steps to try:

To Be Precise (Specify the Problems)

This is really a matter of organizing and focusing what you've learned from your own perspective and the notes or comments of others. Once you've gotten all the input you can, it's time to sit down and organize all the consistent comments and problems others have mentioned, as well as those you've come up with yourself. If your notes seem vague, take the time now to figure out exactly what problem they're indicating. Statements like "the middle is boring" or "the character doesn't work" will not do. Which parts are boring—and where exactly does the script lose energy? Which beats? What aspect of the character is creating the problem? Exactly when is the character not working? What aspect of the character has inconsistencies or seems underdeveloped? Make lists of everything that occurs to you, in discreet categories.

Track Your Man (Isolating Each Component)

Basically, tracking means unweaving the various elements of the story into separate strands so you can examine each one independently and see more clearly where each problem lies. With tracking, the screenwriter checks to see if story, images, characters and dialogue are consistent from beginning to end, as well as if there are any unintended lapses or gaps. This is done by isolating the one element being tracked from everything else.

WAR STORIES

Robin

One of my students had written a screenplay in which the antagonist simply vanished for almost forty pages; because so much interesting stuff was happening to the other characters, the student hadn't noticed that the core conflict of the story had therefore gone into hibernation. By isolating where the antagonist appeared—and noting the page numbers—she was able to restructure that part of the script to keep the conflict focused properly.

For example, if you want to track a particular character, then you'd make a copy of your script and cut out everything but that one particular character's appearances and dialogue. With the character's arc and dialogue lined up without interruption, you can now easily check to see if there is a consistent speech and thought pattern, or if she suddenly starts speaking like someone else or makes unprepared-for leaps of logic, understanding or action. Tracking the dialogue helps you catch redundancies and wordiness as well as lapses.

Tracking can be done with any element: locations, environment, theme. If the world seems chaotic or ill-defined, or at cross-purposes with your characters' journey, isolate and look at how you've structured the sequence of images from scene to scene. See if they reflect or properly contrast with the intended purpose and meaning of each scene. If there's a problem with an ally or other secondary character, you can isolate them and see if their roles are properly set up, carried out and concluded. As with dialogue, tracking characters also helps eliminate redundancy. You might find that two secondary characters are repeating each other's actions, in which case they might better be combined into a single character. Instead of two or three weak characters, you'll have one strong one. Tracking subplots and secondary characters also helps catch loose ends and plot holes that otherwise might slip by unnoticed.

It's especially important to track the working out of your theme. If there are scenes or dialogue that don't express what your story is about, they must be altered or cut. Don't wander away from the spine, because that's where the emotional power and structural coherence of your story come from.

Your Head and the Wall, Part One (Brainstorm Possible Solutions)

Once the problems have been identified, the "machinery" of the script taken apart and laid bare, it's time to find the techniques that will solve each problem. Go back to the basics. Is there conflict? Does it increase properly, scene by scene? Are your characters consistent, or are they doing things that seem out of character? Is your theme clear? Be specific in your solutions. You can't rewrite using vague ideas.

It's really the same process you went through when you first outlined your story. For all your planning, inevitably, some unanticipated problems have arisen—but the techniques for solving them are the same, after the fact. Rewriting is sort of like re-outlining, honing each element so that it fulfills its previously intended role, or cutting it if it now seems unnecessary.

Your troubleshooting chart, with the techniques to solve the problems, might look something like this, although you'd want to be much more specific:

Problem	*Technique*
The story drags.	1. Raise the stakes; right now only Bill's job is at stake. Have his life and that of his daughter Emily in jeopardy, too.
	2. Too much narrative devoted to description of environment and mood rather than the action of the story. Trim and focus.
	3. Too many pages between major events. Eliminate the subplot where Jill's car goes on the fritz.
	4. Dialogue is meandering away from the issues. Look at what Bill is really trying to say.
The protagonist doesn't seem very likable.	1. Add a piece of "sugar." Give Bill a dog, some homeless mutt who keeps following him around until he accepts it.
	2. Weak motivation, not enough positive reasons for his actions. Related to the stakes, put Bill's life in danger.
The protagonist seems shallow, one-dimensional.	1. Add a character flaw or "ghost." Internal conflict: Bill wasn't there for his brother when his brother died in a similar situation.
	2. The character has too much self-awareness; rewrite dialogue so that he isn't so sure of why he's doing what he's doing. Give him a false motivation or excuse, hiding the deeper reason.

Problem	Technique
The conflict seems weak.	1. Make the antagonist more powerful than the protagonist. Right now Bill gets the upper hand too quickly. 2. Increase the consequences of the protagonist's actions. Have what he tries to do create more problems.
The exposition is too obvious overall.	1. Use the environment to reflect the exposition rather than having them talk about it. 2. Add conflict to the moments where the exposition becomes obvious. Bill tells Jill his life story while they're running from the cops, rather than over dinner.
A scene with the fiancé is too long.	1. Enter the scene as late as possible and exit as early as possible. 2. No conflict in scene; just yakking. Actually, just cut the scene, it doesn't add anything.
The script is 130 pages, too long.	1. Edit. Look at every scene and subplot. The ones with Jill's fiancé are all dispensable; don't need his character anyway. Cut them. 2. Check the narrative; is it too wordy? Can the same thing be said with fewer words?
The story seems to be all over the place.	1. Redo scene cards and track the entire movie. Study the structure; does it follow a logical cause-and-effect structure? 2. What is the protagonist's objective; does each scene of the movie follow the spine of that objective? 3. Does the story follow the correct strategies for its genre?

Of course a troubleshooting chart like this could go on for pages, and in a way it does: this whole book is one big troubleshooting chart. The point is, once you acquire objectivity and use these basic techniques to solve a script's problems, you'll discover that rewriting can be far more fun than writing. Rewriting is where average scripts can become great scripts.

Your Head and the Wall, Part Two (Turn Off Your Inner Critic)

One roadblock to problem-solving is allowing yourself to be too critical of your ideas. So don't edit your thoughts right away. Writers are more creative when they come up with many imaginative possible solutions and hold off critical judgment until later. One study placed a group of scientists in a think tank with a problem to solve. They were told that once they came up with a possible solution, they should all immediately and analytically judge the idea. After a day of thinking and judging, they failed to solve the problem. The next day they were given an equally difficult problem to solve, but this time they spent the morning pitching possible solutions without critically judging them or even considering plausibility. That afternoon, the scientists returned and were asked to critically judge each solution they had come up with that morning. It worked. One of their morning pitches solved the problem. By at first turning off the critical side of the brain, they succeeded in increasing creativity.

The same is true for screenwriters. By constantly judging your ideas as they occur, you can stifle the creative side of your brain. The next time you have a problem to solve, write down as many possible solutions as you can, without being critical. Don't judge whether they will work or not. Soon you'll have a list of possible solutions. Then, later, try to logically make each solution work—or, in other words, use the critical side of your brain—and you'll have a better chance of solving the problem. But once you've turned on your internal editor, listen to it. Don't gloss over or ignore new problems you know are arising, or you'll simply have to solve them later in your next draft.

FINAL THOUGHTS

The Baby vs. the Bathwater In Hollywood there's a rather crude saying: "Kill your babies." What this means is that if you are really attached to something in your script, if it's "your baby," you should edit it because it probably doesn't play to the rest of the world. Often this is true: a writer will keep a scene or line of dialogue in spite of knowing in her heart that it just doesn't belong in this story. It may even have been the scene or image or line that gave you the idea for the script in the first place, but like the writers mentioned above, you may simply have to say, "What horse?" Screenwriters should be ready, even eager, to rewrite anything that doesn't work.

But this shouldn't be an absolute, knee-jerk reaction. Sometimes it's "your baby" because it's marvelous writing and it works! In order to know which babies to keep, a screenwriter must first gain objectivity, then troubleshoot and finally apply the techniques needed to solve the problems. And then, if you're lucky enough to sell your screenplay, get ready to do it all over again.

EXERCISES

1. Have a reading of your script. Be quiet and objective. Sit in back where your note-taking won't bother anyone. Be sure to have a copy of the script so you can make notations—but listen, don't read.

2. Take one small problem within your script and follow the three basic steps for problem solving: specify the problem, break the problem into manageable components (track it) and brainstorm possible solutions to each component.

3. Write your own troubleshooting chart. In one column, list your screenplay's problems. In the second column, list the technique you'll use to repair each problem.

PART FOUR

MARKETING

MARKETING THE SCRIPT

THE PITCH

15

Marketing the Script

It's Called Show Business

FADE OUT--THE END. It's taken months to reach these words and many more to rewrite and polish what came before them. Finishing your mega-smash-hit screenplay is a great achievement, yet it's only half the battle. Selling a screenplay can take years of work, countless letters, contacts, networking and an intimate knowledge of the crowded Hollywood market. It's estimated that 300 times per day, some screenwriter types the words FADE OUT--THE END and a new would-be, mega-smash-hit enters the world. There are tens of thousands of screenplays written each year, yet less than 2,000 will sell, and only 300 or 400 will be made into movies.

Faced with such severe competition, the first step is to make sure that your screenplay is ready. Just like any product you want to sell, yours must be as marketable as possible. This means that you have an original, catchy premise, good structure, strong characters, proper format and, of course, it's been proofread. First impressions are important, so the script must have an impressive look as well as an impressive hook, a jump-started story and commercial appeal. In short, it must be a "page-turner." A page-turner is a story so exciting, so well-written, that the reader can't put it down. A page-turner is a script that's easily read in one sitting.

Once you have a solid product to sell, it's time to find an agent, to approach studios and/or independent production companies, to network and hustle. In order to do this, a writer must have a basic understanding of the WGA, registration, copyright, agents, producers and the market.

THE WRITERS GUILD OF AMERICA

Hollywood is a union town. There are unions that represent actors (SAG—the Screen Actors Guild; and AFTRA—the American Federation of Television and Radio Artists) and directors (DGA—the Directors Guild of America). There is even a union for extras (Background Actors Union). Just about everyone who works in television or motion pictures—other than in very low-budget productions—in front or behind the camera, is a union member. The union that represents writers is the WGA (Writers Guild of America). The WGA is a closed-shop union. This means that you must be a member of WGA in order to write for a signatory company. A signatory company is any film or television producer, studio or show that has signed a Minimum Basic Agreement with the WGA. The list of signatories is very long. It includes all the major networks and studios like NBC, ABC, CBS, Paramount, Columbia, Fox, Warner Brothers and hundreds of other studios and film companies. Only very small companies are occasionally not signatories and are usually fly-by-night operations or produce low-quality, straight-to-video product. Signatory companies agree to hire only WGA writers, and WGA writers agree to write for only signatory companies.

Unfortunately, you can't just walk in and join the Writers Guild of America. WGA rules state that you can't write for a signatory company unless you're a member of the union, yet you can't become a member of the union unless you write for a signatory company. It's a Catch-22, but there is a way in. To become a member, you must sell a screenplay or teleplay to a signatory company or compile twenty-four "units of credit." The rules on compiling these units of credit are rather complicated. Each writing job is worth so many units. For example, selling a story you've pitched to a signatory television program that is less than thirty minutes long is worth four units. If you sell a story to a television program that is ninety minutes long, or a story for a feature-length theatrical motion picture, then you get twelve units. If you write and sell a feature-length screenplay to a signatory company, it's worth a full twenty-four units. For more detailed information about units of credit check out the Writers Guild website at *http://wga.org/subpage_whoweare. aspx?id=84.*

What the WGA Is, What It Does and Why You Should Care

Once you've succeeded in selling a script (or compiling enough units), you must join the union. You'll automatically receive a bill from the WGA for your membership fee of $2,500.00. Next, you will be required to pay 1.5 percent of your yearly writing income to the union. Both are expensive, but worth it, for the union keeps wages high, looks out for the writer's interests, and provides health insurance and pension plans (if you meet wage and time requirements). The WGA also monitors and collects both domestic and foreign residual payments, conducts arbitration, maintains a credit union, library, work rules and calls strikes.

When the WGA strikes (which doesn't happen that often), all its members stop work, technically shutting down network television and movie production companies. Soap operas are the first to feel the pinch; sitcoms and hour-length dramas go into reruns, and eventually film companies grind to a halt because they can't buy new scripts or get rewrites on scripts in development. The WGA is a powerful union and they come down hard on strikebreakers. If the WGA is on strike, all writers are expected to honor its picket lines. If you write for a signatory company during a strike, you'll be blackballed from membership in the WGA for life—even if you're not yet in the union. There have been stories about talented college writers who cross picket lines only to find, after the strike is over, that they can never again write for Hollywood.

The WGA was formed in 1933 during the Great Depression. Before this, all screenwriters had was a loosely knit group called the Screen Writers Guild, which was more a social club than union. It had a clubhouse, activities, exchanged professional information, but it did not defend writers' economic and creative rights. When Louis B. Mayer, the head of MGM, tried to use the Depression as an excuse to cut writers' wages by 50 percent, the WGA was born. This was a time of great anti-union sentiment. The studios attempted to block the creation of the WGA by forming their own company-controlled union called the Screen Playwrights Guild. The battle between these Guilds lasted almost a decade. It was not a clean fight. Early WGA organizers and members were accused of being left-wing "Commies." It wasn't until 1942 that the Screen Playwrights Guild died and the Writers Guild of America was officially recognized as the sole collective bargaining representative for motion picture writers. In the years since, the WGA has also come to represent television, cable and interactive writers. It will soon represent animation writers as well (they have their own guild, but it has little clout).

Today, there are over 12,000 members of the Writers Guild. More than half are retired or are writers who've sold perhaps one script and never worked again. This means that there are relatively few full-time, working writers in Hollywood. The vast majority of films, sitcoms, soap operas and dramatic shows are written by about 4,000 people (2,500 write for television, 1,500 for the movies). It's an exclusive club, but membership in the Writers Guild does not guarantee employment or riches. Of its members, less than half are employed during any given year. The average union member's yearly earnings is only $60,000 overall and $130,000 a year for those lucky or talented enough to be employed. This is your reality check.

For more information about the WGA, explore their Web site, located at *http://www.wga.org/*. This site has valuable advice, interviews, lists of agents and agencies, research links and databases.

Written By—The WGA Journal

The WGA's official monthly magazine is called *Written By* and is a must-read for all screen and television writers. Each issue contains articles by WGA members that cover the art, craft and business of writing in Hollywood, as well as TV market contacts, which shows are open to new submissions, and reference information, such as research sites. WGA members get their subscription for free, but nonmembers can also subscribe. You can subscribe by calling (323) 782-4699 or going to *www.wga.org*. *Written By* is also available at most larger bookstores and some newsstands in big cities.

Copyright vs. WGA Registration

Before you market a script you may want to copyright it or get a WGA registration number. Copyrighting and WGA registration are not the same. When you copyright a script, you are guaranteeing yourself exclusive rights to your creation. A copyright is a form of protection provided by the laws of the United States to the authors of original works. WGA registration is only a legal record of the date you completed your screenplay.

All screenplays are technically copyrighted from the moment of their creation, but this doesn't mean you shouldn't prove ownership through the Copyright Office of the Library of Congress. Copyrighting is easy. All you need is a form "PA." Write to:

> Register of Copyrights
> Copyright Office
> Library of Congress
> Washington, DC 20540

Or you can call the Library of Congress Forms Hotline at (202) 707–9100 (24 hours a day). It'll take several weeks for the form to arrive (or you can also download these forms from their website, which is listed below). Send the completed form and script, along with a $40.00 money order to cover the specified nonrefundable filing fee, to the Register of Copyrights. Be sure to mail the form, your check and the script in the same envelope. It may take up to sixteen weeks, but eventually you'll receive a Certificate of Registration, which is your official record of the copyright. For detailed recorded information on copyrights call (202) 707–3000 (24 hours a day). To speak with an information specialist, call (202) 707–3000 from 8:30 a.m. to 5 p.m. Eastern Time, Monday through Friday. Better yet, check out the Library of Congress copyright Web site at *http://www.copyright.gov*.

You can copyright plays, books, articles, screenplays, and even treatments. You cannot copyright titles, character names, short phrases or bits of dialogue. You also cannot copyright ideas, but the *expression* of an idea (i.e., a script) can be copyrighted.

WGA registration is not a copyright, it's a service provided to writers to assist them in establishing the completion date of particular pieces of their literary property. In other words, registration is merely evidence of the writer's claim to authorship. What the WGA means is that their registration is merely evidence of the writer's claim to authorship and a date of completion. The date is important because if someone should attempt to plagiarize or steal your script, with a WGA registration number you can prove that you were the original creator. Unlike a copyright, which is good for the writer's lifetime plus seventy years, WGA registration lasts only five years (it can be renewed for an additional five years). At the end of five years, if it's not renewed, the material is destroyed without notice. So why do screenwriters often use WGA registration when a copyright does everything a registration does plus more? Because WGA registration is quicker and easier and, for WGA members, cheaper.

You can register scripts, treatments, synopses, outlines, television and theatrical motion picture scripts, video cassettes/discs, interactive media, plays, novels, short stories, poems, commercials, lyrics and drawings, but as with copyright, you cannot register a title.

The WGA registers well over 30,000 works annually. This service is available to members and non-members. Registration can be done in person, by mail or, most conveniently, through their website. You can find information on exact formatting requirements, addresses, etc. at their registration website: *http://www.wgawregistry.org/webrss/regmail.html.*

FAQ (Copyright and Registration)

Q: *WHEN SHOULD I RE-COPYRIGHT OR RE-REGISTER A SCRIPT?*

A: Only when the script has been significantly altered, meaning that there is at least thirty percent new material (characters, events, dialogue) should you bother with re-registration or re-copyrighting.

Q: *WHAT IS A POOR MAN'S COPYRIGHT?*

A: This is an unofficial way to copyright. The writer takes his script and mails it to himself. The writer then puts the unopened envelope into storage. This way he can prove he wrote the script by that particular postmarked date. A poor man's copyright is neither legally defensible nor recommended. You can also send it to yourself certified or registered mail, which provides another measure of protection.

Q: *IS PLAGIARISM A PROBLEM IN HOLLYWOOD?*

A: There are a few celebrated cases, such as Buchwald vs. Paramount, but it is not a frequent occurrence. If you're worried, be sure to copyright or register your script, send dated follow-up letters referring to the script by name to anyone to whom you've shown the script, with a copy sent to yourself by registered or certified mail. (This "reminds" them that what they've seen is yours, and creates a "paper trail" to prove who had access to your material and when, if you ever go to court.) Also, keep all rejection letters. There is, however, no cause to be paranoid. For one thing, if your script is good enough to be plagiarized, the producer will still have to pay someone to do so, and most will simply buy what they like in the first place. For another, studios and production companies are very wary of lawsuits. Most professional writers don't worry too much about this and many who have agents don't even bother to register their scripts, because the agency will maintain a paper trail on every script it submits.

Q: *DOES THE WGA ALSO HAVE A COPYRIGHTING SERVICE?*

A: No. The only organization that copyrights a manuscript is the Library of Congress.

Q: *WILL REGISTRATION HELP ME BECOME A MEMBER OF THE GUILD?*

A: No. Registration is just a service the WGA provides; it will not help you become a member. Nor will the Guild provide any legal advice or assistance beyond providing proof of registration.

Q: *IS IT WISE TO GET BOTH A COPYRIGHT AND WGA REGISTRATION?*

A: No. You are wasting your money if you get both.

WAR STORIES

Robin

I once tried to get my agent—a good friend—to represent another writer whose work I believed in. She read this person's work and agreed that the writing was excellent and the characters well-developed, but the premises of the two scripts were only interesting. And being interesting wasn't enough. In order for her to take on a new writer, the stories had to be drop-dead wonderful. I then took this person's work to a likely producer friend, to get an independent opinion (and maybe generate a sale, which would surely grab my agent's attention). But the opinion was the same. Good writing, interesting premises . . . no sale. This happened wherever my friend took her work and she remains unrepresented. So concentrate your efforts on making your scripts the best they can be, on all levels, before submitting them to an agency.

WAR STORIES

Bill

Years ago, I signed with a top television agency. They were interested in me as a sitcom writer, but in my spare time I knocked out a screenplay that was good enough to interest the Academy Award–winning screenwriter and author Stirling Silliphant (*The Poseidon Adventure, Towering Inferno, In The Heat Of The Night*). As a favor, Stirling took the script to Filmways, a financially strapped production company, who agreed to option it for $5,000. The chances of actually getting the movie made were small, but writers always take chances, and I was thrilled at the possibility of working with Stirling Silliphant. I took the script and the good news to my agent. He read it, called me in, chucked the script on the floor, and said, "What do you want from me?" Wasn't it obvious? I wanted him to look at the contract, make the deal. He said, "No." He didn't like the script, didn't think it ever had a chance of being made, and so it was a waste of his time. I left the office insulted and hurt. It wasn't until years later that I stopped to look at the situation from my agent's point of view. The option fee was only $5,000. The agency's take would be only ten percent, a mere $500. Most of his writers were earning more than that a week. Getting the agency's lawyers to look at the contract was going to cost more than that. To top it off, Filmways was a small player with huge financial problems. In the end, he was right. Filmways went into bankruptcy, the great Stirling Silliphant died, and, with him, interest in the script. Good agents have a nose for money, and they can smell it if a project has potential. They can also smell it if it doesn't.

REPRESENTATION

Agents

Few Hollywood studios, production companies or producers will consider work that is not submitted through an agent or manager. The days of young writers pounding out a script, folding it under their arm and bumping into just the right person at Schwab's drugstore are pretty much over. Today, you need an agent, but it's a waste of time looking for one if you are not ready. How do you know you're ready? First, you should have at least two complete, wonderfully written screenplays. These scripts should be so good that you have a hard time telling which one is better. You need several scripts because agents are not in the business of nursing young writers, they want to represent talented, professional, prolific writers, not one-script wonders. They want to be sure you can do it again. The other reason you want more than one script is because agents will often ask for a second sample. If they like your writing, but this particular script is not what they're looking for, they'll often ask "What else ya got?" You want to be ready with a second script. This is not to say that it can't be done with only one script, but the more you write, the greater your chances for success.

We're not just saying this to sound coldly professional. It used to be that it wasn't that hard to get an agent if you had a pretty well-written script, but this has changed. With the higher profile of the film industry and the exponential increase in scripts being written, it is now extremely difficult to find representation, at least good representation (and bad representation is worse than none at all). Put yourself in the agent's shoes. They receive hundreds of scripts and query letters a week. They are overworked and inundated by people who think they can write, as well as people who actually can. And the business has become much more competitive. In recent years, the costs and expectations for movies have made it almost impossible for an unproduced writer to get a writing assignment, once the bread and butter of lower-level writers; unless your spec looks like a no-brainer, sure-thing sale, a good agent—meaning a busy one—will not want to waste his time on it. He already represents many other proven writers who are easier to sell to the studios. Agents simply do not have the time or inclination to nurture talent. It must be there, full-blown, or they will not consider representing you. Their goal is to make money, pure and simple. It's not personal, it's a business; if your script can't make them money they aren't interested.

Where to Find an Agent

Once you have several great scripts and make the effort to understand the agent's point of view, you'll need a list of agents and a dynamite query letter.

The WGA does not assist writers in finding an agent, nor does it recommend individual agents, but it will provide any writer (member or non-member) with a list of signatory agencies that can serve as a good starting point. A signatory agency is one that agrees to abide by WGA rules, which are designed to protect writers. For example, signatory agencies agree not to charge a reader's fee. Some unsavory agencies will charge you a fee just to read (and reject) your script. To avoid this, use only WGA signatory agencies. You can find the list at *http://wga.org/agency/agencylist.aspx*. The WGA list no longer tells you if a particular agency is open to new writers, so you may have to explore a bit. Many agencies limit from whom they will accept submissions. Some have all the writers they need and are not interested in new submissions, others will consider submissions only through referral or only if the writer is a member of the WGA. Of the agencies that are open to all writers, some want the full script, while others will accept only a query letter, based on which they'll decide whether or not they'll read your script. The WGA list gives you the information you need so that you will not waste your time and postage mailing to agencies that are disreputable, closed or limited to new submissions. The WGA list gives the names, phone numbers and addresses of agencies, but not names of individual agents. Each agency has from one to a hundred agents working for it, and you'll want to do some homework to find the right individual to contact—write to a particular agent, not just the agency. "To Whom It May Concern" is usually the death of a great query letter, unless you the writer happen to have a story that's been in the news or have the rights to a bestselling novel—in which case, agencies most likely will already have contacted you.

Using these sources, you should be able to compile a list of a few dozen agents; some may be at the same agency (but you'll only want to contact one at any given agency at a time). The next step is to write a query letter and mail it or email it to everyone on your list. In Hollywood, simultaneous submissions (submitting to more than one agency at a time) are perfectly acceptable.

Query Letters

Few agents have time for unsolicited scripts. An unsolicited script is one that shows up in the mail, no one asked for it, no one requested it, and most of the time no one will read it. However, many agents will read a short, well-written query letter. A query contains a sentence or two of introduction, a dynamite pitch of your screenplay, a little about yourself, and any information that might make them want to read your script. If you're sending a query by snail mail, you can add to this succinct letter is a SASE (self-addressed stamped envelope) that the agent can use to request your script. If they say yes, your script becomes a solicited script and will be read, if not by the agent, then at least by an assistant.

Introduction The introduction of your query letter should contain a hook, something to make the agent stop and say, "Maybe this writer is different." A hook can be that you both know somebody in common, even better if that someone has recommended you: "I was talking to your client J. J. Abrams and he said I'm the type of writer you're looking for"—but don't make this information up, because the agent would rather spend five minutes calling the person up to confirm it (on the chance you are lying) than waste two hours reading your script. The hook can be something you've done: "I'm a graduate of the UCLA film school," a professional success, "My screenplay was a finalist in the Nicholls Fellowship contest," your job (especially if it's related to your screenplay), "I am the lawyer who represented Jeffrey Dahmer, and I've written a screenplay based on the case," or something else that makes you special, such as, "I was Jeffrey Dahmer's cellmate in prison." The hook must be short, clear and to the point.

Pitch Next you want to pitch your idea. You are only allowed a few sentences to tell the story. You want a crisp pitch that states a compelling premise in a short paragraph or two, of not more than three or four sentences each—not much longer than the brief movie descriptions on Netflix, Amazon or film guidebook/websites (see Chapter 16 on the art of pitching in person).

Closing In a short sentence, thank the agent for his or her time and invite a reply to your letter. If snail-mailed, point out that there is a SASE enclosed and all the agent has to do is write the word "Yes" on this letter. Some writers use a postcard rather than a SASE and invite the agent to place their response on the back of the card.

On the next page is a sample of how a query letter might look.

Acceptance

If 5 percent of the agents you've contacted ask to see your script, you are doing great! The vast majority of your queries will be rejected. Most queries are never even answered, they simply disappear into the great circular time-space continuum that is Hollywood. Some will come back with a form letter containing the standard rejection lines:

> "It's not something we'd be interested in."
> "We're too busy."
> "We're not taking new clients at this time."
> "It's not right for us."
> "Our slate is full."

If you should be lucky enough to get an invitation, then send the script with a short note thanking them for reading it, reminding them of the pitch, and telling them how much you're looking forward to their response. When you send the script, you might want to place the words "REQUESTED MATERIAL" on the envelope or email header, so that the agent knows this is something that was actually asked for, not just another of the hundreds of unsolicited scripts that crowd their mailbox/trashbin. If you send a hard copy of your script and want it back you'll have to include a large self-addressed envelope with return postage. If you don't want the script back, place a note on the script and in your letter stating that it's perfectly acceptable to toss it, but do enclose a small letter-sized SASE so they can send their comments or rejection. Don't hold your breath, though. And if you're one of the five or six writers on the planet who actually still uses a typewriter, send a copy—*never, ever, under any circumstances send your only copy of your script*! Even with a SASE you more than likely won't get it back.

James K. Polk
1600 White House Drive
Los Angeles, California 90024
(213) 555-8879 ● Fax# (213) 555-8879 ● e-mail Polk@usa.com

July 12, 2001

Ethel Mertz
The Fred Mertz Agency
1459 Desi Arnaz Blvd.
Beverly Hills, CA 90201

Dear Ms. Mertz,

I've been studying screenwriting at UCLA Extension, and my instructor, Roger Jetson, thought you might be interested in my newest screenplay, BRAD HAWK. It was recently a semifinalist in the Austin Screenwriting Contest.

BRAD HAWK is a comedy about a handsome kid (Johnny Depp) with the perfect con. He goes into a town, finds a girl from a rich family, seduces her, and makes sure that her family hates his guts. The payoff is that he always receives a handsome sum not to marry into the family.

He has the perfect life, until he's profiled on *Oprah*. Realizing the deception is up, he decides to pull one last, major con before retirement. He finds the only place in the USA where no one watches *Oprah*: Stanford University. His goal? The daughter of the President of the United States.

This is my third screenplay. If you'd be willing to read it, just write "Yes" on this letter and return it in the enclosed self-addressed stamped envelope. Or you can call me at the above number.

Thank you for your time,

James K. Polk

James K. Polk

Rejection

Most scripts that are sent to agents are rejected without comment. Never call an agent demanding feedback or an explanation as to why your script was rejected. Most agents don't have time to explain their decisions, and you'll only irritate them if they take your call at all. Don't expect a quick response. Most agencies will take several weeks to respond to a query, and as much as three months to respond to a screenplay submission. If you haven't heard by then (assuming your script was requested) you can make a polite follow-up call or email to be sure your script or query hasn't been mislaid. If you don't hear after that, you won't. They've rejected it and simply forgotten to tell you.

Occasionally a rejection will come back saying that they are not interested in this idea, but they like the writing, and to "keep them informed should you write another script." This is an opportunity. Keep a list of all the agents to whom you've sent scripts or queries, which scripts were sent, the contact person (agent or assistant), their reaction, and any other information that will help you next time you submit. Database programs like Filemaker are perfect for this. Then, either send along your second script or start working on a new one. By the time you get your last rejection letter on this script, you should be well on your way to finishing your next.

Ten Ways to *Increase* Your Chances of Getting an Agent

1. Write a remarkable script.
2. Write a good query letter with a great pitch.
3. Polite, gentle persistence.
4. Professional credits.
5. Live in Los Angeles (or New York).
6. Attend film school.
7. Win or place in a screenwriting contest.
8. Endorsements, recommendations and comments from friends of the agent, especially if anyone is a producer.
9. Already have an agent while looking for a new one.
10. Get a director, producer or actor interested in your script.

Ten Ways to *Reduce* Your Chances of Getting an Agent

1. Write a long, complex query letter that makes you sound more like a philosophy professor or used car salesman than a writer.
2. Ignore typos and horrible grammar.
3. Write a generic, uninteresting or silly pitch, "*Star Wars* meets *Bambi.*"
4. Use faint dot matrix printing, 10 point type or smeared photocopies.
5. Send crude or inappropriate material.
6. Constantly phone the agent to ask what's taking so long.
7. Apologize for the letter and pitch.
8. Be defensive and overly cautious about the agency stealing your exceptional idea.

9. Lie: State that a director, producer or actor no one knows (or everyone knows) is interested in your script.
10. Submit a script that isn't ready.

Tricks to Getting an Agent

Beginning writers are always looking for schemes to manipulate an agent into saying "Yes." The best scheme is to have a great script, but there are little ways some writers do increase their chances of getting a "Yes."

First, look for new, young agents. Almost every agency has a few agents who have just moved up from the mailroom, are just starting out and are therefore more likely to be receptive to new clients. If you politely ask the secretary, he might just give you the name of the newest agent. When you call an agency, always be kind to the secretary or assistants; they have been known to help polite young writers by giving inside information or moving their scripts to the top of the pile. There's a saying in Hollywood, "This week's secretary is next week's agent (or studio head)." Be polite to them now, as they may remember you later.

Other writers try to get an endorsement. Agents are naturally more interested in scripts that have been recommended by someone they know. Young writers in Hollywood are constantly networking, pressing the flesh, trying to get professional writers, directors and producers to read and recommend their work to their agents. It can be hard to find these endorsements because, when someone does recommend it, he is putting his reputation on the line. But remember, the least impressive endorsement is that of another writer. Agents need writers, but don't listen to them, even those they represent. Writers are a mysterious and often unruly lot whose lives seem to be devoted to making life difficult for them. Directors aren't much better, unless the director has the power to get a movie made and wants to make yours. But agents do listen very carefully to producers and development executives at production houses and studios. Why? Because agents are sellers and these people are their buyers. So if a buyer tells the seller, "Hey, I think you should sell this product," the seller listens. So if you can get a development person or producer to read your script—and if they like it—that's the person to ask for an introduction to an agent.

Many writers get introduced to agents by hiring an entertainment attorney first, if they've already landed a job that requires a contract to be worked out; see below for more on lawyers.

Another thing to look for is an agent who has had success with your particular kind of screenplay. For example, if you've written a science-fiction thriller, go to the movies (or video store) and write down the name of the writer(s) on this year's science fiction hits. Next, call the WGA and ask for the "agency department." They will connect you with an assistant who will give you the name of each particular writer's agent. You are allowed to ask for only three writer's agents per day. Now write a dynamite query to an agent you select, pointing out that your screenplay may interest her because you share the sensibilities of another writer she represents.

Does Size Matter?

Big Agencies The advantage to signing with a big agency (WME or CAA) is that they have clout. The disadvantage is that a young writer can get lost in the shuffle. Your agent may be too busy with more important clients to return calls or give you the personal attention you need.

Packaging Agencies Packaging agencies attempt to attach their directors and actors to a script and then sell it to a studio as a "package," thereby collecting several commissions. If your script meets the needs of their directors and actors, great; if not, they couldn't be less interested. Most big agencies are also packaging agencies.

Boutique Agencies These are smaller agencies that have specialized in, or are known for, one particular type of writer: those that specialize in television, or animation, or reality, or indie features--and have become players in that specific market.

Small Agencies With fewer clients, smaller agencies can give the writer more personal attention, but they might not have the clout you need. Be careful not to sign with any agent or agency that is not a signatory with the WGA. It's a sure sign that they are either unethical or ineffective. As a general rule, no agent is better than a bad agent.

Once They Want You

It may take several scripts and a few years, but your persistence and talent may pay off. When an agency wants you, they will ask you to sign a contract guaranteeing they are your exclusive agency for a period of (generally) two years. This exclusivity may be in regard to writing only, or it may include directing, producing or other kinds of work. This means they not only represent you in those areas, but will take 10 percent of whatever you earn in them, too. So if, say, you're an established freelance writer for magazines and don't want to have to pay the agency a percentage of your earnings from that source, you'll want specifically to exclude it in your contract so there's no ambiguity. The contract must be carefully read. If you are signing with a WGA signatory agency—the only kind of agent with whom you should sign— then you know the agent agrees to follow WGA rules. These are designed to protect you. (For example, if you sign with a WGA signatory agency, there must be a ninety-day clause in the contract stating that if they do not make a sale in ninety days, you can leave the agency.) If you are not sure if an agency is signatory, call the WGA.

Once you've signed with an agent, there is generally a honeymoon period in which the agent will send you out on various meet-and-greet or pitch meetings. If you're lucky enough to sell or option a script, the agent will take 10 percent and pay a lot of attention to you. Agents make their living by getting paid a percentage. The standard WGA approved rate is 10 percent, no more. But if you don't sell quickly, well...

Hip-Pocketing Occasionally an agent will "hip-pocket" a young writer. This means that he will send the script to various producers and production companies, but he does not sign the writer officially. In other words, he agrees to market an individual script, not the writer. When the script comes back rejected, the writer is cut loose, in the cold, with nothing, not even an agent. Hip-pocketing isn't all bad; it will get your script to the readers at various production companies. But it isn't the same as having an agent—a person who is pushing for your success, interested in all your scripts and constantly looking for an opening where your style, your talent, your writing is exactly what they're looking for.

If an agent wants to hip-pocket you, it should be taken as a compliment—the agent feels that your script is worth sending out. But you should seriously consider the consequences. If the script is accepted, the agent will sign you immediately and everyone will live happily ever after, but if and when the script is rejected (as most scripts are), you won't have an agent and often won't even know where your script was submitted or who rejected it. The script is now dead and the writer loses. By the way, agents seldom call it "hip-pocketing;" this is a writer's term. If an agent wants to hip-pocket you, he'll say something like, "I'd like to send it around, see what happens," or "Let me fly it up the flagpole and see if anyone salutes." You want them to say, "I like your writing; I want to sign you."

Agents—The Good, the Bad and the Ugly

There's an old joke concerning agents. It goes: One day a young writer comes home to find his house in flames. He runs up to a fireman and gasps, "What happened?" The fireman replies, "Your agent came by, killed your whole family, took your car and set fire to your house." Stunned, the writer smiles joyfully and says, "My agent came to my house?!" Agents have a tendency to be rather remote. Occasionally, a writer finds an agent who is also a kind, caring friend, but this rare and special relationship doesn't occur often. Most agents are all business, and every moment spent talking to you is one they aren't spending talking to someone who might buy something. And even so, most writers never think their agent is doing enough to sell them. Ask most writers and they'll tell you they lined up the majority of their jobs themselves.

But after all, it's your career, so you should be active in promoting it. Get out there. Just because an agent signs you does not mean you've arrived. Agents can't do it all; they can only open doors for you that would remain firmly shut without their help. And that's a lot. But the writer must still hustle, promote, pitch and, most importantly, write new scripts.

Managers

A growing alternative to having an agent is getting a manager. Some writers have both. Managers have long been commonplace for actors and are supposed to take a more active role in helping their clients guide and shape their careers. Theoretically, managers can provide the same access to producers

WAR STORIES

Bill

When I got my first agent, I was thrilled; my wife and I went out to dinner to celebrate. A week later, nothing had happened, a month later, still nothing. Two months later I called to see how things were going, what meetings had been set up, and the agent said, "Where's the next script?" A year and three scripts later still nothing had happened, so I left and moved to a more prestigious agency. A month went by, nothing, two months, still nothing. Then I had a reading of a comedy one-act play of mine at a small local theatre. It was a success, everyone laughed. After the reading, an audience member approached and asked if I had ever written for television. It just so happened that his old college roommate was now the executive producer of an NBC sitcom. He offered to show him a spec. I just happened to have twenty spec scripts. Remember, chance favors the prepared mind. Two weeks later my agent called and told me that through her "hard work and perseverance," she managed to get my script into that particular executive producer and I had a job. I just swallowed my pride and kept swallowing. Having an agent is important, but it's no substitute for hustle.

and studios as agents and are in general more approachable. They will also usually try to help their clients get agency representation as well. There are some drawbacks, however. For one thing, they may charge a greater commission (up to 20 percent, although 10 or 15 is more common). For another, because managers are not required to be WGA signatories, there is more room for abuse. They are not legally allowed to negotiate deals for their clients, but many will do so informally. They may require you to hire an attorney to cut the deal after they've made a successful submission, and this will cost you an additional fee. Also, although agents are not allowed to attach themselves as producers to their clients' work, this is common practice among managers. This means that when submitting your script, they may present themselves (and their fees as producers) as being included in the deal. Many agents and producers have recently created their own management companies and are more open to new writers for exactly this reason—they can get more out of a potential sale. And most—though not all—managers will agree not to charge the writer a commission if they succeed in getting a producer's fee of equal or greater value, an arrangement that can be attractive to the writer. If your manager is powerful and well-connected, he or she can be a great asset in protecting the project in their role as producer. But more often than not, the potential buyer will view their attachment (and fees) as unwanted "baggage;" the buyer may want to get the script without any encumbrance and be free to produce it themselves or attach another producer of their choice. With this caveat, in today's extremely difficult and competitive market, a manager may be your best alternative when seeking representation.

Lawyers

Another common alternative (or addition) to getting an agent or manager is to hire an entertainment attorney. Attorneys can be hired for an hourly fee or for a 5 percent commission of anything you sell. Some attorneys will act as surrogate agents and charge the agent's 10 percent. Since they are legally empowered to negotiate contracts and deals, and are also somewhat more approachable (because it's a simple business relationship), they may be a good way to enter the business. They can also provide access to the buyers (though usually on a more limited basis, since agenting is not their primary activity and they'll have fewer contacts and less time to devote to it) and they'll try to help you get an agent if you want. At some point, you're going to need an attorney anyway, since even agents will want to have them look over the complex legal documents attending any script purchase. Only big agencies use their own legal staff. So this is another attractive gateway to representation.

PRODUCTION COMPANIES

We aren't going to talk much about the studios or "mini-majors" (large, independent production companies that are either owned by or associated with one or more of the studios), because these are largely inaccessible to anyone without good representation; and if you've got an agent or manager, they'll help you to navigate those waters.

But there are also a host of small independent companies, or "indies." This is both good news and bad news. While the ability of the independents to produce and distribute films waxes and wanes on a cyclical basis over the years, with some managing to carve out a niche for themselves and stay afloat, most are in business for just a year or two until their financing runs out. Most of these companies produce very low-budget films and are not Guild signatories, which means that they are not bound by WGA standards of payment or other obligation. They are much more open to new writers, and many young screenwriters get their start this way, but usually these companies try to acquire scripts for as little as possible. For example, it's common for them to offer to pay one dollar to option the rights (see below) to the script for a year; and even if the movie is produced (full payment for the screenplay usually happens at the start of principal photography, when the cameras are actually rolling), the writer may make only several thousand dollars. Collecting residuals is almost unheard of, again because they do not have to abide by Guild rules on ancillary payments (such as video sales). Roger Corman was famous for underpaying—but giving a break to—many beginning filmmakers, some of whom went on to become very famous (such as Jim Cameron).

But this is rare, and the world has changed. It used to be possible to theatrically distribute marginal films in the days before cineplexes and then to sell them to a product-hungry video market. But now the major distributors have a virtual lock on the theaters and the video market is glutted. So most small companies struggle, trying now to figure out how to make money over the internet, and most do not survive. However, with cable and satellite and some growing sophistication on how to monetize websites, there are still opportunities out there.

There are basically three kinds of independent production companies:

Art House

One is the art house company, which produces eclectic, higher quality, low-budget films aimed at the festival circuit and theaters specializing in the unusual or offbeat. Most of these companies concentrate on acquiring finished films that have been privately financed, but they do occasionally finance films themselves. They are also reasonably approachable, but have very little money and are extremely picky. If they buy your script you'll get peanuts, but if the film is made it'll probably be something you'll be proud of.

Exploitation

The second type is the exploitation company. Exploitation means they exploit a certain well-worn genre, such as horror, violent action or erotic thrillers. Again, these are produced nonunion and on a shoestring, as movies go, and the producers have no intention or illusion of creating quality films. They simply provide salable product to cable, video and the foreign market, which has a surprisingly large appetite for junk. These companies will also pay you peanuts and the product will reflect the quality of what they buy. (Hint: They're not looking for art, just for inexpensive-to-make formula scripts.)

Cable and Television

The third kind of independent feeds the better cable networks. These companies produce a wide range of films and limited series exclusively for television. The range of quality is equally wide, but the pay is better, because most of them are Guild signatories. However, they are rarely, if ever, open to new writers, preferring to work with experienced writers who are on approved network or cable lists. It can happen that you'll sell them an original script, but more often they'll buy an idea or the rights to a story and hire someone else to write it.

Release Forms

If your script is not being submitted by an agent, you'll almost always be asked to sign a release form. This is a short contract that basically says you give the producers permission to read your work, that they are not responsible should the script be stolen, lost or destroyed in transit, that there is no implied obligation to you of any kind, and that you will not sue them if they produce something similar. (They need to protect themselves before they even take a look at your story, because they may have a similar story in development.) Release forms are standard operating procedure. Read the contract, and if you are comfortable, then sign. Probably you won't be, but if you don't sign, they won't read your script. It's that simple.

Purchases, Options and the Right to Shop

While this isn't a book about the details of selling your script, you should be aware of the three basic approaches a producer has to acquiring material (screenplays). First, and least common, is an outright purchase, negotiated with your agent or lawyer and involving a whole raft of clauses devoted not only to the purchase price, but to secondary payments such as residuals or performance bonuses, the potential to write a sequel, scales of payment if the movie is used as the basis of a TV series, and so on. It's very rare to sell a script outright except to a studio, because it's a large initial outlay of money that the producer either may not have or may want to devote to overhead and organizing pre-production of the film. And even studios like to hedge their bets.

It used to be more common for a producer or studio to option the screenplay for a percentage of an agreed-upon purchase price, but this is rare now. If your script is optioned, WGA signatories must pay at least 10 percent of the basic minimum purchase price. What this means is that for a certain period of time (usually one year or eighteen months) and a small fraction of the purchase price, the producer essentially owns the rights to the screenplay; more precisely, the producer owns an exclusive option to buy those rights and can therefore pursue other financing or stars and directors without worrying about having the script "shopped around" by anyone else. This makes good sense from their point of view, because even after laying out money for the option, the producer or studio knows that, more often than not, the film will not be made. So it's better to spend a smaller sum on the gamble.

The eventual purchase price of the script is often not fixed, but tied to the production budget of the film, with a "floor" and a "ceiling." For instance, you might be paid a $10,000 option toward a purchase price equaling 3 percent of the production budget, but with a floor of $100,000, meaning they will not pay any less than this (even if 3 percent of the eventual budget is less than this), and a ceiling of, say, $300,000, meaning they will not pay more than this (even if 3 percent of the eventual budget is higher). Most scripts are bought for between 2 percent and 5 percent of the budget. Sometimes, to sweeten the deal, a bonus clause will be added to promise the writer some more money if the budget is enormously higher than anticipated, or if the profits are. Payment does not commence when the film is green-lighted, or approved for production, but upon "principal photography," meaning when the cameras are actually rolling.

Producers and studios know that anything can go wrong, right up to the last day before production begins (and sometimes after), so they still hedge their bets. Normally, there is a negotiated right to renew the option for another period of time, for an additional option payment. The first option payment is commonly additional to the purchase price (so the writer eventually will get 110 percent of the purchase), with any subsequent option payments being applied toward it.

Nowadays, with the escalating costs of movies and the glut of screenplays, an interesting change has been taking place. Straightforward, 10 percent options have become a rarity. Rather, if a studio or major producer perceives a screenplay to be an obvious blockbuster, they'll "option" it for perhaps 75 percent of the final price, with the remaining 25 percent being paid upon principal photography to seal the purchase. Although it's not an outright purchase, it's a large enough upfront percentage to persuade the writer to accept the offer, while still somewhat reducing the studio's exposure. Conversely, if the script is something a producer (not a studio) wants to try and make, but doesn't perceive as a surefire home run, these days he'll simply ask your agent for permission to "shop it around"—for free. Often an agent will give several producers the right to shop, each one limited to bringing it to a particular studio with which they have a deal or good relationship. No purchase price is suggested or negotiated; it's all left up in the air until one of the studios bites. While some producers will still option a script if they want to bring it around to all the studios and other financing sources without competition, most—who realistically have only a few places to take it—much prefer not having to pay at all for the right to do so. This growing practice has meant that fewer and fewer writers get the small, but still significant, payments that options used to provide.

NETWORKING

Networking is more than just schmoozing, it's the art of meeting people and being in the right place at the right time. Everyone knows someone who knows someone else who just happens to be the perfect contact. Networking means keeping an organized log of every person in the industry you have ever met (including descriptions, so you can later put a face to the name), sending out holiday and thank-you cards, never turning down a party invitation, never leaving a bar mitzvah without someone's business card, staying after and meeting the guest speaker at seminars, taking classes, making contacts and creating opportunities. In short, networking is treating your screenwriting career as a business and your social life as an aspect of it.

There are a few general rules when networking. First, never seem desperate or overconfident. We know that's easier said than done, but people in this high-stakes, high-stress business are suspicious of the latter and detest the former. Remember, you're just a good writer with a good idea. Let your own personality and wonderful short pitch speak for themselves. Desperate writers are like the homeless guy begging for change that you wish would just go away. Overconfident writers are obnoxious, overwhelming and suspect. So don't slam into that startled producer with, "I've got the best script you've ever seen, a lot better than that piece of crap chick-flick that came out last week." For one thing, you come off as a jerk. For another, this guy might have produced that chick-flick. Which leads us to...

Knowledge Is Power

Listen before you speak; find out about the people you're meeting, get to know them and their work. You must be up on who's who in Hollywood. It is imperative that you subscribe to and study the trade magazines and websites—*Variety, The Hollywood Reporter, donedeal.com* and *deadline.com* (any or all of which might have gone out of business or been replaced by the time you're reading this); in short, the daily industry journals known as "the trades." These are where the subtle seismic shifts in the business are noted on a day-to-day basis: which company bought which script, who brokered the deal, which development exec has moved from one company to another. These are far more important than knowing the weekend grosses or your favorite actor's intimate thoughts on love and dieting. At first it will all seem like gibberish, a bunch of names and companies that mean nothing to you. But as you clip and note those that are making the kinds of films you'd like to make and that seem to be attracted to your kind of material, you'll begin to see that in the ever-flowing, ever-changing currents of Hollywood, the same major players keep cropping up again and again. These are the people who will hopefully be your colleagues and buyers. The trades also publish constantly updated lists of movies and TV shows in or going into production, lists that can be enormously valuable. Say you are about to sit down and write that great Joan of Arc script, when you open *Variety* and see that not one, not two, but four Joan projects are in active development or production. Still think that's how you want to spend the next six months of your life? Get to know the names, know what's going on. At a recent Hollywood party, a gentleman walked up to an Academy Award–winning actress and asked her if she had ever been in a movie. This is not a good opening line when you want to get a script read.

Remember, however, not to overdo it when introducing yourself. You want to keep your name in their memory, but you want that memory to be positive. It's a good idea to send out thank-you cards and follow-up correspondence, but some writers go too far and end up defeating themselves. One writer we know sends out a bi-monthly newsletter to keep everyone he has ever met informed of his progress. Mom and Dad are thrilled, but for others it has become an embarrassment.

Also, never make excuses for your script. You're at a party, you meet a producer, you start talking about your script. You say, "I don't know, it's sorta not ready yet, and not very good, but would you read it?" How appealing! Busy producers just can't *wait* to read something that isn't finished and is not very good. The meek may inherit the earth, but they don't sell screenplays.

Finally, networking can be done almost anywhere connections are made, at the laundry, the gym, funerals, but you're obviously more likely to find success if you live where the action is—Hollywood. But, in the end, networking is no substitute for writing a great script. Once you've met the right person, you must have the right product.

Networking on the WWW and in Magazines

There are organizations, magazines and sites on the internet that allow screenwriters to pitch or even upload parts of their scripts—for a price. The idea is that producers and agents will read these showcased ideas and request the full script. Some organizations claim incredible success rates for screenwriters who subscribe to their particular service. The only problem with pitching your screenplay on these open billboards is that anyone can see them (the loglines at any rate, if not the entire scripts). The writer has no record of who has read the idea, what they thought, or who might lift the idea. Remember, ideas cannot be copyrighted. Secondly, you're paying for this access. It might be worth it, but then again these sites are run by people who make their money by signing up subscribers—not by selling scripts. Before you subscribe to one of these services, be sure to check them out and know the risks. And do some homework; investigate to be sure their claims are accurate.

Don't Get Hustled!

Perhaps the best word of advice we can give you is this: *Don't do any work for anyone else for free* (unless you have a long, pre-existing and productive relationship with that person). If you're a member of the WGA, you are forbidden to do free work for producers, and signatory producers are prohibited from asking you to. But in the course of meeting people in Hollywood, you will inevitably come across would-be producers who have a killer idea they'd like you to work on with them. The pitch is something like this: "Listen, you sound like someone I'd like to work with. I've got this great story (fill in the story) and I have a hot actor (or financier, distributor, director) who is really, really interested. And I have half the money in place. But I need a screenplay (or treatment) to clinch the deal. So won't you sit down and write it for me? I can't pay you anything now, but we can work out a good back-end arrangement." Back-end means you don't get paid until the movie is actually financed or, more often, actually produced. This is a great thing if the film is already greenlit, and many stars and top directors will take lower upfront fees if they're guaranteed a high percentage of the film's earnings. But what it almost always means with these hustlers is that you'll never see a dime, because their contacts are tenuous or nonexistent. They're all hoping to come up with something they can sell, and they're only too happy to ask you to spend months of your life giving it to them. They will present themselves as extremely real, well-connected and on the verge of huge success, and you *will* be very tempted. They seem bright, honest, aggressive…what if this is your chance? *It isn't, ever.* If you agree to write something for them based on their story, they and not you will control the rights to it because they own the underlying material, and so you can't even try to sell the script when their contacts dry up and the house of cards they're building falls apart. Instead, spend the time writing your own screenplay.

The same goes for doing free rewrites for producers who have optioned or bought your screenplay (again, this is expressly prohibited for WGA writers and signatory producers, but that doesn't mean they won't occasionally ask). Usually a purchase price will include a set of rewrites and a polish as part of the deal. But if a rewrite isn't in your contract, don't do it unless you're paid. You'll feel guilty and obligated—after all, they did pay you something, and you want to be a team player—but you must resist. Hollywood often seems to run on guilt. But if a producer is for real, he'll pay for any additional work. If he doesn't want to, then be grateful for what you've already made, politely tell him you'd love to rewrite it if in the future he's willing to pay you to do so, and move on. Your time and your skills have value—so value them.

FILM SCHOOLS

It may seem odd to include film schools in a chapter on marketing, but in fact they are trade schools and geared to help you enter the business. Film schools came into prominence in the 1970s when a group of alumni suddenly hit it big. The success of Francis Ford Coppola (UCLA), Steven Spielberg (Cal State Long Beach), George Lucas (USC) and many others put film schools on the map. Today, the competition to get into them is fierce. The number of schools offering degrees has doubled and doubled again, but so have the number of people wanting to attend. Most major film schools have hundreds of applications for only a few dozen positions. A list of film schools is located in Appendix D, but on everyone's list of top films schools are:

> UCLA (University of California, Los Angeles)
> USC (University of Southern California)
> NYU (New York University)
> Columbia University
> Chapman University
> Florida State University

We used to include AFI (the American Film Institute) on this list, but recently it's been so wracked by staff and faculty turnover and internal problems that we can only now recommend it with the warning that you check it out very carefully and be sure you know with whom you'll be studying and what you'll be getting out of the experience. Come to think of it, however, that's not bad advice no matter where you're thinking of applying. We also, perhaps immodestly, would recommend the writing programs where we teach, at the University of California, Riverside, and the University of Wyoming.

Most major film schools offer an MFA (Master of Fine Arts) in directing, criticism and screenwriting (each usually as a separate degree program). These degrees take two to three years to earn. Film school can be expensive, but it offers screenwriters an opportunity to spend several years perfecting their craft by studying with other screenwriters; at the better schools, these are almost without exception seasoned industry professionals. Film school graduates do have an edge in Hollywood. Not only do agents actively look for new graduates, but graduates tend to be well-connected, as their years in school are also spent networking with current and future players in the industry. Film school isn't a replacement for talent and luck (in fact, you'll need both just to get in to any of the five schools listed above), but if you get into a film school, your road to success may be a lot easier.

FINAL THOUGHTS

That's Showbiz There's an old saying that screenwriters succeed not by ability, but by persistence. They don't fail, they quit. And most of them do quit, even after going to film school, figuring (correctly) that there must be easier ways of making a living. It's tough; no matter how hard you work at it, rejection is an integral part of being a screenwriter. Lots and lots of rejection. You may write ten or fifteen scripts for every one you sell, and you'll probably have that one rejected by dozens of companies before it finds a home. And that's only if you manage to get an agent—the rejection process starts long before you get that far. One reader will call you brilliant, the next will label you an amateur, without any apparent rhyme or reason. You'll have to learn to deal with it and keep going. There are two reasons a screenplay doesn't sell; the script isn't good enough or the script can't find its market. The blame for the former is the writer's alone, of course. But even though blame for the latter can be laid at many doorsteps, it's still up to the writer to advance his or her own career and see that the script gets to the proper people. A writer in Hollywood must be part artist, part real-estate salesman. First you must build the property, and then you must sell it.

For a list of books on how to market your script see Appendix B.

EXERCISE

Write a query letter to an agent, pitching yourself and your screenplay. Read it aloud to your class and see how your fellow students respond to it.

16

The Pitch
"Godzilla" Meets "Titanic"

"... it's totally high-concept! The big crazy lizard wrecks the ship in an act of insane rage—but then he falls in love with this beautiful chick who's actually a herpetologist—what? No, it doesn't mean she has herpes, it means she studies reptiles—and together they end up saving everybody—even though the lizard dies facing off against the sharks...or DOES HE?! It's four-quadrant with huge tentpole and sequel potential!" Okay...so what does that all mean? "High concept" means there's a clear, simple premise that will hook a large audience. Obviously the writer is drawing upon two big, well-known movies to sell his idea. "Four-quadrant" means it will appeal to every "quadrant" of the audience: old, young, male and female. A "tentpole" is a huge blockbuster that may support the studio even if all its other, less high-concept movies fail. And obviously if it's that successful, it should be designed to spawn a line of sequels. But let's take a step back and look at what we're doing here.

"Pitching" means going to a producer's office and telling them a story idea you hope they'll buy. It's selling ideas rather than scripts. If a producer likes your spec script, they might invite you in for a meet-and-greet and ask you to pitch a few of your story ideas. If the producer likes an idea, she might buy it and hire you to write it. However, sometimes the producer buys it and hires another writer to write it. Pitching is a common way to get a job in television, but it only accounts for a small percent of movie sales; for information on pitching for television, see Chapter 17). Even with such a small percentage of sales based on pitches, taking meetings and pitching is still a regular practice for Hollywood writers.

TO PITCH OR NOT TO PITCH

There are basically two schools of thought about pitching. School One: It's a worthless waste of time and energy that could be better spent actually writing a script, instead of talking about what you'd like to write. Some writers feel that talking about their story actually drains the psychic energy from it, so that it becomes stale and flaccid before there's a chance to capture its essential juices on paper. School Two: Pitching is an essential way to try to sell more story ideas than you'd ever have time to sit down and actually spec. Also, far from draining your story, telling it again and again helps to refine it, and forces you to address problems that may arise. Hey, it sure didn't hurt Homer; the *Iliad* and *Odyssey* where both spoken poems before they were ever written down.

We come down in the latter camp. Yeah, we know that many writers are shy, delicate creatures who may rupture an artery if put in a room and forced to talk to people. They're wonders on the page, but incapable of condensing their long narratives into easily digested verbal presentations. We know many producers who feel that writers are often the worst people to pitch their own stories for that very reason. But that doesn't change the fact that pitching is a valuable tool in a competitive business where every advantage must be pursued. And if you're hoping to write for television you simply cannot avoid pitching, because it's how that market works (see Chapter 17). So no matter what your reservations, our advice is to get over them, suck it up and get out there. Here's why:

More Irons in the Fire

It takes a minimum of several months to complete a screenplay worth sending out. The most prolific writers rarely manage as many as four scripts a year; most are happy if they complete two. But most also have many other good ideas in reserve, and Hollywood buys ideas, as well as finished screenplays. If you don't want to sit on those ideas until you have time to write them (some time in the next decade) then there's only one way to see if someone might want to buy them. You have to go out and pitch. In fact, there are those (like the legendary Bob Kosberg) who do nothing but sell pitches to studios, attaching themselves as producers, while farming the stories out to other writers who actually write the screenplays. Such pitch-meisters may sell up to a dozen stories a year. So, if you're good at it, pitching can be the most time-efficient way to get paid for your stories. Of course, as a writer you'd probably want to write the story you're pitching yourself, and while a pitch usually doesn't sell for as much as a completed script—it's still just an idea that the script may or may not be able to deliver—it's nice to be writing for real money right up front.

Know and Be Known

It's important to make yourself known to those who are in a position to buy your material and to advance your career. Film is a social business—who you know and who knows you are important. So if a producer or development executive can attach a friendly, intelligent person to that otherwise faceless screenplay submission, you're in a stronger position to be remembered and considered. Most agents want their writers to have a pitch to go out with along with a new spec screenplay submission so that if the producer likes the writing, but doesn't go for the script, he or she might buy another story from the same writer. Some agents have their writers actually pitch their completed screenplays while submitting them, to ensure that the busy producer or development exec will remember this particular project and writer.

Who Wants What?

By getting out and meeting people, you'll also get a much better sense of what the buyers are looking for. You need to follow your own muse and be true to your personal vision, but if you want to sell, you also need to know what people want to buy. There are trends and currents in the business, a general sense that "teen comedies are going to be hot next year" or "big-budget action films are losing steam." You can tap into these trends only by talking with people who swim in these currents. You might learn that you'd be better off developing that romantic comedy and letting that period drama you were about to spend six months writing sit for a while. You'll also certainly get a better sense of the individual tastes of the people you're meeting for future reference.

Say It Again, Sam

Pitching is a great way to refine your outline. When you tell somebody a story, you quickly become aware of what feels essential and entertaining and what feels like it's off the point, dragging or slowing the story down. You may find that you never seem to recount scenes or whole sections that you've put into your outline; if so, there's a good chance you won't need those scenes or sections in your screenplay. You may discover that you need to know more about your story's world, or that you don't really know why your characters are doing what they're doing. When you tell someone a story, character motivations or their absence become much more obvious. So do problems with theme, event sequences, even lines of dialogue. A good producer or executive will often ask hard questions that you may not have thought about. That doesn't mean you won't need to answer them sooner or later. Far from draining the energy from your story, pitching it can hone, reinforce and revitalize it in ways you might never have accomplished had you never gone and tried it out on somebody.

Don't Waste Your Time

The worst waste of time for a screenwriter is writing a screenplay no one wants. You probably don't want to hear this, but it's valuable advice. If you eventually find that no one seems interested in the story you're pitching—because it actually isn't that interesting a story—you'll have saved yourself months of time you would have spent writing it. We don't mean that you should lose confidence after the first "no thanks"; take it around to everyone who'll agree to hear it. But if you're getting nowhere—especially if the reasons for your story being rejected seem consistent from meeting to meeting—then you should seriously think about pursuing a different story. There's an old expression which goes, "If everyone tells you you're drunk, you're drunk."

Of course, those who've failed to respond to your story may all be wrong, and if you truly believe in it so strongly that you simply can't let go of it, then you should write it anyway. It may come across much better on the page than in the pitch. You may not be capable of pitching as well as you write. But you need to hear what the people to whom you're pitching are saying. They are your buyers and, if they aren't buying, you need to re-evaluate what you're selling. You may resent this paragraph now, thinking we're crassly telling you to abandon your original vision. We're not. But the fact remains that your screenplay must appeal to a very limited group of people and, if it doesn't, after all the hard work you've done to write it, it will simply end up occupying space in a drawer or on your computer hard drive. We promise you that at that point you'll remember this section and wish you'd paid attention.

One Is the Loneliest Number

Last, but not least: writing is the loneliest part of the filmmaking business. You are the only one who sits in a room by yourself, month after month, trying to create a new world that, hopefully, will be translated into a movie. If you want to feel connected to the world outside—the one you've chosen to live in—and to the people who may actually bring your written world to the screen, then you need to get out and meet them.

GETTING IN THE DOOR

Without an agent, getting a pitch is hard, just as it's hard to get a producer to read your script without an agent or some other meaningful introduction. Your agent, if you have one, will set up the pitch with the executive highest up the ladder that is possible to reach (see Chapter 15 on getting an agent). If you don't have an agent, however, all is not lost. You just have to look a few rungs lower on the ladder. Do some homework: learn which companies seem to be producing which kinds of movies. By companies, we mean production companies, not the major studios themselves. Studio executives usually only take pitches from well-known writers with whom they already want to do business. Production companies—often with studio deals and offices on the studio lots—are where most new material is found and generated. So look for the names of these production companies in the credits of recent movies that are in the ballpark of your story type. Get a subscription to IMDBPro.com or www.donedealpro.com and learn who is the production company's "Director of Development" or "Creative Executive." Disregard anyone with a "Vice President" or "President" title, unless they're the only one listed at the company with a "development" or "creative" tag. They're usually too high up the ladder to consider meeting with an unrepresented writer. What you want is someone young, hungry and accessible.

Once you've got a name, do some more homework: what else has the company produced? Lots of info is available at the above sites and elsewhere on the internet. Visit last year's online archives from *Variety* and *The Hollywood Reporter* and *http://www.deadline.com/hollywood/* (as of this moment—these sites are bound to change, so stay current by doing your own searches) for references to the company and to the person you're hoping to meet. See if that individual has expressed a particular story preference in print, or if the person's boss has. Knowledge is power, so learn all you can about your prospective buyer. Usually, this will be a bright twenty-something who is working at his first or second job, and who is full of energy and passion to find the undiscovered project that will impress his boss and make his career.

When you've done your homework, call that person and see if he will meet with you. Your phone call should be brief and to the point. Let's say you're approaching John Smith, the Director of Development at Hot Tamale Pictures, on the Foxx lot. You've found his email and/or phone number and are ready to get in touch. Email is the easiest and least traumatic way to go about it, if you're timid. But calling has its advantages: When talking to a real person (you), the secretary or assistant on the other end of the line (them) can't simply hit "delete" and may in fact display a glimmer of humanity by giving you a chance. First of all, don't call at 9:00 a.m. No one gets to the office in Hollywood before 10:00. Then they're usually in meetings until around noon. Lunch is between 1:00 and 3:00, so call between noon and one, or after three. A secretary or assistant will answer. The conversation will go something like this:

> SECRETARY
> Hello, Hot Tamale Pictures, please hold.

(five minutes go by)

> SECRETARY
> Hello, can I help you?

> YOU
> Yes, my name is Jim Beam. I'd like to speak with John Smith, please.

> SECRETARY
> Will he know what this is regarding?

(Uh-oh, the first roadblock. If you're old enough, you suddenly remember old *Saturday Night Live* routines with David Spade as the obnoxious assistant: "And you are...?" That's okay, just take a deep breath and continue.)

> YOU
> No. But I'm a screenwriter, and I'd like to talk with him about setting up a pitch meeting.

(If you were referred to him personally by someone you know, state that now, as well).

```
              SECRETARY
    I see. Please hold.
```

(Then, after another five minutes, you'll either be connected, or asked to leave your number so John can call you back. The latter is more likely. At the end of the day, or the end of the week, after all his more important calls have been made, John will call.)

```
              YOU
        (answering the phone)
    Hello, Jim Beam here.

              JOHN
    Hi, this is John Smith from Hot Tamale
    Pictures. Returning your call.

              YOU
    Oh, hi, John!
```

(Yes, call him by his first name; only a total newbie would say "Mr. Smith.")

```
              YOU
    The reason I called is that I loved Hot
    Tamales' last film, The Big Hoo-Hah, and
    I have a story I'd like to pitch along
    those lines.

              JOHN
    Oh, really? Do you have an agent?
```

(Another, perhaps fatal roadblock. But not necessarily. You knew he'd ask, so you're prepared. As prepared as you can be. Contain that nervous chuckle and push on.)

```
              YOU
    No, not at the moment. But I do know
    (fill in the blank if there's anyone even
    conceivably known to this person) who
    thought I should bring my pitch in to
    you; he/she speaks most highly of you.
```

(This is, of course, probably a lie. He knows it, you know it, but it's still a nice touch. Try not to make it too much of a lie, since he may call you on it.)

```
                      YOU
         John, I know you must be very busy, but
         I'd love to have a chance to come in and
         pitch you my story. I really believe it's
         something Hot Tamale might like.
```

At this point, John will either tell you they don't take unsolicited pitches, or he'll ask you for a brief description of your story. Have this prepared, written out in front of you if you need to. Don't stammer, denigrate it, mumble or make excuses. Keep it to one sentence, two at the most, and make it sound like the greatest thing he's going to hear this year, or any other. If you sound intelligent, reasonable and enthusiastic, without being desperate, John will chew his eraser for a second or two, then probably decide he might as well meet you—who knows, you might really have something, and it'll help fill his calendar. If you have a choice, schedule your appointment early. Avoid late afternoon, when John will be tired, behind schedule and cranky because he's anxious to get out of there. Most likely, you'll be given a 5:30 p.m. slot.

Okay, you've got your appointment, next Thursday. Time to get to work. Although John may have slotted you in for half an hour or even forty-five minutes, in fact you'll have about ten minutes of grace time (roughly equivalent to the first ten pages rule, see Chapter 10) to catch his interest. After that, he'll either find a way to excuse himself and get rid of you, or he'll want to hear more. What you need to come up with are two versions of your story: a short pitch to hook him, and a longer pitch, richer in detail, in case the short one works and you get that far.

How Do You Get to Carnegie Hall? Practice, Practice!

Before you go to your meeting, be sure to practice your pitch on everyone who will tolerate you, friends, family, and especially people who are in the business and can give you informed opinions. Don't be defensive: listen. Are you taking too long to get to the point? Are you confusing them? Are you maintaining eye contact and a confident sense of your story, or are you

---

WAR STORIES

Robin

When I set up my first pitch meeting, my wife insisted that I put on a suit and tie so I'd look professional. I encountered a producer in frayed denim shorts, a tank top, and flip-flops. Needless to say, I was the one who looked unprofessional. So don't overdress. Wear what you feel comfortable in, unless that includes a suit and tie, in which case, just wear some jeans, a polo or T-shirt, and maybe cowboy boots or scuffed Oxfords. Baseball caps are considered an acceptable accessory.

mumbling into your navel? Does your story make sense? Are your characters interesting and consistent? Are there plot holes, where the logic falls apart? Try to locate and solve as many of these problems as you can (in effect, you're re-outlining your story). You won't catch them all, but you'll greatly improve your pitch going in. By the way, if you find that you keep losing your place or having to backtrack to fill in details you forgot to mention, it's a good sign that your scenes don't grow naturally and inevitably out of each other, that your story may be too episodic (see Chapters 7 and 8), or that you simply don't know your story well enough to pitch it yet. Don't go into a meeting unless and until you know your pitch cold.

Anatomy of a Pitch Meeting

Pitch meetings only seem informal. In fact, they are ritualized performances that follow roughly the same script every time. First of all, you want to look right. Writers in Hollywood dress with studied casualness.

Next, be punctual, in case John is ready to see you at the appointed time (he won't be, but miracles do happen), so plan to get there in plenty of time to enter the studio lot and find parking. John or his assistant will have told you on the phone how to get onto the studio lot, and that they'll have a pass waiting for you at the guard gate. However, they may forget or the computers may be down, and the guard will have to call in and confirm your appointment. The guard will hand you a pass and tell you where to park. Since you're a nobody, you'll probably have to park in a visitor area a good ten-minute walk away from the office you're going to, so plan for it.

Once you arrive at the proper office and identify yourself, an assistant—perhaps the one you spoke with—will tell you that John's running just a few minutes late, but will be right with you. You'll be offered a seat in the waiting area and something to drink. By all means accept it, even if you're not thirsty. It'll help calm your nerves and give you something to do while you wait. But keep it simple. Don't ask for a can of peach nectar, just a Coke or water or coffee. But don't drink it all, keep some for the meeting. For one thing, you don't want the call of nature suddenly interrupting you. More importantly, your drink is a prop. More on this in a moment.

After between ten and twenty-five minutes (depending on how important you're perceived to be), either an assistant or John himself will appear, apologize for the delay, then lead you back to his office. Usually John's assistant will join you. This person is there to take notes and will rarely speak. Don't let it get to you. Take a comfortable seat that isn't facing a window, so you won't have to squint to read John's expression as you tell your story. Avoid the deep leather couch, because you'll sink in and feel silly.

There are a requisite four or five minutes of chitchat, during which you praise the view from his office as well as the last film Hot Tamale produced, and John apologizes for the messy state of his office (they're in the process of moving) and finds out a little more about you. You might want to ask (if you've learned a bit about him) how he likes the change from Cold Fish Productions, where he used to work. He'll be flattered that you've followed his career, such as it is, and may be more receptive. Then he'll say something like, "So what have you got?" It's time to pitch. Start off with your short one.

The Short Pitch   A short pitch clocks in at not more than ten minutes. There are differences of opinion as to how a writer should approach this. Some feel that you should just dive into some early, exciting moment in the story, without any hint as to where you're going; the mystery itself will engage interest. Others, including the authors of this book, feel that producers and executives take pitches because they want to know what your story is and anything you can do to help them follow the narrative is a good thing. So we advocate beginning your pitch by telling them what genre it's in, and perhaps identifying a couple of other (successful) films that it might resemble, as per the example that led off this chapter—but obviously better thought out. This may seem almost cartoonishly hackneyed, but it's how producers generally lock onto a new idea. For instance: "My story, *High Tide*, is a futuristic action-thriller set in the world of the Coast Guard's drug interdiction operations in the Caribbean. It's kind of like *The French Connection* meets *To Have and Have Not*." (These are very old references and if you can find more recent ones, use them—for instance, you might try: "It's kind of like *Avatar* meets *Fast Five*, set in an alien paradise a lot like the Caribbean." But stick to old classics if they're the best comparisons you have.)

Then go into a brief, visual description of your exciting opening, complete with a brief, visual description of your exciting hero, antagonist and central conflict. It's okay to refer to major stars that you think might be perfect for the role—especially if your research has told you that this company is looking for a "vehicle" for a certain movie star. You'd never want to do this in your screenplay, but in a conversational pitch it can be useful. Then outline the general course of the story, stopping to highlight two or three more of your most exciting scenes with a brief, visual description (getting the point?), and perhaps a few cool lines of dialogue, if you've got them.

When you pitch the story you should be passionate. There is no rule that says you have to stay seated; some writers get up and pace the room as they sell the story. They are moved by the spirit of the characters as the story's dramatic tension manifests itself within them. It's a performance. Some writers in Hollywood actually take acting classes so that they can learn how to tell a wonderful exciting story. Whichever way you tell the story, the one thing you don't want to be is boring.

Until you become practiced at pitching, you're going to be nervous, and you may get lost in your story. You should always have a small crib sheet with a list of a few key words written down so you don't lose the thread of your story. By the way, this is where your drink may come in handy. If you do lose your place, pause to clear your throat and take a sip of your Coke or coffee—just enough to recapture the thread and get back on track. Or, your throat may just be dry.

Throughout, maintain eye contact with the person or people to whom you're pitching. First of all, you're telling them a story and want to keep them interested. Secondly, you can see if their attention is flagging, if their eyes are drifting off to that report they still need to write, or if they're checking their watches in anticipation of clocking out. If that's what you see, you're being too windy—and probably you've gone longer than ten minutes. So cut out anything but the most exciting, salient parts of your story and try to reel them back in. Then bring it to a dramatic, satisfyingly emotional conclusion—emotional in that you focus on how your central characters end up. You may also want to include some reference to the thematic point of the story and how your protagonist's journey exemplifies it.

Here is an example of one writer's pitch that worked. In this case, he dove right in.

```
          JOHN THE PRODUCER
     (on the phone.)
Hold my calls. Thanks.


          WRITER
We come up on a Porsche. In the passenger
seat is Brad (Johnny Depp). The driver is
a woman who's not good enough for him-
-too many Abraham Lincoln moles. He says
"Shall we do it?" She agrees, starts up
the car and drives into a huge, gated
estate. Inside we find the library and
the girl's old fart father behind a tank
of a desk. He asks his daughter to step
outside, he wants to have a private word
with Brad. Once she leaves, he says,
"You're not going to marry my daughter."
Brad argues, "I've asked her to marry me,
she loves me." The old man takes 20,000
dollars out of the desk and spreads it
out in front of Brad; "You're not going
to marry my daughter." Brad's totally
insulted; "She's old enough, we don't
need your permission." Another 20,000
is added to the pile. Brad is more
righteous, "How dare you sir! You can't
buy love!" The old man shoves another
heap of bills onto the pile; "You're not
going to marry my daughter." Brad looks
at the mountain of bills, glances out to
the cobblestone drive, thinks a moment
and says, "Throw in the Porsche." Cut to
the autumn leaves flying as Brad Hawk
pulls out of town in the Porsche.


The phone rings. John answers. The writer waits five
minutes.
```

                        JOHN
            Sorry about that. Go on.

                        WRITER
            This is a movie about a handsome kid
            who's got the perfect con ... he goes
            into a town, finds the richest girl, gets
            her to fall in love with him, makes sure
            the parents hate him and gets paid off
            not to marry into the family. It's *Don
            Juan DeMarco* meets *The Music Man*.

The phone rings again. John curses, then answers. The
Writer knows he's hooked. He doesn't mind waiting five
minutes. The call ends.

                        JOHN
            Sorry, crisis on the set. Go on.

                        WRITER
            Okay, so Brad's in the islands,
            enjoying his loot. Pool bar--Oprah's on
            television. Suddenly he sees a composite
            picture of himself and Oprah interviewing
            his last "love" victims. They're all
            happy that they knew him, for they all
            learned about men and love through him.
            But they want his nuts. He realizes the
            game is up and decides to pull one last,
            major con before retirement. He has to
            find the one place in the country where
            the women aren't that attractive, their
            fathers are wealthy and no one watches
            Oprah. The answer Stanford. His goal, the
            daughter of the President of the United
            States.

The phone rings. John, upset, answers. The Writer waits
one minute. John slams down the phone and yells to his
assistant.

                        JOHN
            Debbie, will you please hold my calls!
            Sorry about that. Go on.

John leans forward. The assistant scribbles furiously.

                    WRITER
At Stanford he starts the con ... it's
working perfectly. It takes no time for
the President's ugly daughter to fall
madly in love with him. He's invited
to the White House and begins to turn
the family against him--he makes a pass
at the first lady, the brother and the
downstairs maid. But, back at school,
there's a problem--he keeps seeing
a pretty graduate student who seems
to be following him (Secret Service,
Reporter?). He finally confronts her and
she admits that she saw him on Oprah. But
she doesn't want to turn him in. Instead
she wants to write her graduate thesis
on the mating habits of the American
Male, with Brad as the star specimen. Or
else she'll bust him. He agrees. The con
continues, just as beautifully. But it's
not so easy. Brad is beginning to fall in
love for the first time in his life with
none other than the winsome grad student.
He tries to tell her how he feels, but
all he can manage are his trite, old
lines. Which she puts into her thesis.
The payoff day arrives. But the President
says, "You're an S.O.B., son, I'm an
S.O.B. ... welcome to the family. Oh,
yeah--and if you let my baby girl down,
I'll kill you." The Secret Service are
assigned to make sure Brad won't run, his
bank account is emptied and his pretty
Porsche impounded.

The phone rings again. John glares out the door and
ignores it.

                    WRITER
There's nothing Brad can do but go
through with the nuptials. After one
last attempt to tell his grad student
sweetheart how he feels, he apologizes
for his actions and heads for the church.
It's a huge church, thousands of people
are there. He walks out in front of the
crowd, there are TV cameras and klieg

> lights and then Oprah Winfrey struts out,
> turns to the cameras and says, "Ladies
> and gentleman, we caught him!" From the
> back of the auditorium, the President
> gives Brad the finger. Brad faces the
> music.

The phone rings in the outside office, finally.

>   WRITER
> Two hours later, Brad finds himself
> penniless, carless and dateless as he
> attempts to hitchhike out of town. He's
> cold and tired, when a small V.W. bug
> pulls up. It's the graduate student. And
> for the first time, he's able to express
> his love; "Love is infatuation with
> knowledge. If you know someone, know all
> of their idiosyncrasies and shortcomings
> and you're still infatuated, then you're
> in love." The grad student admits that
> she, too, must be in love. They ride off
> into the sunset together.

At this point, given this description of events, John will either want to hear more, or ask you when you can come back and pitch to his boss. He really liked it. And you're really going to meet his boss. You're halfway there.

The Long Pitch If he wants to hear more, this is where your longer pitch comes in. You should have a reasonably clear idea of all the major scenes, characters and thematic issues, so you can pick up on any part of it that he chooses to ask about. But this is still just a pitch, so if John asks something you really can't answer, don't try. You'll start digging a hole for yourself that you can't get out of. Just tell him you haven't worked that out yet, but you will.

The Real World

More likely, after your short pitch, he'll thank you very much and usher you out with the sad news that this just isn't for them, or they've got something too similar in the works, perhaps add a cruelly optimistic promise to talk to those higher up, and they'll get back to you (they won't). If he's ending the meeting, don't try to keep it going. It's over, and you lost. (Yes, meetings are won and lost, as Lynda Obst points out in her essential, insider account *Hello, He Lied*.) So don't overstay your welcome; leave John with the sense that you gave it a good shot, and maybe he'd like to hear what else you come up with in the future. Don't drag it out and annoy him.

Bill

Years ago I was at Greenblatt's Delicatessen on Sunset Boulevard, when I heard a deep, resonant voice I had heard many times before. I turned to find the actor Billy Dee Williams standing beside me ordering a sandwich. I seized the moment and said, "Hi, I'm a UCLA Screenwriting student and I just finished a new screenplay." He gave a polite "go away" smile. He wasn't interested. Then I pitched, "It's a modern version of *Othello* using Chicago cops." He smiled and said, "I'm sorry, but I don't . . ." Then he stopped, thought for a second, and finished, " . . . I'd like to read that!"

Some writers like to bring in a second pitch or third pitch, just in case the first one gets shot down right away (such as when you've just opened your mouth and they interrupt with, "Sorry, we're doing one just like that"). This is a good idea, if you've got another pitch (or pitches) of equal quality. But if it's just a rough idea, don't pitch it, because you probably won't sell it on the odds, and this is what they'll remember you by. Also, don't bring in half a dozen stories to shop at one meeting, because then it doesn't seem you're invested in any one of them. Your excitement and commitment to your story is their first clue that it might be worth theirs. Don't confuse them. (This does not apply to pitching to a television show. In a television pitch, four to seven ideas are the norm. For more information on pitching to a television show, see Chapter 17.)

Once you've answered their questions, ask them if there's anything else. If not, then thank them, and ask if there are any other particular kinds of stories for which this company is currently looking. Often they'll just say, "Oh, just something good," but once in a while you'll learn a very specific need. (John might say something like, "Well, we are looking for an action vehicle for Jessica Chastain—she'd like to do something like *La Femme Nikita* with us.") If you just happen to have such a script or pitch, then tell them about it; they'll want to read it or set up another pitch meeting. If not, shake hands, thank them again, and leave. You're not getting anything else out of them. Even if they intend to buy your pitch (which wouldn't happen immediately unless the president of the company was there), they probably won't tell you. They'll want to talk about it and get back to you.

Before you go, you'll probably be asked if you have anything written down, such as a treatment (a five- to fifteen-page prose description of the story). Again, there are two schools of thought as to whether you should leave one, if in fact you have written one. Some people feel that if the pitch went well, it's better to leave your animated, verbal impression unmarred by something that isn't a finished screenplay, and can only suffer by comparison. Others believe that it's better for the higher-ups in the company to get your story in your own words, rather than the rough story notes taken by the silent assistant in the meeting. It's a toss-up as far as we're concerned. If you feel you've got a terrific treatment written up, then you might want to leave it. If all you have are rough notes, then you probably shouldn't. But there's no right or wrong.

Once you've gone home, take a moment to jot John a letter thanking him for taking the time to meet with you to discuss your story; be sure to include the title and one-sentence story description. Then send it by certified mail. Keep a copy for yourself. This is partly to remind him of who you are, since he hears about twenty pitches a week. It's partly to remind you of where you've pitched which story. But it also creates a clear, dated paper trail that will protect you in case the company you've pitched to "borrows" your story and you decide to sue. It will also hint to them that you know enough that it wouldn't be a good idea for them to steal your idea in the first place. This hardly ever happens—honestly. Overt story theft is in fact quite rare in Hollywood—most companies are far too wary of litigation—but it does happen once in a while.

FINAL THOUGHTS

Life's a Pitch   Pitching can create possibilities, and in the end, possibilities are where realities begin. Pitching doesn't always work. In fact, most of the time it doesn't, but screenwriters should always be ready to pitch their exciting, wonderful ideas. Pitching can open the doors. At the very least, it gets you out of your own door, into the life of the industry.

EXERCISES

1. Come up with a short, ten-minute pitch of your favorite movie. When the movie is reduced to a short pitch, what are the important points? Which lines, which events, which moments hold the story together?

2. Rehearse a pitch of your story. Don't memorize it. This will only make it sound rehearsed. Instead, allow yourself to sell the story, as if you were telling a friend about an exciting event that just happened.

PART FIVE

ALTERNATIVES

WRITING FOR TELEVISION

WRITING WEBISODES

WRITING FOR VIDEO GAMES

17

Writing for Television
Down the (inter)Tube(s)

Let's not sugarcoat it: getting a job writing for a television show is not easy. The jobs are few and the competition is fierce; in fact, there are far more writers trying to break into television than into features. Yet writing for television can seem less daunting (writing a half-hour or hour script rather than a two-hour feature) and more lucrative: a working TV writer can have a regular gig with a high salary and attractive benefits. However, there is a price. The pace and pressure are relentless, and because there are often so many writers involved in the process of developing each produced episode, it can sometimes (depending on the kind of show) bear only a passing resemblance to the original writer's script.

There are two types of television writers: staff and freelance. Staff writers are full-time employees who work all or part of a show's season and receive a weekly salary. Their title can be Staff Writer (sometimes called Term Writer), Story Editor, Associate Producer, Producer or Executive Producer. Freelance writers are self-employed writers who sell spec scripts or are hired by a show to write individual episodes. They may write episodes for several different shows in the same season. Ordinarily a television show hires between eight and twelve staff writers (from term to producer) per season. Staff writers write the vast majority of episodes but sometimes they also hire freelance writers to write individual episodes. This means that there are only a few hundred jobs available. Thousands of writers fight for their piece of this very small pie.

The strong competition for jobs is well justified when we look at salary. Staff writers earn from $5,000 to $10,000 a week (some who have reached the executive producer level make a great deal more). On top of this weekly salary, the writer sometimes gets a payment for each episode written; that fee currently stands at about $18,000 for one episode of a sitcom and $27,000 per episode of an hour-length show. There can also be residuals. Residuals are a type of royalty payment a television writer receives every time an episode airs. If a show goes into syndication, the residuals through the years can add up to more than the original fee. Landing a job with this kind of salary requires a long-term commitment, setting goals, the stamina to write every day and, of course, talent.

There are three forms of television writing (sometimes called teleplays) that we'll cover: sitcoms (short for situation comedies), hour-length dramas, and movies of the week (known as MOWs). We will not cover skit writing (such as for *Saturday Night Live* or other late night shows that include sketch comedy) or writing for soap operas or reality television. At this writing, reality show writers are not members of the WGA (for more on the WGA see Chapter 15), although the union is hoping that someday they will be included. With soap operas only head writers are members of the WGA. The head writers decide on the storylines for the entire season and then the episodes are divvied up between a throng of non-WGA episode writers who are paid only a few thousand dollars to knock out scripts. Skit writing depends more on writing gags than formal storytelling, the subject of this book. And besides, most of these writers got their jobs by being successful writers in other fields (e.g., as playwrights, standup comedians, hour-length television writers, and so on).

In Hollywood, everyone has a story about how they were "discovered." From chance meetings, to knowing the right person, to wild coincidence, each story is really about being in the right place at the right time. Unfortunately, luck does play an important role in getting a job, but there are many things writers can do to increase the chances of luck invading their lives. Louis Pasteur, the great French chemist and microbiologist, said, "Chance favors the prepared mind." Preparing for a writing job in television means learning how to write "spec" scripts (written on speculation), moving to Hollywood, getting an agent, writing more spec scripts and pitching.

WRITING A SPEC

The first step in landing a job is to write several great spec scripts (remember "spec" is short for speculation, see Chapter 1). Specs are the writer's calling card; they show that the writer has talent. Writing one spec is never enough. It takes several specs to learn how to write for television in the first place and perhaps many more before agents begin paying attention. Spec scripts rarely sell; they are written primarily to prove that you can write. They are the television writer's audition.

Spec scripts rarely sell because producers seldom respond well to a spec for their own show. The reason is that the producers (who are the writers) are very possessive about their particular show. They feel they know everything there is to know about their characters and situations and so they're hyper-critical. Therefore, even if a spec writer thinks she's caught the exact tone of the show and voices of the characters, the producers will automatically sense something slightly askew, or see that the spec story is at variance with a direction they intend to take their show in future episodes, so they'll reject the spec. Instead, producers want to see a spec script for a different show, one in which they are not invested, and therefore can read without prejudice or preconceptions.

While there are occasional lucky exceptions, it's not uncommon for struggling TV writers to pound out between ten and thirty spec scripts before they get their first job. Here are a few things to keep in mind when writing a spec:

They Are Not Looking for a Pilot (or Maybe They Are) A pilot is the first episode of a brand-new series. The conventional wisdom used to be that writing spec pilots was a waste of time. For one thing, a spec pilot is a poor example of how well you can write for an existing show, because the producers can't compare it to anything they've read or seen. For another, no matter how good it is, agents and producers are usually not interested in pilots written by beginners. New shows are usually developed and written only by writers who have paid their dues with years of experience, or who are being courted by networks because they've had great success in standup comedy or features. After you've worked your way up from staff writer to story editor to producer, then you can think about creating a pilot. So for now, write specs for successful shows that are already on the air. HOWEVER: Partly due to a number of studio initiatives and the spread of competitions allowing for pilot entries, in recent years a number of spec pilots scripts have in fact been bought, if not actually produced and/or brought to completion. Ideas have also been generated by web blogs and posts (for instance, *$#*! My Dad Says* was a comedy series developed from Justin Halpern's hilarious Twitter feed. It only lasted one season or so, but still).

Pick a Winner When you write a spec, choose only those well-known, successful, established shows that earn good ratings and critical acclaim, and are going to be around for a while. Occasionally writers create specs for hot new shows, hoping that agents and producers have not yet been inundated by scripts for them and are not yet sick of reading them (spec scripts arrive in Hollywood by the truckload). This isn't a bad idea if you already have several great specs for more popular shows, but be assured that the producers of any new show already have an arsenal of scripts to last at least one and probably two seasons, so you're not really much more likely to sell it to them than to a more established show. Above all avoid shows that have gone off the air. This means that those wonderful *Seinfeld*, *Cheers* or *Frasier* specs you wrote are now worthless.

You know a show is popular when, at the proverbial water cooler the next morning, everyone is discussing last night's episode. The national water cooler test for television shows is called the Nielsen rating. Nielsen numbers are listed by rating point and share. For example, a show will have a rating of 11.9 and a share of 20. One rating point is equal to 1 percent of the total number of U.S. households that have TVs (in other words, everyone). So if a show has a rating of 11.9 that means that of all the households in the United States (approximately 103 million of them) 11.9 percent watched that particular show. Share is the percentage of households that have their TV sets turned on and tuned to that particular show (not all households have their TVs on all the time, it only seems that way). If the show's share is 20, that means that of all the households watching television at that particular moment, 20 percent of them are tuned into that show. Show ratings are listed in most major newspapers, in trades like *Variety* and *The Hollywood Reporter* or elsewhere on the web. The value of these ratings continues to be debated as channels multiply and other internet outlets continue to be explored.

Few Outside Characters   Generally you don't want to create a spec for an existing series in which a new or outside character dominates the story, so that wonderful episode idea you have about the main character's eccentric great aunt coming for a visit is dead on arrival. Producers and agents want to see how well you can write *existing* characters, not those of your own creation.

Involve the Main Characters Directly in the Story   You want to focus the story on the stars of the show. Make sure that the main characters are at the center of every conflict and resolution.

Don't Mess with the Premise   All television shows have a premise, a fundamental situation and assumption that never changes from episode to episode. Characters begin and end in essentially the same place. They might learn a lesson about life, but the premise of their lives remains the same (this is why it's called episodic television). In other words, writing an episode in which a character's mother dies is not a good idea. The mother can go into the hospital, but in the end she must be home so that everything can turn back to the status quo. Yes, occasionally shows do change the premise, but these decisions are made by the networks and/or the executive producer and should never be done in a spec.

Use Existing Sets   Try to use the standard locations of the show. This is particularly true of sitcoms, unless they are in the *Seinfeld*, *Bored to Death* or *Hung* mold, and even then they primarily rely on standard sets. You want to show that you can create a story that uses the standard, existing sets.

Get the Story Rolling   Competition is fierce. When agents read specs, they generally give you a few minutes. If you haven't snagged their interest by page four or five, it's off to the rejection pile, so state the major problem and begin the conflicts as close to page one as possible.

Getting a Good Idea

How often have you watched a really awful episode and thought, "I could write something better than that." The truth is that you're right, maybe you could. Unlike television writers, you have time to go back, rewrite, put it down for a while, come back to it and knock off a dozen drafts. Network television writers, on the other hand, must operate under a crushing deadline. They turn out material at a frantic pace. In television there is an old saying, "I don't want it good, I want it Tuesday!" Sitcom writers, for example, are given only one week to write an episode. There's a famous story of a young staff sitcom writer who was asked how long he needed to write his first episode and he sheepishly answered, "two weeks?" The stunned producer leaned forward and said, "Son, in two weeks, I could rewrite the Bible, with jokes." The lesson here is that when you write a spec, it must be better than anything on the air. You have the time to make your audition script perfect.

That perfection starts with a wonderful story idea, an idea that's new and distinct, yet does not deviate from the show's style. All shows have established structures, storylines and characters that cannot be altered or you change the essence of the show. After a show has been on the air for a while, unique story ideas can be hard to come by. You certainly don't want to write something they've already done, so you must seek the rarest of all commodities in television, a new idea—or at least a good one that hasn't been seen for a while.

The small screen eats up original ideas so fast that it's often forced to re-hash, spit-shine and reinvent old ideas. An original, new idea is always best, but it's also perfectly acceptable to use an old idea, as long as you disguise it and make it appropriate for and unique to whichever show you're writing. Story ideas come from watching television, reading the show descriptions (sometimes called slugs or log lines) on IMDB.com or the series' own websites, and from studying old movies and plays. The test is how good you are at inventing (or re-inventing) an idea that feels original and new but fits the show exactly. As a producer once said, "I want the same thing, only different."

Start by writing down one idea after another as they come into your head. At first, don't allow yourself to be critical. Creative and critical thinking come from opposite sides of the brain and seldom operate in unison. Constantly judging your ideas as they occur will cause the creative gridlock known as writer's block. Ask "what if": What if this happened, what if that happened?

Once you have a list of story ideas, go back and allow your critical side to judge each one logically. Does it fit the show? Have they done it before? Is it consistent with the show's style? Does the situation you've created contain enough surprise and conflict to sustain the comedy or drama of the show?

Structure

Once you have a good idea, it must be tailored to fit the unique structure of the show. Each television show has a singular structure. The best way to understand a show's structure is to stop watching it for enjoyment and start dissecting it. Dissecting a show is done by scene-carding several episodes, or "breaking them down" (scene cards are discussed in detail in Chapter 9). When breaking an episode down, the scene card process is reversed. Record an episode and then play it back, one scene at a time. After each scene, hit PAUSE and briefly write out on a scene card what the scene was about, where it took place, how long it took, who was involved, how it moved the story forward and what comprised the major conflict.

Once you have scene-carded an episode, the show's structure (or skeleton) should become clear. Lay it out in order, indicating teasers, tags and acts. A teaser, sometimes called a "cold opening," is a short scene just before the opening credits. For example *The Office* and *Breaking Bad* start with a teaser. A tag is a short scene or epilogue that falls after the last commercial and right before the closing credits or sometimes during the closing credits. Some shows have teasers, some have tags, some have both or neither. In television, an act is everything that happens after the teaser and before the tag, and between commercials. Today there are no set rules when it comes to how many acts a sitcom has, some have two acts, some three, some more. Hour-length shows usually have five acts, but again there are many exceptions. The only way you'll know is to watch and scene card several episodes.

With your scene card breakdowns laid out in front of you, study the show's structure. Notice that almost all acts end with a plot twist. The writers know that the audience members clutch remotes, their fingers on the button, ready to change to any one of 500 other channels, so they end acts on a moment of suspense, revelation or with a dramatic question that will hopefully make the audience endure the commercial without touching the button. You want to structure your story with these same end-of-act cliffhangers.

Some shows have more than one story within the same episode. These are known as "A" and "B" stories; occasionally there will be a "C" and even a "D" story, too. The "A" story is the main plot of the episode, the "B" story is a secondary or smaller plot, the "C" story, a running gag. For example, the "A" story might be that (Name Your Protagonist) has found a new love but keeps having a recurring dream that "she" is really a "he," while the "B" story is that (Name Your First Regular Character) must attend a tractor pull with his father. The "C" story might be the fact that someone keeps drinking (Name Your Second Regular Character)'s soft drink and he doesn't know who until the end. Each story is complete, with a beginning, middle and end. Sometimes the two stories start separately, but by the end of the episode they collide into one ending (Name Your Protagonist's new love wins the tractor pull). A good "B" story will have some thematic relationship to the "A" story; for instance, both "A" and "B" stories could deal with the issue of characters nervously trying to prove their heterosexuality. You want your spec to match exactly the number of acts, "A-B-C" story, teaser/tag configurations and overall structure that are the standard for that particular show.

Once you've dissected a few episodes, you should have a clear idea of the show's overall formula. You want to take your story idea and structure it using the same formula. Deviation from formula is not what television is about and will not look inventive to the producers, only incompetent.

You must also keep in mind that television is a fluid medium, and things keep changing. In an interview with Robin, Steve Peterman, the producer and/or executive producer of enormously successful shows from *Murphy Brown* to *Hannah Montana* to *Blah, Blah, Blah with Boys*, described the state of sitcom this way:

> What's happened in television…is a combination of a whole lot of outlets for people to watch, a lot of alternatives, which means the attention span is shorter, which means you have to hook people faster. Along with that is the fact that you have an audience that is so much more sophisticated in terms of the vocabulary of television that they know the shorthand, so you don't have to spend as much time setting up a story as you used to. *Seinfeld* is the classic example…it went from a show that told one story primarily, maybe two. But it soon began telling four main stories,

around its four main characters…they'd have four different stories going on, and multiple scenes, and what had started as a show with two acts of three scenes in one and four scenes in the second, by the time you got to the later years had twenty-two, twenty-five scenes. It turned television into a more cinematic way of telling a story. You came into a story much closer to a climactic moment. You'd sometimes see *Seinfeld* start an episode with something like George in a taxi with a woman he'd obviously been dating for a while. You'd never seen the woman before, you hadn't seen them meet, you hadn't seen their first date, you hadn't seen him talk about her to the others. In the old days you would have seen all that in the setup to the story. Now they don't bother with that. They say, let's get into the relationship right near the crisis point. This is becoming more true for all sitcoms. We hear from the network, "Don't feel you have to tell your story in such a traditional way, find a more unusual way, give the audience credit for being faster."

Characters

When dissecting a show, you must also analyze the characters, understand their style, motivation and idiosyncrasies. All the questions asked when creating a character (Chapter 5) must now be asked when dissecting an existing character. The key to writing a preexisting character is to know how they speak and behave. Each has trademark speech patterns and modes of behavior that result from their own unique thoughts, logic, comedy, education, history and environment, but most of all because of the particular actor who plays the role. Personality is revealed by analyzing what people say and how they say it, as well as by how they physically act and react to particular situations. Television writers must take it one step further and be able to reproduce these patterns.

To successfully match a character's speech, it's necessary to listen to the actor play the role over and over again. This can be very time-consuming. One trick is to record an episode and play it back on that long drive to work everyday. Listening to the voice will train your brain to hear the particulars of the character and actor's voice. Once the voice is firmly implanted in your mind, you should be able to write dialogue that closely matches it. Once you've written your spec, the reader should be able to cover up the character's name in the script and know exactly which character is speaking by the dialogue alone. Test this by whiting-out all the character names and having a friend who knows the show identify each character's lines. If she can't tell which character is which, the script is not ready. The challenge is to catch the character's nuances and still have them say something fresh and surprising.

Even though TV relies more on dialogue than features do, teleplay dialogue is lean. Every line must present the immediate conflict, reveal the characters, advance the plot (or in the case of sitcoms, be funny). If a line does not satisfy one of these needs, then it is excess fat and must be cut.

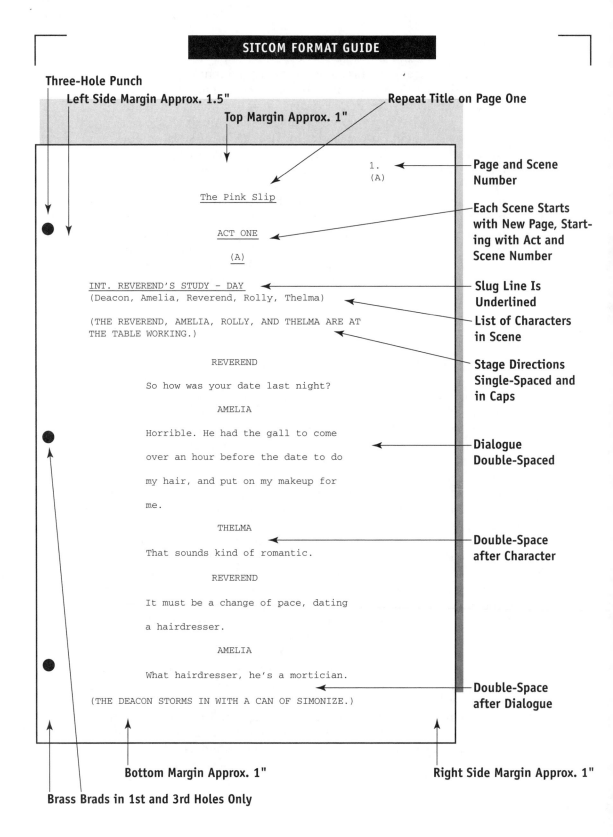

SITCOM FORMAT GUIDE

Three-Hole Punch

Left Side Margin Approx. 1.5"

Top Margin Approx. 1"

Repeat Title on Page One

1.
(A)

Page and Scene Number

The Pink Slip

ACT ONE

Each Scene Starts with New Page, Starting with Act and Scene Number

(A)

INT. REVEREND'S STUDY - DAY
(Deacon, Amelia, Reverend, Rolly, Thelma)

Slug Line Is Underlined

List of Characters in Scene

(THE REVEREND, AMELIA, ROLLY, AND THELMA ARE AT THE TABLE WORKING.)

Stage Directions Single-Spaced and in Caps

REVEREND

So how was your date last night?

AMELIA

Horrible. He had the gall to come

over an hour before the date to do

my hair, and put on my makeup for

me.

Dialogue Double-Spaced

THELMA

That sounds kind of romantic.

Double-Space after Character

REVEREND

It must be a change of pace, dating

a hairdresser.

AMELIA

What hairdresser, he's a mortician.

(THE DEACON STORMS IN WITH A CAN OF SIMONIZE.)

Double-Space after Dialogue

Bottom Margin Approx. 1"

Right Side Margin Approx. 1"

Brass Brads in 1st and 3rd Holes Only

Format

There are basically two formats when it comes to television writing: one-camera and three-camera. One-camera television shows are shot on location or on sound stages without an audience. They are just like movies, only produced on a much smaller budget and with commercial breaks. *Homeland* and *Mad Men* are examples of one-camera shows. The traditional definition of a three-camera is a show is one that is confined to a sound stage, and seldom, if ever, goes on location. Sitcoms like *King of Queens* and *Two and a Half Men* are traditional three-camera shows. The term "three camera" came from the 1950's when sitcoms like *I Love Lucy* were taped using only three cameras. Modern sitcoms actually use more cameras. Similarly, many cameras are rolling on a one-camera show like *Homeland*, but the handles have stuck.

In the old days three-camera shows were taped in front of a live audience, had few characters, and were limited to three or four sets. Today three-camera shows have no limits. Some have dozens of sets; some shoot on location (as does a one-camera show) and some are even animated. There are also no industry wide consistent rules when it comes to formatting. Some sitcoms use one-camera format, some three camera. The only way to know if you are using the right format is to get a copy of the script.

Getting a Script   There are still some mail-order bookstores that sell sitcom and hour-length scripts, but you can also download many from a variety of websites. In contrast to feature scripts you may download or order, with TV you want to make sure you're getting the genuine article, the final script of a produced episode, not some writer's first draft or spec. Real scripts usually have a show number on the title page, a cast of characters page and a list of sets needed for that particular episode.

They also often have little asterisks (*) in the margins of the script to indicate where line changes have been made. In production rewrites, instead of giving the actors, director and crew a totally new script every time lines are changed, they are given only the pages with changes. Each round of rewrites is marked by a new page color. Monday's changes, for example, might be on yellow paper, Tuesday's on green and so on. By the end of the week, a television script is a rainbow of colors. (The same is true, by the way, of feature film production scripts.)

Next, an asterisk is placed in the margin next to each change so that everyone knows exactly what's new on that particular page. If you have a photocopy, the pages will, of course, no longer be colored, but the revision key on the title page and the asterisks in the margins should still be there, and you'll know whether you have a genuine script. Often, rewrite pages will appear partial, because they are inserts dealing only with a portion of a pre-existing page. This is not how the original draft looked.

Formatting Software   The same advice we gave for formatting software for feature films applies here as well. A program like Final Draft or Movie Magic contains standard formats for all forms of screen and television writing. Once you have the program installed you can even go to their websites and download templates for specific shows. These programs aren't cheap, but can cost less if you can use their student discounts. If you are really strapped for cash and you have the time, you can create your own formatting templates (Check your word-processing program under "templates" or "style" for more information.) You can also download screenplay and sitcom templates for both Macintosh and PC from the web, but as you know, when you download anything you are taking a chance. (See Appendix A for one- and three-camera, i.e., sitcom, templates.)

Title Page A spec television script has a simple title page. You don't want a fancy, clear plastic or colored cover, just a plain white sheet of paper. About three inches from the top of the page, type the name of the series in caps and underline it (<u>TWO AND A HALF MEN, CSI: MIAMI</u>). Centered and double-spaced under it place the title of your particular episode. Although these titles seldom appear on the air, all television episodes are given a title. Give your spec a fun, funny, dramatic or intriguing title. This title should be in lowercase and in quotation marks ("Why Singers Don't Get Nose Jobs," "Shy Kidneys"). Put your name about an inch under the title (Written By Bill Smith). In the lower right-hand corner, put your address, e-mail and phone number(s), or those of your agent if you have one. That's it, nothing else is needed.

Things to Leave Out On the very next page, after the title page, start the first page of your script. Production scripts will often have several pages of casting and production notes, but these should not be included in a spec script.

Binding Television scripts use the same type of binding used on a screenplay: three-hole punch with metal brads in the first and third holes. Again, nowadays any place that has actually agreed to read your script will probably accept an emailed PDF.

Length One-hour shows are generally fifty to sixty pages long, while MOWs have around 100 to 105 pages. Length is important in a teleplay because each episode must fit into an exact time slot (though precise running time is handled partly in editing, and is not the writer's responsibility alone). When you cut out all the commercials and credits, hour-length dramas are only about forty-six minutes long. The scripts are longer than forty-six pages because of the act breaks. Unlike a feature screenplay, where one page generally equals one minute of air time, for a sitcom, each page equals only thirty seconds, so a script is anywhere from forty-five to sixty pages long. When you cut out all the commercials and credits, sitcoms are only about twenty-three minutes long.

WRITING COMEDY

All the usual elements of good storytelling apply to sitcoms: character, conflict, complication, suspense, crisis and climax. Of course, the key to writing a good sitcom spec is that it must be funny, but more, it must match a show's particular style of humor. Some shows deal with controversy, some have a nine o'clock time slot and have hard-hitting or sexual humor, some have eight o'clock (family hour) time slots and don't even allow sexual innuendo. You must match each show's sense of humor, not your own.

There are three ways of testing to see if your script is funny enough. First, draw a big red line across each page about halfway down. Then check to make sure that there's at least one funny bit above the line and one below. In other words, you don't want to go more than a half a page (fifteen seconds) without something funny happening or being said. Second, have a reading of the script (see Chapter 14, Rewriting).

Remember that, in most cases, humor does not come from characters telling jokes, but rather from their comic reactions to or commentary on the situation—it's a situation comedy, not a joke comedy. If your script isn't funny but your premise and situation is, your problem may be overwritten dialogue: too many words can cloud the humor. Comedy is lean; dialogue must be sharp and punchy.

Here is an example of comic dialogue that fails because of too many words. First read the scene with all the lines, then re-read, leaving out the crossed-out words. Notice that with fewer words, it still makes sense, and it's funnier.

                    MILES
~~Settle down everyone, I have an important~~
~~announcement to make.~~ It's no secret our
ratings are slipping; it's time to take
action.

                    MURPHY
What happened to ratings with dignity
~~that you were so hot about?~~

                    FRANK
~~I hate to admit this but~~ it didn't work.

                    MILES
I've been trying to figure out how to
tell you this. ~~This isn't easy.~~ I came up
with three different ways.

                    MURPHY
How about ~~telling~~ the truth.

                    MILES
~~I hadn't thought of that.~~ All right, four
ways. ~~I've made an executive decision.~~ I
signed Jerome Reardon as a new member of
the FYI team.

                    MURPHY
          Not that malicious little columnist for
          the New York Times?

                    MILES
          Pulitzer-Prize-winning-malicious-little-
          columnist.

                    FRANK
          ~~Oh, I know him.~~ Wasn't he a theatre
          critic?

                    JIM
          Yes, but he gave that up after the
          assassination attempt. ~~They missed.~~

                    MURPHY
          You hired Satan and you didn't check with
          us first!

                    MILES
          I only had a small window of opportunity
          before 20/20 grabbed him.

                    JIM
          Remember Lanford Benley? That talented
          young man who wrote "Gay Nam Vet"? ~~Great~~
          ~~writer.~~

                    FRANK
          Incredible play.

                    JIM
          ~~Well,~~ Reardon panned it. Poor playwright
          was so upset he ended it all.

                    FRANK
          He killed himself over a review? ~~I don't~~
          ~~believe it.~~

                    JIM
          No, he sold it to Danny DeVito for two
          point five mil, moved to Crete and never
          wrote again.

                    FRANK
          ~~On that is~~ tragic. Most tragic.

```
          JIM
I was a consultant on the Viet Nam aspect
of the play. Yes, we put those actors
though hell. Made them sleep in foxholes
behind the theatre, get up at four a.m.
and go to the bathroom in a hole in the
ground. The actors just couldn't take it.
Three of the cast members actually suffer
from flashbacks. Now that's real acting.
```

YOU NEED AN AGENT

All of this initial effort and preparation is done in order to get an agent. In television writing, you must have one. Unless you have a personal "in" with a producer, almost no network television producers will read an unsolicited script for their own show sent to them by a writer. No matter how wonderful your cover letter, no matter how great your script, it will be returned unread. There are two reasons for this cold wall between television producers and spec writers. First, producers don't want to open themselves up to legal liability: if you send them a spec that happens to be similar to a story they're developing (and with the thousands of scripts being submitted, odds are some will be similar), you might sue them for stealing your idea. You'll probably lose, but it will still cost them energy and money to defend themselves. Rather than dealing with this possibility, producers usually only allow specs to be submitted through agents. Agents know what the different shows are looking for and keep records as to what was submitted and when. The second reason shows only allow agented submissions is to winnow out the weaker scripts. Agents want to keep a good relationship with producers, so they won't waste time submitting weak or average scripts. The assumption is that an unagented script is most likely a weak one, or the writer would have representation.

It is not, however, impossible to get someone to read a spec for a different show, in hopes of getting in for a pitch meeting or an assignment. Steve Peterman offers the following advice:

> If you have some kind of a personal relationship with a writer on staff, that writer can get your spec to the attention of the executive producer. There are certain times of the year when [producers] have time to read unsolicited scripts. At the end of the season—most shows finish up in late February, March or early April—that time of the year is a good time to send a very gracious and begging request, if you do it with a little bit of humor and sincerity. You might get somebody to read your spec then, because they're coming to the end of a season and they have a little bit more time.

But again, remember, producers will not read an unsolicited spec for their own show, ever!

Once you have several great specs—and again, make sure they are absolutely as good as you can make them—your next step is luring an agent. You will need several specs because agents want to be sure your writing is consistently good before they sign you (see Chapter 15 for more detailed information on how to write query letters and get an agent). But remember: you want an agent who is located in Los Angeles. There are agents all over the country, but for television you only want to consider agents who are located in the heart of the industry.

L.A. IS WHERE YOU WANT TO BE

While it is possible (difficult at first, but possible) to be a feature screenwriter and live somewhere other than Los Angeles, this is not the case with television. Just as you want your TV agent to be based in L.A., you need to be there too. Success depends on talent, being prepared, who you know and being in the right place at the right time. All but talent involve living in Los Angeles, at least when you are getting started. Los Angeles is the center of the universe for sitcoms and dramatic shows. True, a small percentage are taped in New York, Chicago or Canada, but the nucleus of "the Industry" is Los Angeles. Want to work for a network show? Then be where you can "network" with people working on network shows. And you have a greater chance of bumping into the right person in L.A. than in Iowa City. While you're trying to break in, there are jobs in agencies as production assistants and as script secretaries that can both help you pay the bills, meet the right people and serve as stepping stones to writing jobs. If nothing else, you'll get to see how the business really works from the inside. Also, when writing a spec, especially for a sitcom taped in front of a live audience, it's always good to try and see the taping of an episode, which you can only do—guess where?

And even when you've broken in, you'll most likely have to be in Los Angeles. Unlike feature screenwriters, who (after they've gotten an agent) can live just about anywhere and still have a chance for success, network television writers are doomed to failure if they don't live in Los Angeles, unless they're among the lucky few who already have jobs on one of the handful of shows produced elsewhere. TV is a fast-moving, deadline-driven industry that cannot wait for anyone. Agents and producers expect writers to be available for meetings on short notice and, if you're lucky enough to land a staff position, you have to come to work at the studio. Even in this age of high-speed modems, the web and video/telephone conferencing, television writers are expected to live within a stone's throw of the industry. Maybe some day this will change, but for the foreseeable future television writers must be where the action is.

Before you move to L.A., take the time to test your talents by writing several specs. *Geographic location and bumping into the right person will not help you if you're not prepared to make the most of the contacts you meet.* What good is it to meet a friendly script supervisor if you don't have any good scripts to show him? Don't pack your bags until you're really ready.

WAR STORIES

Bill

Once, while pitching to the Sherman Hemsley sitcom *Amen*, I noticed a white board on the producer's wall with a list of episode titles that were currently being written. Although I didn't get a job, the pitch had gone well, and they asked me back to pitch again. This time I came in with a story that I thought matched one of the titles on the wall. That was the first idea I pitched. Halfway through, the producer stopped me and said, "I'm so sorry, nobody knows this but we already have that idea set for this season." Then he added, "You really know this show, don't you?" The very next pitch, they bought. By clueing in on something they had in development, I proved to them that my thinking was in line with the show—but I had also come in with stories they hadn't thought of.

While writing for *My Two Dads*, Paul Reiser's first sitcom effort, I was amazed by how many writers pitched a story about the existence of a "third dad." The producers were sick of it—they'd heard the idea a hundred times. The writer who does his research will avoid tired subjects and ideas. Steve Peterman notes that in general, "You want to come in with a story that has a clear beginning, middle, and an end, and a clear attitude from the main character toward that story at every moment. You need a B and C story, but you don't need as much there as long as you can tell where the areas of 'funny' might be.

PITCHING FOR TELEVISION

So you've written some great specs and nailed an agent. Now you can just sit back and wait for the offers to start pouring in, right? Wrong. All you've done is lay the groundwork (no one said this was going to be easy). While your agent is sending out your specs, you must always be writing new specs. Agents need a steady supply of new scripts; they can't keep submitting the same old things. Sometimes your agent will tell you which shows he wants you to spec. Listen to him, he's on the phone all day with producers and knows what they're looking for. Meanwhile, with luck, some producer will like one of your specs and invite you in for a pitch meeting.

Pitching to a television show is much like pitching to a movie producer (Chapter 16), with just a few exceptions. First, unlike a movie pitch, where you're bringing in totally original material, here you're working with an existing concept and set of characters. Before you come in to pitch, you'll first be sent a show's "bible." This contains information about the show's characters, particulars, a complete list of the stories they've already done and sometimes a script or two. They send you this because they don't want you to waste their time pitching ideas they've already tackled in previous seasons.

After studying the "bible" and watching as many episodes as possible, you must come up with five to eight story ideas. Each idea must be fully worked out, with a beginning, middle and end. You're given about a week to do this and then you head into the studio on your appointment to pitch.

There are several keys to good television pitching. First, cut down on the number of unknowns: do some research. Ask your agent for details about this particular producer's likes and dislikes. Producers do like a writer who seems to really know the show.

Next, once you've come up with your stories, you must rehearse your pitch. Never go in cold; there's no time once you're there to fumble around trying to remember the beats of your story; that will make you look unprepared. Also, your stories may not sound as good or be as funny out loud as they look on the page. After you have come up with your ideas, practice pitching them to friends. Run them over and over until you can do them in your sleep. (For further details on the actual process of pitching, see Chapter 16.)

Next, you also want to try and pitch to Producers, Associate Producers or Executive Producers, not Story Editors. Story Editors lack the power to okay an idea, so you're less likely to sell; at best, if the Story Editor likes one of your stories, you'll be asked to come in and pitch it all over again to someone who can say "Yes." Of course, the writer often doesn't have any choice as to who on the show takes the pitch, but your agent should push for someone as high on the food chain as possible. Whoever takes your pitch, try to come in knowing everyone's name and rank. People like it when you know who they are.

Giving Them the Treatment

Writers Guild rules state that a writer cannot be asked by a producer to write an outline or treatment of his verbal pitches. Even if you are not in the Guild, it's generally a good policy to follow, because producers are only too happy to have someone give them work for free, which you do not want to do. However, it's acceptable to leave a pitch outline behind if you already have one prepared, and it can be helpful. Wouldn't you rather have them look to your words than their notes to remember what you pitched to them?

How'd It Go?

After the pitch meeting, the writer calls his agent and tells him how things went (were the producers excited about the pitches, or were they bored, or too busy to be bothered). The agent now calls the producer and finds out if one of the stories interests them. If there is no sale, then it's over, at least with these pitches at this show. The agent sends the specs off to other shows, the writer goes back to writing specs and hopes for the phone to ring again.

If an idea sells, then the process moves to the next level, a story meeting. In a story meeting, the staff writers meet with the freelance writer and kick around the ideas, pitch jokes, test lines of dialogue and try to structure the episode. (Yes, you already structured it, but now it's fair game for everyone, and it's going to change shape whether you like it or not. Your structure basically just proved to them that you knew what you were doing and now it's their turn.) The freelancer is expected to take detailed notes. This meeting can go on for many hours and often does. Once it's over, the freelancer heads home and takes a few days to write a detailed outline: a double-spaced narrative, six to ten pages long, broken into scenes and acts, and written in the present tense. Dialogue samples are often allowed. This story outline must accurately reflect the structure and ideas that were agreed upon in the story meeting. When the outline is turned in, the writer is given more notes and is sent home to write the episode. In some rare cases, after the freelance writer has finished the story outline he is simply paid story money, sent home and a staff writer is given the assignment of actually writing the script. Story money is about $4,000.

A LIFE IN TELEVISION

In Hollywood, television is called the writer's medium. This is relative to features. Novels, plays, short stories and poems offer writers far more creative freedom than television. Yet, when compared to writing for the movies, television is far more writer-friendly. On the big screen, directors and producers reign supreme, while writers live a life of quiet servitude. On the little screen, the power structure is different. Writers can often work their way up through the ranks to become both executive producer and head writer, while directors are largely hired hands there to service the story. This means that on a television show, there are far more opportunities for writers to gain positions of power. Writing for television can also be more a team effort no matter whether you are a freelance or staff writer.

Team Writing

Writing teams are common in television. Working with a partner has some great advantages, particularity in sitcom writing, simply because there is always someone there to bounce your ideas and jokes off of, and because two people can often generate ideas and material more quickly than one. Also, it is less lonely. But there are some serious drawbacks to consider as well. You must not enter a writing partnership casually. It is like a marriage; in fact, in some ways it is closer. You will spend most of every day working intensely with one another and so you'd better be very sure that you really get along and respect each other's talent. In fact, if you decide to work with a partner, make sure you pick a partner who is better than you. You don't want to "carry" a writer who has less talent, less experience, or less desire, or you will soon resent her. Another major consideration is that teams are paid as if they were one writer, so if you do pair off with a partner, know that you will be splitting your salary as well as all future residuals. And if you sell a co-written script, you will be identifying yourself as one-half of a team for the foreseeable future, joined at the hip with your partner from then on as far as producers are concerned. They know that you've worked well together, but will have doubts about you individually: maybe only one of you was talented, and if so, which one? If you do split up, it will be almost as painful as a divorce, and it will also take a whole new set of successful specs to break free and re-establish your own identity as an individual writer.

The Life of a Freelance Writer

Freelance writers spend a great deal of time watching and recording network television shows. They seldom know in advance which show they'll be pitching to and so they record many different shows in order to build up a large library. This way, when they are called in to pitch, no matter what show it is, they have several episodes to study. Some freelance writers prefer to do only freelance work; the stress of a staff job is not to their liking and so they work on their reputation of being a good writer and hope that the phone rings. But most are freelancing only until they can land a lucrative staff job.

The Life of a Staff Writer

Being a staff writer is stressful. Typically, staff writers arrive at the studio at around ten in the morning and rarely leave before ten at night. They can easily put in fourteen-hour days. While a staff writer's contract will state how many episodes she is guaranteed to write, she must still pitch ideas, just like freelance writers. The first draft is usually written by the staff writer alone, but then the team takes over and the script is written and rewritten and rewritten again by everyone involved. Dialogue is changed all week long, right up to taping. Generally, May is staffing season, when all the shows hire writers for the fall season. Writers are hired in thirteen- to twenty-week periods. In other words, if you don't measure up, your contract will not be renewed at the end of thirteen weeks. Every two to three weeks the directors and actors take a hiatus, or week-long break, but the writers seldom have this luxury. They are too busy writing the next episode.

FINAL THOUGHTS

TV or Not TV   The French playwright Molière said, "Writing is like prostitution. First, you do it for the love, then you do it for a few friends, and finally you do it for money." And television writing does pay handsomely, but there's a cost as well. True, network television writers have more power compared to feature screenwriters, but there are many restrictions on subject matter, limited time to create, and strict formulas that must be followed. Ratings, not art, control the industry; as television producer, writer and actor Garry Marshall said, "If you want to do art, go home and write poetry. On the other hand, if you wanna buy things…" While there are those special shows that transcend the medium, it's good to remember the wisdom of Ernie Kovacs, a great television comic during the golden age of TV. He quipped that the boob tube was a lot like a steak: "It's a medium that is neither rare nor well done."

For a list of books about writing for television see Appendix B.

18

Writing Webisodes

Doing It Yourself

The online Merriam-Webster at this moment defines a webisode as "an episode especially of a TV show that may or may not have been telecast but can be viewed at a Web site." That definition is already dusty; webisodes are more and more likely to have been produced specifically for online consumption, and have not (and never will be) broadcast on TV. We acknowledge that this chapter itself is likely going to be out of date almost before it's published. That said, we felt it important to include some thoughts and guidelines for one of this active and exciting new area of storytelling, and one which looks to be more and more important as the internet becomes more and more the source for our entertainment.

Felicia Day, the award-winning creator of the popular webisode series *The Guild (watchtheguild.com)*, said that she started writing, directing, and starring in webisodes after she received a pile of rejections from Hollywood. During her acceptance speech at the Streamy Awards (the Oscar-inspired award ceremonies for online videos) she said webisodes are for all those who don't want to wait for permission to make their art. She's right. If your desire is to sidestep the Hollywood gatekeepers and start seeing movies based on your screenplays, webisodes are an increasingly popular (and affordable) way to go.

Before we proceed let's be clear: we are not talking about video blogs or webcams or uploading a video of your cat playing the piano or footage from a camera strapped to your dog's head to show everyone "A Day in the Life of Fido." Such videos can be very entertaining and perhaps lead to millions of hits on the web, but they will do nothing to advance your screenwriting career unless they also contain the elements of story. This chapter is about web based miniseries that you will probably direct yourself, and edit yourself using programs like Adobe, Final Cut, or even iMovie; they will have a production budget no bigger (and hopefully a lot smaller) than your bank account or Visa card credit limit. And we are going to concentrate on the script—the story element—because there are plenty of good books out there about how to direct and edit your own movie. Most of the lessons in the other chapters of this book will also apply to writing webisodes, but this chapter will focus on some of the writing techniques unique to this new form. And if you manage to create a combination of whatever makes some uploads go viral with a good story, then you'll have hit gold.

The dream is that you will write that mind-blowing web series that gets 10,000 hits a day, and 3 million viewers in its first year, after which Disney offers you a lucrative contract, but just as you are about to sign, the President of Paramount knocks on your door, doubles Disney's offer, and includes a massive signing bonus. You go on to become an Oscar-winning screenwriter with a Porsche and house in Beverly Hills. And then one day you truly come to understand the sweet smell of success when you are invited back to your alma mater, where you give an awe-inspiring commencement speech about how you "refused to play the Hollywood game" and sing Frank Sinatra's "My Way." And to think it all started with a webisode you shot in your garage. Or if you approach it with your feet on the ground, webisodes are a great way to take your stories to the screen, in a form that may find an audience for your ideas, and to learn a lot about screenwriting. In order to get started on a great script, the first thing you need is a great premise, a hook.

WEBI-PREMISE

Let's not sugarcoat it, a lot of webisodes are crap. And there are tens of thousands of them on the Internet. Over 200,000 videos a day are uploaded to YouTube and hundreds of those are webisodes. Add to this thousands of webisodes that are available on sites like Atom Uploads, Blip.tv, Break.com, Brightcove, Crackle, FlickLife, Go Fish, Jumpcut, Meacafe, Revver, and a dozen other webisode internet libraries and it's easy to see that the webisode—even though this word is now just being added to dictionaries—is nothing new. The Wild West days of short independent online movies was the late 1990s, so if you are just getting into the market, you are a latecomer. So how do you rise above the crowd?

The key to setting yourself above and apart is to have a great premise, a hook or concept that is unique and so catchy that it will propagate like wildfire through the web via social networks and blogs. There are dozens of webisode parodies of medical shows, sitcoms, comic books, horror movies, and *Battlestar Galactica*, that are all really just a form of fan fiction—those won't give you a unique premise. There are thousands of too-generic webisodes about love, death, cancer, mental wards, being single, murder mysteries, soap operas, and teen wolf stories. There is nothing new under the sun—or is there? Look at the webisode series *Gaytown* (available on Crackle), which does have a unique, catchy premise: a heterosexual man trapped in a world where everyone is gay. In one episode he is caught in a bathroom stall sting operation when he tries to play fantasy football with what he thinks are two other straight men; in fact they are undercover gay cops. This is a current, inventive idea, something that has not been done before or is, at the very least, a fresh take on an old idea.

Speaking of bathrooms, limited locations are obviously an advantage—another series happens to be called *Bathroom Confidential*, about a plumber who's been hired by a film production company to keep the toilet working in the creaky old house they're using as a location. His dream is to somehow transform this lowly service into a Hollywood career. The writing team includes Rob Rinow, Val Stulman, John Shannon, A. H. Gullett, Tim Furlong and Chuck Cummings, all working feature, theatre and TV writers, actors or producers, and they approached the writing side very seriously. Before beginning production, they came up with six webisodes and a complete bible for the arc of the first season (twelve in all), character bios, roles/functions and backstories, as well as a smart, standard six-beat format for each four minute webisode: a ten-second teaser to grab attention; introducing the current problem outside the bathroom; a real world attempt to solve it, which fails; a fantasy comic sequence that inspires the solution; the solution applied; a cliffhanger in which the following webisode's problem is introduced. It's a lot of story to pack into a short time, so every line is re-examined to make sure it's both funny and necessary. Each webisode is a stand-alone story, but each has a character or story element that will be picked up on later in the series. This setting might have been a trap as far as jokes are concerned, but they've avoided relying on bathroom humor; rather, the humor is situational and character-based. As of this writing, you can check the series out at *bathroomconfidential.com*.

Where do unique concepts come from? Simple (not!): Have something personal to say about how the world is or how it should be, and have a singular, innovative point of view about things that matter to a lot of people. You want something with broad appeal, but with a game-changing premise. One thing that can help is to watch a lot of webisodes. Novelists read lots of novels; poets read lots of poems; and webisode writers watch lots of webisodes. If you see your idea already playing on the net, then you'll know your idea isn't unique. Next, consider your audience: they own computers, smart phones, and they spend a lot of time online. Felicia Day became a "webiname" by using that very fact as a premise for her series, *The Guild*, a series about characters who are addicted to online video games. It was such a good idea that it led to over fifty episodes and millions of addicted followers. Keep in mind that webisodes are fast moving, brash, usually brief, and aimed at an information-overloaded audience, so your premise should not be complicated, and it will probably work best if there's irony involved (true of most storytelling, by the way). If you cannot state your premise in a sentence or two that contains a catchy, ironic hook, it is probably not a good concept for a web series.

WEBI-STRUCTURE

There are no set rules when it comes to the length of a webisode. For example, at half an hour per episode, the comedy *Goodnight Burbank (goodnightburbank.com)* is one of the longest, while the drama *Sam Has Seven Friends* (*www.samhas7friends.com*), which has two-minute episodes, is considered short. Most average four to eight minutes. There is also no rule about how many episodes a web series should have, but most average ten to twenty. It's important to remember that people who watch webisodes are probably doing it on their iPhone during a coffee break, or sneaking a quick hit between e-mails. Webisodes are a compact form of storytelling told to an audience with a short attention span.

Webisodes generally fall into two categories: those that follow the arcing structure of a serial movie and those that conform to the episodic structure of a sitcom. The ones that follow serial movies must be watched in sequential order to make sense of the plot, while the ones that follow the episodic structure of a sitcom can be watched out of sequence because each video is a complete story in itself and only loosely connected (through character) to the others.

From the 1920s to the 1950s serial movies (often called just "serials") were a mainstay of America's moviegoing experience. Before each feature film audiences would arrive early to watch a cartoon, a newsreel, and a serial about comic book heroes like Captain Marvel, sci-fi adventures with Flash Gordon, and especially Westerns—lots of Westerns. Each serial was about fifteen minutes in length and had eight to twelve episodes, with a new episode premiering each week. So, in this age before television, if you failed to go to the movies for a week you'd fall behind on the serial story. Serials were much like modern soap operas, except that the story was split into weekly instead of daily chapters. In order to entice the audience not to miss an installment, each serial generally ended with a cliffhanger. A cliffhanger is a precarious situation, a shocking revelation, and/or a dramatic question that leaves the audience in suspense and wanting more. Movies that are intended to have sequels do that today: For example, each installment of the horror film series *Saw* ends with a cliffhanger, making the audience want to come back again for another helping of torture, gore and blood. Modern serial webisodes use this same structural device, so not only must this kind of webisode follow the structural outlines found in Part Two of this book, it must also be designed so that each two- or ten-minute (or whatever your length is) episode ends with a hook that pulls the audience back for more. It's like ending each chapter with the words "To Be Continued."

One way to make cliffhangers work is by asking a dramatic question and then answering it with another dramatic question. Every script is populated with small dramatic questions. For example, say that at the beginning of a webisode a son comes home from the army and tells his mother he's been dishonorably discharged, but he doesn't want to talk about it. Of course, the dramatic question is: Why was he dishonorably discharged? The writer wouldn't answer that question immediately, but instead would tantalize the audience by delaying the answer. And once the question is answered (at the start of the next episode, perhaps) the screenwriter does so by then asking a new dramatic question. The soldier might, at the end of the new episode, tell his mother that he was discharged for "psychological problems?" Of course, this them leads to the question: what type of psychological problems? And on that question you fade to black, forcing the audience to click on the next episode in order to satisfy their curiosity.

Episodic webisodes, like many modern sitcoms and hour-length television shows, have a beginning, middle and end for each episode which stands on its own as a single adventure. This means that there is no (or limited) overall arc to the characters—instead they are pretty much the same at the end as they were at the beginning of each episode, which simply place them in different escapades and situations. This is the origin of the phrase "situation comedy" (or sitcom) because the humor and story are derived from the unique situations into which the writers put the characters, not on how the characters grow over time. Episodic structures work well for television because of syndication. When a show goes into reruns (syndication) it is easier if they can be aired in random order and not sequential installments that demand that the audience knows what's happened in prior episodes. Episodic structure is not limited to television: the action adventure 007 movies are also episodic because the character of James Bond does not change (except perhaps because different actors will play him over time). Writers create the story by placing Bond in a new situation for each adventure. One wrinkle that's become popular, however, is to create an "origin" episode for otherwise episodic characters like Bond or other superhero types. But essentially these movies stand on their own.

When it comes to webisodes both structures are perfectly acceptable, you just have to make up your mind. Is your story about characters who have an arc and grow over time, or are your characters pretty much set and the story comes from placing them in unique situations? Are you going to follow a serial structure like the groundbreaking webisodes *Sam Has Seven Friends*, or the episodic structure of comedies like *Gaytown*?

WEBI-CHARACTERS

As far as characters are concerned, everything that applies to a full-length screenplay also applies to webisodes. So be sure to read Chapter 5, which covers everything from motivation to internal conflict. The problem with webisodes is that you don't have a lot of time for character development. There is no room for that three-minute monologue where your protagonist talks about how he was abandoned as a child and had to fight his way out of the Amazon jungle with only his wit and an app store compass. You can solve this problem by concentrating on four critical elements that all screen characters have in common: what they want, what they need (not always the same thing), what they do about it (action), and what or who stands in their way (source of conflict). Screen characters must have deep unfulfilled desires, and be willing to (or forced to) take action to get what they want or need. At its most basic, character is that simple: in essence a character *is* what he wants and needs and how he chooses to act upon those things. If you write about a man who wants to give the girl he loves a diamond engagement ring and shoplifts it from a local jewelry store, you have written the character of a crook. If he is willing to sell his prized 1963 Corvette so that his best friend can buy the ring to marry a girl he himself loves, you've written the character of an altruist (or maybe a masochist). And if he crashes his 1963 Corvette into a jewelry store, kills all the shoppers, and then as an afterthought pockets the ring, you've written either a psychopath or a Quentin Tarantino protagonist. The key is that no character (no protagonist at any rate) can simply wish for what they want. They must take action. With the compressed nature of webisodes it is critical to show the character's want as early as possible. Make your character desire something within a half a page of entering, even if it is a cup of coffee. And as soon as you can, make her take some sort of action, even if it ends in total failure.

If you are writing a serial webisode you will want to consider the character's arc or how the character will change over time. Character arc can include how her viewpoint, personality, needs, or personal philosophy will change over time, and why. In the movie *Tootsie*, Dustin Hoffman's character starts off as a self-centered actor (is there any other kind?) and something of a male chauvinist, but through the action of the movie he turns into a man who understands women because he's been forced to pretend to be one.

If on the other hand you are writing an episodic webisode, you'll want to make sure that your protagonist is so compelling that he or she will remain interesting no matter what situation you place him or her in.

WEBI-PILOT

In writing a feature script, you've got five to ten pages (five to ten minutes) to win over your reader. In webisodes, you've got maybe one short minute—which in web-time is an eternity (don't believe us? How many online vids have you passed on because there was a ten-second ad you'd have had to sit through before you could see them?). There are tens of thousands of webisodes out there, at least one for every hopeful screenwriter with a camera, all competing for your audience's ever-shrinking patience, so you had better win over your viewer damned fast or they are not going to linger. The first minute of your pilot episode, your first episode, had better be fascinating. Years ago network television would occasionally keep a low-rated show on the air because they felt it would eventually build an audience. Shows like *Seinfeld* and *Cheers* were at the bottom of the ratings pile when they first debuted, but over time became hits. Although your pilot will be available and waiting there online once you upload it (as opposed to the pre-DVR days of TV when you either watched something at a certain scheduled time or you missed it), if you don't hook your viewer early, it might as well not be online. You must shine right out of the gate.

One way to approach this is to follow the old Ten Percent Rule in screenwriting. The Ten Percent Rule has been around for decades and is a staple of screenwriting books and classes. What it means is that you want the moment when the clouds of conflict appear, when the primary action of the story clearly declares itself, to happen about 10 percent of the way into the script. This structural moment has been given various names including: The inciting incident, the call to adventure, the catalyst that leads to the film's first turning point, and the banana peel your protagonist slips on that starts the action of the story. We'll call it the point of attack. It is the moment when Bruce Willis gets shot in *The Sixth Sense* (on page nine). In a 100-page screenplay the point of attack usually happens on, around or before, page ten. In *Juno*, it happens much sooner, when she confirms she's pregnant by page four). So, in a ten-page webisode, the point of attack needs to happen by the end of page one.

In a full-length screenplay you might have a few pages to introduce the characters, establish the environment, and provide relevant exposition; in a webisode you don't have that kind of time. You must get the story rolling. One way to jump to the action is to start with a brief narration. For example, the pilot episode of *Gaytown* begins with a forty-second narrated montage where the protagonist explains the premise. And then, because *Gaytown* is not a serial—it can be watched out of sequence—each subsequent episode begins with a ten-second version of the same narrated montage to let viewers who missed the pilot in on the premise (pretty much the same technique that TV has used for decades, and radio before that, as when each *Superman* episode began with "The Adventures of Superman—Faster than a speeding bullet! More powerful than a locomotive! Able to leap tall buildings in a single bound!").

Or just cut out the exposition. Start the story and jump right to the point of attack, with a person wanting something and going after it. They will define themselves and the premise by what they do. For example, the pilot of the comedy web series *Goodnight Burbank* just starts. It's another day at work and things, very funny things, happen in the very first minute. The background information is incorporated into the action. You'll be surprised by how little exposition or beginning you need. Let's face it, if your webisode needs more than a minute of narrative or action in order to make sense, it most likely is not a good idea for a webisode.

It's also a good idea to write more than just the pilot episode before you start shooting. If you are writing a serial then you need to write or at least outline a majority of the episodes before you go to camera. Even if you are writing an episodic series, have at least eight or ten episodes scripted. Having a substantial chunk of the writing done allows you to see the series as a whole: Beginning, middle and end. By doing this many writers discover that their third or fourth webisode makes a better pilot than the one they'd originally planned to upload. During the writing process you will make discoveries about characters, story and conflict that will need to be set up in the pilot. It also allows you to plan your shoots more efficiently: remember, you've got to get the most production value for the least money, so being able to shoot several episodes at once while your set, actors, cameraperson, etc., are there makes sense. Always remember, writing is cheap, production is expensive. A good webisode artist spends 75 percent of their creative time writing.

Whatever you have planned for your pilot episode, above all else, cut out the opening credits. It sure feels great to see your name in lights, but no matter how wonderful the music or how brilliant your title sequence you are going to bore the hell out of everyone—the exception being everyone listed in the title sequence and your mother. Show the title card and go. If you need credits place them in the lower corners of the first scene. You got one minute, that's it, one short minute, and you don't want to blow it with credits.

WEBI-CHEAP

Webisodes are generally dialogue heavy for two simple reasons. Reason One: As noted above, dialogue is cheap. And cheap is good—isn't that part of why you're doing this? So, from the very first draft, take expense into account. That sequence you might have written for that feature spec, where your protagonist is shot at by a space alien who misses and blows up a water tower by mistake and that comes crashing down on City Hall could have been brilliant, but it doesn't belong here. Notice that the web series *Goodnight Burbank* is not the story of a bigtime news program but of a tiny, local, underfunded nightly program. This is not because the creators wouldn't love to make it about a network news show, but because they don't have the money (yet). *General Elevator* is a parody of medical shows—that takes place entirely within an elevator at a hospital. This is not only cheap, but funny. However, there are ways to open up your location possibilities while keeping your expenses down by scouting locations even before you write. If you have a friend who owns an auto dealership and is willing to give you access—*voila!*—write an episode in which a car dealership is central to the story. If you find out that a local water tower or abandoned building is scheduled to be imploded and you can get there in time to shoot it, maybe it's time to start writing an episode where that's part of the story. Oh, yeah…Reason Two: Though not as compelling as Reason One, webisodes are not written and produced for the big screen, but rather for the small, or very small, screen, so the primary emphasis on the visual that feature films demand does not apply here.

WEBI-FORMAT

Generally webisodes use a standard screenplay format covered in Chapter 2. Even if you are going to direct, act, edit and produce it yourself you want to follow the standard Hollywood formatting rules—if for no other reasons than to look professional and be consistent: proper format gives you a rough idea of the length of each episode. One page equals approximately one minute of screen time. If you are just starting out it is not necessary to buy one of the expensive screenwriting programs (Movie Magic, SceneWriter Pro, Final Draft), although these are very good for longer and more involved projects, and for exporting to production and scheduling software. There are now two pretty good free screenwriting programs you can download, Celtx (celtx.com) and Scripped (scripped.com). Or, if you want, you can create a simple style sheet or template in Microsoft Word that will work. Just search for "Screenplay formatting + Word + Template" on the web and you'll find sites telling you how to do this with your particular version of Word.

WEBI-TALENT

When it comes time to actually film your webisodes, find good creative people who if possible have some knowledge of film production. Your script may be brilliant, but if the finished product has poor production values you will never have the chance at giving that commencement speech we talked about earlier. The (apparently) simplest thing, like getting a clean recording of your dialogue, or cutting together takes of two people talking, requires people who know what they're doing (sound and continuity in these cases) or you'll have useless footage and beat yourself up trying to "fix it in post."

WEBI-SCRIPTS

It can be hard to locate sample webisodes scripts. They are seldom published and you generally cannot find them on the web, as you can with movie and television scripts. To give you an idea of what such a script looks like, here is one called *Headshots*. It's about actors trying to make it in Hollywood and was written by Todd McCullough, who also wrote the National Lampoon movie *Van Wilder: Freshman Year*. Read, enjoy and then go online to watch the final product.

HEADSHOTS

by

Todd McCullough

Episode #4:

"MUGGING FOR THE CAMERA"

INT. THE HOUSE - BATHROOM -- DAY

TODD stands at the mirror, cleaning up for work. He bends down to use the sink. When he comes up, MIKE is there.

              TODD
   Jesus!

              MIKE
   Hey, buddy, whatcha doing?

                    TODD
          I'm--

                    MIKE
          Hey, remember when you said we should be
          doing more to further our acting careers?

                    TODD
          Yeah.

                    MIKE
          And that we should make our own
          opportunities?

                    TODD
          Yeah.

                    MIKE
          And that you'd do anything to help me?

                    TODD
          Don't remember that.

                    MIKE
          I need three hundred dollars.

                    TODD
          Excuse me?

INT. LIVING ROOM -- CONTINUOUS

Todd comes out of the bathroom. Mike follows.

                    MIKE
          I wanna buy a video camera so I can start
          shooting my own stuff.

                    TODD
          You have a camera--

                    MIKE
          I need an HD camera. People need to see
          this shit times ten. I just need to put
          three hundred down.
                    (takes out a checkbook)
          Now, I already wrote out the check--

                    TODD
          What are you doing with my checkbook?

                    MIKE
     I was trying to save you some time.

                    TODD
     I You forged my signature!

                    MIKE
     You gotta admit, it's pretty good.

                    TODD
          (tearing up the check)
     No. This is not happening.

                    MIKE
     That's fine. Cash works.

                    TODD
     What makes you think I have three hundred
     dollars just lying around?

                    MIKE
     You're working that big party at the
     restaurant tonight, right? You'll make
     three hundo in tips, easy.

EXT. HOUSE - CONTINUOUS

Todd goes outside, heads to his car.

                    TODD
     Why would I give you money when you still
     owe me for rent?

                    MIKE
     Here we go again. Dude, how many times
     do I have to tell you? This is America.
     People don't just get kicked out of their
     homes because they don't pay their rent.

                    TODD
     Yes, they do! Every day! The fact that
     my parents own this place doesn't mean we
     get to live here for free.

                    MIKE
     Well, it's not my fault your parents
     don't love you. Now, are you gonna give
     me the money?

                         TODD
            No! Now clear the driveway.

Todd gets in the car, takes off. Mike watches him go.

INT. THE RESTAURANT - NIGHT

Todd is counting his tip money. His boss, DEB, takes
some, stuffs it in her cleavage.

                         DEB
            Reach in there and get it.

                         TODD
            No.

                         DEB
            Come on. You want your money, don't you?
            Reach in there.

                         TODD
            No.

                         DEB
            Pussy.

Deb walks off. Todd sighs.

EXT. THE HOUSE - DRIVEWAY -- NIGHT

Home from work, Todd gets out of his car. Suddenly
a MUGGER in a hoodie and ski mask jumps out at him,
holding a knife.

                         MUGGER
            Wallet!

                         TODD
            What?

                         MUGGER
            Wallet, motherfucker!

Terrified, Todd hands over his wallet.

                         TODD
            Here! Here!

The mugger takes it, runs off.

```
INT. LIVING ROOM -- LATER

Todd, still shaken, sits on the couch in his robe,
holding a mug of hot cocoa. Mike enters with a shopping
bag.

                    TODD
          Where have you been?

                    MIKE
          Why? What happened?

                    TODD
          I got mugged.

                    MIKE
          Mugged? Like, by a mugger?

                    TODD
          I'd just gotten back from work and this
          guy jumped out with a knife and took my
          wallet. He got all my tip money.

                    MIKE
          What? Aw, shit. That sucks. Did you call
          the cops?

                    TODD
          I'm gonna go to the station. They said--

                    MIKE
          Hey, they're gonna get him. They're gonna
          get this piece of shit.

Mike sits, takes a new HD video camera out of the bag.

                    TODD
          God, my heart's still pounding. I've
          never been mugged before. I was just
          getting out of the car, and then-- What
          is that?

                    MIKE
          Camera.

                    TODD
          Where did you get it?
```

                    MIKE
        Store, dumb shit.

                    TODD
        No, I mean where did you get the money to
        buy it?

                    MIKE
        From an actor friend of mine.

                    TODD
        Who?

                    MIKE
        You don't know him.

                    TODD
        Oh.

Beat. Todd walks out of the room, returns a moment
later.

                    TODD
        Did you rob me?

                    MIKE
        What?

                    TODD
        You robbed me!

                    MIKE
        What are you talking about?

                    TODD
        Well, it's just very strange. I mean, you
        needed money for a new camera, you knew I
        was working that party tonight, I just so
        happen to get mugged, you just so happen
        to get a new camera....

                    MIKE
        I can't believe this. You actually think
        I would rob you at knifepoint? If I
        was gonna rob you, I'd use a gun. Bam!
        Glock to the clock. Dead bitches mean no
        snitches.

                    TODD
          I wanna know where you got the money to
          buy that camera. Look me in the eye and
          tell me.

They get right in each other's faces, eye to eye.

                    TODD
          Where'd you get the money?

                    MIKE
          From. A. Friend.

                    TODD
          Which. Friend?

                    MIKE
          George.

                    TODD
          "George." George what?

                    MIKE
          George Wash...

Todd raises an eyebrow.

                    MIKE
          ...burn.

                    TODD
          "George Washburn." You got the money from
          your good chum, George Washburn. Ol'
          Georgie Washburn gave you the money for
          that camera. Ol' G-Dub.

                    MIKE
          That's right.

Beat.

                    TODD
          I'm going down to the police station to
          file my report.

                    MIKE
          What're you gonna tell 'em?

> TODD
> I'm gonna tell 'em the truth.

Todd exits.

EXT. POLICE STATION - ESTABLISHING

Todd comes out of the local police station.

EXT. HOUSE - DRIVEWAY -- LATER

Returning from the police station, Todd parks in the
driveway. The mugger jumps out. Same outfit, same knife.

> MUGGER
> Gimme your money!

> TODD
> Oh, what the hell...?

> MUGGER
> Now, bitch!

> TODD
> You already took my money, remember?

> MUGGER
> Then gimme your phone!

> TODD
> Screw you, Mike, take the mask off.

> MUGGER
> Bitch, I will cut you!

> TODD
> (tilts his head back)
> Okay, cut me. Go ahead and cut me. I'm
> waiting....

Suddenly, Mike runs up and CLOCKS HIM. The mugger drops.

> TODD
> MIKE?!?

                    MIKE
          Get outta here! Call the cops!

Mike starts kicking the crap out of the mugger. Todd
runs off. As soon as he's gone, Mike stops kicking.

                    MUGGER
          Ow! Fuck, man! Stop it!

Mike stops, helps the mugger up.

                    MUGGER
          You didn't say you were gonna kick me!

                    MIKE
          Sorry, man. I got carried away.

                    MUGGER
          I've got an underwear commercial tomorrow
          and I'm gonna look like Tina fuckin'
          Turner.

Mike hands the mugger a few bills.

                    MIKE
          Here. For your trouble.

                    MUGGER
          I have sensitive skin. Dick.

The mugger walks off.

                    MIKE
          I owe you one, George!

UNDER THE CLOSING CREDITS:

George tries to explain things to the cops as he's
arrested.

THE END.

Writing for Video Games

You're in the Driver's Seat

We start this chapter with a disclosure: Neither of us has written for video games. These games, however, are fast becoming the first entertainment choice of the new generation. Since games such as *Grand Theft Auto* (*GTA*), *Halo*, *The Elder Scrolls* and *Call of Duty* have gross receipts rivaling or exceeding those of the biggest Hollywood blockbusters (in fact, game sales have outstripped those from every other sector of the entertainment industry), we felt it important to add a brief chapter that provides a few relevant game-scripting concepts and suggestions.

Assisting us in preparing this chapter were Prof. Derek Burrill of UCR, an expert in games and game theory; computer graphic designer and game artist Jeff Kunzler (who participated in the landmark 2008 *EVE Online* Goonswarm event); and Patrick Seitz, director and writer of, and actor in, countless anime series and video games (including directing the voice-over and facial motion capture for *SoulCalibur V*, and voicing Scorpion in the most recent *Mortal Kombat* release). Many of the insights are theirs; all of the mistakes are ours.

YOU ARE THERE

"In games there are three voices: there's the voice of the creator, there's the voice of the game and there's the voice of the player.... We're invited by the artist to inject our own morality, our own worldview, our own experiences into the game as we play it. And what comes out is wholly different for everybody that experiences it."—*Chris Melissinos, curator of the Smithsonian's "The Art of Video Games."*

The primary attraction of computer games, aside from whatever immediate visual and auditory appeal they may have, is that the player becomes a participant in an adventure—in fact, the adventure's protagonist, with whom the player identifies visually, aurally and through its journey of action and acquisition. Depending on the game, the player may be represented by an "avatar" (a personal image used in a game environment) or may participate in a game world from a first-person perspective, or perhaps guide the actions of whole armies from above, like a chess player.

Unfortunately, until very recently games were almost purely action-driven, not character-driven; what a character learned wasn't as important as helping it acquire more weapons, skills, or powers to overcome new obstacles or foes. Also until very recently, game characters were primarily driven by the game's architecture (instead of the character's "personality"), determining its various conclusions via encounters with an assortment of possible environments, pathways, discoveries and opponents. But this is changing rapidly, as computer advances allow the video game to embrace ever more deeply nuanced characters, stories, environments and decision-making processes.

FIRST THINGS FIRST

As a game writer, your first creative task is to choose the general world and nature of the game you'll develop. (Some types of games may be more suited to a given writer's talents than others.) Perhaps a good place to start is with the four game categories chosen to guide visitors through the Smithsonian American Art Museum's 2012 exhibit "The Art of Video Games." Its curator, Chris Melissinos, is founder of JavaGaming.org and PastPixels, and Sun Microsystems' former Chief Gaming Officer.

The four categories are Action, Target, Adventure and Tactics. Within each of these very broad and often overlapping designations are many, many game genres and subgenres, which also more often than not overlap each other. Jeff Kunzler points out, "A number of people in the games industry take issue with modern genre conventions and how games are labeled; for example, *Mass Effect* is an RPG [Role-Playing Game] but also a Third-Person Shooter, and it's hard to classify it.... *Dark Souls* at first glance is an RPG, but within that it is Masocore [masochistic games that are extremely difficult and unforgiving to the player].... There [are] genres, subgenres within those genres, and it can get pretty deep classifying games."

For this chapter's purposes, though, the following will help clarify these categories:

- The **Action** category that contains such popular genres as platform games, shooter games (both first-person and third-person varieties) and fighting games. It has a history that dates from the archaic *Pac-Man* (1980) to the more recent *Gears of War 2* (2008), *Uncharted 2: Among Thieves* (2009) and *Super Mario Galaxy 2* (2010).
- **Target** is a category that includes series ranging from *Space Invaders* (1980) to *Blast Works: Build, Trade, Destroy* (2008) and *Flower* (2009).
- **Adventure** includes many role-playing games, from *Pitfall!* (1982) to the action-adventure *The Legend of Zelda: Twilight Princess* (2006) to *Mass Effect 2* (2010) and the 3-D interactive thriller *Heavy Rain* (2010).
- **Tactics** can include strategy games and puzzle games. This category has a long history, running from the primitive *Combat* (1977) to *Lord of the Rings: Battle for Middle Earth II* (2006) and *Zack and Wiki: Quest for Barbaros' Treasure* (2007).

If all you're after is a really cool environment in which to engage in one or another forms of combat, then *story* might not seem to involve much more than setting up that environment and the kinds of weapons and tactics you're planning, i.e., the gameplay mechanics. But that is more the game designer's turf. For instance, Jeff Kunzler notes that in first-person shooter games like *Modern Warfare 2* (2009) the plot is an afterthought, written to string together the action set-pieces after the lead designers have developed them. Before jettisoning most of your plot and character elements, bear in mind that with today's rapidly advancing computer technologies, such action games can now be much, much more. Patrick Seitz notes that the newest version of the old fighting game *Mortal Kombat* (first developed in 1994, with a completely revised version introduced in 2011) takes the original franchise's disparate elements and integrates them into a much more satisfying single plotline experience by applying the traditional elements of character and drama development. In the best game design situations, writers and designers work together to create fully developed, innovative worlds rich in both story and gameplay content.

Generally speaking, the advancing complexity of video games, a direct offshoot of advances in computer technologies, is making the introduction of interesting, original and dramatic story ideas and characters a very real and increasingly common aspect of all categories and genres. Media scholar and USC professor Henry Jenkins suggests, "What we've seen from games so far is just the beginning of what this medium is capable of doing."

Kids in a Sandbox

What really helped advance the integration of compelling story and character ideas into video games was the emergence of "sandbox" games (also known as "open-world" and "free-roaming" games), which may embrace any game category or genre. A sandbox game is said to be just like a kid's sandbox, in that there are always new areas to explore, new things to find and new villains to battle. In essence, the player of a sandbox game may maneuver more or less freely through its virtual environment.

Although video game historians date the first stirrings of this sort of game environment to the mid-1980s, the 2001 release of the 3-D action-adventure game *Grand Theft Auto III* seems to have done the most to popularize it. *GTA* in its various iterations and locations has combined a lot of genres, including racing, role-playing and adventure, in landscapes that could also be explored for their own interest. Character storylines, though still simple, became more important: In *GTA IV*'s *Liberty City*, for instance, you start with only the knowledge that you've come from Europe to look for your brother—then you're free to explore a world filled with parodies and references to all sorts of New York icons and personalities, picking up information that helps you advance in the game but that also makes your experience more involving.

In sophisticated games like the action-role-playing *The Elder Scrolls V: Skyrim*, when the player creates her own avatar she creates its race, appearance, qualities, frailties and combat styles in a way that isn't just cosmetic but actually affects the kind of story she'll experience—there are racial and social prejudice and distinctions at work, for one thing. Also, avatars can chart their own journeys without actually following the game's predetermined pathways. More and more, the better the stories, the better the game experience.

Let's look briefly at some of the story tools game writers use, and at both what they share with and how they differ from what screenwriters use.

The Decision Tree and Checkpoints

For a video game, the decision tree is the map—a branching diagram—of the possible antagonists, pathways and levels that a player encounters. It operates like a series of funnels, with wider possibilities at the start of each, but always invisibly guiding the player, narrowing her options until she reaches a "checkpoint"—a location where the game changes level and/or direction—that allows her to move to some other aspect or area of the game. The term "decision tree" comes from game theory, a branch of applied mathematics used in various disciplines from economics to biology to political science. To paraphrase Nobel laureate economist Roger Bruce Myerson, game theory mathematically models the interactions—both conflicts and cooperation—between rational decision-makers. It is often used by the military to map out possible war and battle scenarios.

Game theory is also used by multinational companies to strategize their business plans well into the future. For instance, oil companies and countries around the world hire energy consulting firms to "game out" what will happen to the energy economy given various scenarios: What if there's a hurricane or earthquake? What if there's a war or terrorist attack involving certain energy-producing countries? This kind of sophisticated prognostication is now a valuable part of the video gaming world, as game writers use game theory to design believable and compelling options and avenues for players of various sandbox games.

The more invisible to the player the decision tree construction, the better the illusion that the player has actual freedom of choice within the game.

Exposition

The question here is, how do you deliver only as much information as the player will need? In the past, video game players didn't regard exposition in the same way that viewers of film or TV did. A game's exposition was often absolutely straightforward because, unlike in screenwriting, it didn't seem as necessary to seamlessly hide it or blend it into the character's personality and motivation.

A lot of the exposition in a video game is like the pamphlet that tells you how to put a swing-set together: it simply tells players what they need to know to get going. However, not unlike the intro voice-overs of some old movies, it also may be there to tell players about the world they're in—what its history and challenges may be—and to offer clues to finding the hidden powers or weapons they'll need to defeat the enemies the game throws at them. Such exposition (consider the extended voice-overs at the beginning of *The Elder Scrolls* series or *God of War*) can be frustrating for movie-lovers to endure, but it's often a necessary part of helping the player get comfortable in a new world that, unlike with the chiefly passive act of viewing of a movie, is about taking action to move forward.

The recent well-written action-adventure sandbox games *Red Dead Redemption* and *L.A. Noire* present decent hybrids of both approaches, with voice-overs but also flashbacks to fill in the narrative component. Along these lines, Patrick Seitz feels that "a well-done VO or introductory cut-scene—or better yet, an intro cut-scene with moments of player enfranchisement interspersed, à la *Alan Wake* [a survival horror game about a writer, incidentally]—is the best way to get [players] up and running. A good way to get info across during the game or to world-build and flesh out the environment without reducing your NPCs [non-player characters] to walking information kiosks is to include media within the game—emails, scrolls, books, what have you. Fans appreciate the effort, like being able to read them at the time of their choosing, and some games go so far as to make their discovery tied in with an Achievement or Trophy.... The *Mass Effect* franchise does a good job of this, giving you all the background you want on the sundry races and planets without talking your ear off with it during the meat-and-potatoes of the gameplay; it's accessible from the menu system at your leisure, with each initial mention of a new topic unlocking it for later perusal."

As a rule of thumb, sandbox games, which present the player with myriad changes in direction and level (at checkpoints), need less upfront exposition. On the other hand, the more a game is about straightforward action, the more exposition you'll want to get out of the way at the start, so that the player can simply jump into one series of competitions or combats after another without having to stop, impeding his action experience, to learn details.

Lastly, don't forget to pay attention to how introductory exposition pays off: One annoyance of *Skyrim* is that the avatar starts out as a condemned prisoner, but that element really doesn't have much to do with the adventure other than to create a bit of suspense and motivation for the initial escape. Another example is the fantasy role-playing game *Dragon Age II*, in which the Mages are supposedly a persecuted minority, yet a player can play a Mage character and never face any consequences for it. Jeff Kunzler contrasts this with the role-playing fantasy *The Witcher 2: Assassins of Kings*, which he considers a good example of "how to do a fantasy realm full of moral dilemmas, racial issues and heavy ideas."

Non-Player Characters (NPCs)

A non-player character is any character that the player does not control. Carefully choosing and working out the NPCs that a game pits against the player can help writers deepen and develop a game's story aspects. Patrick Seitz feels that NPCs may present writers with ever-expanding challenges as they can reappear in a later version of a game and "remember" situations from earlier versions: "Some studios are now making games where your dialogue decisions and actions not only affect the events of that particular game, but events in the sequels.... With *Mass Effect 3* and potential subsequent releases, they'll have had to script any number of resolutions, side-quests and consequences that have followed the player's avatar throughout the course of the series."

Keeping It Interesting

A player increasingly needs the puzzles, traps and challenges to be varied and interesting, and to increase in spectacle and complexity he moves toward the final confrontation. This provides an opportunity for writers to integrate more compelling story elements into a game's sequence of goals and obstacles, as well as into the "free space" between items and powers collected, "Easter Eggs" (hidden messages or in-jokes that add entertainment value) and challenges. According to noted game designer Warren Spector, "What story does in games is it provides significance: You have to save your brother; you've only got ten minutes; here's the problem you have to solve *to* save your brother. Go!"

Some games have tried to involve stories that allow for different conclusions. For example, *Heavy Rain*, a *noir* psychological thriller, has a sophisticated decision tree that allows the player to arrive at a variety of endings depending on choices both of character and path. (*Heavy Rain*'s writer-director, David Cage, says, "With *Heavy Rain*, I was looking for a way to make the player play the story.") The challenge with this sort of game is to create a really new experience for each branch of the tree. If you don't, few players are going to remain interested enough to replay the game again and again to encounter each ending. But game designers are taking more risks in that direction. *L.A. Noire* allows you to explore practically the entire landscape of 1940s Los Angeles, even if you just want to drive around. Likewise, *Skyrim* is a remarkable experiment in that its challenges are actually less interesting than the avatar design, and its world is created with such detail and humor that a player can simply wander around in it for hours without ever engaging in combat. One can even play pranks on the NPCs, such as putting buckets over their heads so they can't see that you're stealing from them.

According to Video Game Hall of Famer Nolan Bushnell, founder of the Atari Corporation, "One of the things that's really fun with games is the whole idea of the playful mind. How can we make games surprise you?"

How It Works

Writing for video games is a bit like writing for animation: The writer describes the game's world, characters and various other elements such as backstories, opponents, obstacles and powers that can be given or acquired, but then passes it into the hands of teams of artists and engineers who lay out the actual parameters and possibilities.

Spinoffs

New stories are often reverse-engineered and shellacked over an existing game engine. And new games are often developed within companies based on existing successful models, by simply applying a new "skin" and backstory to existing game architecture. *L.A. Noire*, for example, for all its intensive recreation of 1940s Los Angeles, is a lot like *Red Dead Redemption*, which in turn is a lot like *Grand Theft Auto* and other sandbox games. Derek Burrill points out, "If you think about the *Tomb Raider* series, the original design team on that put that whole thing together focused on making it very story-heavy at the beginning, and then developed the architecture for that world, which means that both *Tomb Raider* II and III could be made pretty much on the same architecture, they didn't have to reinvent the whole world."

THE REAL WORLD: BREAKING AND ENTERING

When it comes to finding work in video games, a solid writing background is a plus, because it's still rare and valued in the video game industry. You don't have to know how to code, but it helps, and that knowledge will earn you more respect from the design team responsible for actually making the game a reality. Have both writing and code experience, and you'll be way ahead of the game, so to speak.

That said, it's tough to break in with a spec game. Software houses generally hire from within, so you'll want to start by trying to get a job on an existing project as part of the team. If you've worked on a successful game within the house, you'll probably get a chance to work on another project.

But writers within the industry aren't typically known or identified with a game. The credit tends to go to the software house itself. In some ways these houses, with their distinct types of games, are more like the movie studios of the 1930s and 1940s: in those days an MGM movie had a distinctive identity from a Paramount or RKO film and so on. As Derek Burrill points out, "there are only a few people who have 'branding name' identity, like Peter Molyneux." Molyneux created particular types of games like *Dungeon Keeper* and *Black & White*, and designed them for early computers and consoles like Atari, Amiga and Commodore 64. People identify that sort of game with him. Another well-known writer is Patrice Désilets, creative director behind the first *Assassin's Creed* games.

FINAL THOUGHTS

"You don't need technology to create feelings and love and fear and hate and passion, you need great storytelling."—*Jen MacLeary, video game developer and CEO of 38 Studios*

Writing for games requires a different approach than writing for movies or TV. Game players don't sit down and watch a show; they *do* something.

Your job is to create a fascinating new world for them to *do* something *in*. As Patrick Seitz notes, "The challenge in writing for video games is that players are increasingly coming to expect the best of both worlds: an unprecedented amount of choice and player empowerment, on the one hand, with the most compelling stories and characters linear storytelling has to offer on the other. It's a real tightrope act."

For further reading, we recommend two books:

Interactive Storytelling: Techniques for 21st-Century Fiction, by Andrew Glassner (Natick, MA: A. K. Peters, 2004)

The Ultimate Guide to Video Game Writing and Design, by Flint Dille and John Zuur Platten (Los Angeles: Lone Eagle Publishing, 2008). The basic concepts in this book should remain reasonably consistent, although the field is changing so fast that you'll want to make sure you have its most recent edition, or look for newer resources.

Other knowledgeable resources:

Giant Bomb (www.giantbomb.com), which has highly detailed information and a user-maintained wiki that covers the game universe, is billed as "the world's largest editable video game database."

Let's Play Archive (lparchive.org), which has run-throughs of hundreds of games viewable in screenshot or video form.

FADE OUT...

Final Thoughts on Becoming a Screenwriter

Writing for the movies or television is infinitely seductive, but it's not necessarily right for everyone. It takes years of work, many scripts, life choices that are hard to make and rejection that is hard to take. You can't go into it half-heartedly. There's a story about a cynical, over-the-hill, middle-aged actor who goes to a party at a Hollywood Hills mansion. He's introduced to the owner, a star who seems to have it all. Envious of her young success, he tells her that he too could have been a great star, if it weren't for his dying mother. It seems he had spent years taking care of her and now regrets the lost opportunities. The actress listens to his glum story and answers, "My mother was also very ill, but I became a star." The middle-aged actor can't believe it. How did you do it, he asks, how could you balance both? The starlet answers, "I let her die."

We are not saying that you should "let your mother die"; that's not the moral of the story. But it is true that those who really want something will let little stand in their way—especially in Hollywood. In this case, the regretful actor had not chosen his career over "taking care of his dying mother," and this might be the right path for you as well. You cannot blame yourself if certain things are more important than writing; that's your choice, and your choices define who you are. Either your priorities are organized so that you can become a writer or they are not, but if writing is not first, or a close second in your life, then the chance of being successful is small and even smaller in the world of screenwriting.

Too many young screenwriters think only of success—they spend their time writing with the goal of selling "the big one." Few Hollywood writers get big money. More people have won the California State Lottery than have sold a million-dollar script. The average Hollywood working writer (that means someone who actually works as a screenwriter) makes just over $50,000 a year. Despite this, there are 50,000 so-called writers living in Los Angeles, hundreds of thousands more around the world, trying desperately to break into the industry. Doctors, lawyers, cops, waiters—everyone seems to have a spec screenplay or sitcom script. Even a talented writer in Hollywood faces a massive uphill climb and constant disappointment.

If the picture is so bleak, why write?

The answer is found in the documentary *Wild Man Blues*, on the life and music of Woody Allen. They ask him what his life is like. His answer is simple. He says that he lives the life of a writer: he gets up in the morning, he writes and then he goes for a walk. We must live the life of a writer. We must get up and write every day, then go for a walk and think about what we are going to write tomorrow. Only when we live the writer's life, only when our lives, our loves, our families, our jobs revolve around and support the writer's life, is there a chance at success.

This doesn't mean you have to live a life of poverty because you're devoting every waking hour to your writing. You have to find the middle ground between total obsession and abandoning your dream, between letting your mother die and letting your writing career die. Most writers have jobs, as teachers, copy editors, marketers, attorneys, whatever. It may make sense to get a job where you can practice your skills; especially if you're in Los Angeles or New York, you can try to get work with a production company where you can see how the business works, get to read the scripts coming in and make useful contacts. And with the growth of film production in other areas, such as Dallas, Chicago, Toronto, Vancouver, Baltimore and elsewhere, there are more film-related job opportunities than ever before. But whatever your job, think of it not as a distraction, but as part of your life as a writer. Study your co-workers as potential characters; find material for drama in the conflicts of your own life, your work, your family. Scott Turow, for example, turned his years of experience as a prosecutor into material for his best-selling novels. Look to your own life, passions and experiences for those stories that only you can create. But above all, always, always set aside some inviolable time every day when you can sit down and do what writers do: they write. Don't let anything get in the way if you can help it, and don't procrastinate. There's an old saying that goes, "procrastination preserves the illusion of genius because the illusion is never tested." You can't call yourself a writer if you're just thinking about it.

Years from now, after decades of writing every day and tens of thousands of walks, what if the millions never roll in? What if you're still living in the little bungalow in North Hollywood and not the Hollywood Hills mansion? What if we cannot call ourselves "a success" by Hollywood standards? What then? Then we can at least look back and, unlike that regretful middle-aged actor, be able to say, without regrets, "I chose the writer's life." It can be a wonderful life, full of discoveries, analysis and creativity, a life of the imagination. And who knows? With a bit of luck, and a lot of hard work, you might even be able to "write the picture."

Appendix A:
Templates

These templates will help you set margins for screenplays, sitcoms, and plays.

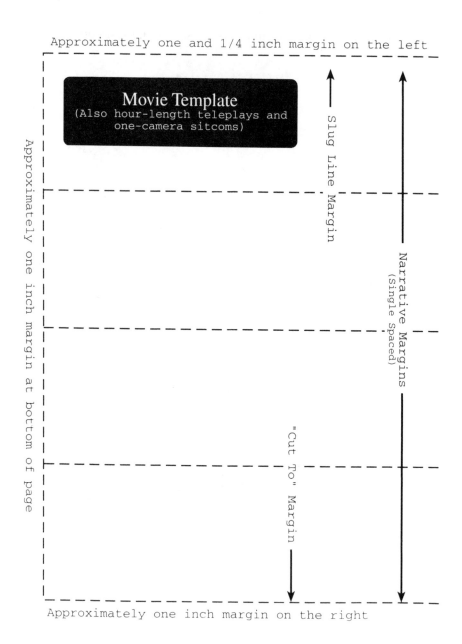

Approximately one and 1/4 inch margin on the left

Approximately one inch margin at bottom of page

Movie Template
(Also hour-length teleplays and
one-camera sitcoms)

Slug Line Margin

Narrative Margins
(Single Spaced)

"Cut To" Margin

Approximately one inch margin on the right

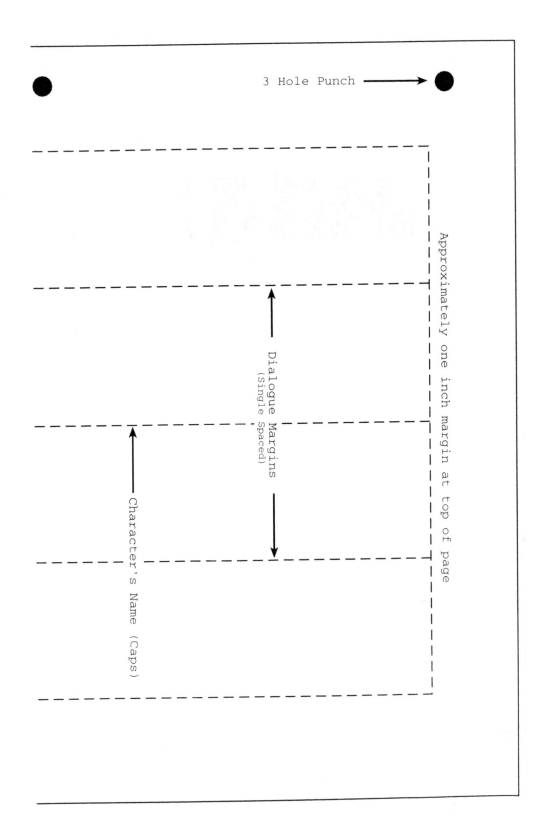

3 Hole Punch →

Approximately one inch margin at top of page

Dialogue Margins
(Single Spaced)

Character's Name (Caps)

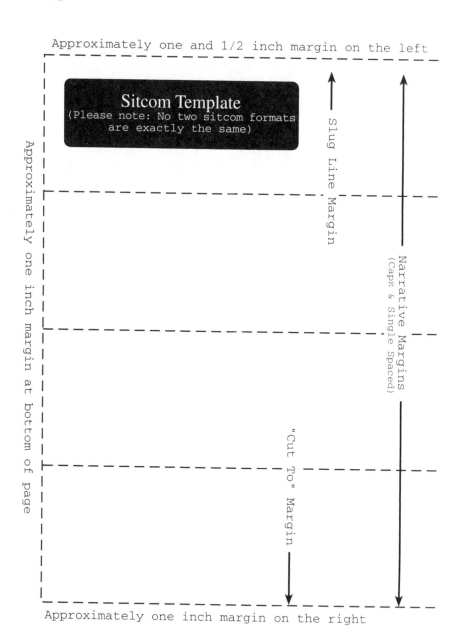

Approximately one and 1/2 inch margin on the left

Sitcom Template
(Please note: No two sitcom formats
are exactly the same)

Approximately one inch margin at bottom of page

Slug Line Margin

Narrative Margins
(Caps & Single Spaced)

"Cut To" Margin

Approximately one inch margin on the right

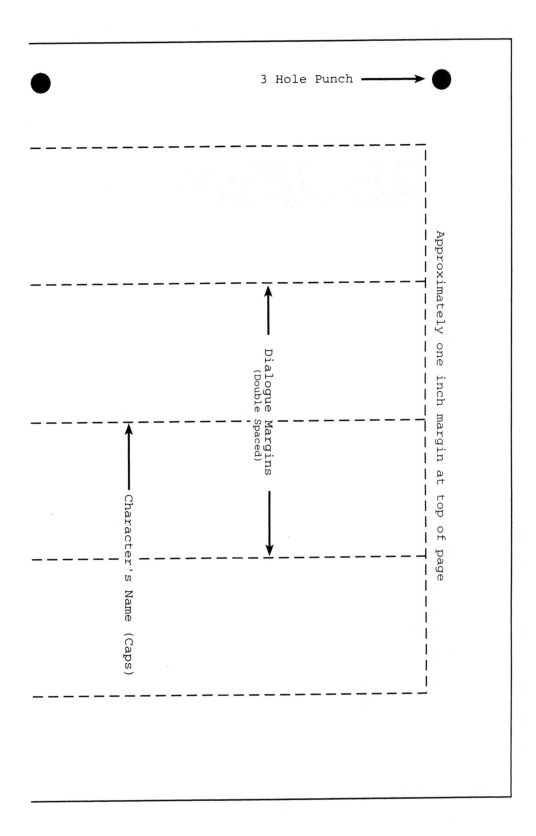

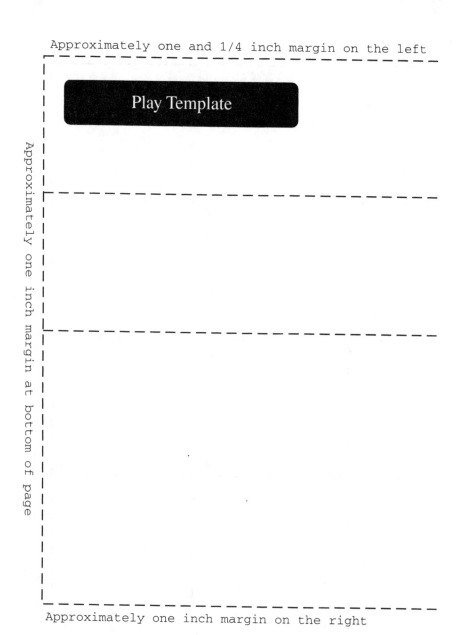

Approximately one and 1/4 inch margin on the left

Play Template

Approximately one inch margin at bottom of page

Approximately one inch margin on the right

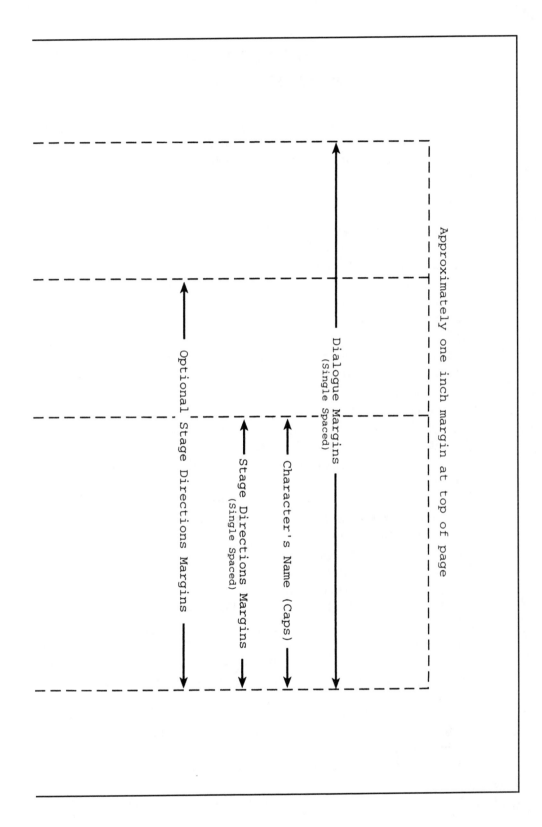

Appendix B:
Suggested Reading

Note: With the rapid changes in the film industry, as well as the vastly increased number of resources on the Internet since we wrote the first edition of this book, we are only including books that we feel still stand the test of time.

Must-Reads

Adventures in the Screen Trade by William Goldman
(New York: Warner Books, 1983)

Aristotle's Poetics by Aristotle
(Trans. S. H. Butcher. New York: Hill & Wang, 1961)

The Art of Dramatic Writing by Lajos Egri
(New York: Simon and Schuster, 2004)

Backwards and Forwards: A Technical Manual for Reading Plays by David Ball
(Carbondale: Southern Illinois University Press, 1983)

Essentials of Screenwriting: The Art, Craft, and Business of Film and Television Writing, Updated Edition, by Richard Walter
(New York: Plume, 2010)

The Hero with a Thousand Faces, 2nd Edition, by Joseph Campbell
(Princeton: Princeton University Press, 1990)

Letters to Young Filmmakers: Creativity and Getting Your Films Made by Howard Suber
(Studio City, CA: Michael Wiese Productions, 2012)

Lew Hunter's Screenwriting 434 by Lew Hunter
(New York: Perigee Books, 1994)

Making a Good Script Great, 3rd Edition, by Linda Seger
(Los Angeles: Silman-James Press, 2010)

The Power of Film by Howard Suber
(Studio City, CA: Michael Wiese Productions, 2006)

Save the Cat! The Last Book on Screenwriting You'll Ever Need by Blake Snyder
(Studio City, CA: Michael Wiese Productions, 2005)

Story: Substance, Structure, Style, and the Principles of Screenwriting by Robert McKee
(New York: HarperCollins, 1997)

The Writer's Journey: Mythic Structure for Writers, 3rd Edition, by Chris Vogler
(Studio City, CA: Michael Wiese Productions, 2007)

Marketing Your Script

Dealmaking in the Film and Television Industry: From Negotiations to Final Contracts, 3rd Edition, by Mark Litwak
(Los Angeles: Silman-James Press, 2009)

How to Write Irresistible Query Letters by Lisa Collier Cool
(Cincinnati: Writer's Digest Books, 2002)

Opening the Doors to Hollywood: How to Sell Your Idea, Story, Book, Screenplay by Carlos de Abreu and Howard Jay Smith
(New York: Three Rivers Press, 1995)

Pitching Hollywood: How to Sell Your TV and Movie Ideas by Jonathan Koch and Robert Kosberg, with Tanya Meurer Norman
(Sanger, CA: Quill Driver Books, 2004)

The Script Is Finished, Now What Do I Do? The Scriptwriter's Resource Book and Agent Guide, 4th Edition, by K. Callan
(Studio City, CA: Sweden Press, 2007)

The Writer's Guide to Selling Your Screenplay by Cynthia Whitcomb
(Waukesha, WI: Kalmbach Publishing, 2002)

Television Writing

Comedy Writing for Television and Hollywood by Milt Josefsberg
(New York: HarperCollins, 1987)

The TV Writer's Workbook: A Creative Approach to Television Scripts by Ellen Sandler
(New York: Delta, 2007)

Writing Television Sitcoms by Evan S. Smith
(New York: Perigee, 1999)

Writing the Pilot by William Rabkin
(Pasadena, CA: Moon & Sun & Whiskey, 2011)

Playwriting

Naked Playwriting: The Art, the Craft, and the Life Laid Bare by William Missouri Downs and Robin Russin
(Los Angeles: Silman-James Press, 2004)

Additional Reading

The Complete Book of Scriptwriting by J. Michael Straczynski
(Cincinnati: Writer's Digest Books, 1996)

Elements of Style, 4th Edition, by William Strunk, Jr., and E. B. White
(London: Longman, 1999)

The Screenwriter's Bible: A Complete Guide to Writing, Formatting, and Selling Your Script, 5th Edition, by David Trottier
(Los Angeles: Silman-James Press, 2010)

Written By: The Magazine of the Writers Guild of America, West
(Los Angeles: Writers Guild of America, West)

Appendix C:
A Few Clichés to Avoid like the Plague

Here are a few clichés to avoid. Many more can be found on various websites, or in Roger Ebert's hilarious little book *Ebert's Bigger Little Movie Glossary*, as well as on his website.

No Applause, Please

A common cliché at the end of many romantic laughter and courage films is to have the lovers embrace and kiss in front of a large group of people, whom, often, they don't know. These people then break into spontaneous, delighted applause. As noted, this is a reaffirmation of the life force, but it's been done to death. If you must resort to group applause, find a new and unusual way to present it.

"Are You All Right?" (aka "Are you OK?")

Almost every writer is tempted to use these words at some point in a script. Try not to give in—it is meaningless filler. If one character wants to express concern for another, find a more specific and interesting way. The same goes for "What are you talking about?" and when an older, usually ally character, declares, "I'm too old for this shit." These expressions are too old for any new screenplay.

Blowing Up Real Good

The worst action movie cliché is when the hero, usually dragging along his helpless female companion, runs from an impending explosion. No matter how capable or athletic, the woman will trip or break a heel along the way. The man will yank her to her feet, they run on and are blown into the air by a huge explosion behind them. Naturally they land unscathed.

No Hookers with Golden Tickers

In spite of the success of *The Owl and the Pussycat*, *Mighty Aphrodite*, *Casino*, *Pretty Woman*, *Leaving Las Vegas* and others too many to list, and in spite of the fact that this character actually exists in the oldest written epic, *Gilgamesh*, try to avoid the Hooker with the Heart of Gold. Obviously this character neatly encapsulates the madonna-whore complex endemic to our society's perception of women but, as a device, she's as old as the hills and twice as dusty (to rephrase another tired cliché).

No Architects, Writers or Advertising/Graphic Artists

These characters have been done to death as well. Find another profession to display your character's heart, smarts and creativity.

CGI Fatigue

As with explosions, audiences have become too sophisticated to be won over by spectacular special effects in general, so don't count on including them to sell your script. Even in a light science-fiction context, there's no substitute for a good story.

The Ezsterhas Corollary (aka "Moore Is Sometimes Less")

Great naked breasts do not constitute great special effects and won't save a movie from a lousy script, either. Witness the Joe Ezsterhas–written *Showgirls*, the Demi Moore vehicle *Striptease* and any number of similarly would-be "tit-elating" films.

Appendix D:
Graduate (MFA) Screenwriting Programs

MFA Programs

American Film Institute
Bard College
City University of New York, City College
Columbia College, Chicago
Columbia University
Florida State University
New York University
Northwestern University
San Francisco Art Institute
San Francisco State University
School of the Art Institute of Chicago
Southern Illinois University at Carbondale
Syracuse University
Temple University
University of California, Los Angeles
University of California, Riverside
University of Miami
University of Southern California
University of Texas at Austin
University of Wisconsin, Milwaukee

Glossary

* An **asterisk** "*" in the margin of a shooting script means that somewhere within the line beside the "*" there has been a rewrite.

A & B Pages These are part of pre-production formatting. In a shooting script the page numbers are set. When there is a rewrite, instead of adding to the page numbers, A and B pages are created. So, for example, page 92 now becomes page 92A and 92B.

AEA Actors Equity Association. The union that represents stage actors.

AFI American Film Institute.

AFTRA The American Federation of Television and Radio Artists.

anticlimax When the conflicting forces in a play fail to come to a confrontation or to arrive at a conclusive decision. An example would be Chekhov's *The Cherry Orchard*.

art director The person on a film crew who is responsible for every aspect of set design and construction, as well as overseeing the production designer, prop master and anyone else involved in creating the look of the film (other than the cinematographer).

backstory Events that took place before the story begins. Exposition.

beat A brief pause. It also means a single unit of thought. It's a small section of the dialogue that's accented by a particular emotion, subject, and/or idea. A change in emotion, subject or idea means the beginning of a new beat.

best boy The first assistant electrician on a film crew.

blue screen A visual effect. An actor is filmed in front of a single-color background screen, usually blue. A computer can then be programmed to replace the background with an image.

boom The telescoping microphone that is used on a set.

CGI (Computer Generated Imaging) A visual effect or image created with computers.

character arc Just as a story has a beginning, a middle and an end, so do most characters. Character arc is the growth or change in a character caused by the events of the story.

cinematographer Also known as the Director of Photography or D.P., this is the person who directs the lighting and filming of the movie. Sometimes he/she will also operate the camera; in bigger productions there will be a separate Camera Operator who is responsible to the D.P.

compositing A visual effect that combines two or more images into a single shot.

dailies A working print of a day's footage.

denouement The solution or unraveling of the plot. The final outcome of the play. A liberal translation of the French "untying of the last knot." Usually comes after the climax and before the conclusion.

deus ex machina *(The god from the machine)* From the ancient Greek theatre, this was a machine that lowered the god from above. Once on stage, the god would resolve the characters' problems and set everything right. Today, *deus ex machina* often means a play that has an unimaginative, sudden ending that may set everything right, but lacks believability. Sometimes these endings are known as "acts of God." An act of God is a massive coincidence that is too unbelievable for the audience to accept. (This type of coincidence only works now in comedies.)

DGA (Directing) The Directors Guild of America.

DGA (Playwriting) The Dramatists Guild of America.

dramatic irony Occurs when the audience perceives a double edge (a second ironic meaning) to the scene that the characters do not perceive.

EXT. (Exterior) Used in Master Scene Headings to indicate that a scene will be shot outside.

fish-out-of-water story A story that simply puts your protagonist into a new or alien environment.

flashbacks A cinematic device in which a scene showing an earlier event is inserted into the normal chronological order.

flatbed A motorized film-editing machine.

gaffer The chief electrician on a film crew.

grips The people who move equipment on a film set.

high concept A movie's premise or storyline that is easily reduced to a simple and appealing one-liner.

hook The key element that makes a story gripping or commercial.

inciting scene or incident An event that causes the opening balance to become unglued and gets the main action rolling.

INT. (Interior) A Master Scene Heading that indicates that the scene will be shot inside.

legitimate drama The term comes from eighteenth-century England when theaters had to hold a license from the king in order to perform legitimately. Today the term denotes a live stage performance rather than movies or television.

logline One-line story description as in *TV Guide* or *TV Log*.

The MacGuffin The "MacGuffin," associated with Alfred Hitchcock, refers to the element in the story that motivates the action of the story, but that in and of itself may or may not have a real effect on the story; it is the excuse for the action. For example, in the *Maltese Falcon* it is the statue of the falcon; in *North by Northwest* it is the microfilm hidden in the PreColumbian statue; in the movie *Mission: Impossible* it is the computer disk with the list of agents; in *Charade* it's the stamp worth $250,000.00. In these cases, it doesn't really matter what exactly it is, other than that it is something that both the protagonists and antagonists are after; the Maltese Falcon could just as easily have been a Chinese Dragon. The term is said to originate with a Scottish story about two men in a train. One asks the other, "What's that parcel you've got up there in the baggage rack?" The second man replies, "That's a MacGuffin." The first man asks, "What's a MacGuffin?" to which the second man responds, "Well, it's a contraption for trapping lions in the Scottish Highlands." The first man laughs, "But there are no lions in the Scottish Highlands!" "Well then," answers his companion, "then it's not a MacGuffin!" The point being, the MacGuffin is simply what you need it to be.

matte A visual effect in which part of the image is blocked out and replaced with a drawing or model.

montage A series of shots in rapid succession.

motif The underlying poetic themes and verbal metaphors of the play or screenplay.

moviola An older-style film editing machine.

MOW Movie of the Week.

obligatory scene The expected clash between adversaries. It's what the audience believes will be the outcome of the action. The obligatory scene is an expected scene or conflict that the writer sets up and therefore has an obligation to pay off. It's the major showdown (also called "scene a faire").

O.C. (or OC) Off Camera. Dialogue or sounds heard while the camera is on another subject.

on the nose When a character says exactly what's on her mind.

option A percentage of the purchase price for a screenplay or treatment that is paid by a producer in order to gain exclusive control of the rights to the material for a certain period of time.

O.S. (or OS) (Screenwriting) Off Screen. Same as O.C.

O.S. (Playwriting) Off Stage or Off Set.

pathos Something that evokes a sense of pity. (From the Greek word for "suffering.")

P.O.V. (Point of View) A camera positioned from the point of view of a particular character.

premise The premise of a film is the "situation." It is usually describable in a sentence or two.

red herring A story device that leads the audience to think the play is going one way when it's really heading in another direction. It is a false setup in which the audience is warned of coming events and problems that never appear. It's a smokescreen.

SAG Screen Actors Guild.

script doctor A writer who rewrites someone else's script, concentrating on polishing and correcting the script's structural or character problems.

spec (short for "speculation") A script that is written without any guarantee of a sale.

special effects (SFX) Includes everything from explosions to bullet hits to rain. Special effects are those effects that can be done live on the set during a shot (see Visual Effects).

spin A spin is an offbeat or different twist in a character or story. It's the one thing that makes this story or character different from all others.

spine The screenplay's central or main action.

subplot The second or "B" plot, which mirrors or contrasts with the main plot.

super (superimpose) The photographic effect of showing one image over another.

superobjective The character's driving force or motivation. Constantin Stanislavski is famous for this term. It's the overall purpose that carries a character though the story. For example, according to Stanislavski, Hamlet's superobjective is "to find God."

talent In this business, it means the actors.

treatment A prose narrative (five to twenty pages long) which recounts the events in a proposed script or movie.

visual effects Effects that do not happen on the set during the shooting but rather are added to the movie by manipulating the filmed image, usually by computer.

V.O. Voice-over.

WGAe Writers Guild of America East. (see Chapter 15)

WGAw Writers Guild of American West. (see Chapter 15)

Index

About the Authors

Robin U. Russin is a Professor of Screenwriting at the University of California, Riverside, where he serves as Director of the MFA in Creative Writing and Writing for the Performing Arts. He has written, produced, consulted and directed for film, TV and the theater, including the box-office hit *On Deadly Ground*; *America's Most Wanted* on Fox; and *Vital Signs* on ABC. His short stories, articles and reviews have appeared in *Script Magazine*, *Verdad Magazine*, *Connotation Press*, *Harvard Magazine*, *The Los Angeles Times*, *The American Oxonian* and elsewhere. He and Bill are also the co-authors of *Naked Playwriting*. A Rhodes Scholar, he received his Bachelor's Degree in Fine Arts from Harvard, and has graduate degrees from Oxford University, Rhode Island School of Design, and UCLA, where he received his MFA in screenwriting.

William Missouri Downs is a Professor of Screenwriting and Playwriting at the University of Wyoming. He holds an MFA in screenwriting from UCLA and an MFA in acting from the University of Illinois. In Hollywood, Bill started as a script secretary on NBC's *Moonlighting* (Bruce Willis and Cybill Shepherd), and worked his way up to staff writer on the NBC sitcom *My Two Dads* (Paul Reiser). He also wrote episodes for the NBC shows *Amen* (Sherman Hemsley) and *Fresh Prince of Bel-Air* (Will Smith). In addition he sold a movie to Ron Howard's Imagine Films and optioned another to Filmways. He is the author of over twenty plays that have had well over one hundred productions, including at the Kennedy Center, the Detroit Rep, the Wisdom Bridge Theatre, New York City Fringe Festival, the International Theatre Festival in Israel, Orlando Shakespeare Theatre, the Charlotte Actors Theatre, the Durban Performing Arts Center (South Africa), Performance Network, the Berkeley Rep, the StadtTheater Walfischgasse (Vienna) and a Rolling World Premiere through the National New Play Network. Samuel French, Playscripts, Next Stage Press and Heuer Publishing have published his plays. He also co-wrote the books *Naked Playwriting* (Silman-James) and *The Art of Theatre* (Wadsworth).